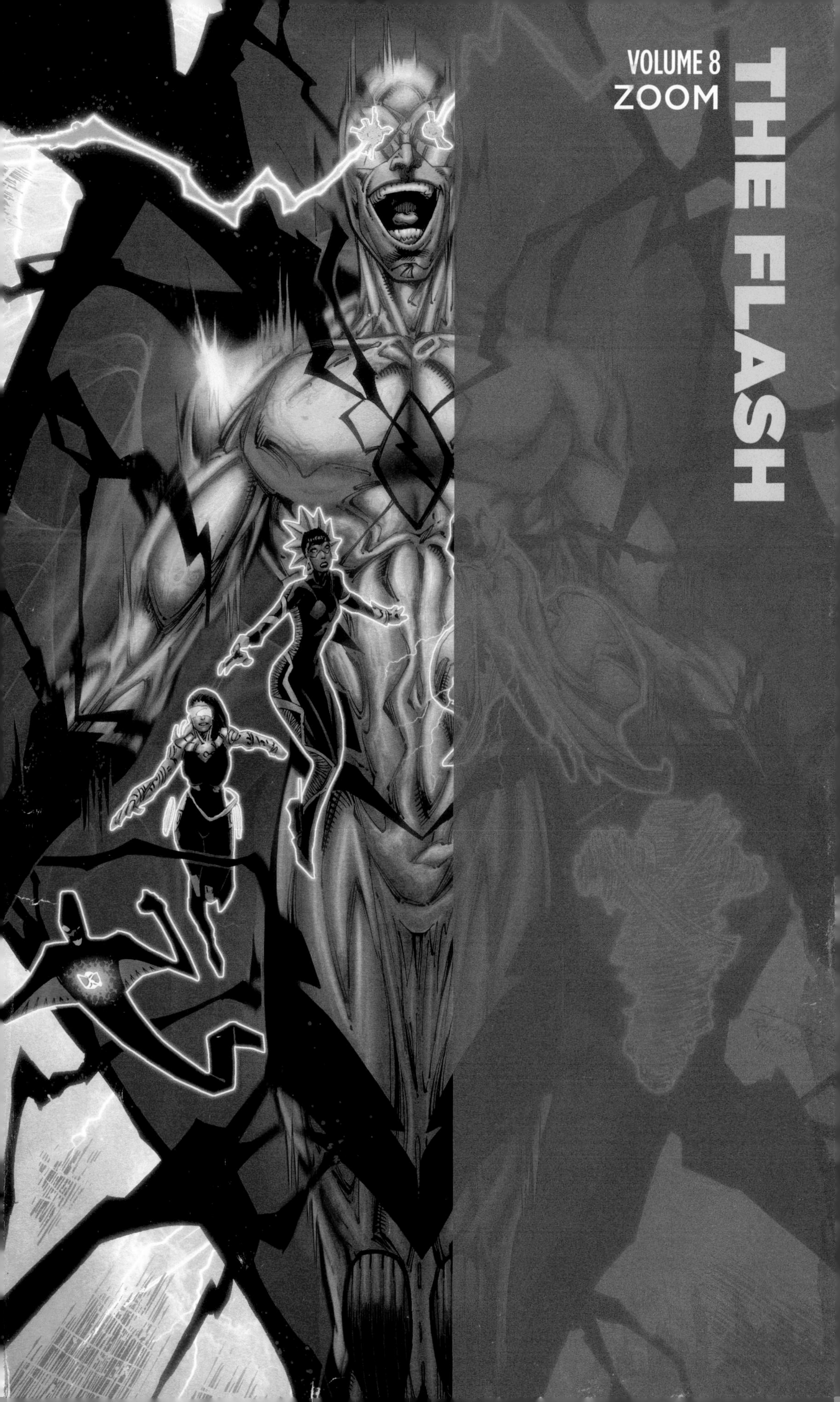
VOLUME 8
ZOOM
THE FLASH

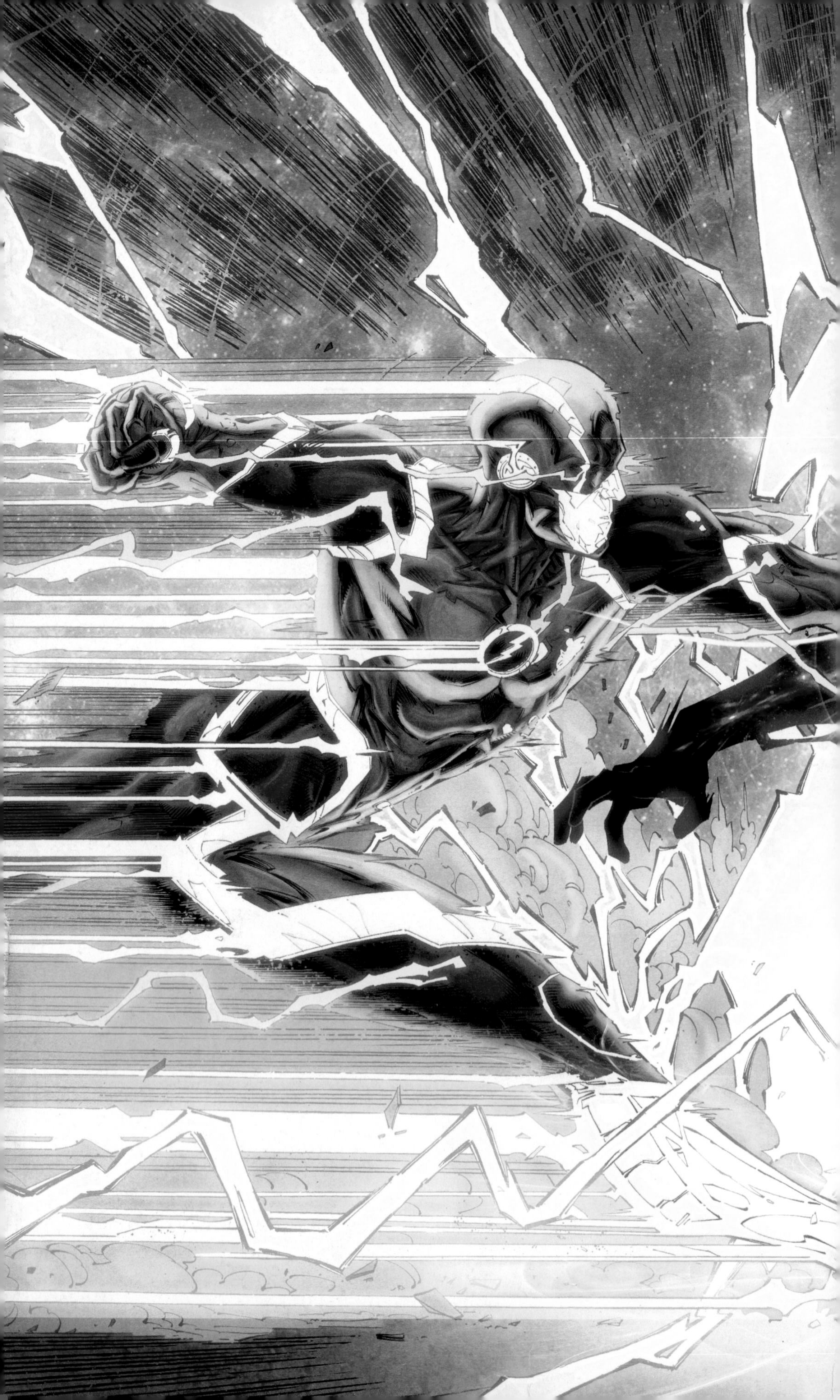

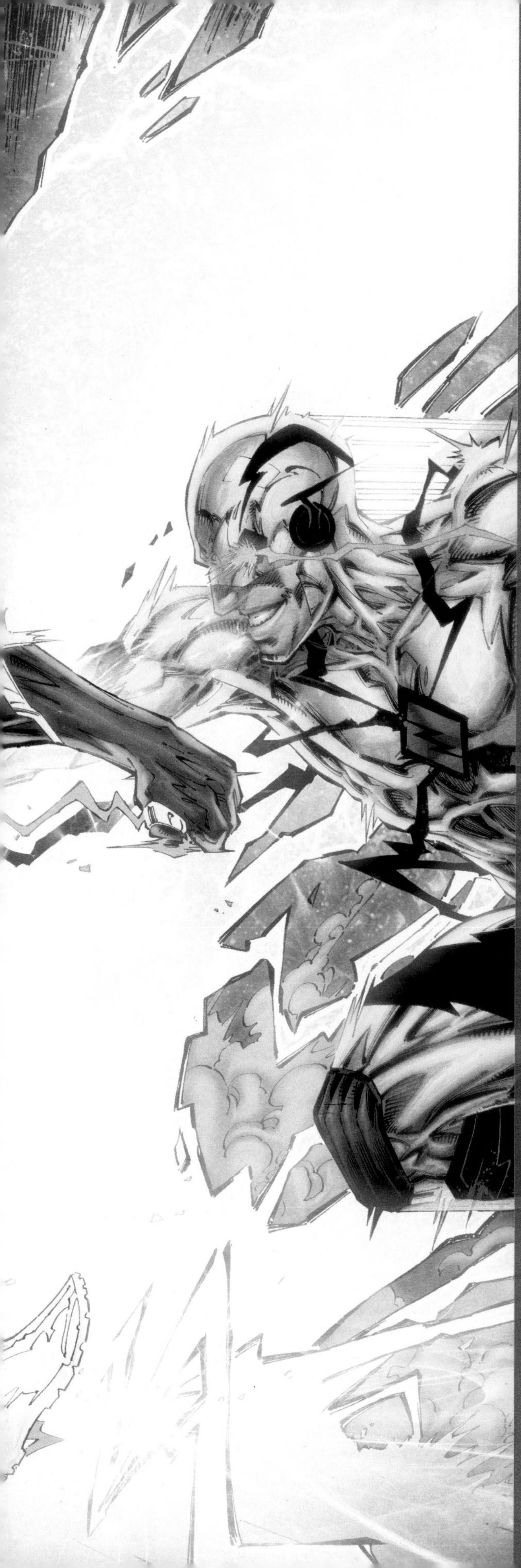

THE FLASH

VOLUME 8
ZOOM

WRITTEN BY
ROBERT VENDITTI
VAN JENSEN

PENCILS BY
BRETT BOOTH
BONG DAZO
VICENTE CIFUENTES
ALÉ GARZA

INKS BY
NORM RAPMUND

COLOR BY
ANDREW DALHOUSE
WENDY BROOME
JEROMY COX

LETTERS BY
PAT BROSSEAU
CARLOS M. MANGUAL

COLLECTION COVER ART BY
BRETT BOOTH,
NORM RAPMUND
& ANDREW DALHOUSE

BRIAN CUNNINGHAM Editor – Original Series
AMEDEO TURTURRO Assistant Editor – Original Series
JEB WOODARD Group Editor – Collected Editions
SUZANNAH ROWNTREE Editor – Collected Edition
STEVE COOK Design Director – Books
DAMIAN RYLAND Publication Design

BOB HARRAS Senior VP – Editor-in-Chief, DC Comics

DIANE NELSON President
DAN DIDIO and JIM LEE Co-Publishers
GEOFF JOHNS Chief Creative Officer
AMIT DESAI Senior VP – Marketing & Global Franchise Management
NAIRI GARDINER Senior VP – Finance
SAM ADES VP – Digital Marketing
BOBBIE CHASE VP –Talent Development
MARK CHIARELLO Senior VP – Art, Design & Collected Editions
JOHN CUNNINGHAM VP – Content Strategy
ANNE DEPIES VP – Strategy Planning & Reporting
DON FALLETTI VP – Manufacturing Operations
LAWRENCE GANEM VP – Editorial Administration & Talent Relations
ALISON GILL Senior VP – Manufacturing & Operations
HANK KANALZ Senior VP – Editorial Strategy & Administration
JAY KOGAN VP – Legal Affairs
DEREK MADDALENA Senior VP – Sales & Business Development
JACK MAHAN VP – Business Affairs
DAN MIRON VP – Sales Planning & Trade Development
NICK NAPOLITANO VP – Manufacturing Administration
CAROL ROEDER VP – Marketing
EDDIE SCANNELL VP – Mass Account & Digital Sales
COURTNEY SIMMONS Senior VP – Publicity & Communications
JIM (SKI) SOKOLOWSKI VP – Comic Book Specialty & Newsstand Sales
SANDY YI Senior VP – Global Franchise Management

THE FLASH VOLUME 8: ZOOM

DC Comics, 2900 West Alameda Ave., Burbank, CA 91505
Printed by RR Donnelley, Salem, VA, USA. 07/01/16. First Printing.
ISBN: 978-1-4012-6366-9

Library of Congress Cataloging-in-Publication Data

Names: Venditti, Robert, author. | Jensen, Van, author. | Booth, Brett, illustrator. | Rapmund, Norm, illustrator.
Title: The Flash. Volume 8, Zoom / Robert Venditti, Van Jensen, writers ; Brett Booth, Norm Rapmund, artists.
Other titles: Zoom
Description: Burbank, CA : DC Comics, [2016]
Identifiers: LCCN 2016017016 | ISBN 9781401263669 (hardback)
Subjects: LCSH: Comic books, strips, etc. | BISAC: COMICS & GRAPHIC NOVELS / Superheroes.
Classification: LCC PN6728.F53 V47 2016 | DDC 741.5/973—dc23
LC record available at https://lccn.loc.gov/2016017016

PEFC Certified
Printed on paper from sustainably managed forests and controlled sources
PEFC
PEFC/29-31-75
www.pefc.org

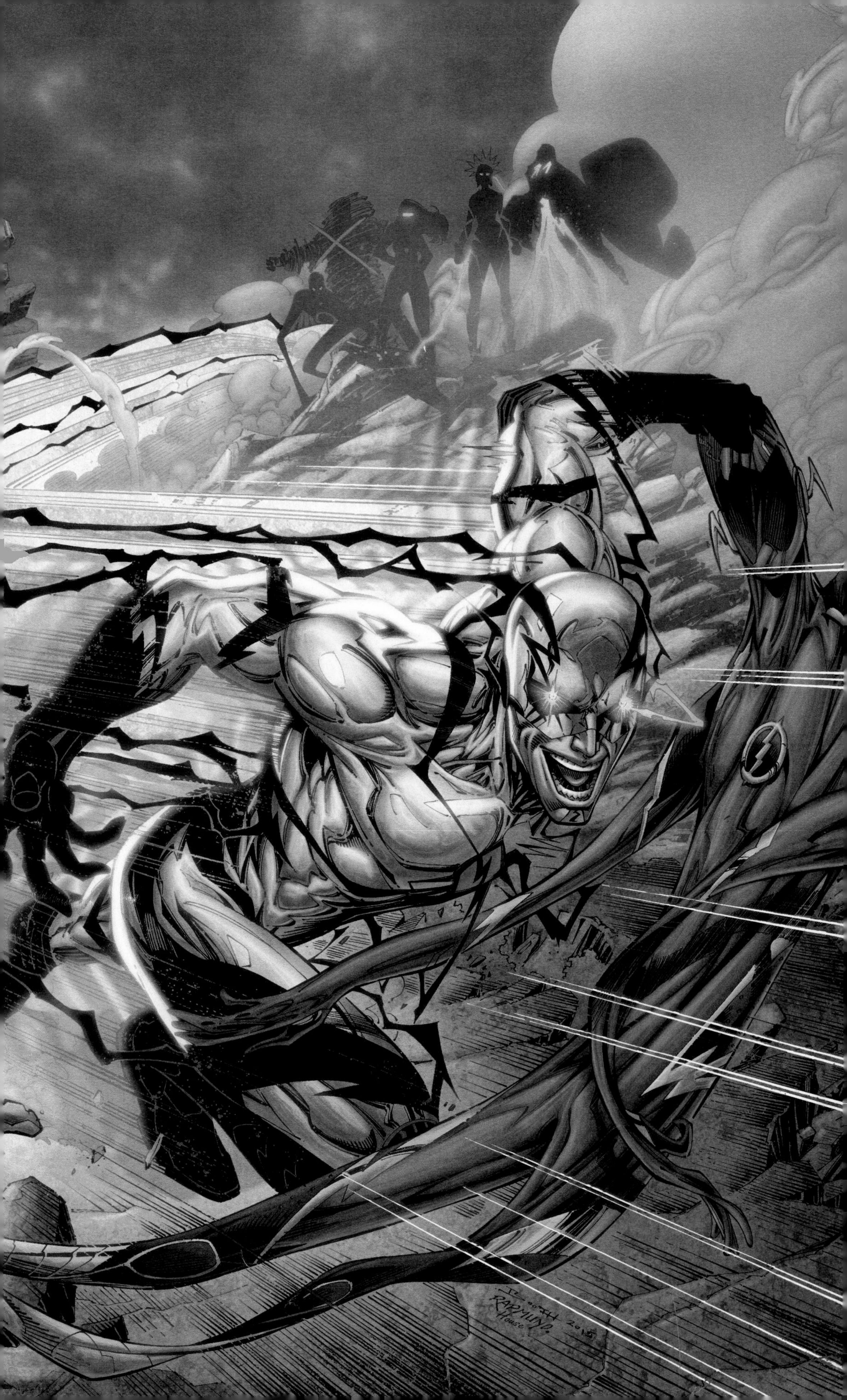

YELLOW

ROBERT VENDITTI, VAN JENSEN writers BRETT BOOTH penciller NORM RAPMUND inker ANDREW DALHOUSE colorist PAT BROSSEAU letterer
cover by BRETT BOOTH, NORM RAPMUND, ANDREW DALHOUSE

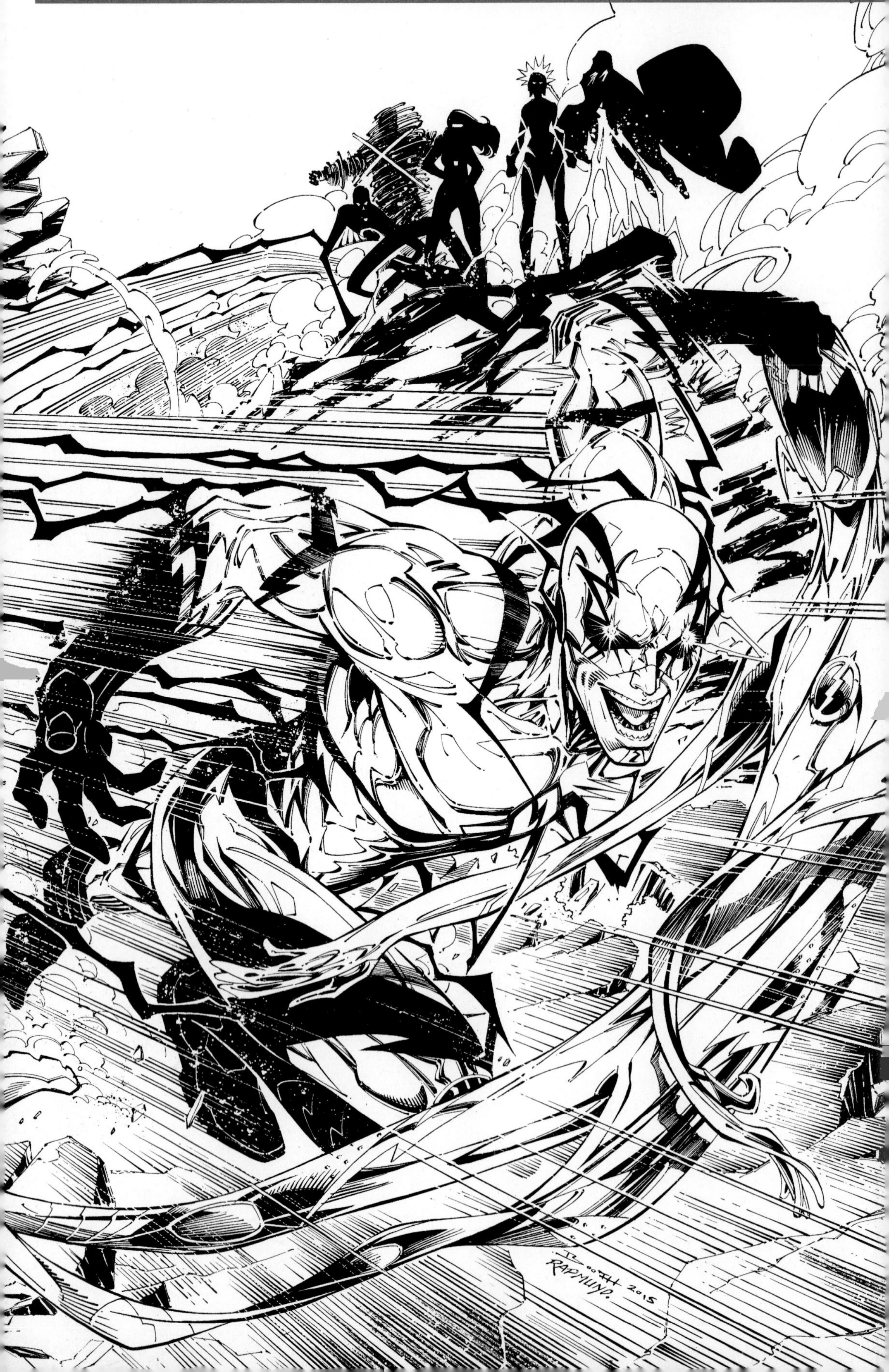
BOOTH 2015
RAPMUND.

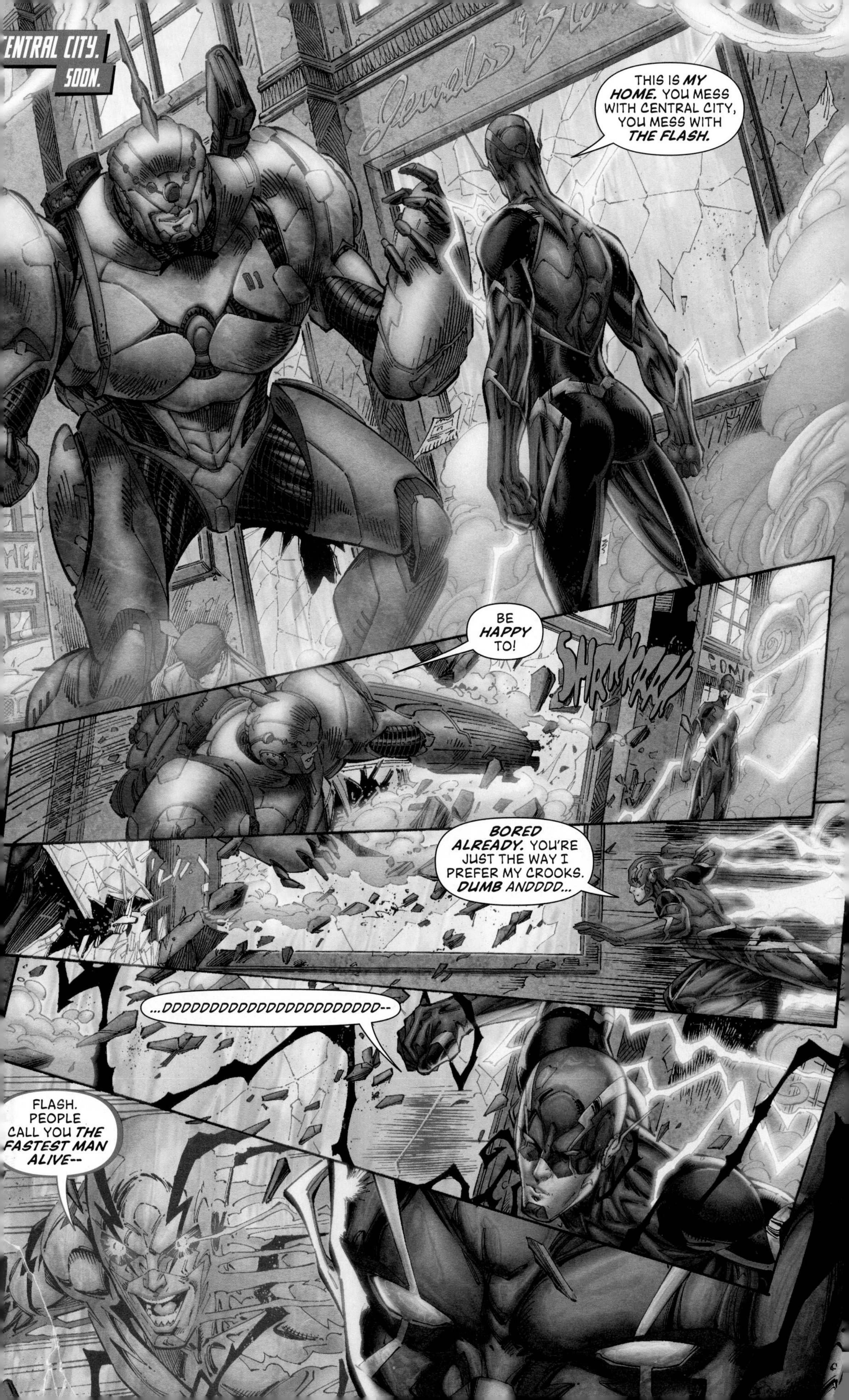
ENTRAL CITY.
SOON.
THIS IS MY HOME. YOU MESS WITH CENTRAL CITY, YOU MESS WITH THE FLASH.
BE HAPPY TO!
BORED ALREADY. YOU'RE JUST THE WAY I PREFER MY CROOKS. DUMB ANDDDD...
...DDDDDDDDDDDDDDDDDDDDDDDD--
FLASH. PEOPLE CALL YOU THE FASTEST MAN ALIVE--

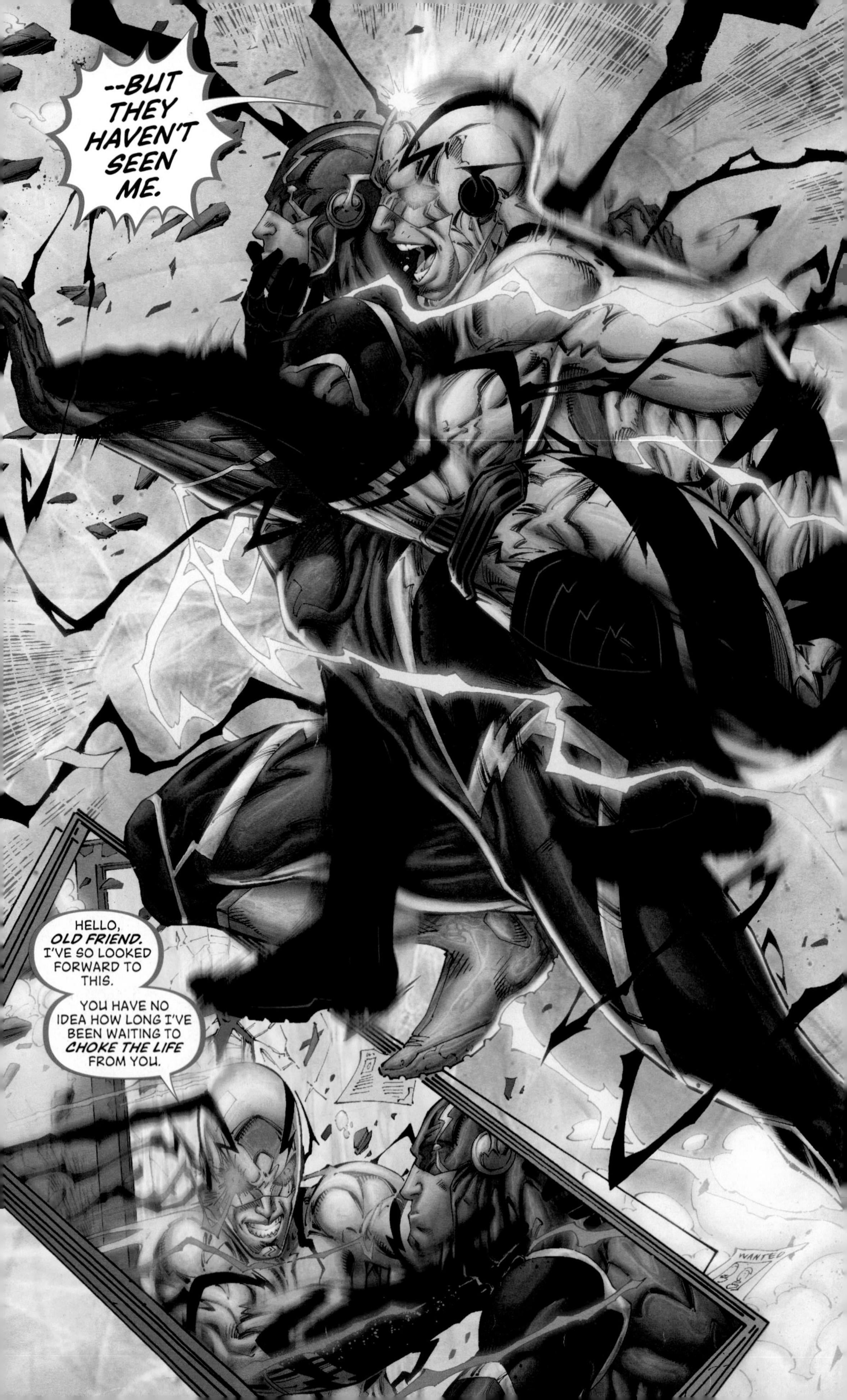
--BUT THEY HAVEN'T SEEN ME.
HELLO, OLD FRIEND. I'VE SO LOOKED FORWARD TO THIS.
YOU HAVE NO IDEA HOW LONG I'VE BEEN WAITING TO CHOKE THE LIFE FROM YOU.
WANTED

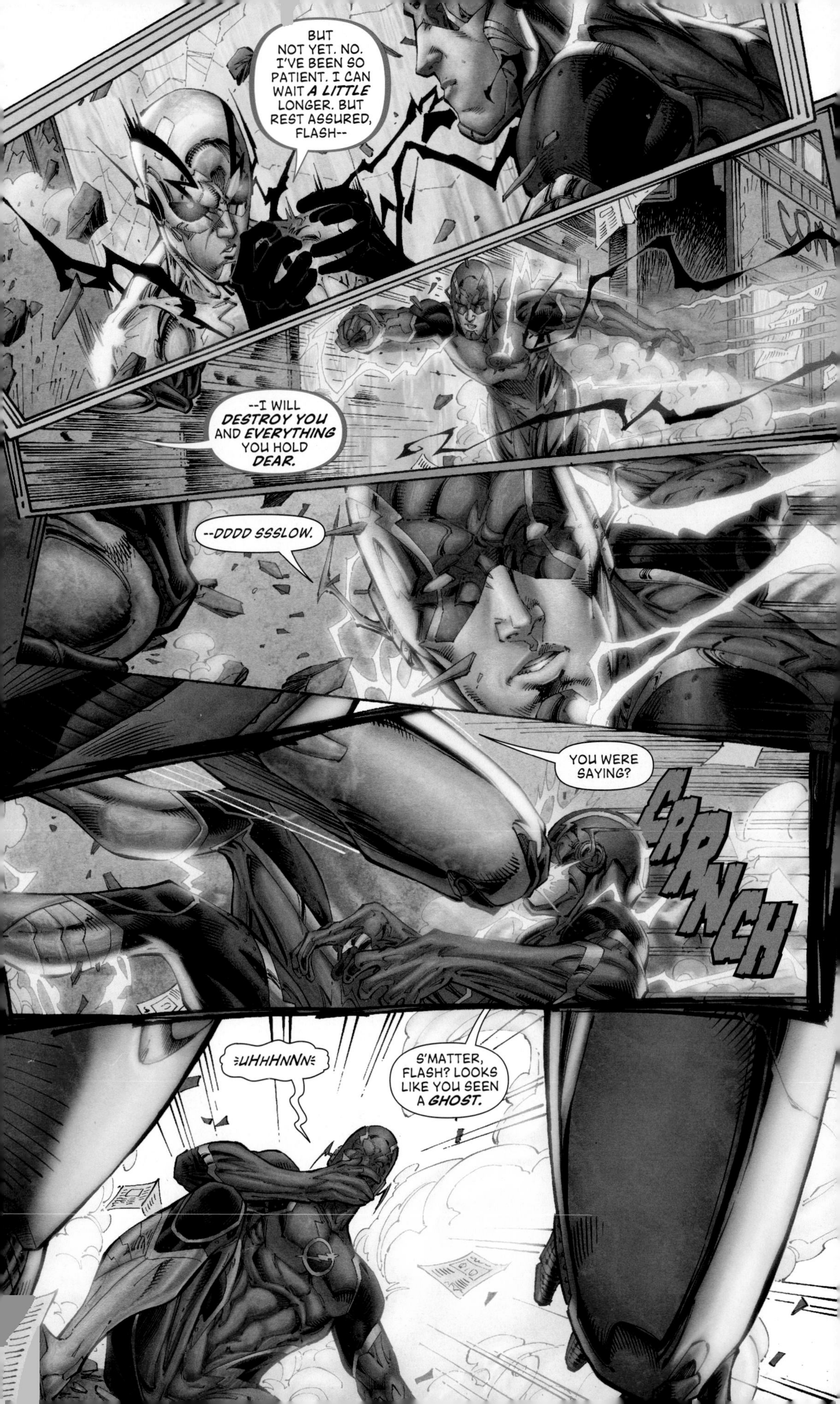
BUT NOT YET. NO. I'VE BEEN SO PATIENT. I CAN WAIT *A LITTLE* LONGER. BUT REST ASSURED, FLASH--
--I WILL *DESTROY YOU* AND *EVERYTHING* YOU HOLD *DEAR.*
--DDDD SSSLOW.
YOU WERE SAYING?
CRRNCH
UHHHNNN
S'MATTER, FLASH? LOOKS LIKE YOU SEEN A *GHOST.*

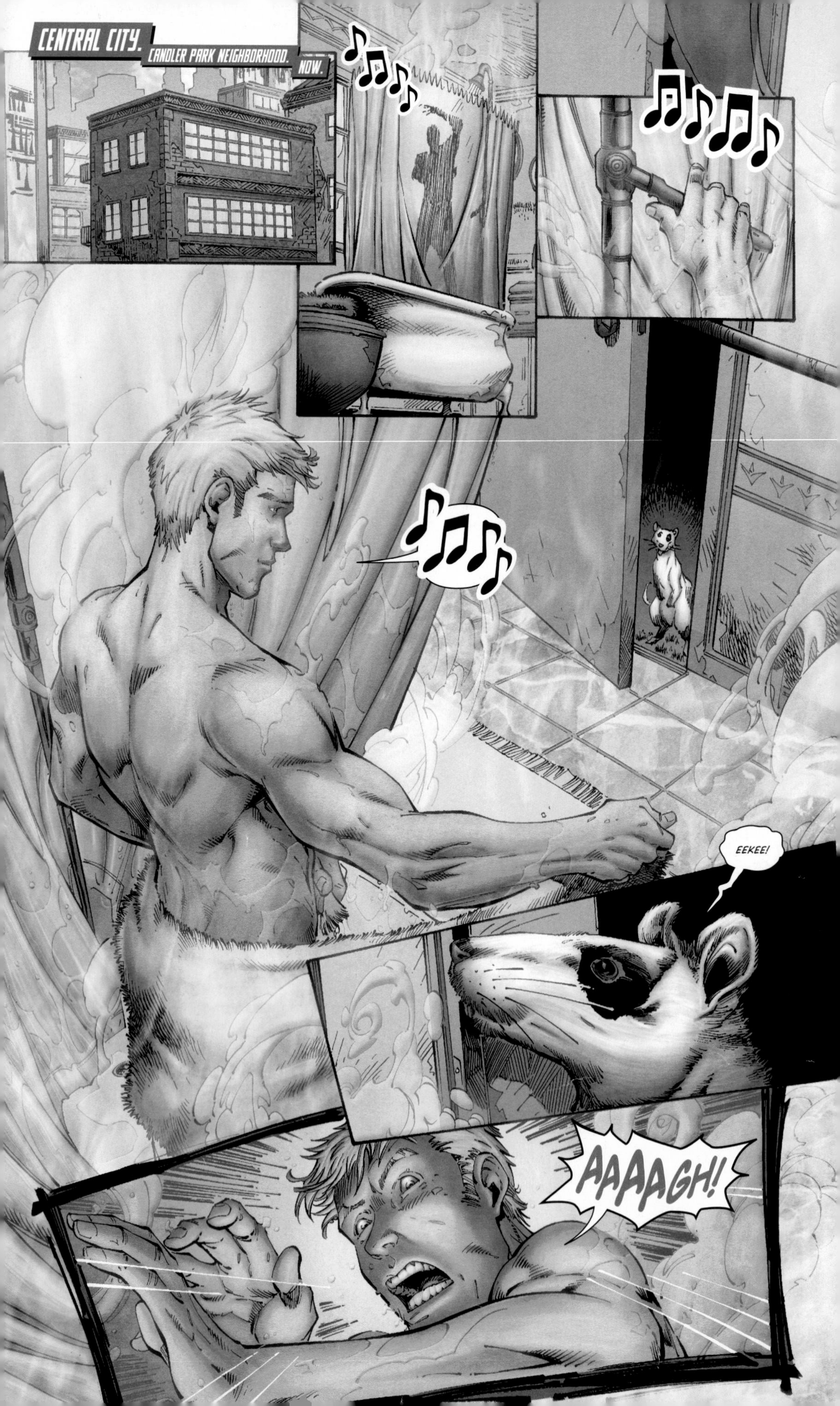

CENTRAL CITY.
CANDLER PARK NEIGHBORHOOD.
NOW.
EEKEE!
AAAAGH!

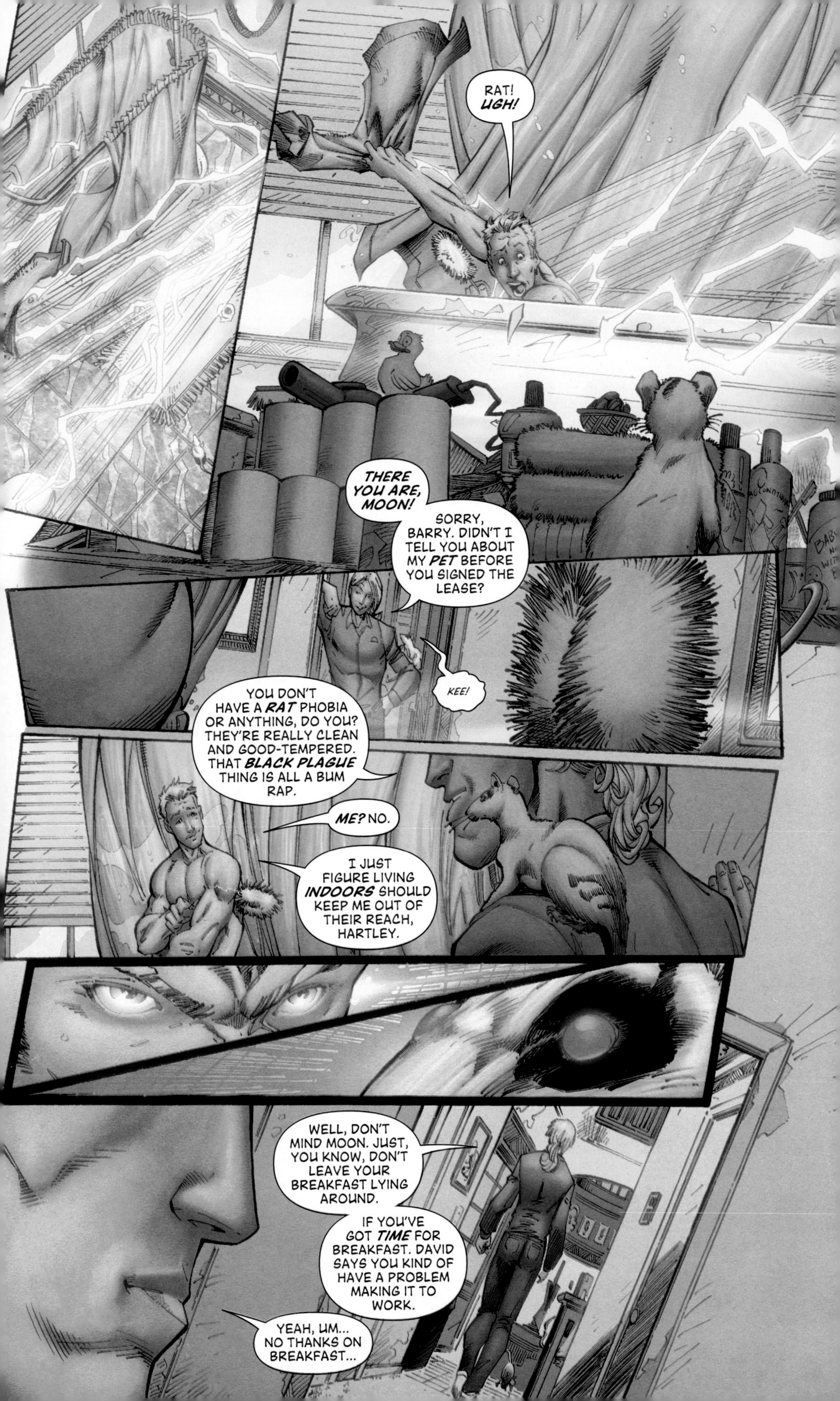
RAT! UGH!
THERE YOU ARE, MOON!
SORRY, BARRY. DIDN'T I TELL YOU ABOUT MY PET BEFORE YOU SIGNED THE LEASE?
KEE!
YOU DON'T HAVE A RAT PHOBIA OR ANYTHING, DO YOU? THEY'RE REALLY CLEAN AND GOOD-TEMPERED. THAT BLACK PLAGUE THING IS ALL A BUM RAP.
ME? NO.
I JUST FIGURE LIVING INDOORS SHOULD KEEP ME OUT OF THEIR REACH, HARTLEY.
WELL, DON'T MIND MOON. JUST, YOU KNOW, DON'T LEAVE YOUR BREAKFAST LYING AROUND.
IF YOU'VE GOT TIME FOR BREAKFAST. DAVID SAYS YOU KIND OF HAVE A PROBLEM MAKING IT TO WORK.
YEAH, UM... NO THANKS ON BREAKFAST...

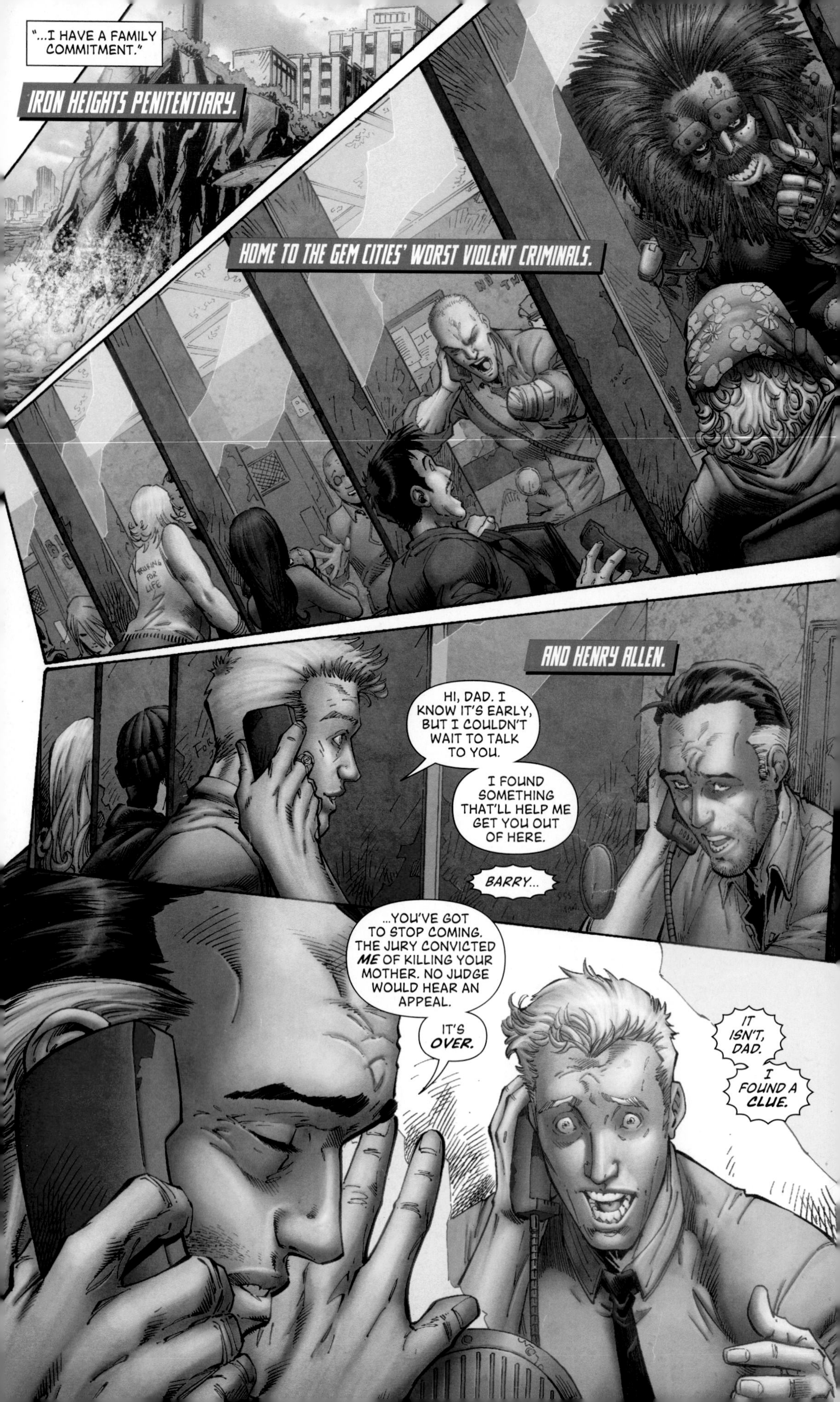
"...I HAVE A FAMILY COMMITMENT."
IRON HEIGHTS PENITENTIARY.
HOME TO THE GEM CITIES' WORST VIOLENT CRIMINALS.
AND HENRY ALLEN.
HI, DAD. I KNOW IT'S EARLY, BUT I COULDN'T WAIT TO TALK TO YOU.
I FOUND SOMETHING THAT'LL HELP ME GET YOU OUT OF HERE.
BARRY...
...YOU'VE GOT TO STOP COMING. THE JURY CONVICTED ME OF KILLING YOUR MOTHER. NO JUDGE WOULD HEAR AN APPEAL.
IT'S OVER.
IT ISN'T, DAD.
I FOUND A CLUE.

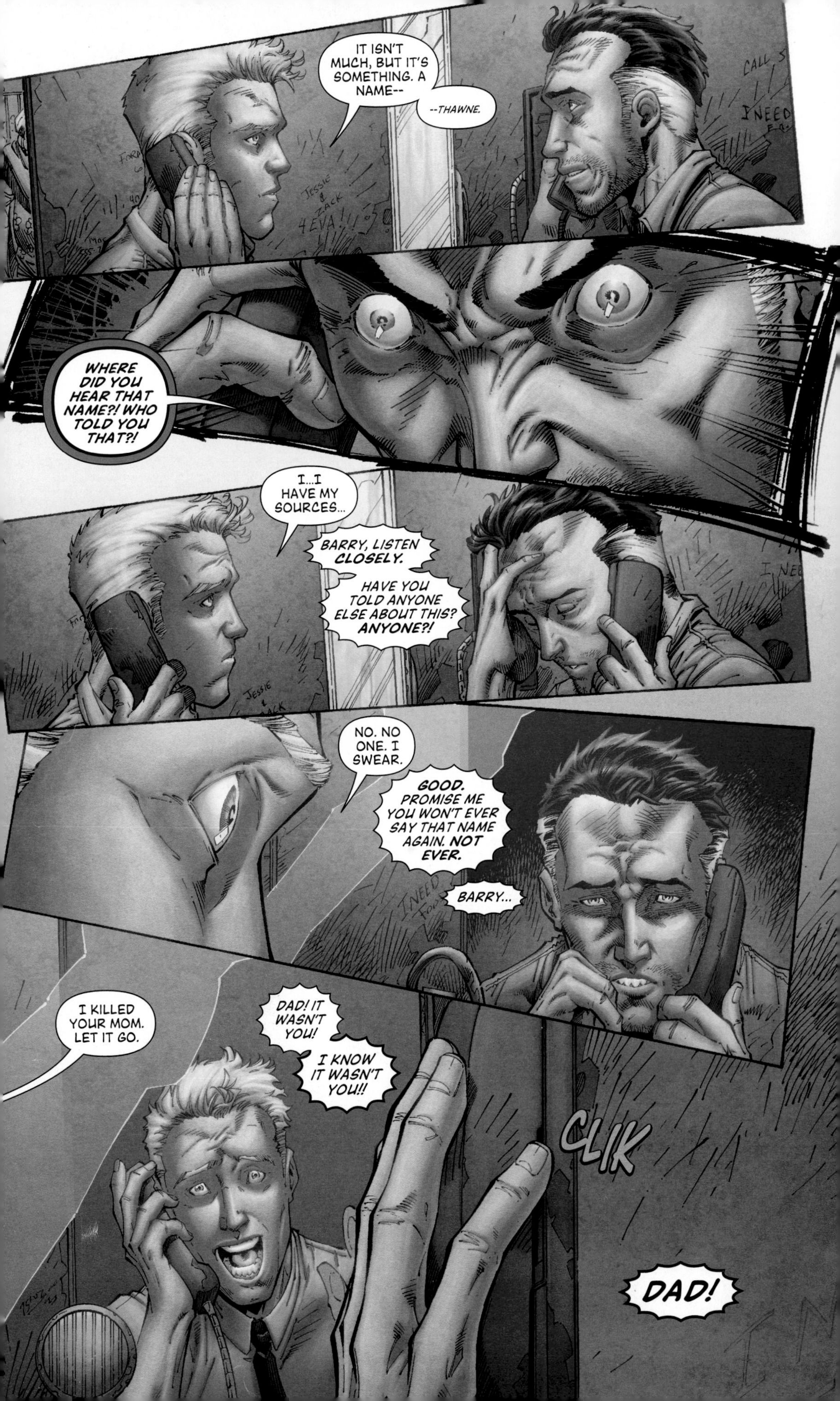

IT ISN'T MUCH, BUT IT'S SOMETHING. A NAME--
--THAWNE.
WHERE DID YOU HEAR THAT NAME?! WHO TOLD YOU THAT?!
I...I HAVE MY SOURCES...
BARRY, LISTEN CLOSELY.
HAVE YOU TOLD ANYONE ELSE ABOUT THIS? ANYONE?!
NO. NO ONE. I SWEAR.
GOOD. PROMISE ME YOU WON'T EVER SAY THAT NAME AGAIN. NOT EVER.
BARRY...
I KILLED YOUR MOM. LET IT GO.
DAD! IT WASN'T YOU!
I KNOW IT WASN'T YOU!!
CLIK
DAD!

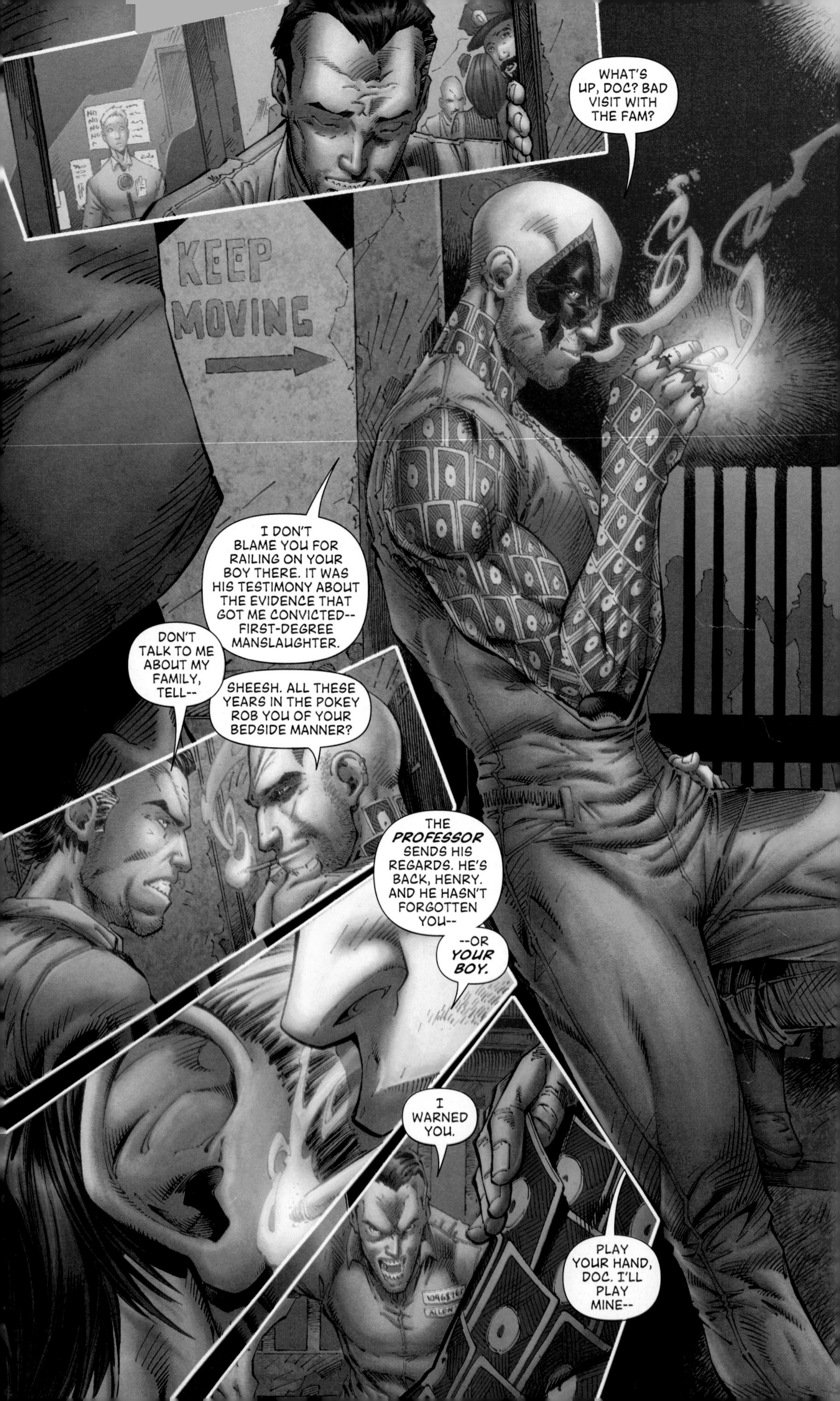
WHAT'S UP, DOC? BAD VISIT WITH THE FAM?
KEEP MOVING
I DON'T BLAME YOU FOR RAILING ON YOUR BOY THERE. IT WAS HIS TESTIMONY ABOUT THE EVIDENCE THAT GOT ME CONVICTED-- FIRST-DEGREE MANSLAUGHTER.
DON'T TALK TO ME ABOUT MY FAMILY, TELL--
SHEESH. ALL THESE YEARS IN THE POKEY ROB YOU OF YOUR BEDSIDE MANNER?
THE *PROFESSOR* SENDS HIS REGARDS. HE'S BACK, HENRY. AND HE HASN'T FORGOTTEN YOU--
--OR *YOUR BOY.*
I WARNED YOU.
PLAY YOUR HAND, DOC. I'LL PLAY MINE--

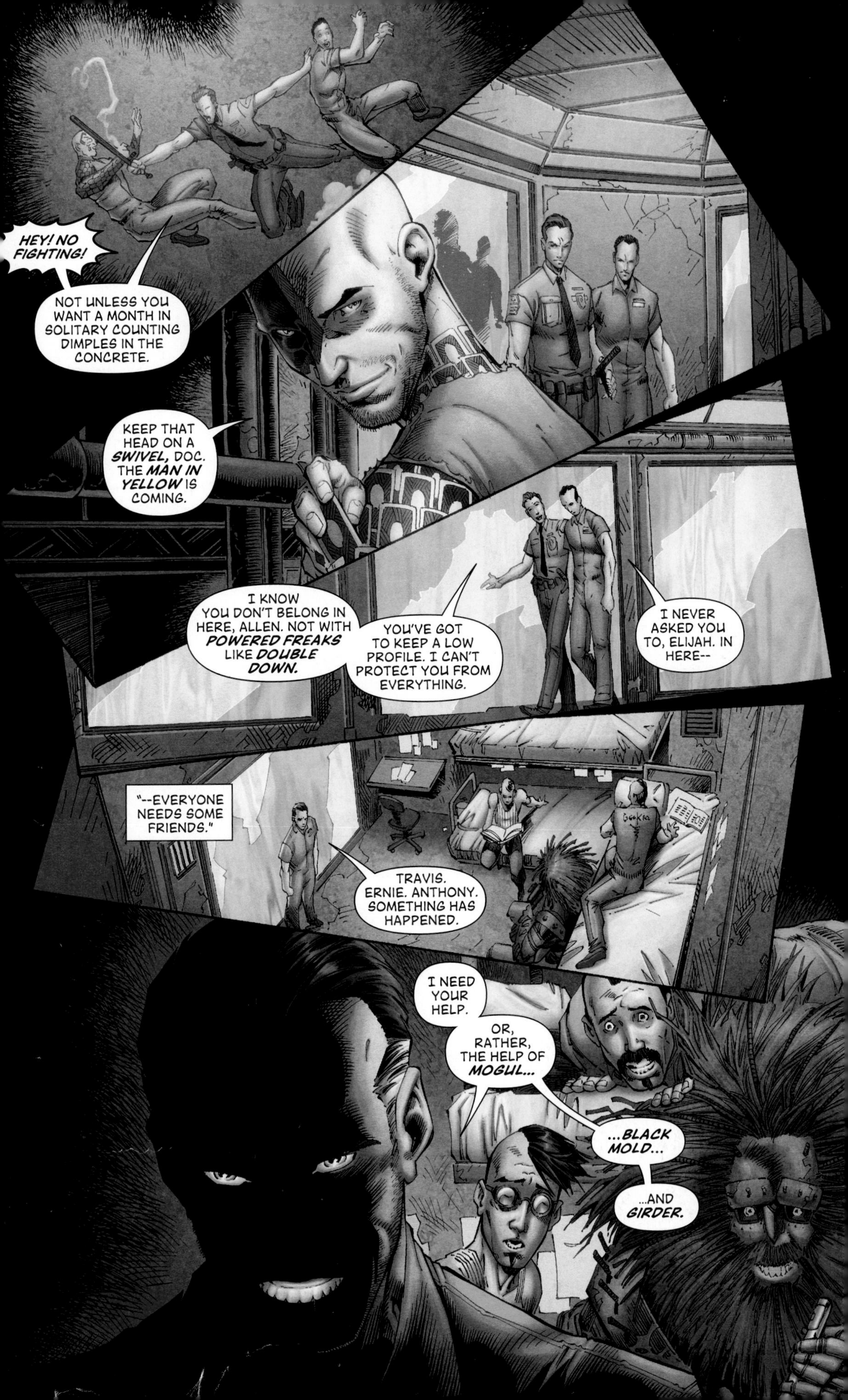
HEY! NO FIGHTING!
NOT UNLESS YOU WANT A MONTH IN SOLITARY COUNTING DIMPLES IN THE CONCRETE.
KEEP THAT HEAD ON A SWIVEL, DOC. THE MAN IN YELLOW IS COMING.
I KNOW YOU DON'T BELONG IN HERE, ALLEN. NOT WITH POWERED FREAKS LIKE DOUBLE DOWN.
YOU'VE GOT TO KEEP A LOW PROFILE. I CAN'T PROTECT YOU FROM EVERYTHING.
I NEVER ASKED YOU TO, ELIJAH. IN HERE--
"--EVERYONE NEEDS SOME FRIENDS."
TRAVIS. ERNIE. ANTHONY. SOMETHING HAS HAPPENED.
I NEED YOUR HELP.
OR, RATHER, THE HELP OF MOGUL...
...BLACK MOLD...
...AND GIRDER.

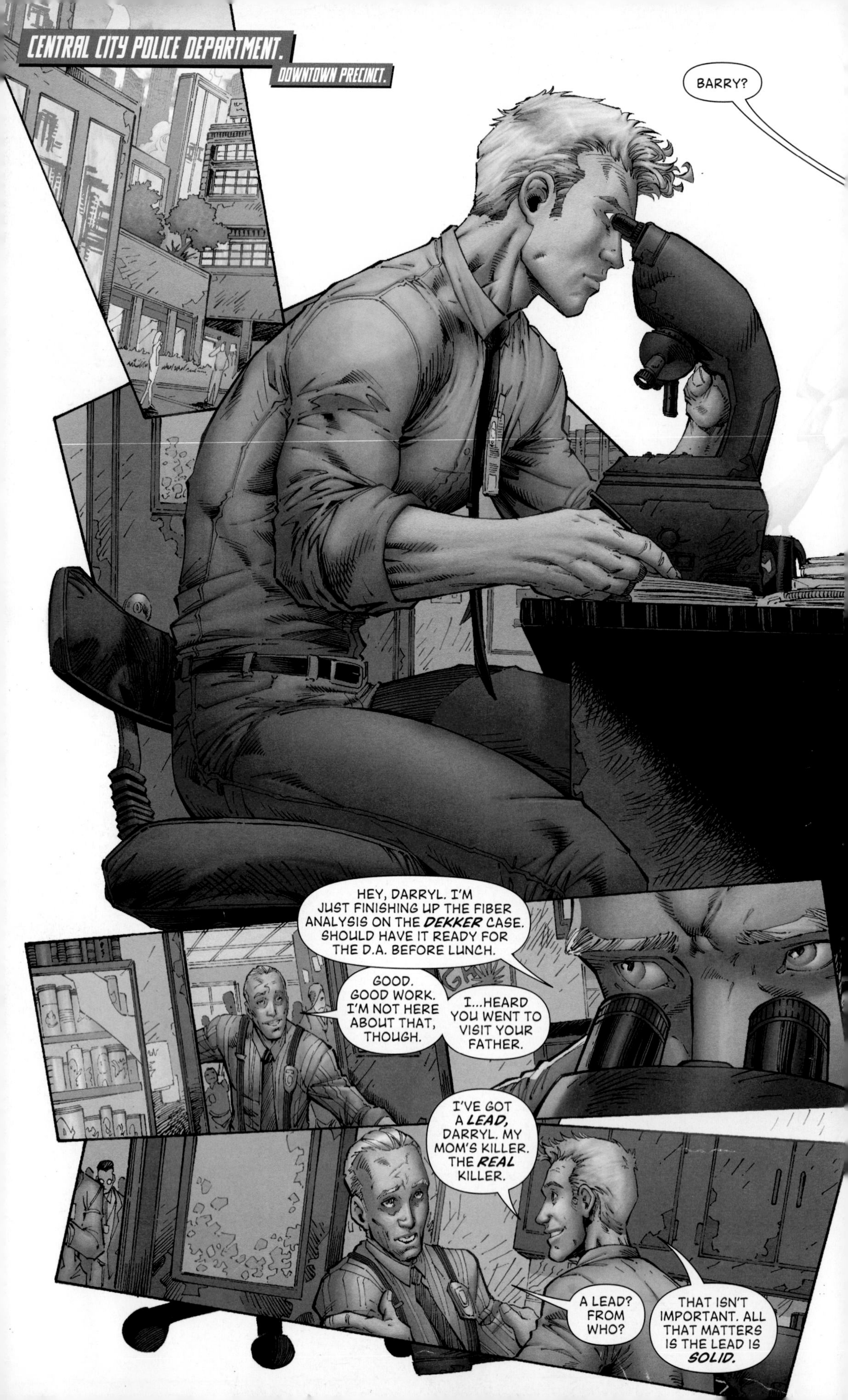
CENTRAL CITY POLICE DEPARTMENT.
DOWNTOWN PRECINCT.
BARRY?
HEY, DARRYL. I'M JUST FINISHING UP THE FIBER ANALYSIS ON THE DEKKER CASE. SHOULD HAVE IT READY FOR THE D.A. BEFORE LUNCH.
GOOD. GOOD WORK. I'M NOT HERE ABOUT THAT, THOUGH.
I...HEARD YOU WENT TO VISIT YOUR FATHER.
I'VE GOT A LEAD, DARRYL. MY MOM'S KILLER. THE REAL KILLER.
A LEAD? FROM WHO?
THAT ISN'T IMPORTANT. ALL THAT MATTERS IS THE LEAD IS SOLID.

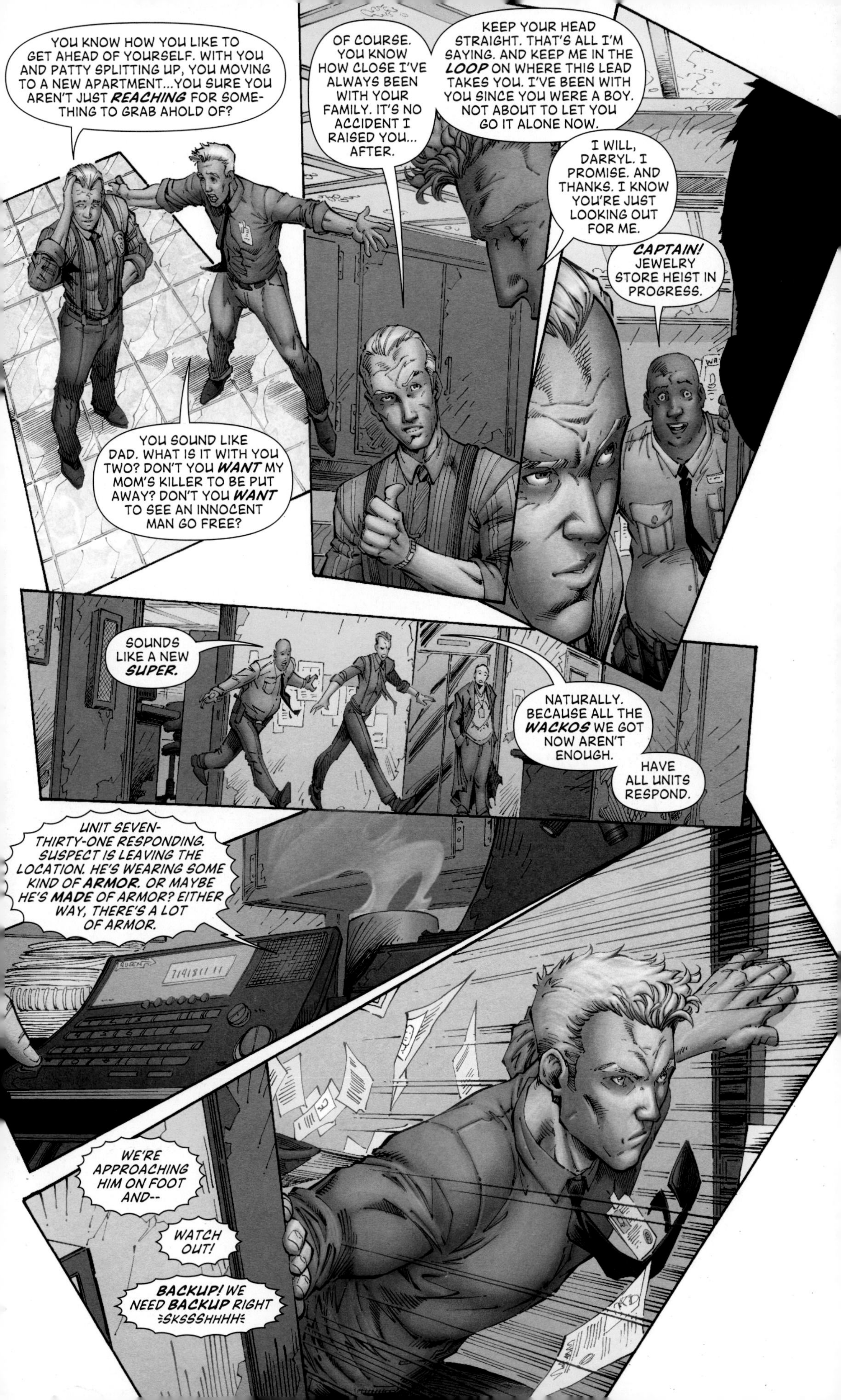
YOU KNOW HOW YOU LIKE TO GET AHEAD OF YOURSELF. WITH YOU AND PATTY SPLITTING UP, YOU MOVING TO A NEW APARTMENT...YOU SURE YOU AREN'T JUST REACHING FOR SOMETHING TO GRAB AHOLD OF?
YOU SOUND LIKE DAD. WHAT IS IT WITH YOU TWO? DON'T YOU WANT MY MOM'S KILLER TO BE PUT AWAY? DON'T YOU WANT TO SEE AN INNOCENT MAN GO FREE?
OF COURSE. YOU KNOW HOW CLOSE I'VE ALWAYS BEEN WITH YOUR FAMILY. IT'S NO ACCIDENT I RAISED YOU... AFTER.
KEEP YOUR HEAD STRAIGHT. THAT'S ALL I'M SAYING. AND KEEP ME IN THE LOOP ON WHERE THIS LEAD TAKES YOU. I'VE BEEN WITH YOU SINCE YOU WERE A BOY. NOT ABOUT TO LET YOU GO IT ALONE NOW.
I WILL, DARRYL. I PROMISE. AND THANKS. I KNOW YOU'RE JUST LOOKING OUT FOR ME.
CAPTAIN! JEWELRY STORE HEIST IN PROGRESS.
SOUNDS LIKE A NEW SUPER.
NATURALLY. BECAUSE ALL THE WACKOS WE GOT NOW AREN'T ENOUGH.
HAVE ALL UNITS RESPOND.
UNIT SEVEN-THIRTY-ONE RESPONDING. SUSPECT IS LEAVING THE LOCATION. HE'S WEARING SOME KIND OF ARMOR. OR MAYBE HE'S MADE OF ARMOR? EITHER WAY, THERE'S A LOT OF ARMOR.
WE'RE APPROACHING HIM ON FOOT AND--
WATCH OUT!
BACKUP! WE NEED BACKUP RIGHT
SKSSSHHHH

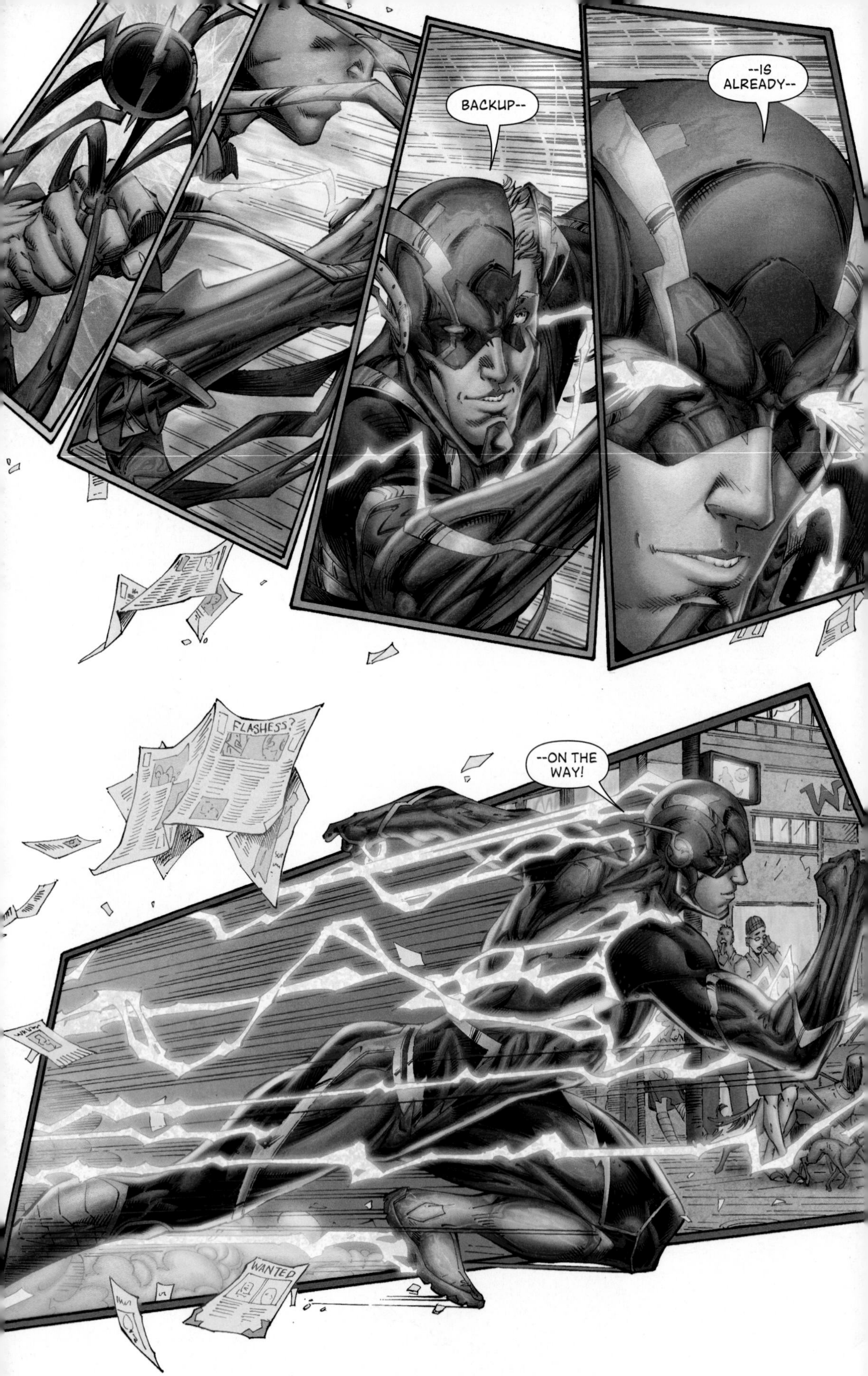
BACKUP--
--IS ALREADY--
FLASHESS?
--ON THE WAY!
WANTED

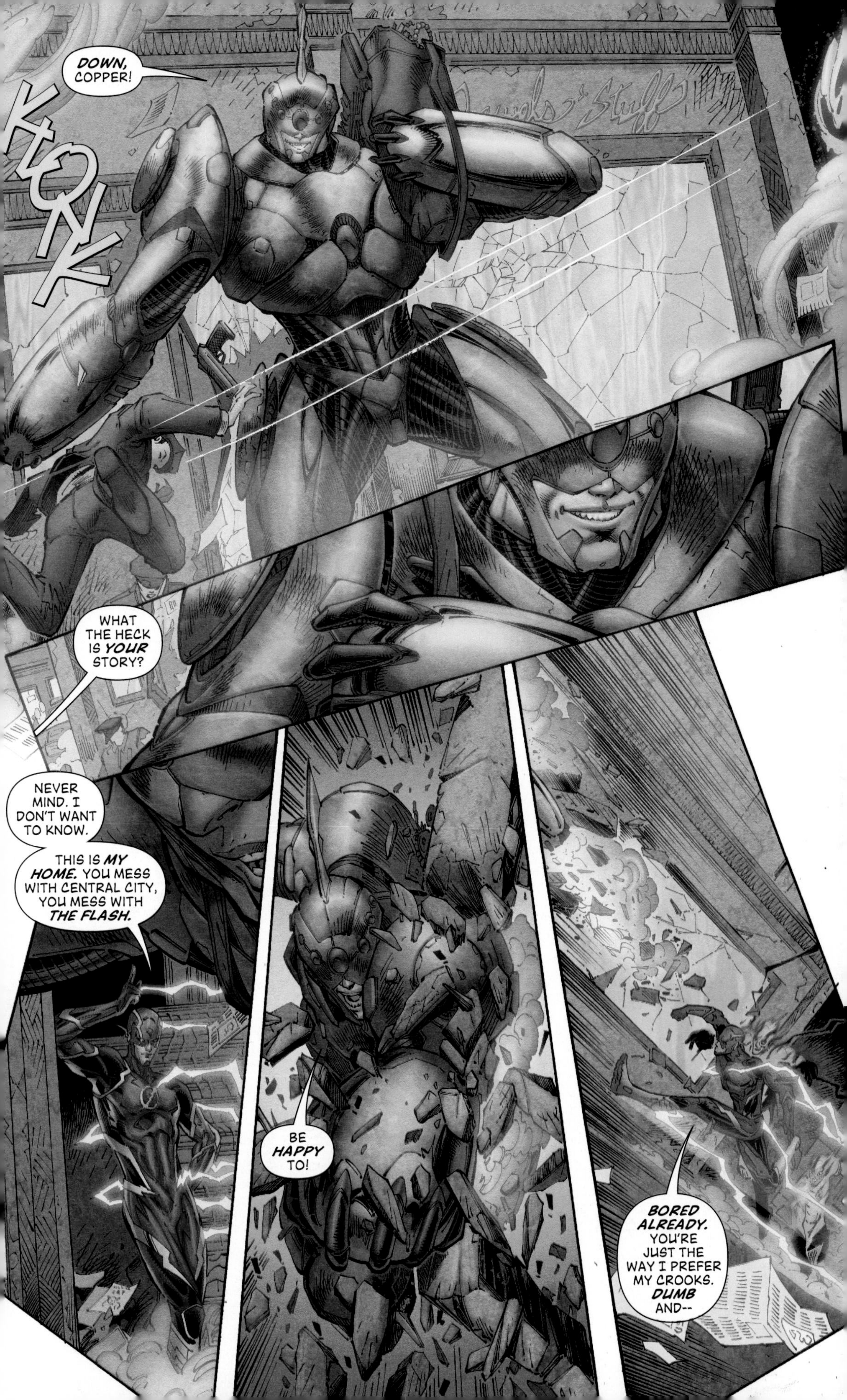
DOWN, COPPER!
KLONK
WHAT THE HECK IS YOUR STORY?
NEVER MIND. I DON'T WANT TO KNOW.
THIS IS MY HOME. YOU MESS WITH CENTRAL CITY, YOU MESS WITH THE FLASH.
BE HAPPY TO!
BORED ALREADY. YOU'RE JUST THE WAY I PREFER MY CROOKS. DUMB AND--

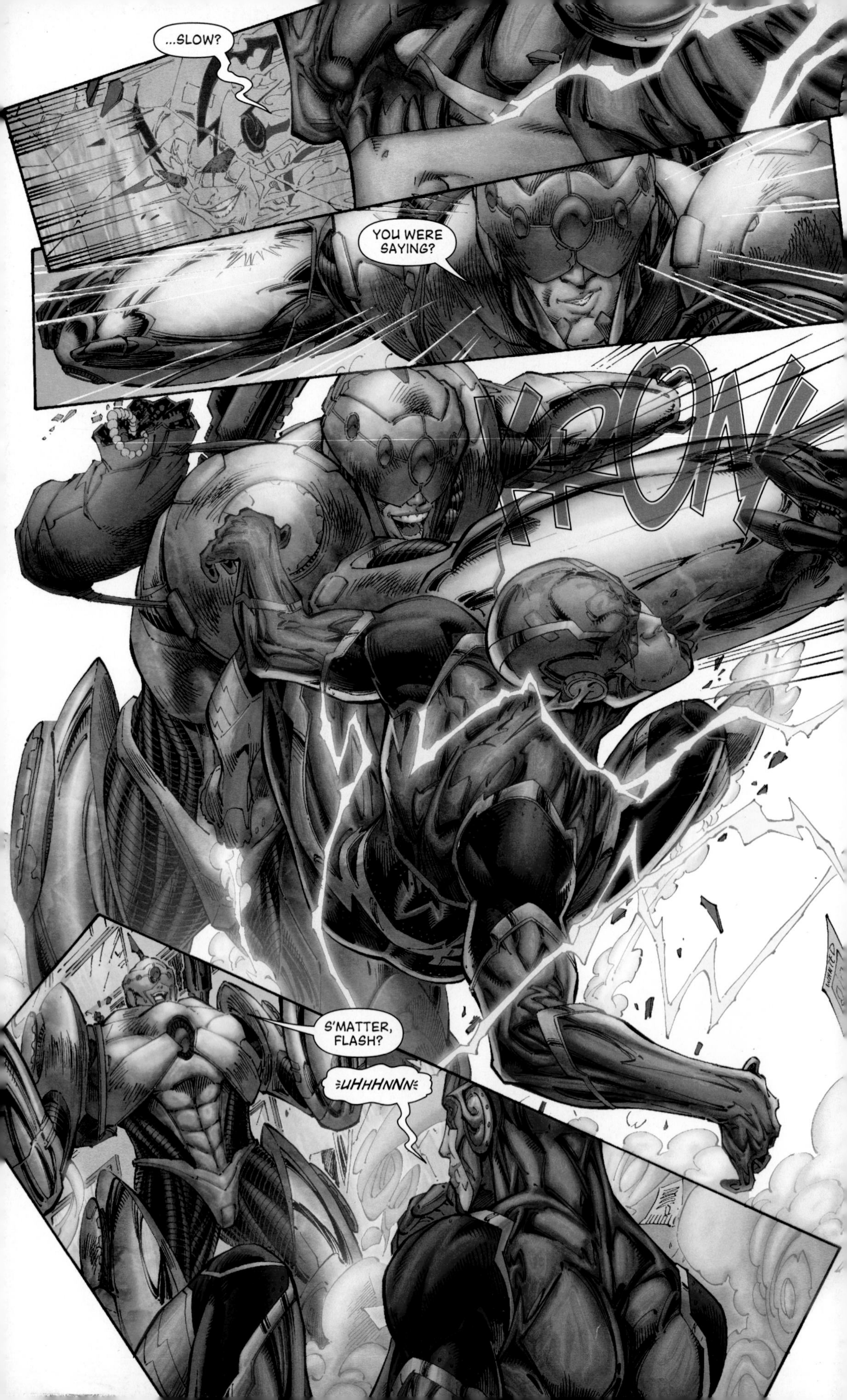

...SLOW?
YOU WERE SAYING?
KRONK
S'MATTER, FLASH?
UHHHNNN

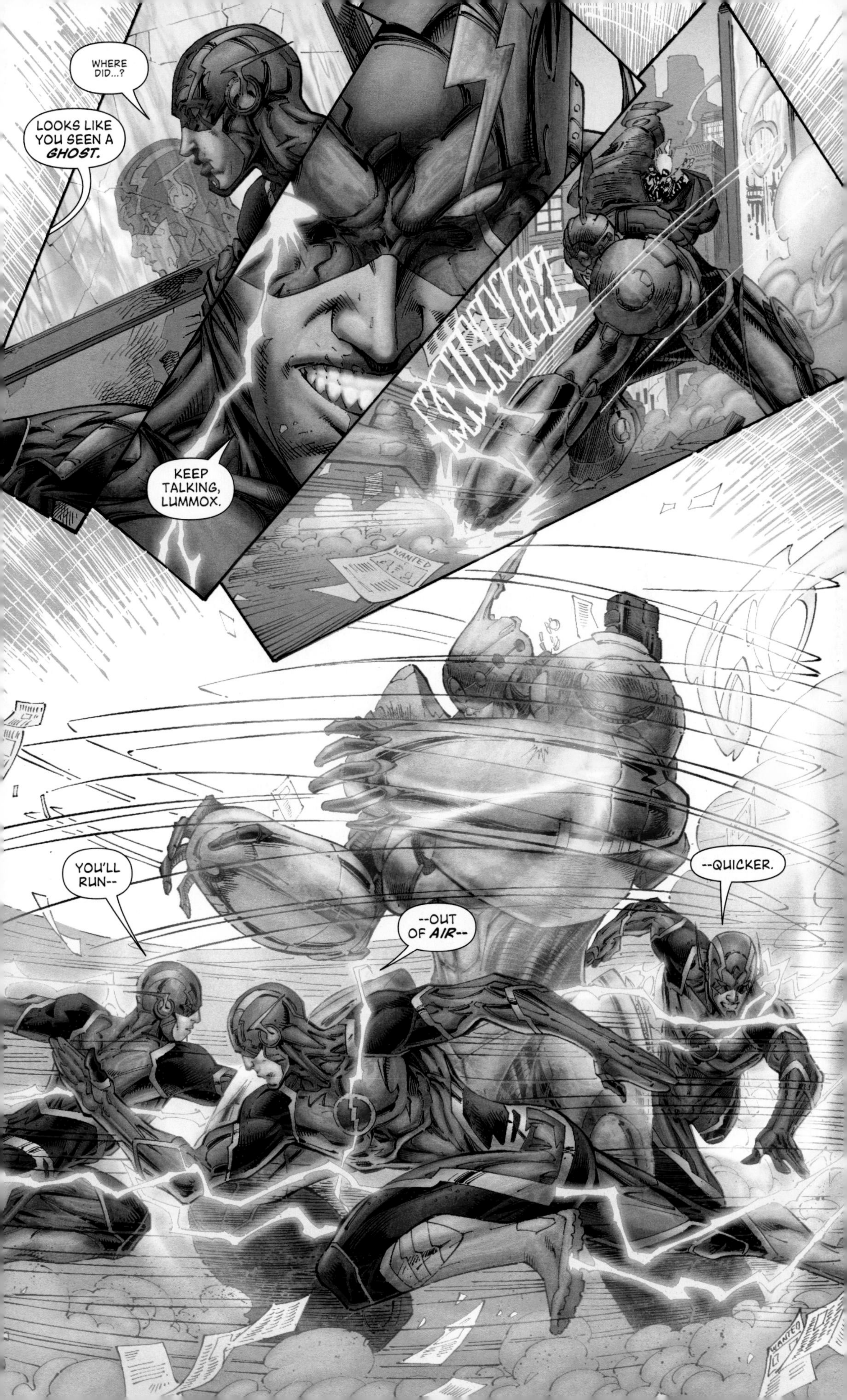
WHERE DID...?
LOOKS LIKE YOU SEEN A GHOST.
KEEP TALKING, LUMMOX.
YOU'LL RUN--
--OUT OF AIR--
--QUICKER.

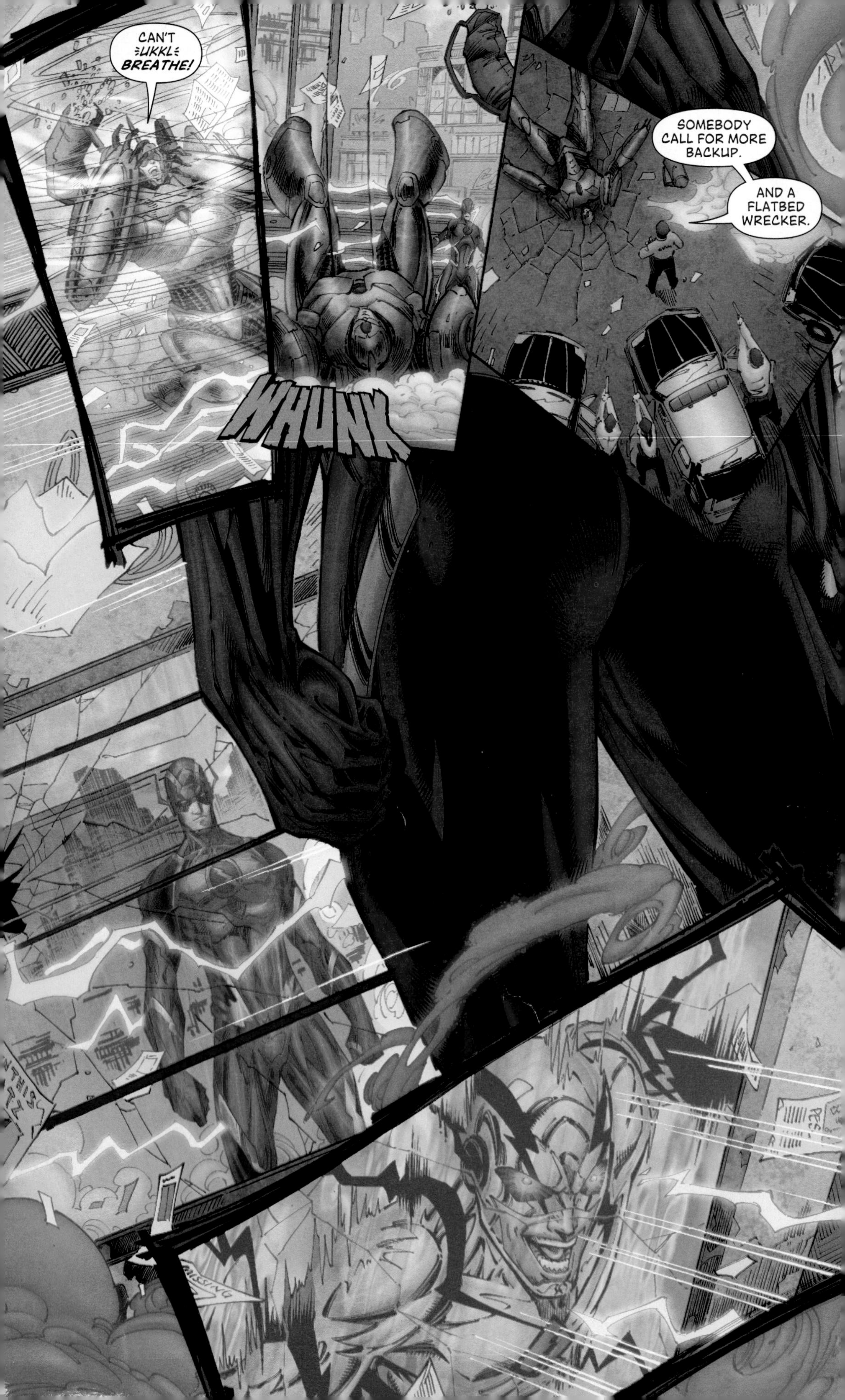
CAN'T ukkl BREATHE!
WHUNK
SOMEBODY CALL FOR MORE BACKUP.
AND A FLATBED WRECKER.

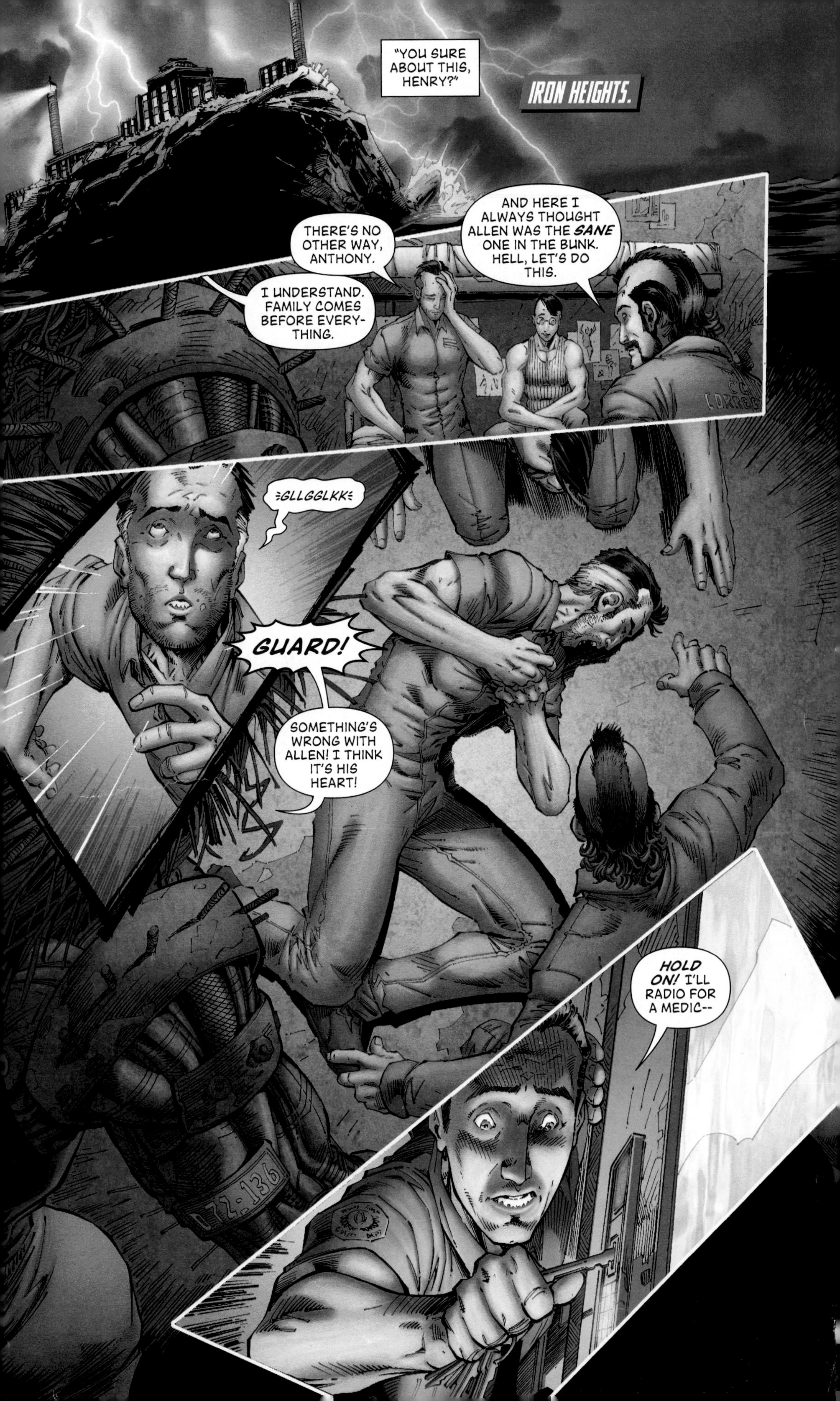
"YOU SURE ABOUT THIS, HENRY?"
IRON HEIGHTS.
THERE'S NO OTHER WAY, ANTHONY.
AND HERE I ALWAYS THOUGHT ALLEN WAS THE SANE ONE IN THE BUNK. HELL, LET'S DO THIS.
I UNDERSTAND. FAMILY COMES BEFORE EVERY-THING.
GLLGGLKK
GUARD!
SOMETHING'S WRONG WITH ALLEN! I THINK IT'S HIS HEART!
HOLD ON! I'LL RADIO FOR A MEDIC--

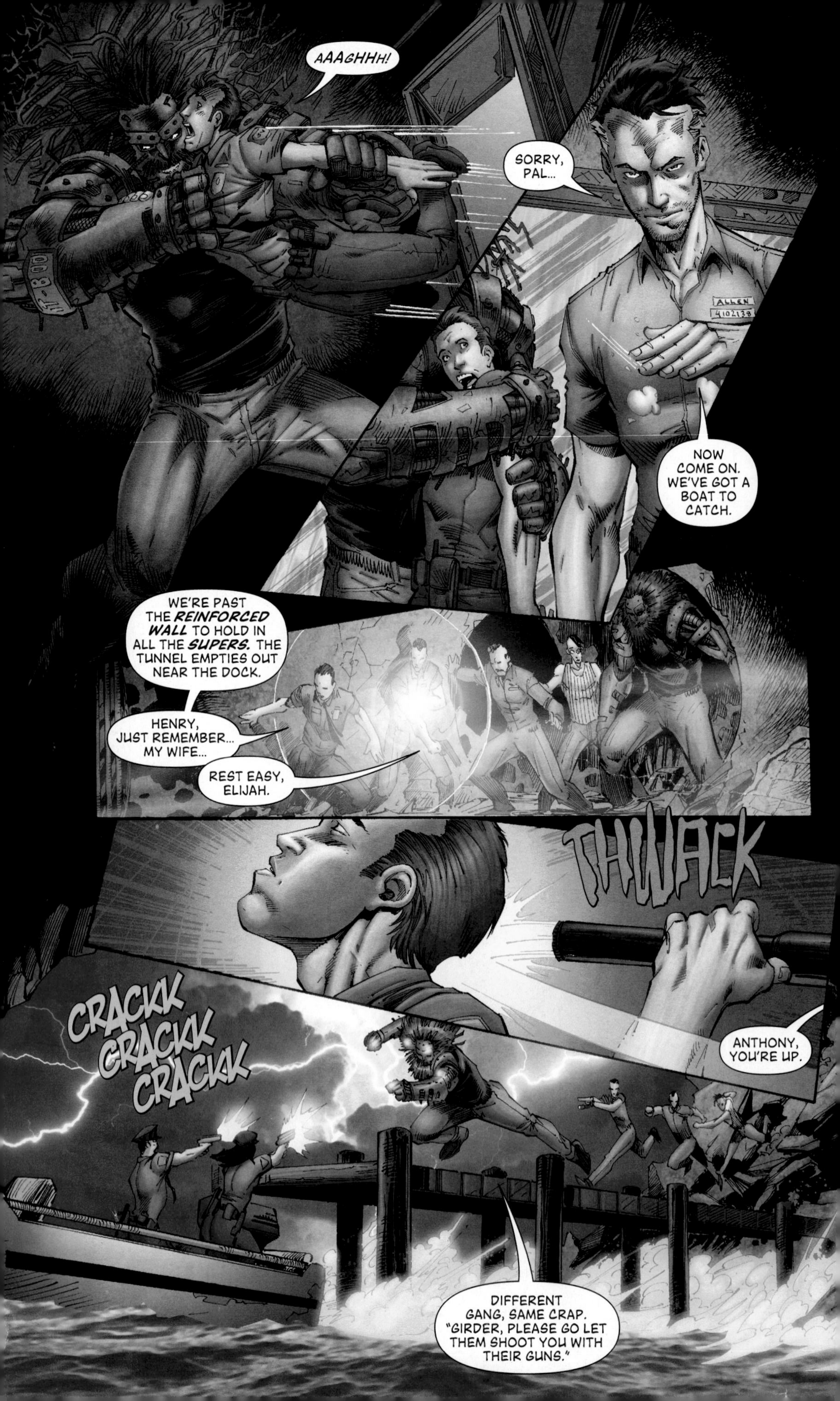
AAAGHHH!
SORRY, PAL...
ALLEN 4102138
NOW COME ON. WE'VE GOT A BOAT TO CATCH.
WE'RE PAST THE **REINFORCED WALL** TO HOLD IN ALL THE **SUPERS.** THE TUNNEL EMPTIES OUT NEAR THE DOCK.
HENRY, JUST REMEMBER... MY WIFE...
REST EASY, ELIJAH.
THWACK
ANTHONY, YOU'RE UP.
CRACKK CRACKK CRACKK
DIFFERENT GANG, SAME CRAP. "GIRDER, PLEASE GO LET THEM SHOOT YOU WITH THEIR GUNS."

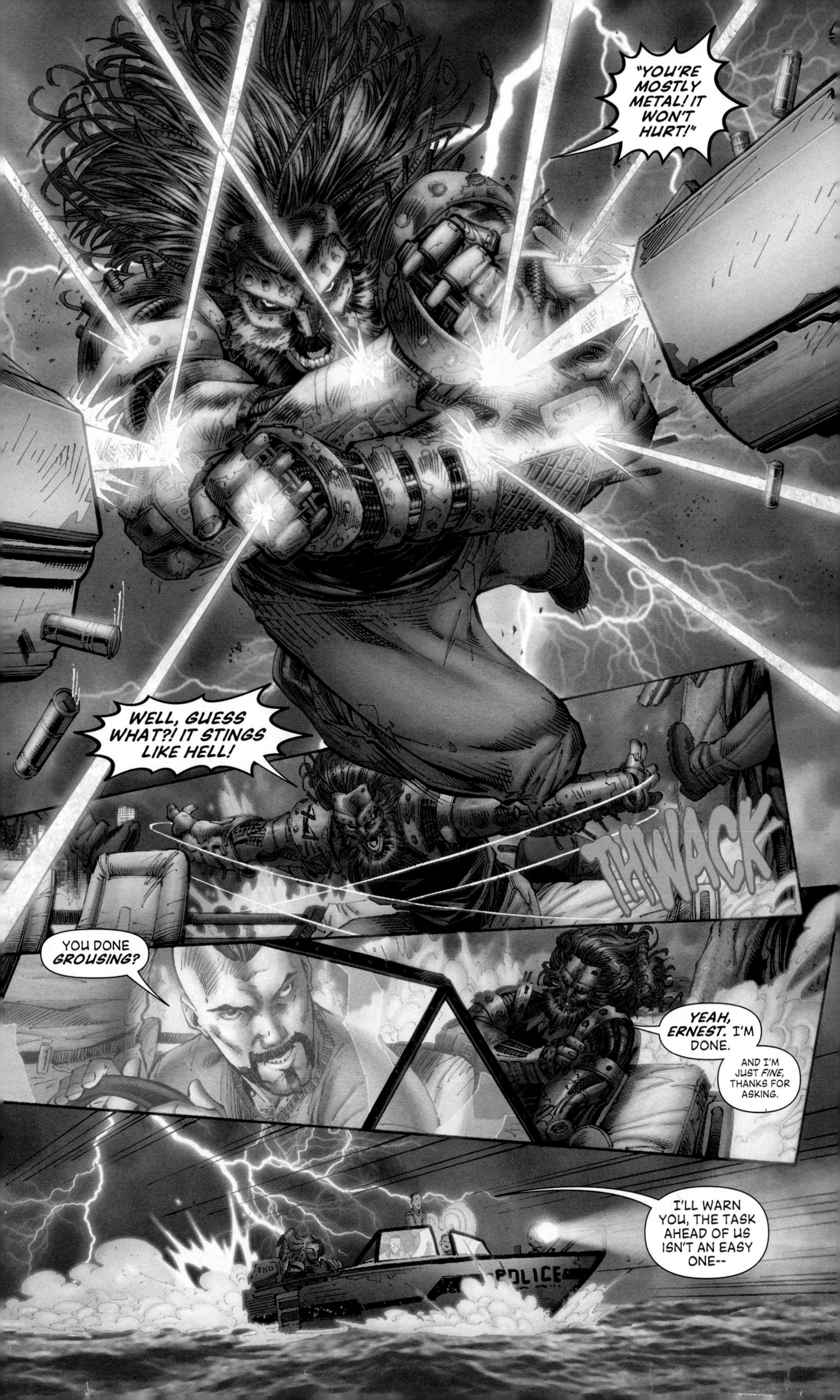
"YOU'RE MOSTLY METAL! IT WON'T HURT!"
WELL, GUESS WHAT?! IT STINGS LIKE HELL!
THWACK
YOU DONE GROUSING?
YEAH, ERNEST. I'M DONE.
AND I'M JUST FINE, THANKS FOR ASKING.
I'LL WARN YOU, THE TASK AHEAD OF US ISN'T AN EASY ONE--
POLICE

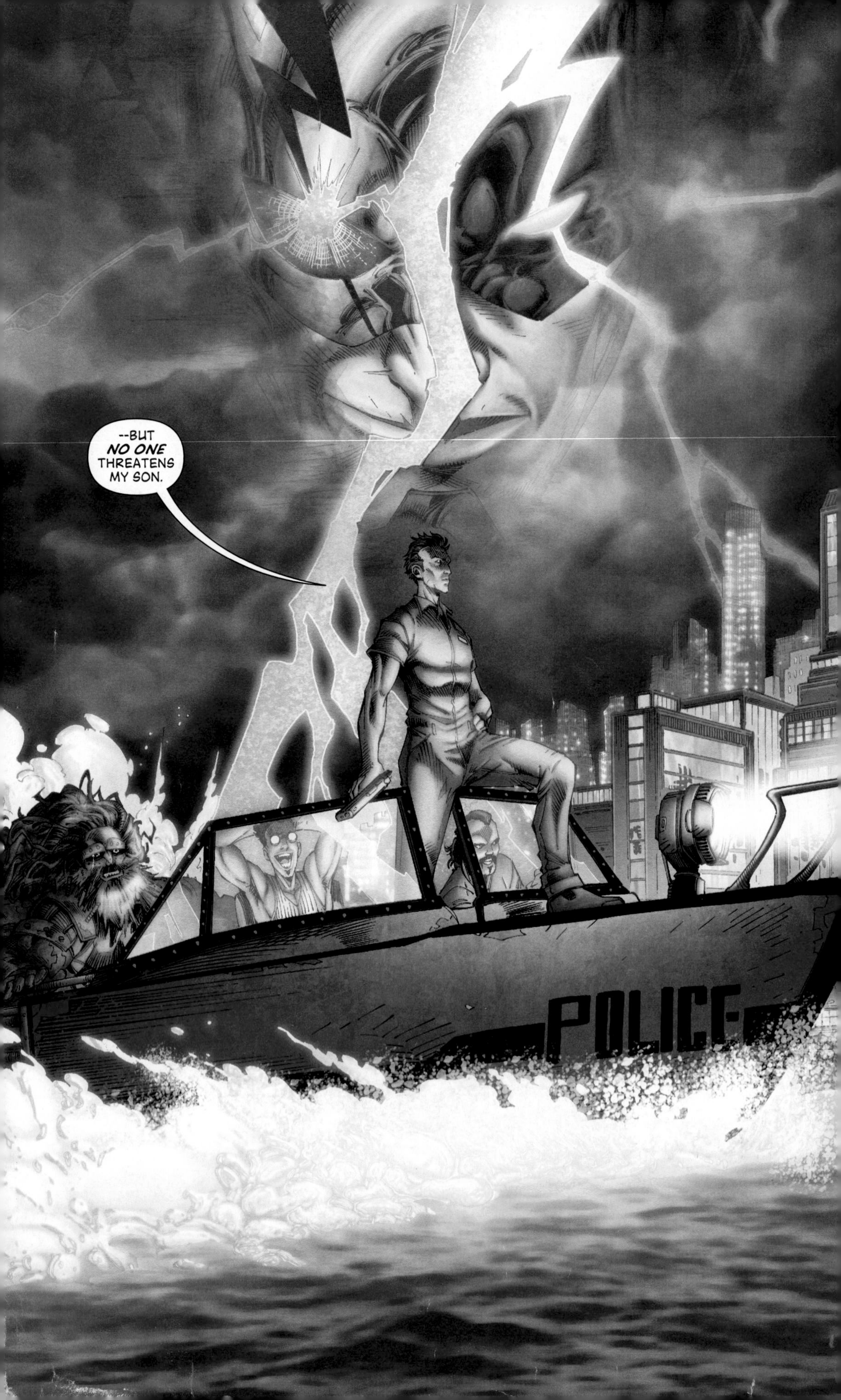
--BUT *NO ONE* THREATENS MY SON.
POLICE

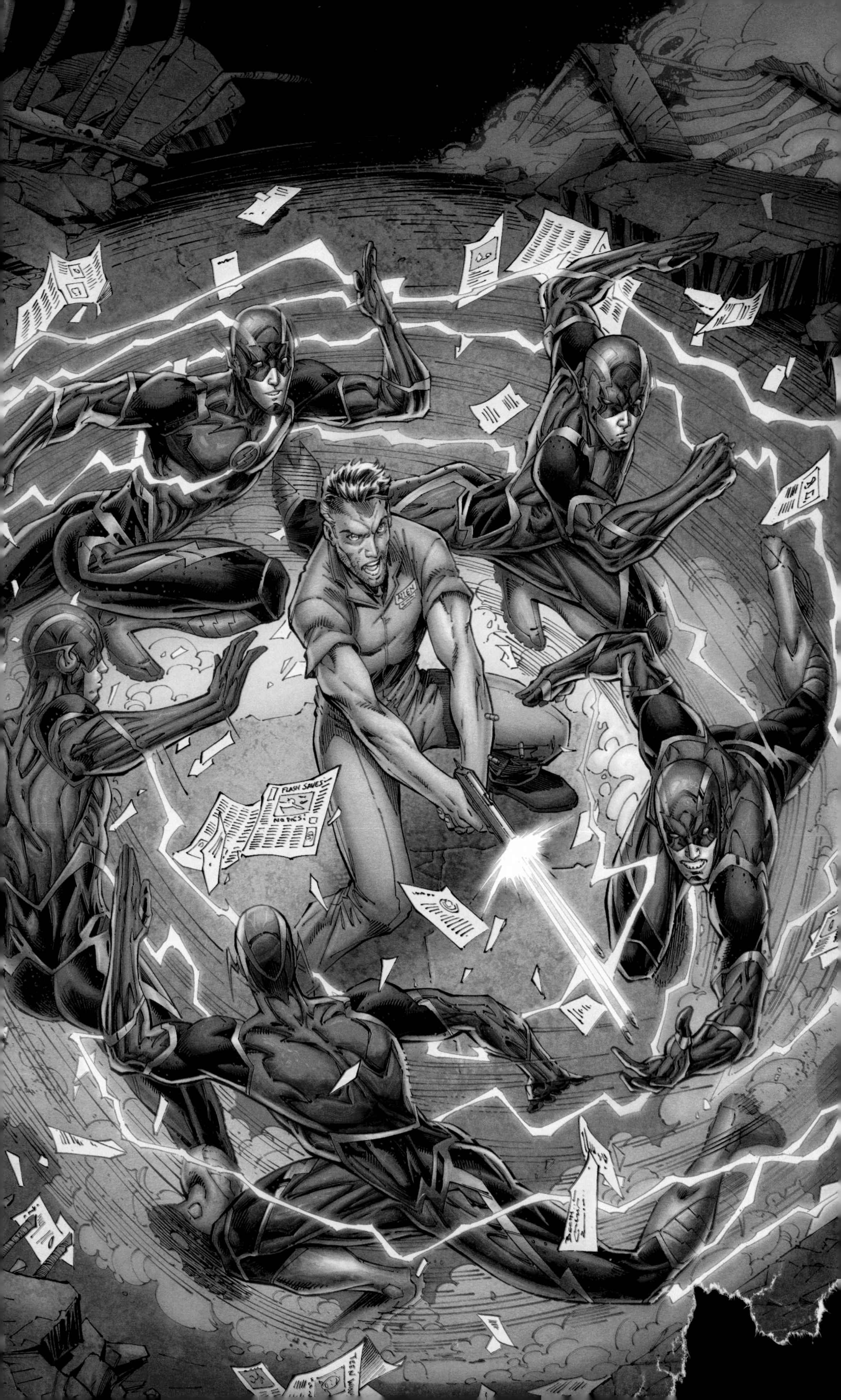
FLASH SAVES
NO PICS!

BLOOD IS THICKER

ROBERT VENDITTI, VAN JENSEN writers BRETT BOOTH penciller NORM RAPMUND inker ANDREW DALHOUSE colorist PAT BROSSEAU letterer
cover by BRETT BOOTH, NORM RAPMUND, ANDREW DALHOUSE

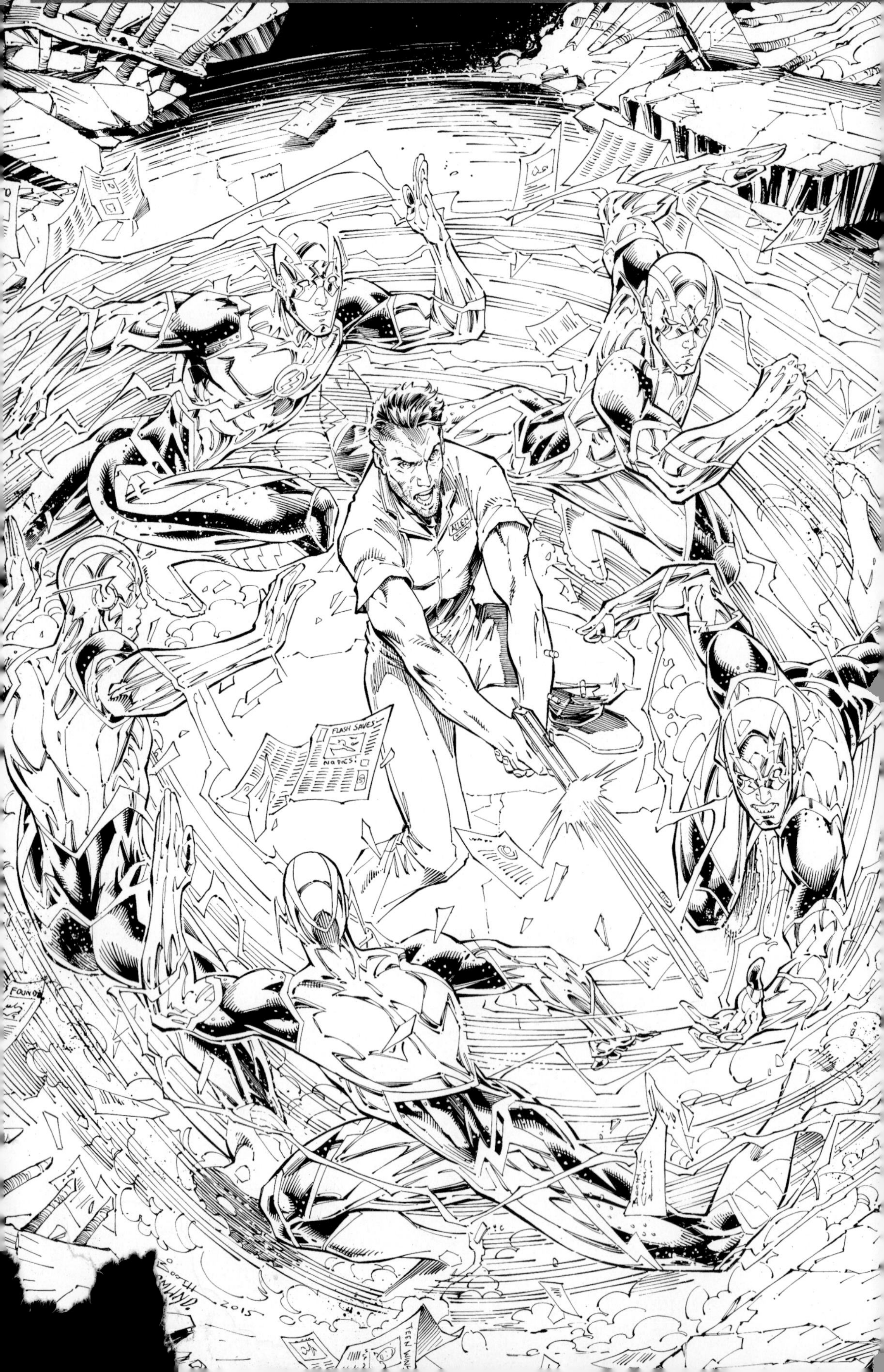

ALLEN
FLASH SAVES
NO PICS!

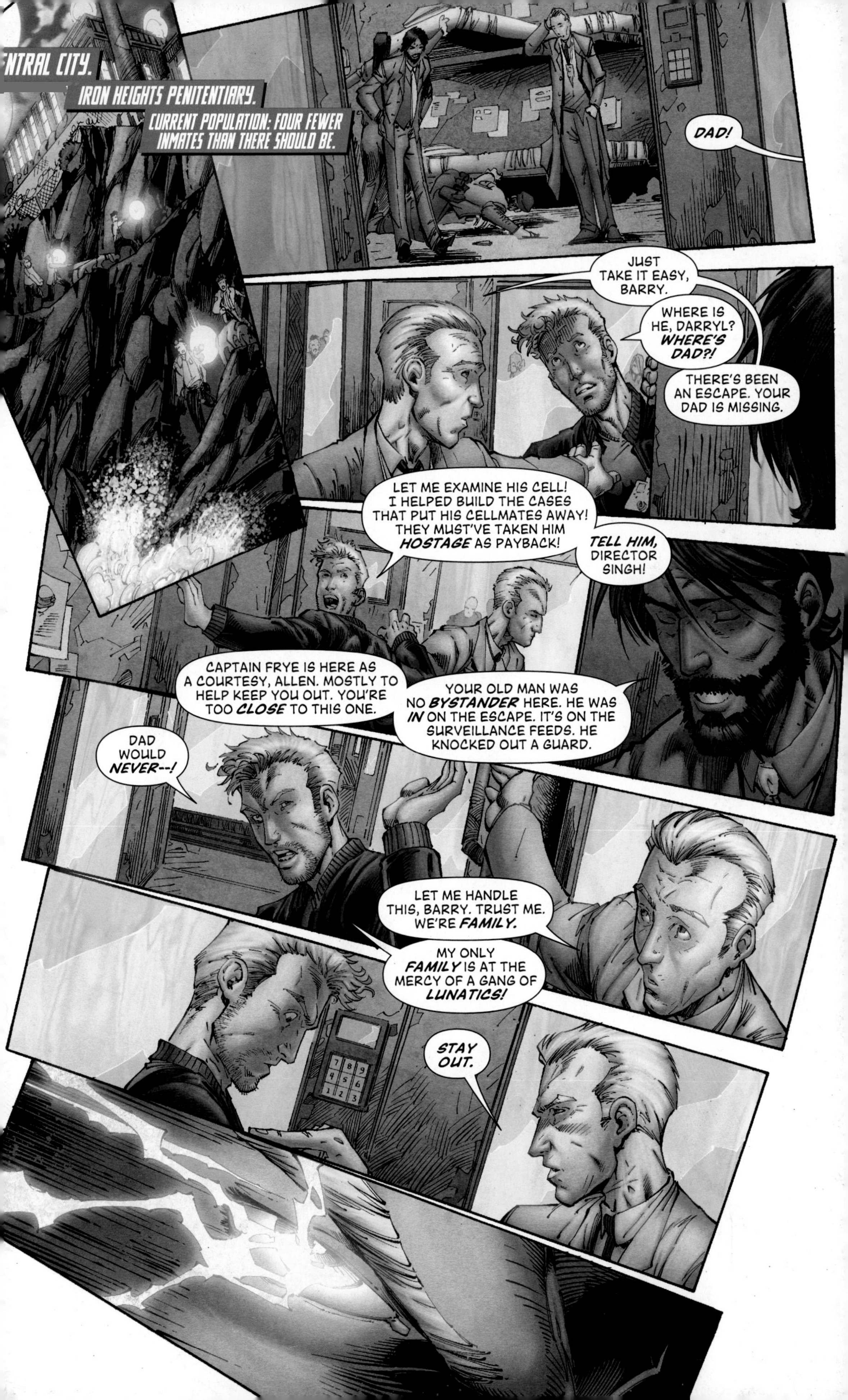
NTRAL CITY.
IRON HEIGHTS PENITENTIARY.
CURRENT POPULATION: FOUR FEWER INMATES THAN THERE SHOULD BE.
DAD!
JUST TAKE IT EASY, BARRY.
WHERE IS HE, DARRYL? WHERE'S DAD?!
THERE'S BEEN AN ESCAPE. YOUR DAD IS MISSING.
LET ME EXAMINE HIS CELL! I HELPED BUILD THE CASES THAT PUT HIS CELLMATES AWAY! THEY MUST'VE TAKEN HIM HOSTAGE AS PAYBACK!
TELL HIM, DIRECTOR SINGH!
CAPTAIN FRYE IS HERE AS A COURTESY, ALLEN. MOSTLY TO HELP KEEP YOU OUT. YOU'RE TOO CLOSE TO THIS ONE.
YOUR OLD MAN WAS NO BYSTANDER HERE. HE WAS IN ON THE ESCAPE. IT'S ON THE SURVEILLANCE FEEDS. HE KNOCKED OUT A GUARD.
DAD WOULD NEVER--!
LET ME HANDLE THIS, BARRY. TRUST ME. WE'RE FAMILY.
MY ONLY FAMILY IS AT THE MERCY OF A GANG OF LUNATICS!
STAY OUT.

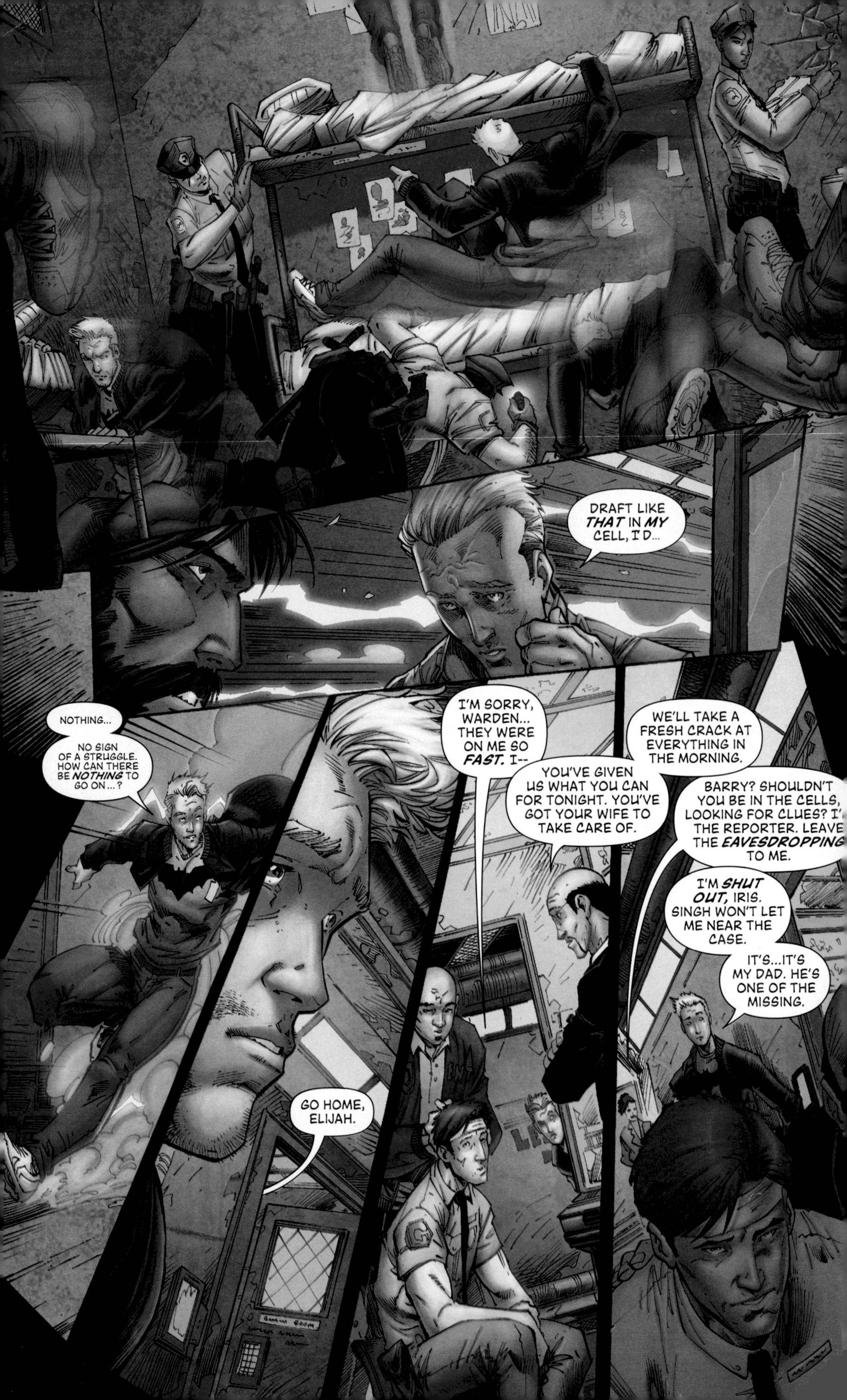
DRAFT LIKE *THAT* IN *MY* CELL, I'D...
NOTHING...
NO SIGN OF A STRUGGLE. HOW CAN THERE BE *NOTHING* TO GO ON...?
I'M SORRY, WARDEN... THEY WERE ON ME SO *FAST*. I--
YOU'VE GIVEN US WHAT YOU CAN FOR TONIGHT. YOU'VE GOT YOUR WIFE TO TAKE CARE OF.
GO HOME, ELIJAH.
WE'LL TAKE A FRESH CRACK AT EVERYTHING IN THE MORNING.
BARRY? SHOULDN'T YOU BE IN THE CELLS, LOOKING FOR CLUES? I'M THE REPORTER. LEAVE THE *EAVESDROPPING* TO ME.
I'M *SHUT OUT,* IRIS. SINGH WON'T LET ME NEAR THE CASE.
IT'S...IT'S MY DAD. HE'S ONE OF THE MISSING.

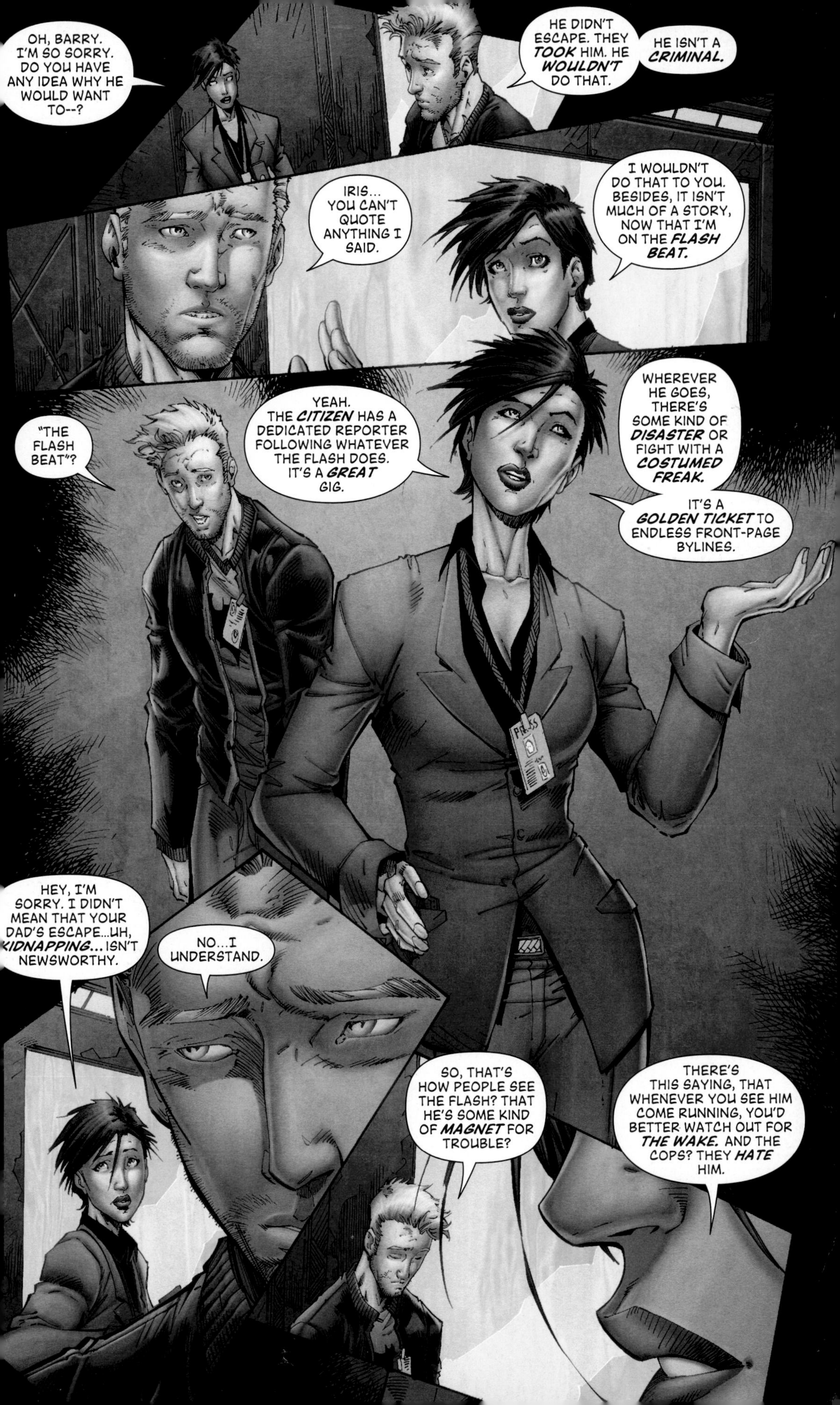
OH, BARRY. I'M SO SORRY. DO YOU HAVE ANY IDEA WHY HE WOULD WANT TO--?
HE DIDN'T ESCAPE. THEY TOOK HIM. HE WOULDN'T DO THAT.
HE ISN'T A CRIMINAL.
IRIS... YOU CAN'T QUOTE ANYTHING I SAID.
I WOULDN'T DO THAT TO YOU. BESIDES, IT ISN'T MUCH OF A STORY, NOW THAT I'M ON THE FLASH BEAT.
"THE FLASH BEAT"?
YEAH. THE CITIZEN HAS A DEDICATED REPORTER FOLLOWING WHATEVER THE FLASH DOES. IT'S A GREAT GIG.
WHEREVER HE GOES, THERE'S SOME KIND OF DISASTER OR FIGHT WITH A COSTUMED FREAK.
IT'S A GOLDEN TICKET TO ENDLESS FRONT-PAGE BYLINES.
PRESS
HEY, I'M SORRY. I DIDN'T MEAN THAT YOUR DAD'S ESCAPE...UH, KIDNAPPING... ISN'T NEWSWORTHY.
NO...I UNDERSTAND.
SO, THAT'S HOW PEOPLE SEE THE FLASH? THAT HE'S SOME KIND OF MAGNET FOR TROUBLE?
THERE'S THIS SAYING, THAT WHENEVER YOU SEE HIM COME RUNNING, YOU'D BETTER WATCH OUT FOR THE WAKE. AND THE COPS? THEY HATE HIM.

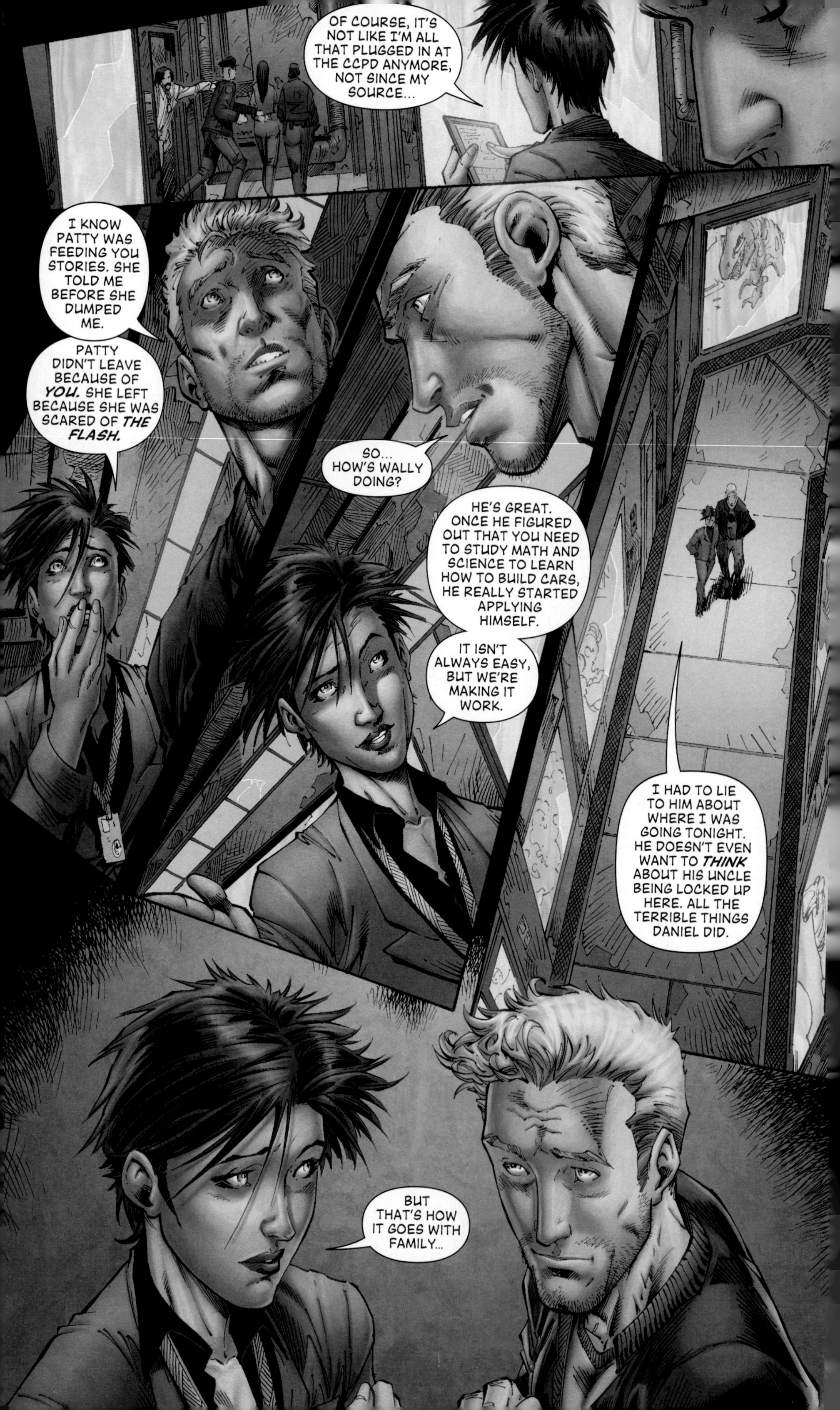
OF COURSE, IT'S NOT LIKE I'M ALL THAT PLUGGED IN AT THE CCPD ANYMORE, NOT SINCE MY SOURCE...
I KNOW PATTY WAS FEEDING YOU STORIES. SHE TOLD ME BEFORE SHE DUMPED ME.
PATTY DIDN'T LEAVE BECAUSE OF *YOU.* SHE LEFT BECAUSE SHE WAS SCARED OF *THE FLASH.*
SO... HOW'S WALLY DOING?
HE'S GREAT. ONCE HE FIGURED OUT THAT YOU NEED TO STUDY MATH AND SCIENCE TO LEARN HOW TO BUILD CARS, HE REALLY STARTED APPLYING HIMSELF.
IT ISN'T ALWAYS EASY, BUT WE'RE MAKING IT WORK.
I HAD TO LIE TO HIM ABOUT WHERE I WAS GOING TONIGHT. HE DOESN'T EVEN WANT TO *THINK* ABOUT HIS UNCLE BEING LOCKED UP HERE. ALL THE TERRIBLE THINGS DANIEL DID.
BUT THAT'S HOW IT GOES WITH FAMILY...

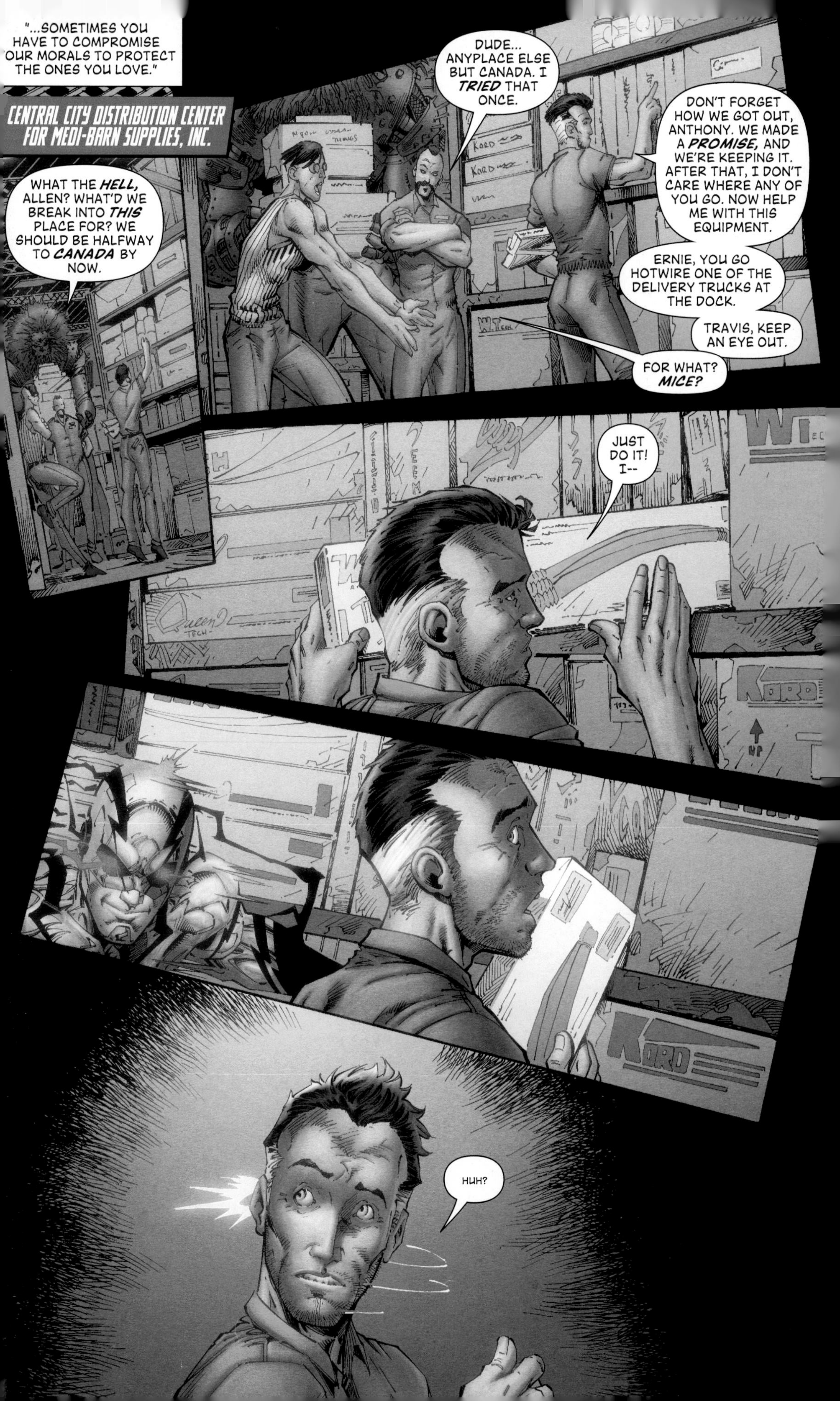
"...SOMETIMES YOU HAVE TO COMPROMISE OUR MORALS TO PROTECT THE ONES YOU LOVE."
CENTRAL CITY DISTRIBUTION CENTER FOR MEDI-BARN SUPPLIES, INC.
WHAT THE HELL, ALLEN? WHAT'D WE BREAK INTO THIS PLACE FOR? WE SHOULD BE HALFWAY TO CANADA BY NOW.
DUDE... ANYPLACE ELSE BUT CANADA. I TRIED THAT ONCE.
DON'T FORGET HOW WE GOT OUT, ANTHONY. WE MADE A PROMISE, AND WE'RE KEEPING IT. AFTER THAT, I DON'T CARE WHERE ANY OF YOU GO. NOW HELP ME WITH THIS EQUIPMENT.
ERNIE, YOU GO HOTWIRE ONE OF THE DELIVERY TRUCKS AT THE DOCK.
TRAVIS, KEEP AN EYE OUT.
FOR WHAT? MICE?
JUST DO IT! I--
HUH?

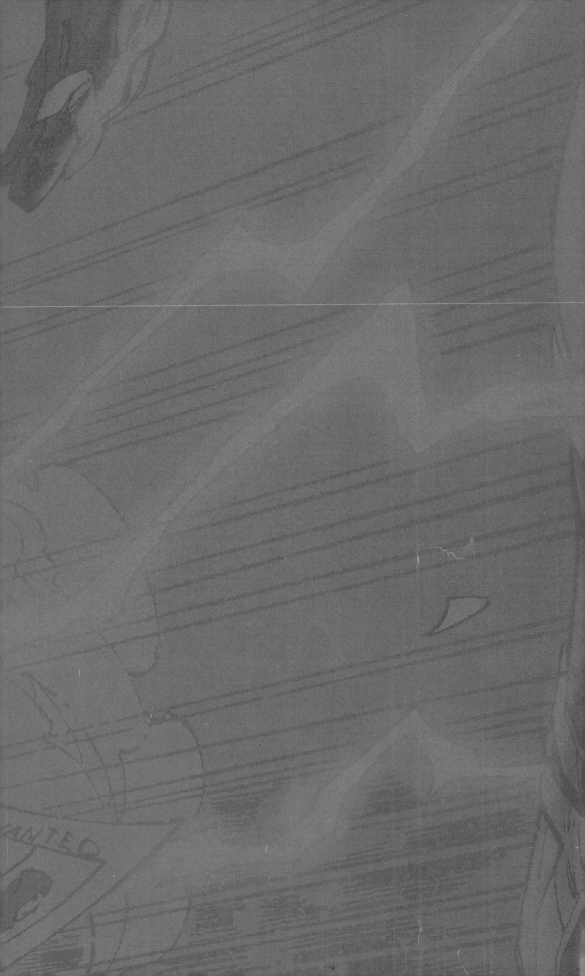

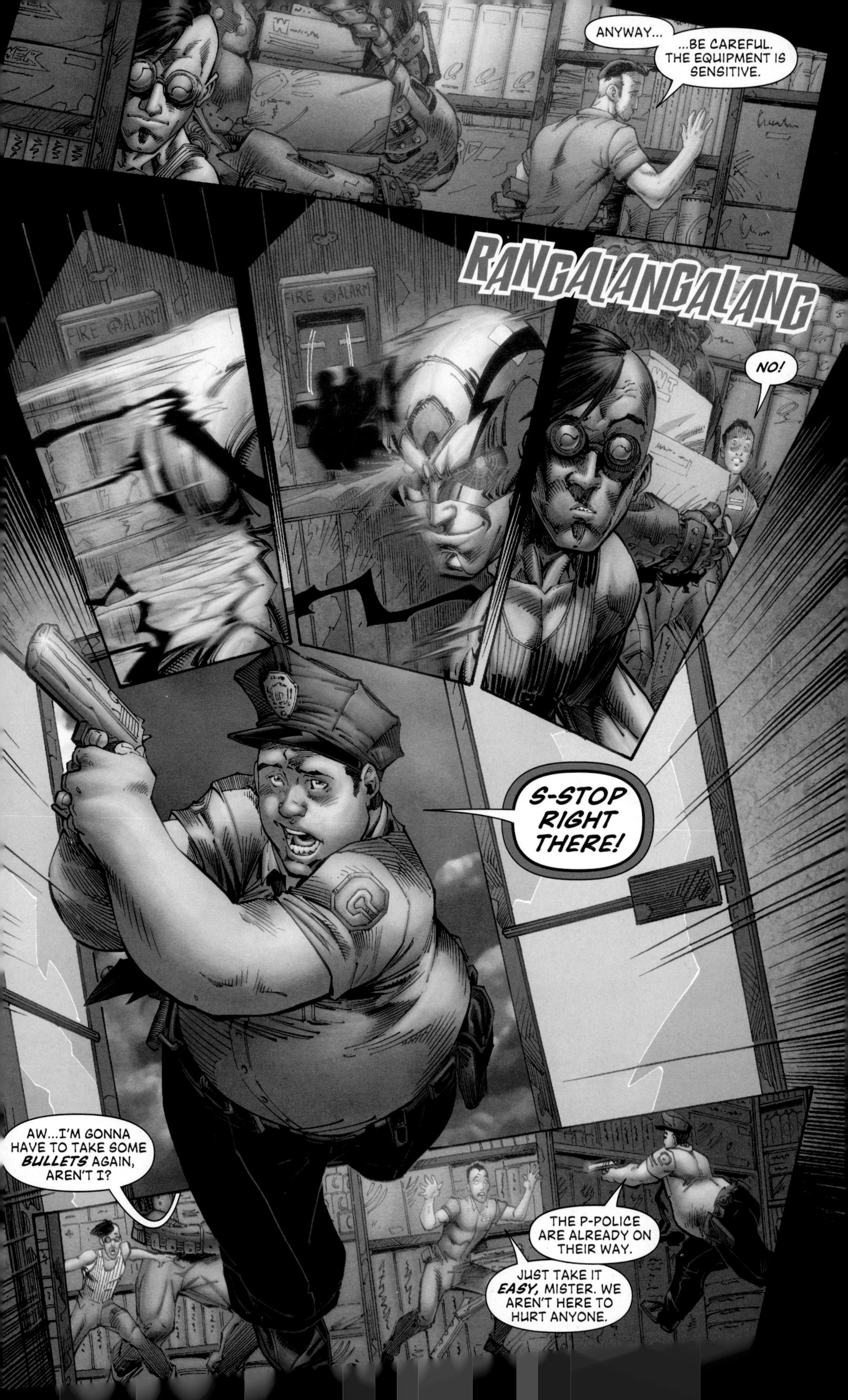
ANYWAY...
...BE CAREFUL. THE EQUIPMENT IS SENSITIVE.
RANGALANGALANG
NO!
S-STOP RIGHT THERE!
AW...I'M GONNA HAVE TO TAKE SOME BULLETS AGAIN, AREN'T I?
THE P-POLICE ARE ALREADY ON THEIR WAY.
JUST TAKE IT EASY, MISTER. WE AREN'T HERE TO HURT ANYONE.

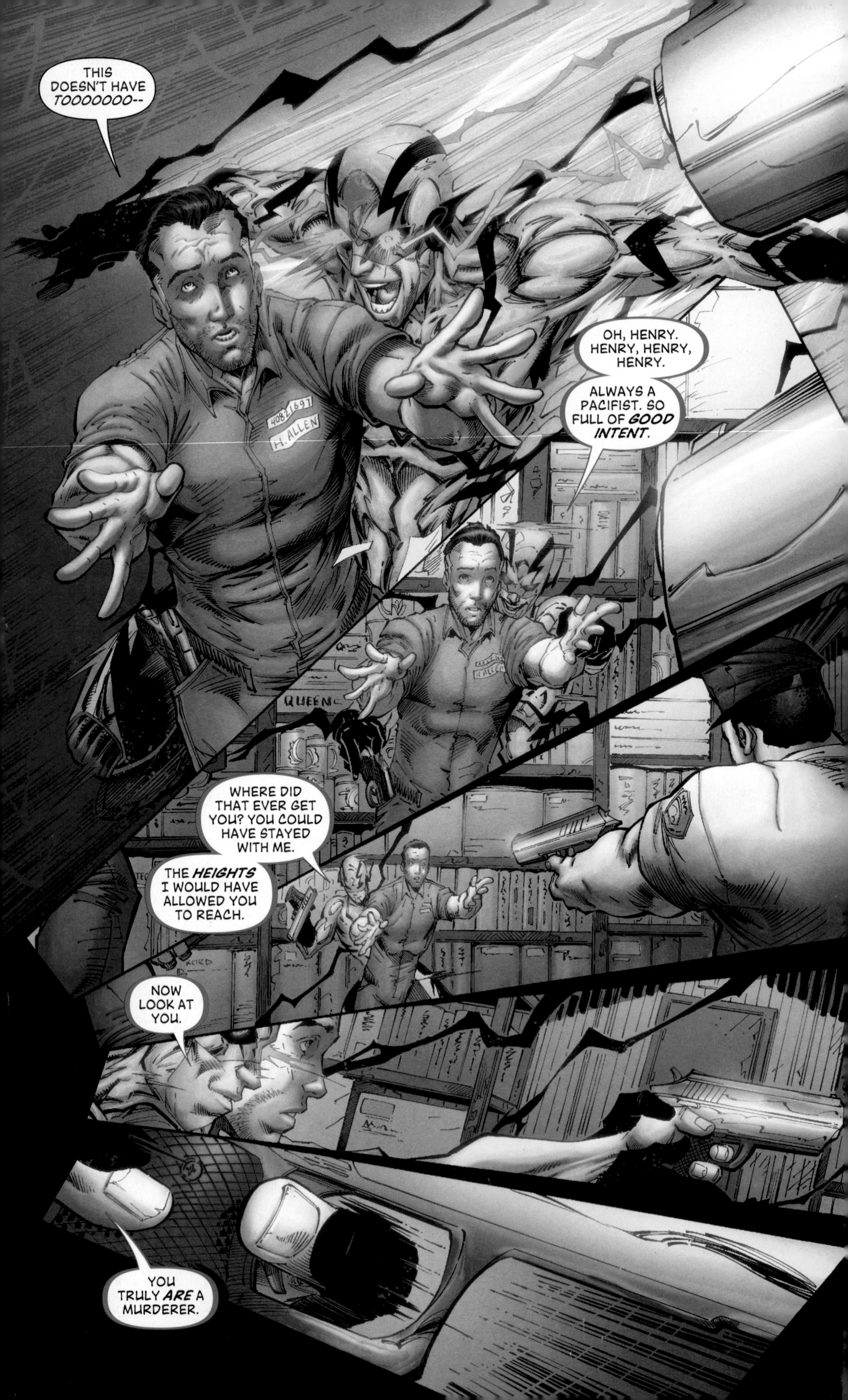
THIS DOESN'T HAVE TOOOOOOO--
OH, HENRY. HENRY, HENRY, HENRY.
ALWAYS A PACIFIST. SO FULL OF GOOD INTENT.
WHERE DID THAT EVER GET YOU? YOU COULD HAVE STAYED WITH ME.
THE HEIGHTS I WOULD HAVE ALLOWED YOU TO REACH.
NOW LOOK AT YOU.
YOU TRULY ARE A MURDERER.

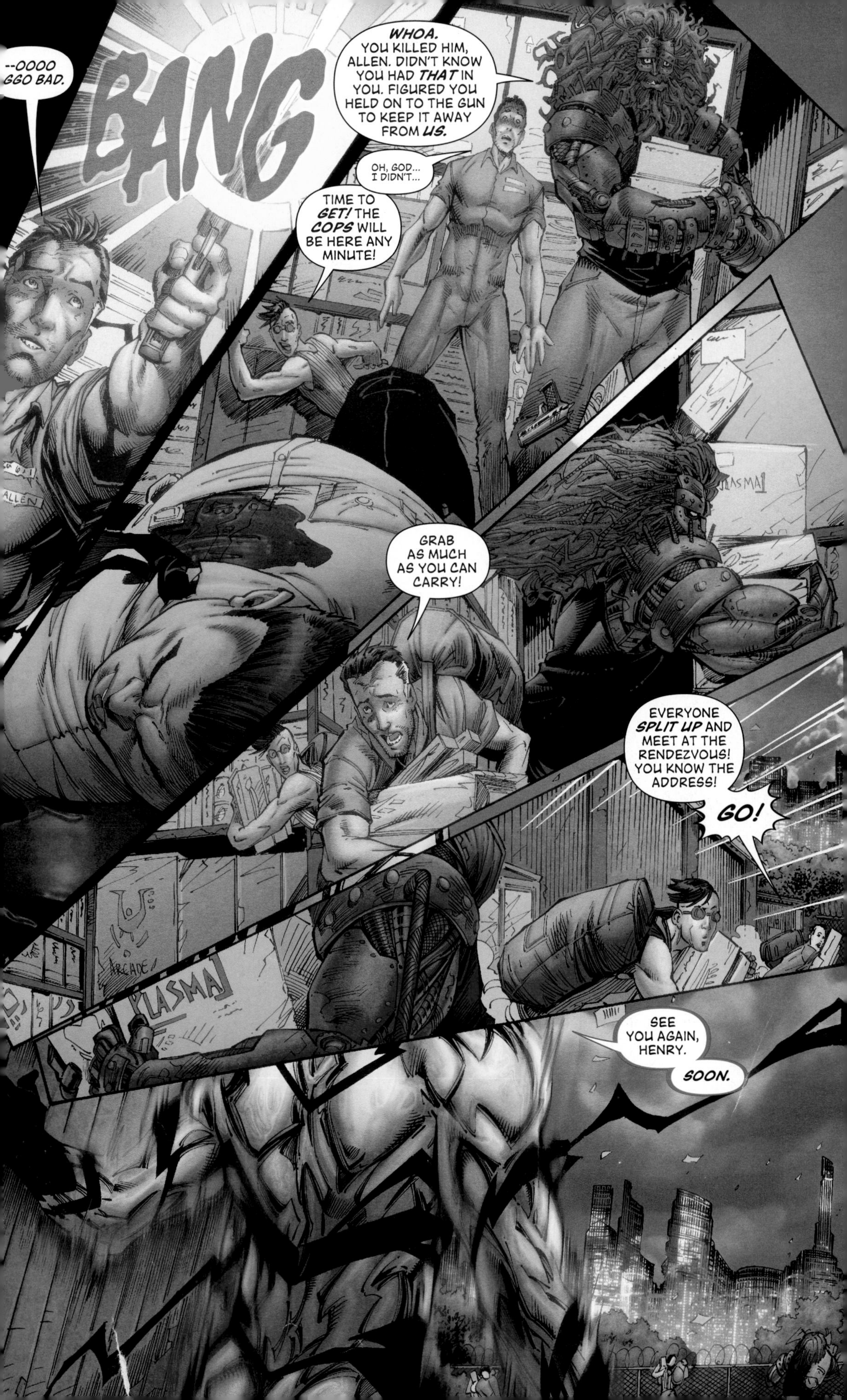
--OOOO
GGO BAD.
BANG
WHOA. YOU KILLED HIM, ALLEN. DIDN'T KNOW YOU HAD THAT IN YOU. FIGURED YOU HELD ON TO THE GUN TO KEEP IT AWAY FROM US.
OH, GOD... I DIDN'T...
TIME TO GET! THE COPS WILL BE HERE ANY MINUTE!
ALLEN
PLASMA
GRAB AS MUCH AS YOU CAN CARRY!
EVERYONE SPLIT UP AND MEET AT THE RENDEZVOUS! YOU KNOW THE ADDRESS!
GO!
ARCADE
PLASMA
SEE YOU AGAIN, HENRY.
SOON.

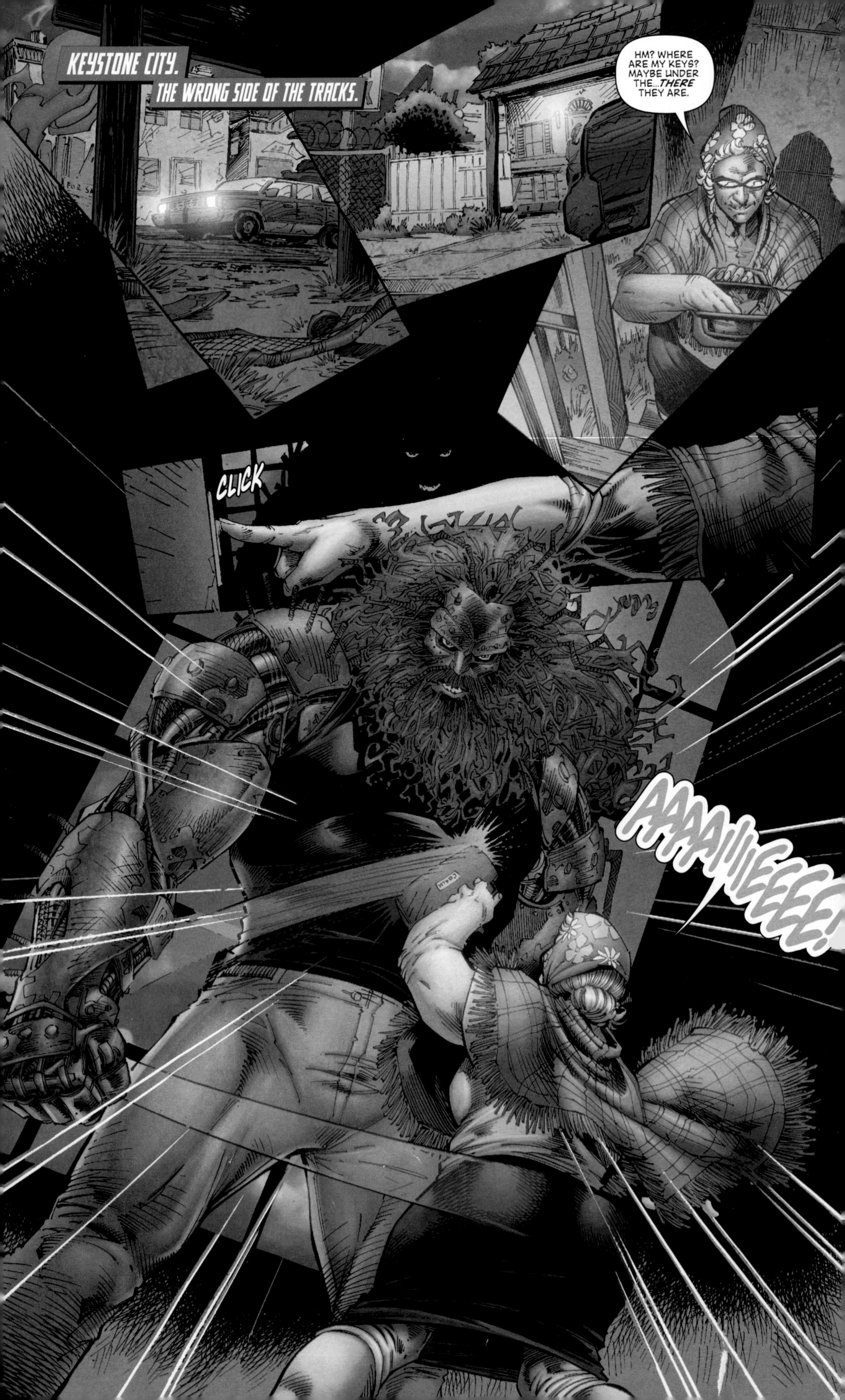
KEYSTONE CITY.
THE WRONG SIDE OF THE TRACKS.
HM? WHERE ARE MY KEYS? MAYBE UNDER THE...THERE THEY ARE.
CLICK
AAAAIIIEEEE!

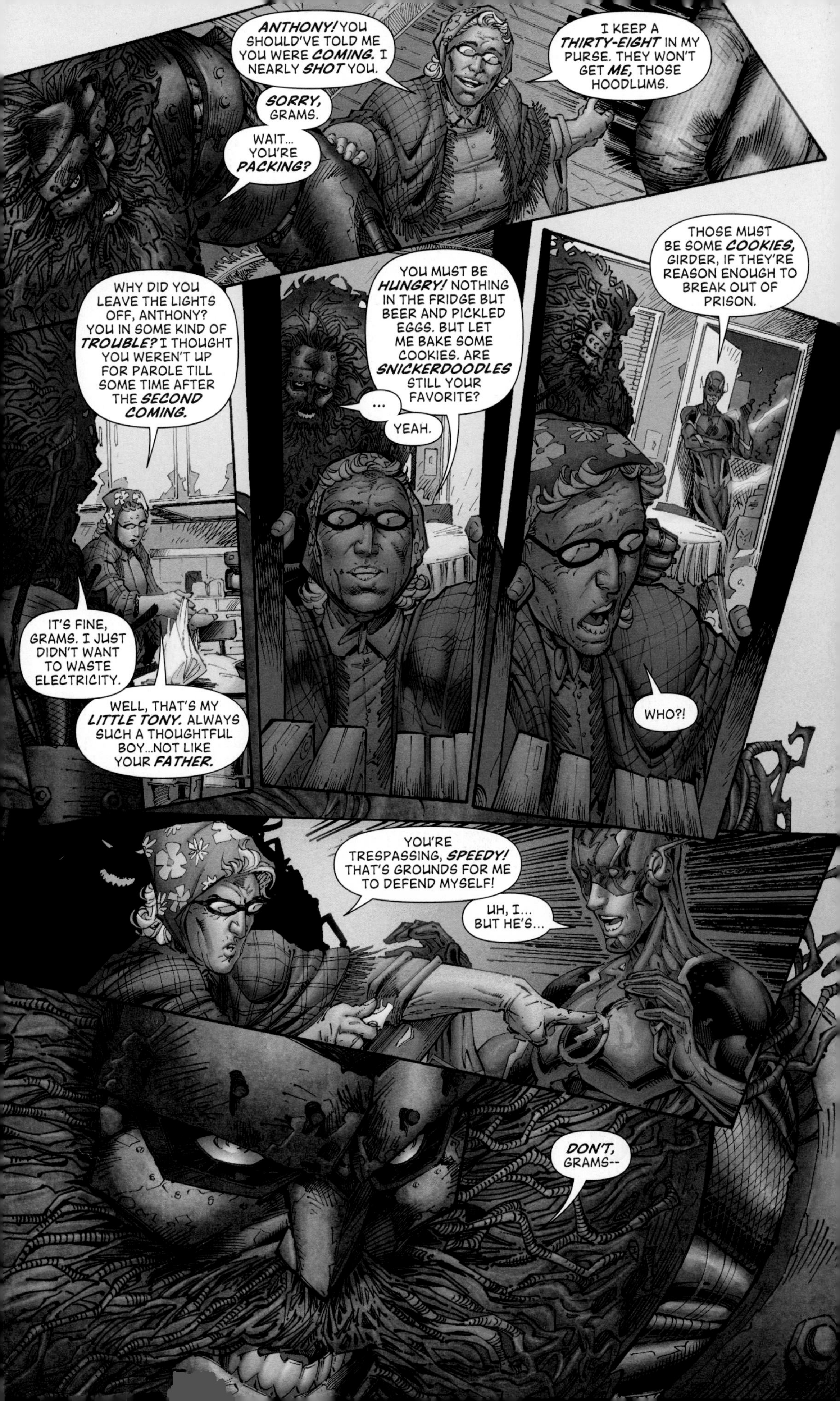
ANTHONY! YOU SHOULD'VE TOLD ME YOU WERE COMING. I NEARLY SHOT YOU.
SORRY, GRAMS.
WAIT... YOU'RE PACKING?
I KEEP A THIRTY-EIGHT IN MY PURSE. THEY WON'T GET ME, THOSE HOODLUMS.
WHY DID YOU LEAVE THE LIGHTS OFF, ANTHONY? YOU IN SOME KIND OF TROUBLE? I THOUGHT YOU WEREN'T UP FOR PAROLE TILL SOME TIME AFTER THE SECOND COMING.
IT'S FINE, GRAMS. I JUST DIDN'T WANT TO WASTE ELECTRICITY.
WELL, THAT'S MY LITTLE TONY. ALWAYS SUCH A THOUGHTFUL BOY...NOT LIKE YOUR FATHER.
YOU MUST BE HUNGRY! NOTHING IN THE FRIDGE BUT BEER AND PICKLED EGGS. BUT LET ME BAKE SOME COOKIES. ARE SNICKERDOODLES STILL YOUR FAVORITE?
...
YEAH.
THOSE MUST BE SOME COOKIES, GIRDER, IF THEY'RE REASON ENOUGH TO BREAK OUT OF PRISON.
WHO?!
YOU'RE TRESPASSING, SPEEDY! THAT'S GROUNDS FOR ME TO DEFEND MYSELF!
UH, I... BUT HE'S...
DON'T, GRAMS--

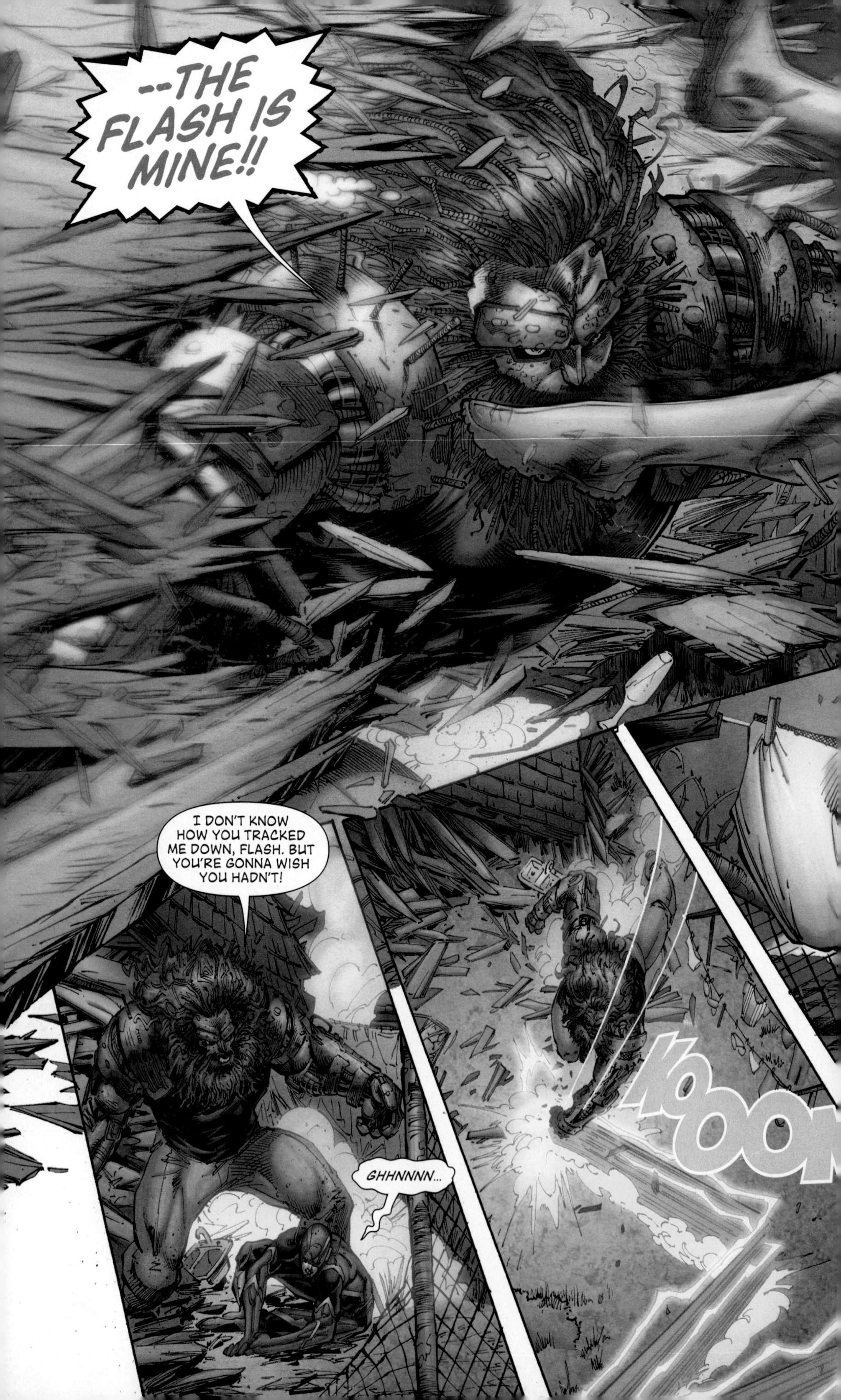

--THE FLASH IS MINE!!
I DON'T KNOW HOW YOU TRACKED ME DOWN, FLASH. BUT YOU'RE GONNA WISH YOU HADN'T!
GHHNNNN...
KOOOOM

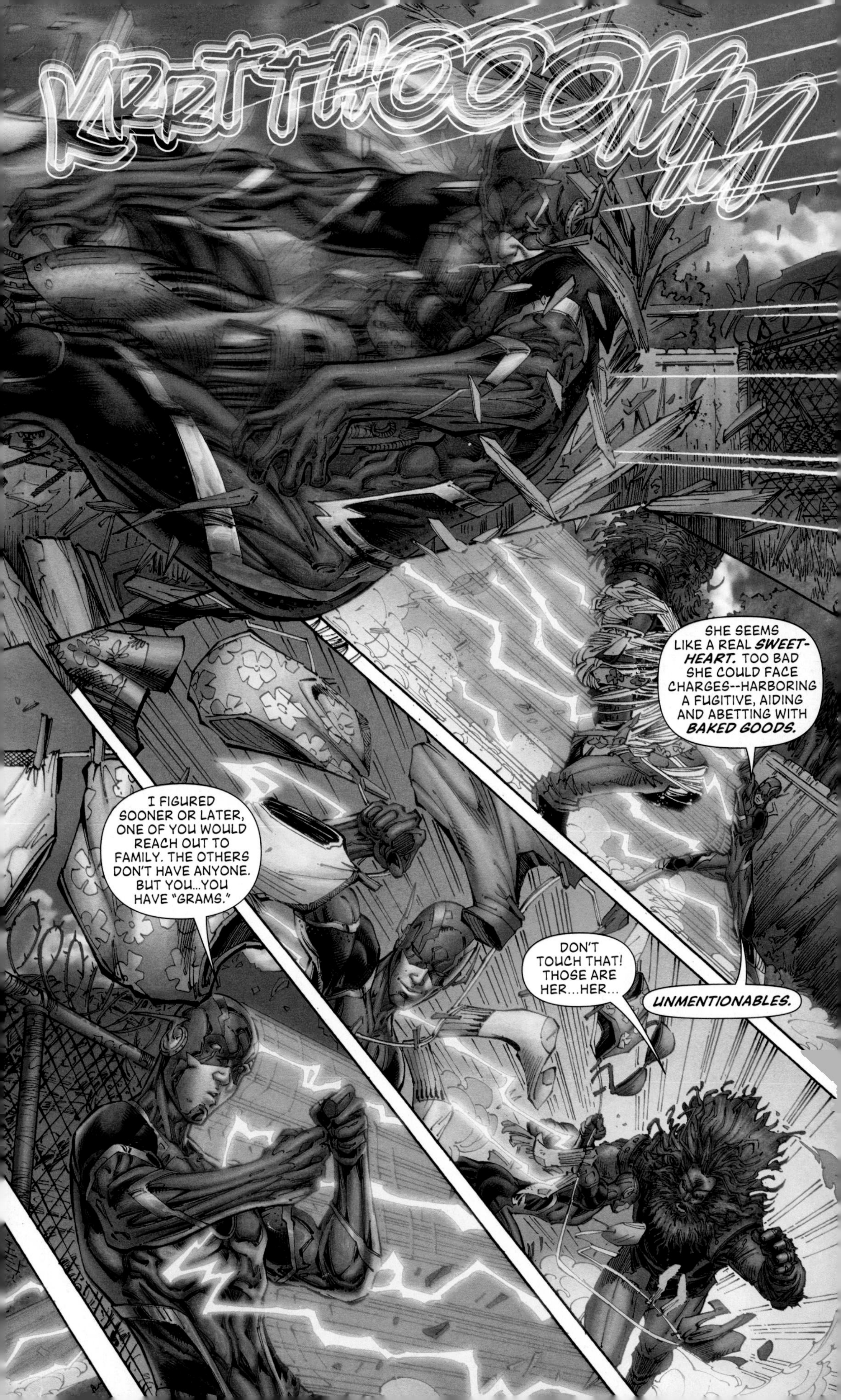
KRRTTHOOOMM
SHE SEEMS LIKE A REAL *SWEET-HEART.* TOO BAD SHE COULD FACE CHARGES--HARBORING A FUGITIVE, AIDING AND ABETTING WITH *BAKED GOODS.*
I FIGURED SOONER OR LATER, ONE OF YOU WOULD REACH OUT TO FAMILY. THE OTHERS DON'T HAVE ANYONE. BUT YOU...YOU HAVE "GRAMS."
DON'T TOUCH THAT! THOSE ARE HER...HER...
UNMENTIONABLES.

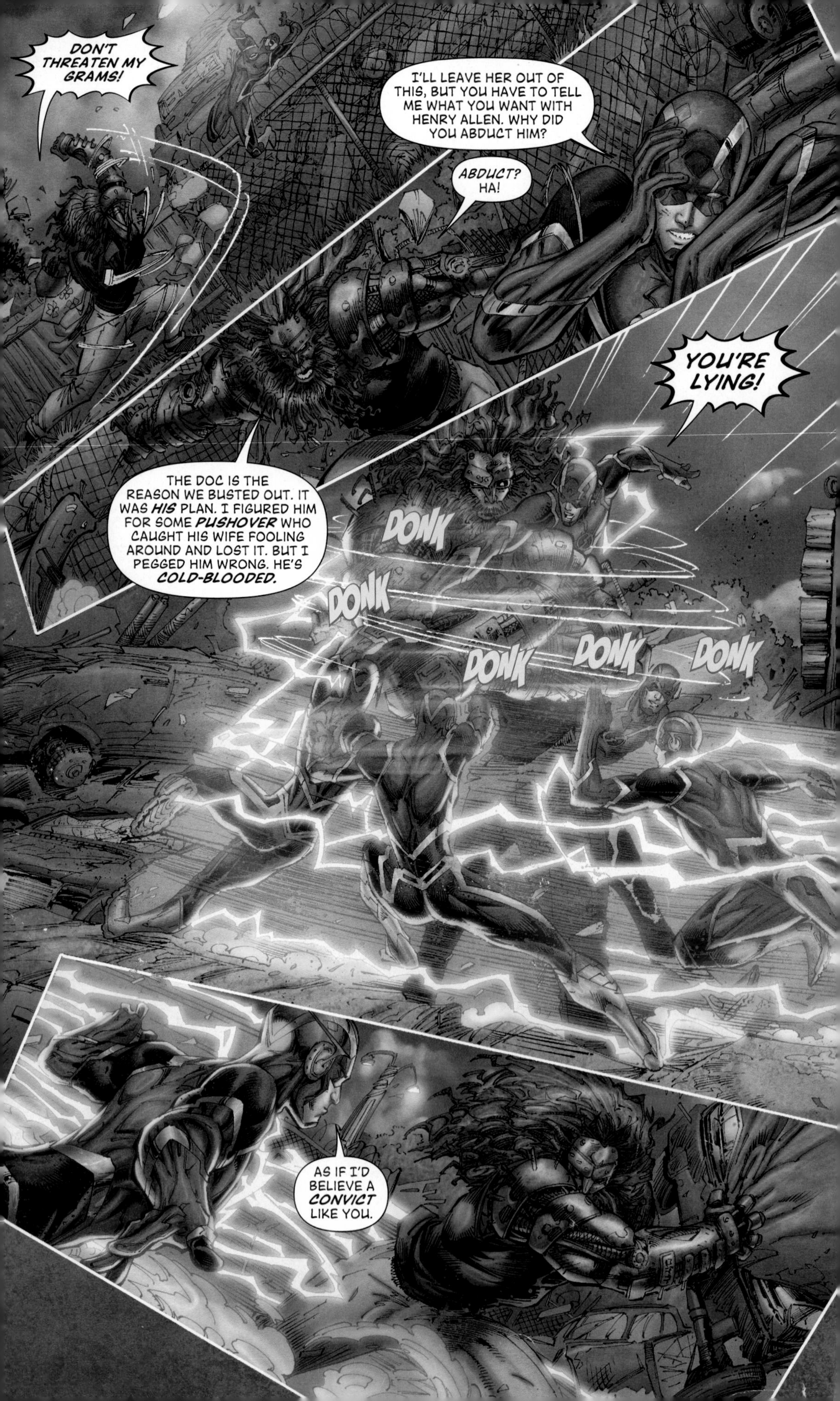
DON'T THREATEN MY GRAMS!
I'LL LEAVE HER OUT OF THIS, BUT YOU HAVE TO TELL ME WHAT YOU WANT WITH HENRY ALLEN. WHY DID YOU ABDUCT HIM?
ABDUCT? HA!
THE DOC IS THE REASON WE BUSTED OUT. IT WAS HIS PLAN. I FIGURED HIM FOR SOME PUSHOVER WHO CAUGHT HIS WIFE FOOLING AROUND AND LOST IT. BUT I PEGGED HIM WRONG. HE'S COLD-BLOODED.
YOU'RE LYING!
DONK
DONK
DONK
DONK
DONK
AS IF I'D BELIEVE A CONVICT LIKE YOU.

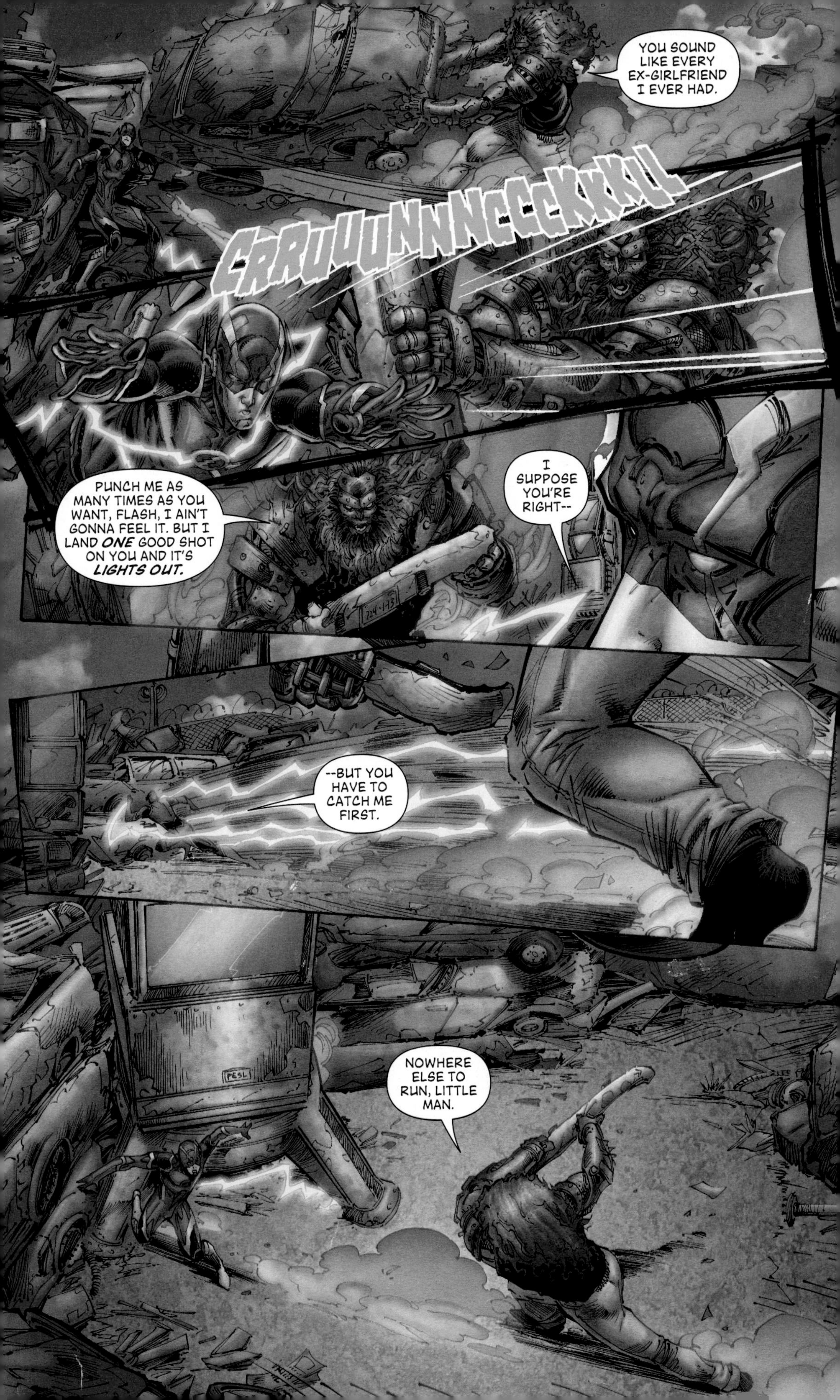

YOU SOUND LIKE EVERY EX-GIRLFRIEND I EVER HAD.
CRRUUUNNNCCCKKKLL
PUNCH ME AS MANY TIMES AS YOU WANT, FLASH, I AIN'T GONNA FEEL IT. BUT I LAND *ONE* GOOD SHOT ON YOU AND IT'S ***LIGHTS OUT.***
I SUPPOSE YOU'RE RIGHT--
--BUT YOU HAVE TO CATCH ME FIRST.
NOWHERE ELSE TO RUN, LITTLE MAN.

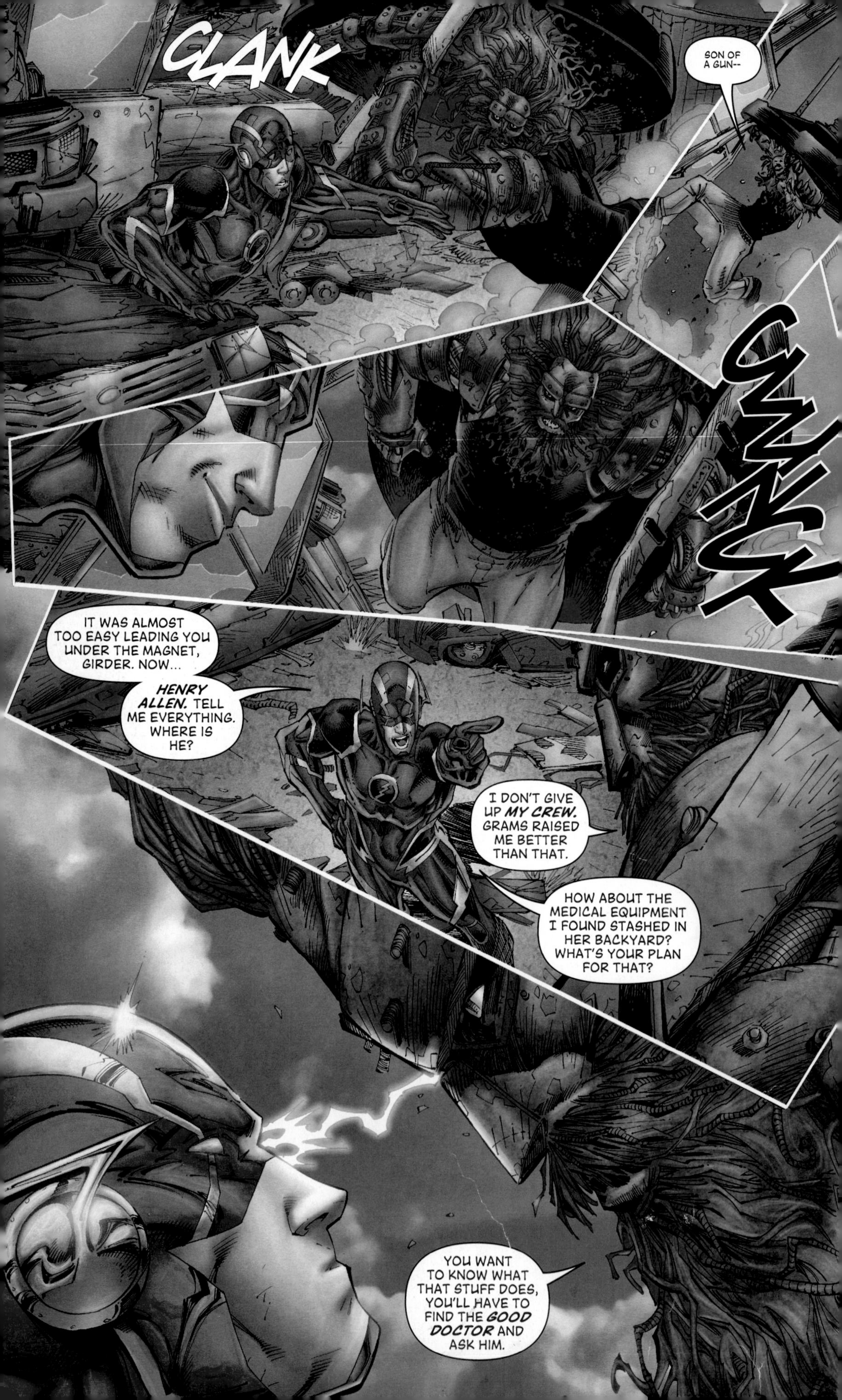
CLANK
SON OF A GUN--
GWUNCK
IT WAS ALMOST TOO EASY LEADING YOU UNDER THE MAGNET, GIRDER. NOW...
HENRY ALLEN. TELL ME EVERYTHING. WHERE IS HE?
I DON'T GIVE UP *MY CREW.* GRAMS RAISED ME BETTER THAN THAT.
HOW ABOUT THE MEDICAL EQUIPMENT I FOUND STASHED IN HER BACKYARD? WHAT'S YOUR PLAN FOR THAT?
YOU WANT TO KNOW WHAT THAT STUFF DOES, YOU'LL HAVE TO FIND THE *GOOD DOCTOR* AND ASK HIM.

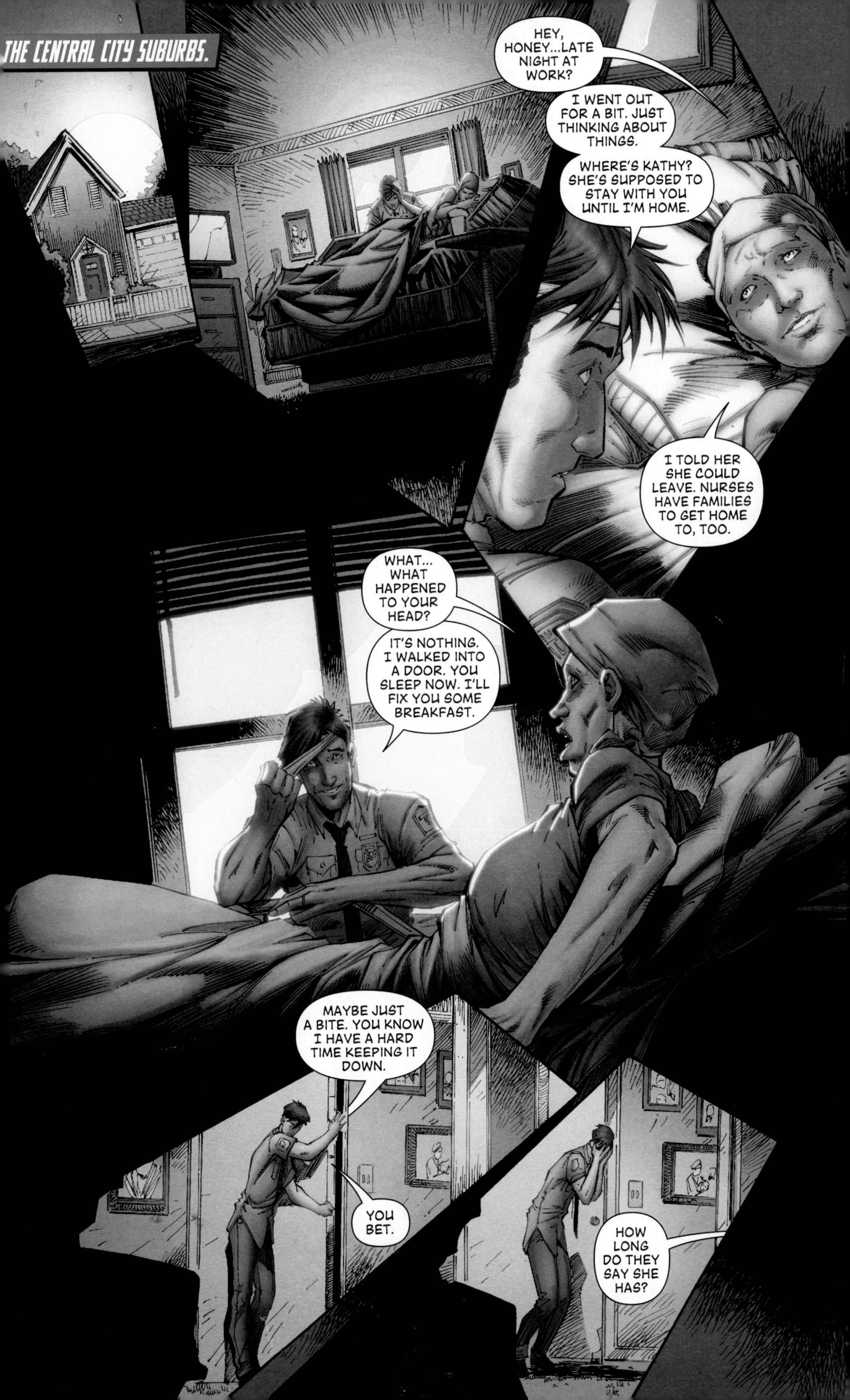
THE CENTRAL CITY SUBURBS.
HEY, HONEY...LATE NIGHT AT WORK?
I WENT OUT FOR A BIT. JUST THINKING ABOUT THINGS.
WHERE'S KATHY? SHE'S SUPPOSED TO STAY WITH YOU UNTIL I'M HOME.
I TOLD HER SHE COULD LEAVE. NURSES HAVE FAMILIES TO GET HOME TO, TOO.
WHAT... WHAT HAPPENED TO YOUR HEAD?
IT'S NOTHING. I WALKED INTO A DOOR. YOU SLEEP NOW. I'LL FIX YOU SOME BREAKFAST.
MAYBE JUST A BITE. YOU KNOW I HAVE A HARD TIME KEEPING IT DOWN.
YOU BET.
HOW LONG DO THEY SAY SHE HAS?

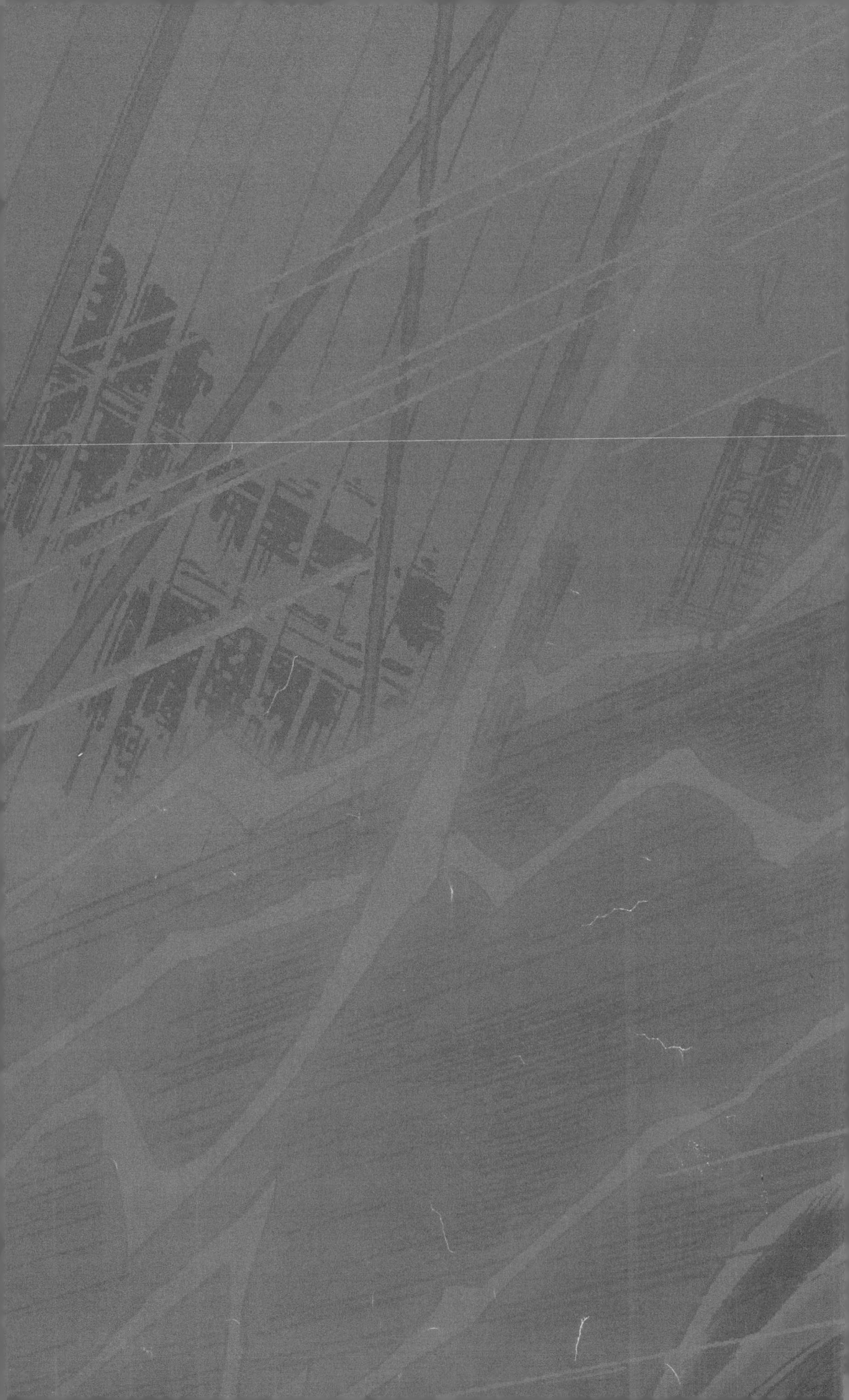

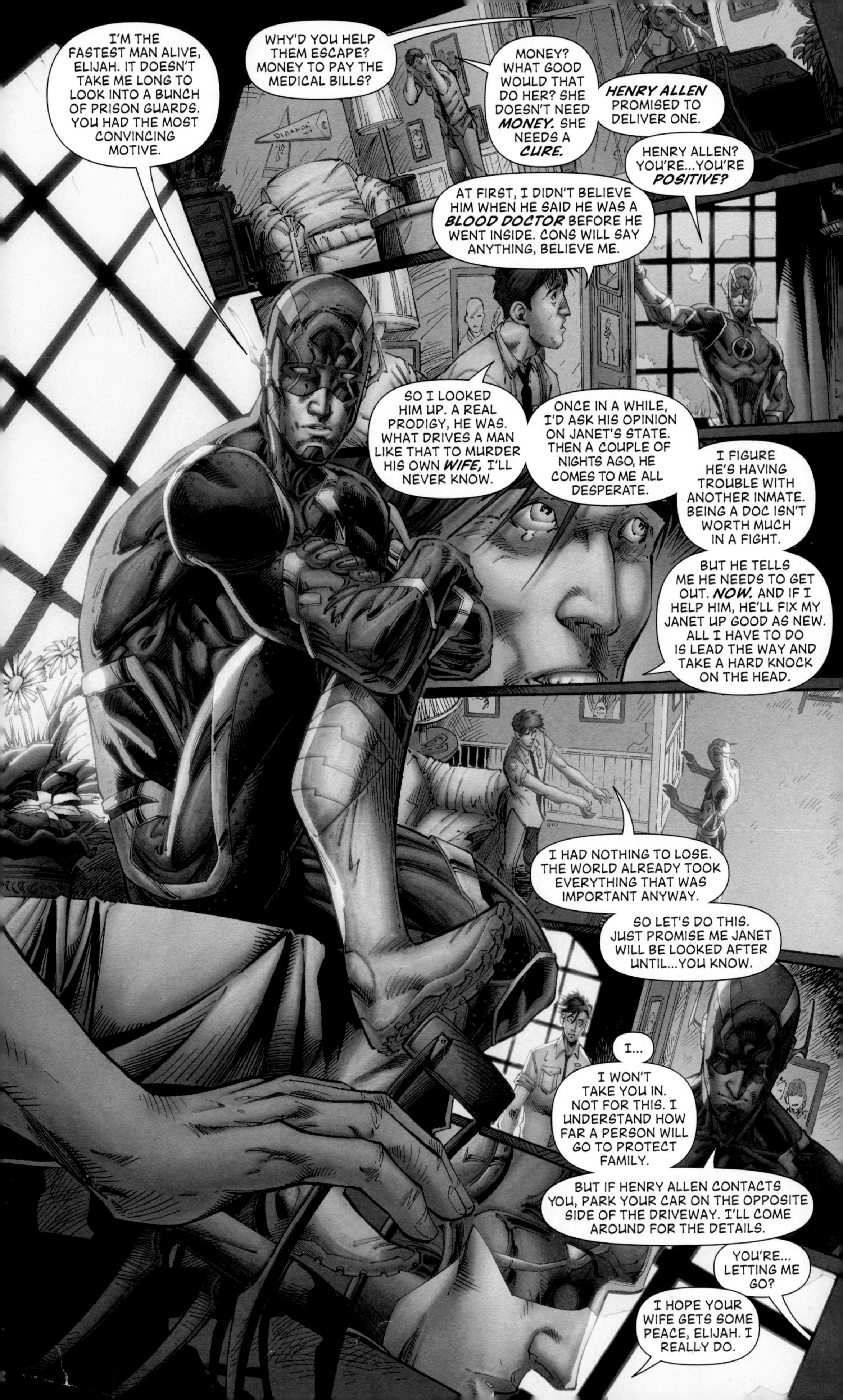

I'M THE FASTEST MAN ALIVE, ELIJAH. IT DOESN'T TAKE ME LONG TO LOOK INTO A BUNCH OF PRISON GUARDS. YOU HAD THE MOST CONVINCING MOTIVE.
WHY'D YOU HELP THEM ESCAPE? MONEY TO PAY THE MEDICAL BILLS?
MONEY? WHAT GOOD WOULD THAT DO HER? SHE DOESN'T NEED MONEY. SHE NEEDS A CURE.
HENRY ALLEN PROMISED TO DELIVER ONE.
HENRY ALLEN? YOU'RE...YOU'RE POSITIVE?
AT FIRST, I DIDN'T BELIEVE HIM WHEN HE SAID HE WAS A BLOOD DOCTOR BEFORE HE WENT INSIDE. CONS WILL SAY ANYTHING, BELIEVE ME.
SO I LOOKED HIM UP. A REAL PRODIGY, HE WAS. WHAT DRIVES A MAN LIKE THAT TO MURDER HIS OWN WIFE, I'LL NEVER KNOW.
ONCE IN A WHILE, I'D ASK HIS OPINION ON JANET'S STATE. THEN A COUPLE OF NIGHTS AGO, HE COMES TO ME ALL DESPERATE.
I FIGURE HE'S HAVING TROUBLE WITH ANOTHER INMATE. BEING A DOC ISN'T WORTH MUCH IN A FIGHT.
BUT HE TELLS ME HE NEEDS TO GET OUT. NOW. AND IF I HELP HIM, HE'LL FIX MY JANET UP GOOD AS NEW. ALL I HAVE TO DO IS LEAD THE WAY AND TAKE A HARD KNOCK ON THE HEAD.
I HAD NOTHING TO LOSE. THE WORLD ALREADY TOOK EVERYTHING THAT WAS IMPORTANT ANYWAY.
SO LET'S DO THIS. JUST PROMISE ME JANET WILL BE LOOKED AFTER UNTIL...YOU KNOW.
I...
I WON'T TAKE YOU IN. NOT FOR THIS. I UNDERSTAND HOW FAR A PERSON WILL GO TO PROTECT FAMILY.
BUT IF HENRY ALLEN CONTACTS YOU, PARK YOUR CAR ON THE OPPOSITE SIDE OF THE DRIVEWAY. I'LL COME AROUND FOR THE DETAILS.
YOU'RE... LETTING ME GO?
I HOPE YOUR WIFE GETS SOME PEACE, ELIJAH. I REALLY DO.

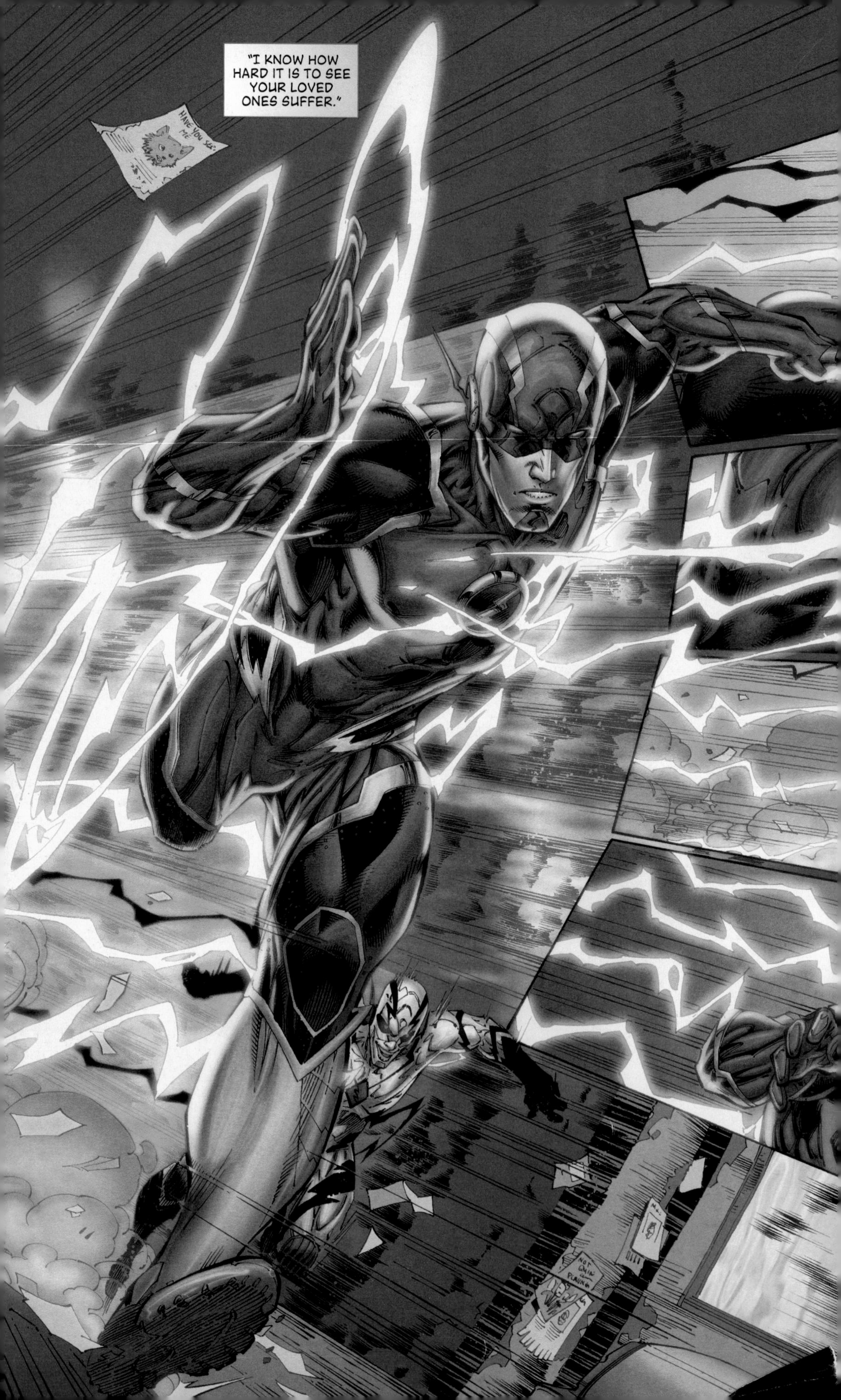
"I KNOW HOW HARD IT IS TO SEE YOUR LOVED ONES SUFFER."

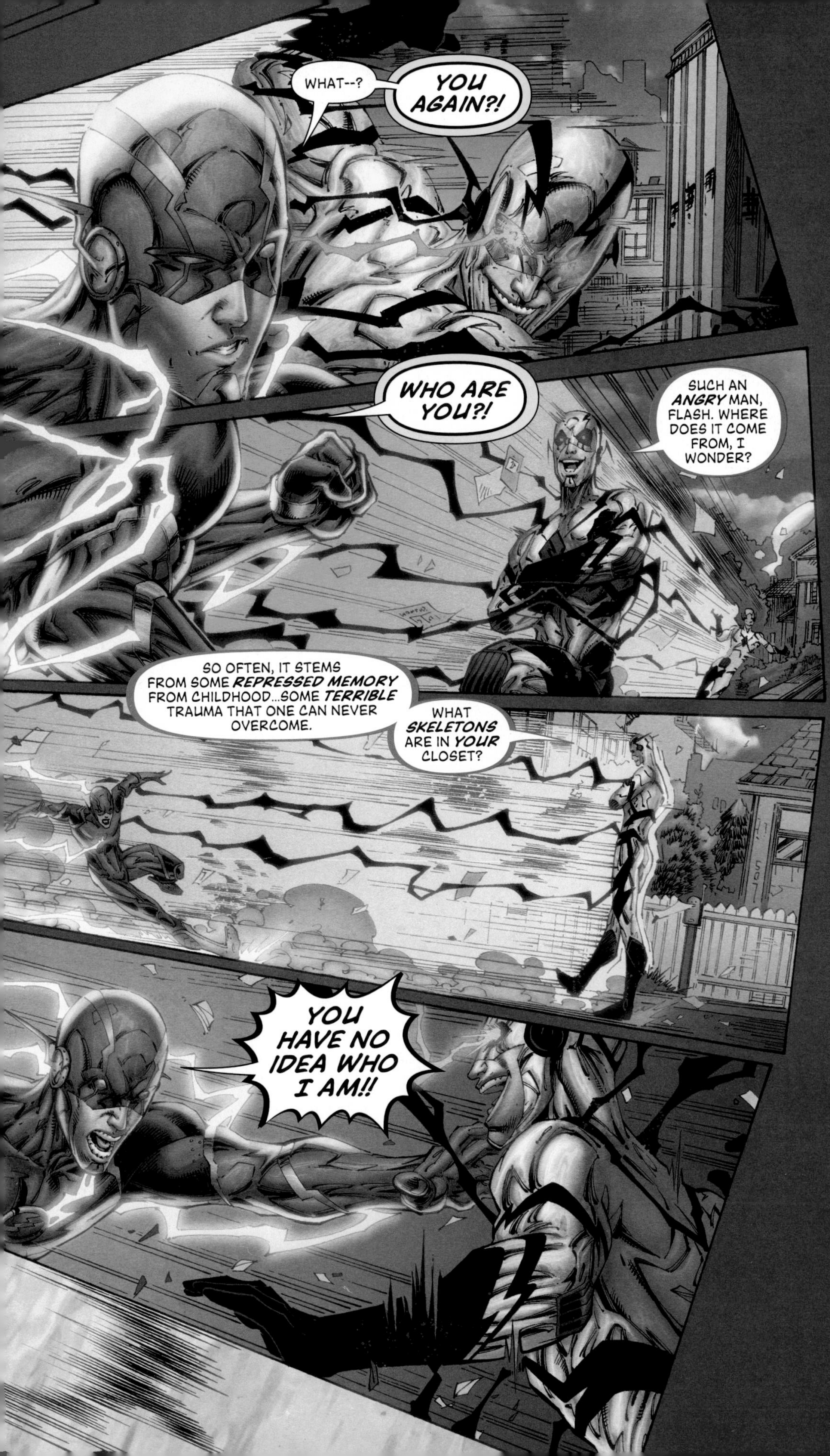
WHAT--?
YOU AGAIN?!
WHO ARE YOU?!
SUCH AN ANGRY MAN, FLASH. WHERE DOES IT COME FROM, I WONDER?
SO OFTEN, IT STEMS FROM SOME REPRESSED MEMORY FROM CHILDHOOD...SOME TERRIBLE TRAUMA THAT ONE CAN NEVER OVERCOME.
WHAT SKELETONS ARE IN YOUR CLOSET?
YOU HAVE NO IDEA WHO I AM!!

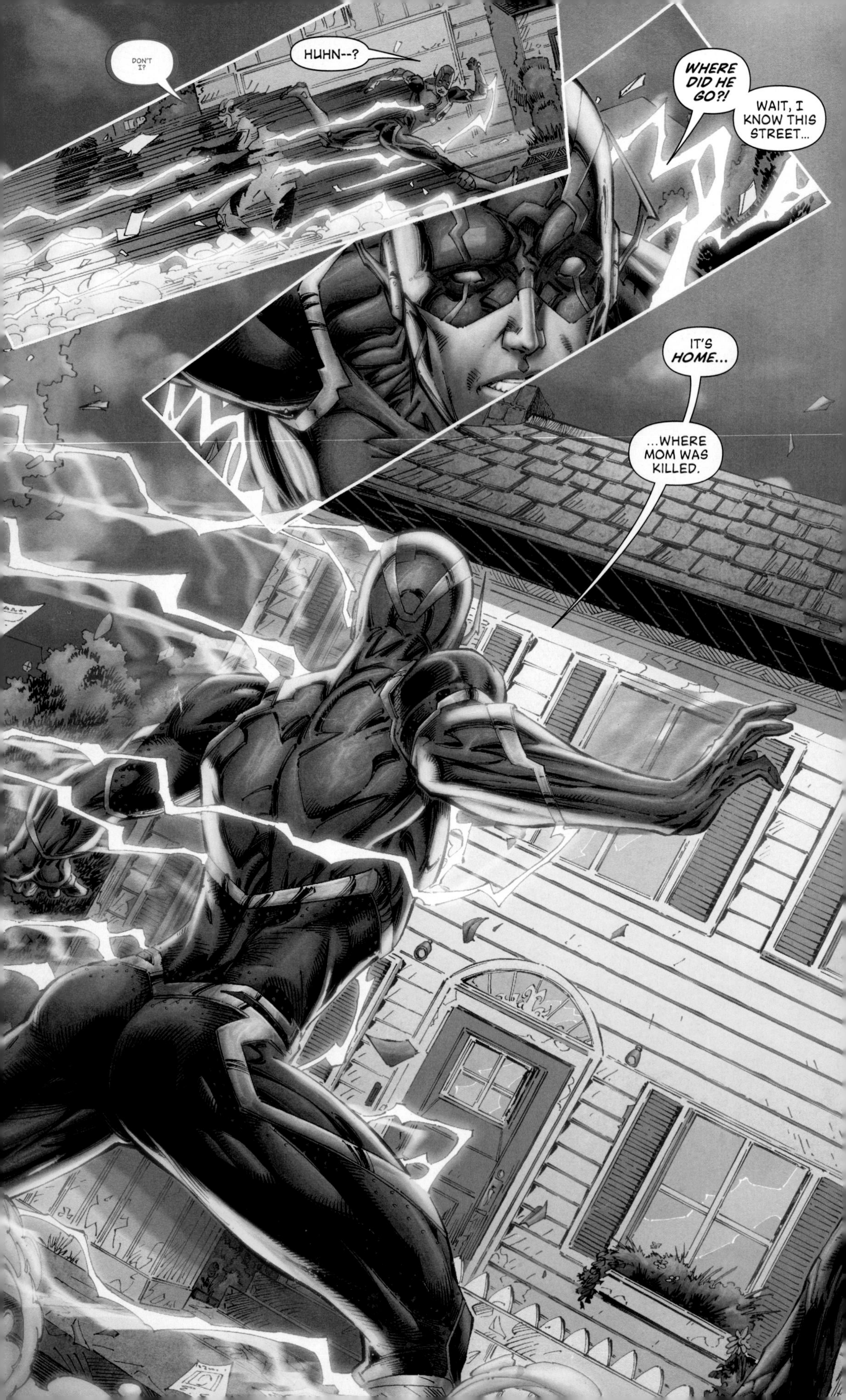
DON'T I?
HUHN--?
WHERE DID HE GO?!
WAIT, I KNOW THIS STREET...
IT'S HOME...
...WHERE MOM WAS KILLED.

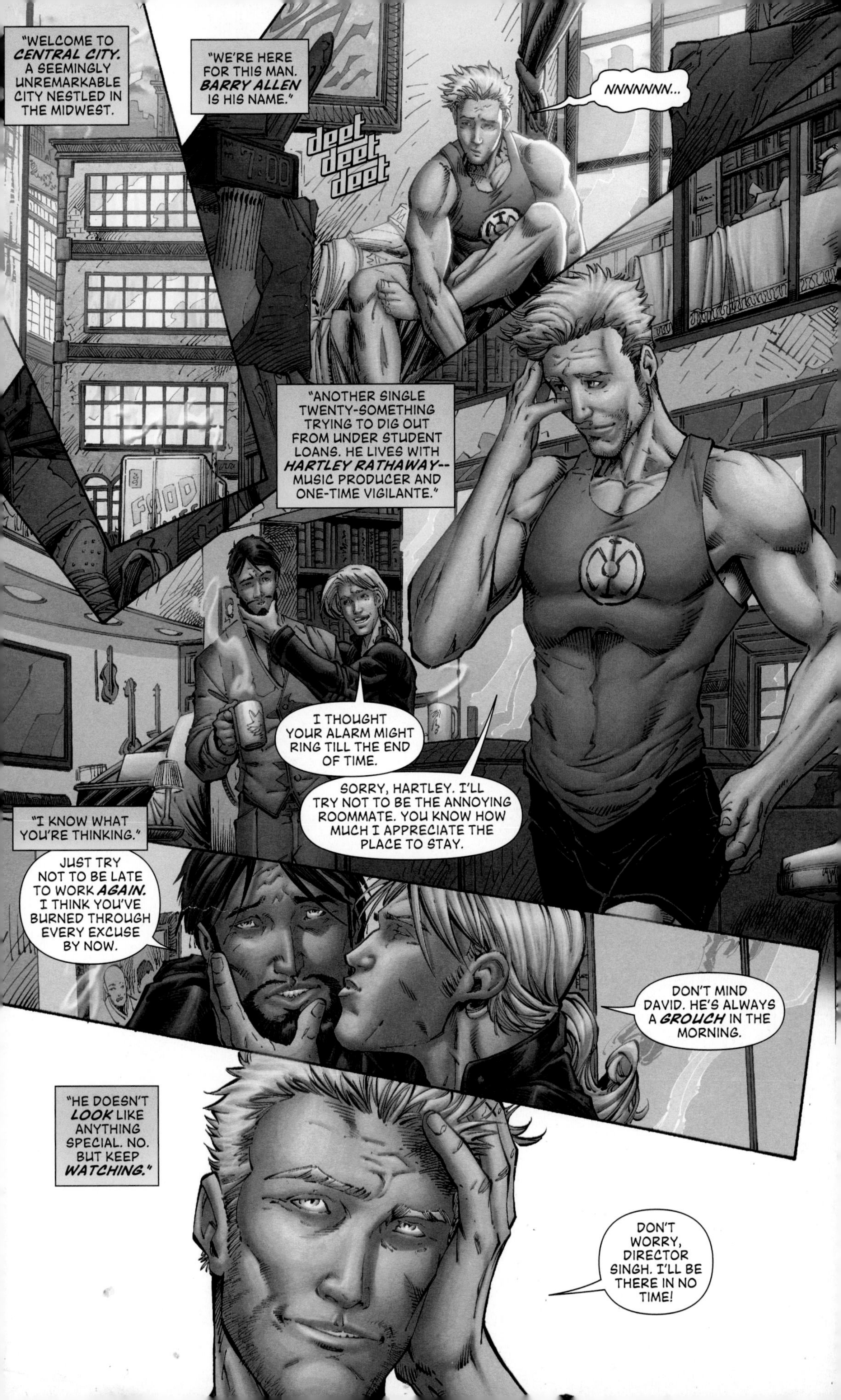
"WELCOME TO CENTRAL CITY. A SEEMINGLY UNREMARKABLE CITY NESTLED IN THE MIDWEST.
"WE'RE HERE FOR THIS MAN. BARRY ALLEN IS HIS NAME."
7:00
deet deet deet
NNNNNNN...
"ANOTHER SINGLE TWENTY-SOMETHING TRYING TO DIG OUT FROM UNDER STUDENT LOANS. HE LIVES WITH HARTLEY RATHAWAY--MUSIC PRODUCER AND ONE-TIME VIGILANTE."
FOOD
I THOUGHT YOUR ALARM MIGHT RING TILL THE END OF TIME.
SORRY, HARTLEY. I'LL TRY NOT TO BE THE ANNOYING ROOMMATE. YOU KNOW HOW MUCH I APPRECIATE THE PLACE TO STAY.
"I KNOW WHAT YOU'RE THINKING."
JUST TRY NOT TO BE LATE TO WORK AGAIN. I THINK YOU'VE BURNED THROUGH EVERY EXCUSE BY NOW.
DON'T MIND DAVID. HE'S ALWAYS A GROUCH IN THE MORNING.
"HE DOESN'T LOOK LIKE ANYTHING SPECIAL. NO. BUT KEEP WATCHING."
DON'T WORRY, DIRECTOR SINGH. I'LL BE THERE IN NO TIME!

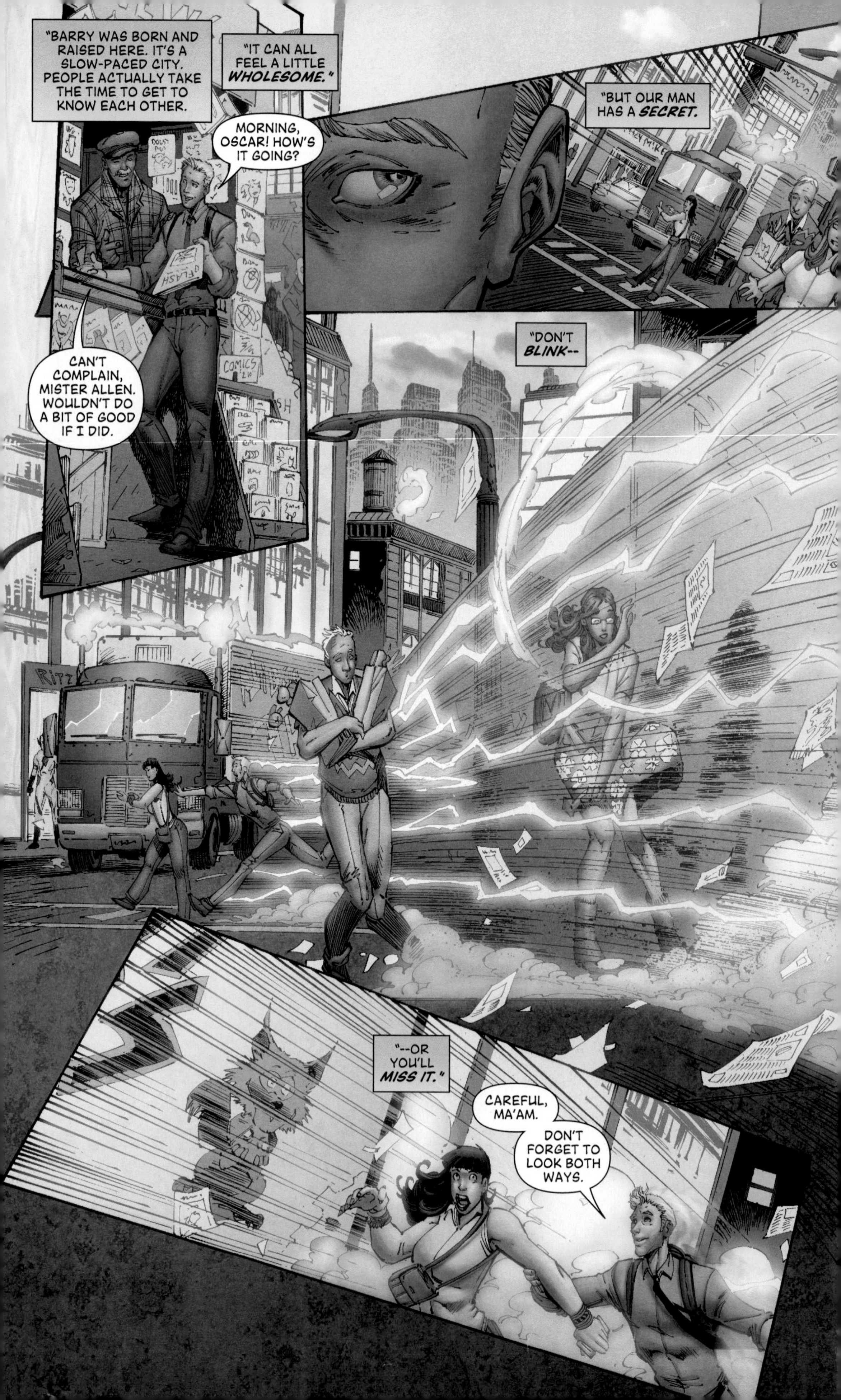
"BARRY WAS BORN AND RAISED HERE. IT'S A SLOW-PACED CITY. PEOPLE ACTUALLY TAKE THE TIME TO GET TO KNOW EACH OTHER.
"IT CAN ALL FEEL A LITTLE WHOLESOME."
MORNING, OSCAR! HOW'S IT GOING?
CAN'T COMPLAIN, MISTER ALLEN. WOULDN'T DO A BIT OF GOOD IF I DID.
"BUT OUR MAN HAS A SECRET.
"DON'T BLINK--
"--OR YOU'LL MISS IT."
CAREFUL, MA'AM.
DON'T FORGET TO LOOK BOTH WAYS.

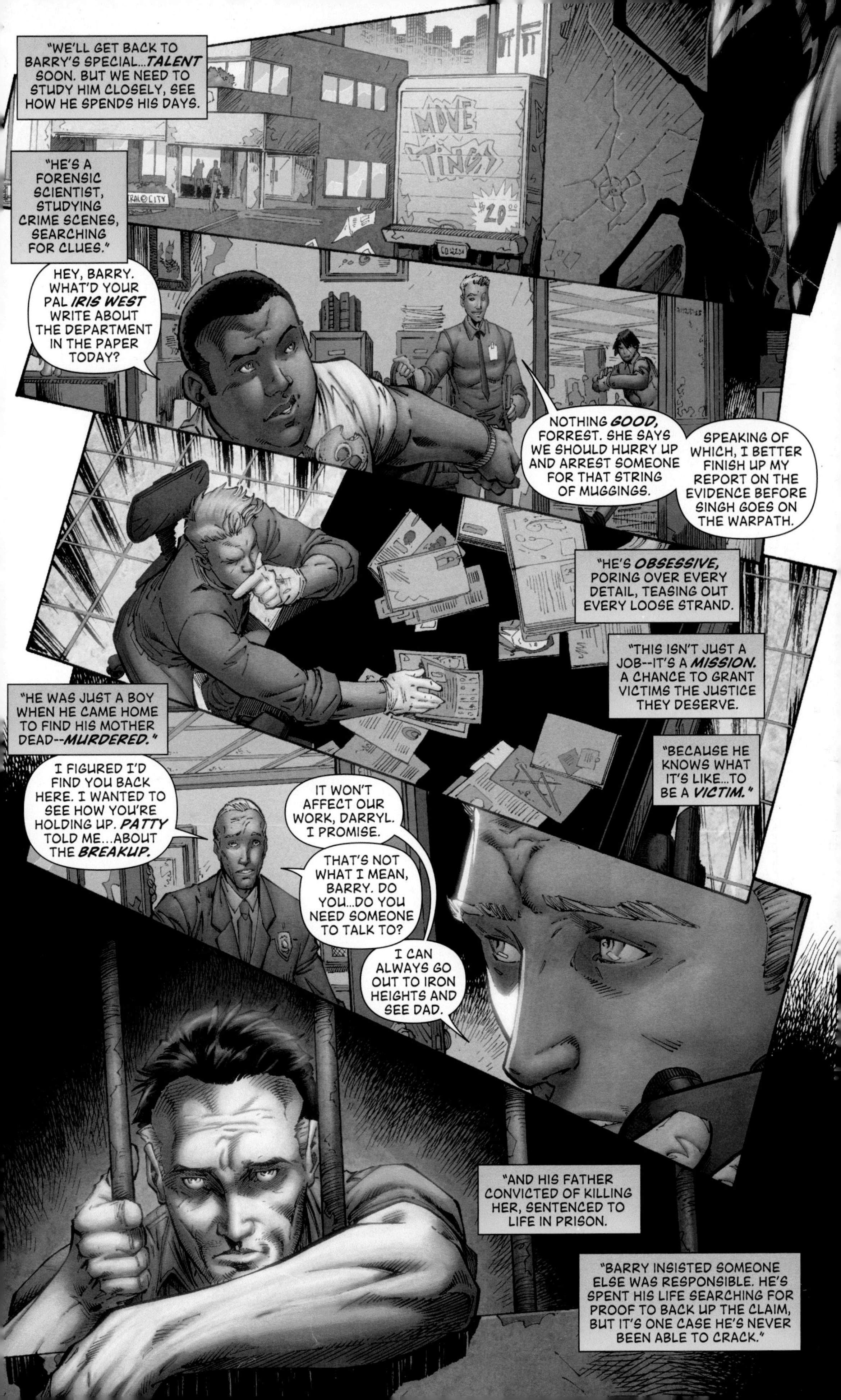

"WE'LL GET BACK TO BARRY'S SPECIAL...*TALENT* SOON. BUT WE NEED TO STUDY HIM CLOSELY, SEE HOW HE SPENDS HIS DAYS.
MOVE TING!
$20.00
"HE'S A FORENSIC SCIENTIST, STUDYING CRIME SCENES, SEARCHING FOR CLUES."
HEY, BARRY. WHAT'D YOUR PAL *IRIS WEST* WRITE ABOUT THE DEPARTMENT IN THE PAPER TODAY?
NOTHING *GOOD,* FORREST. SHE SAYS WE SHOULD HURRY UP AND ARREST SOMEONE FOR THAT STRING OF MUGGINGS.
SPEAKING OF WHICH, I BETTER FINISH UP MY REPORT ON THE EVIDENCE BEFORE SINGH GOES ON THE WARPATH.
"HE'S *OBSESSIVE,* PORING OVER EVERY DETAIL, TEASING OUT EVERY LOOSE STRAND.
"THIS ISN'T JUST A JOB--IT'S A *MISSION.* A CHANCE TO GRANT VICTIMS THE JUSTICE THEY DESERVE.
"HE WAS JUST A BOY WHEN HE CAME HOME TO FIND HIS MOTHER DEAD--*MURDERED.*"
"BECAUSE HE KNOWS WHAT IT'S LIKE...TO BE A *VICTIM.*"
I FIGURED I'D FIND YOU BACK HERE. I WANTED TO SEE HOW YOU'RE HOLDING UP. *PATTY* TOLD ME...ABOUT THE *BREAKUP.*
IT WON'T AFFECT OUR WORK, DARRYL. I PROMISE.
THAT'S NOT WHAT I MEAN, BARRY. DO YOU...DO YOU NEED SOMEONE TO TALK TO?
I CAN ALWAYS GO OUT TO IRON HEIGHTS AND SEE DAD.
"AND HIS FATHER CONVICTED OF KILLING HER, SENTENCED TO LIFE IN PRISON.
"BARRY INSISTED SOMEONE ELSE WAS RESPONSIBLE. HE'S SPENT HIS LIFE SEARCHING FOR PROOF TO BACK UP THE CLAIM, BUT IT'S ONE CASE HE'S NEVER BEEN ABLE TO CRACK."

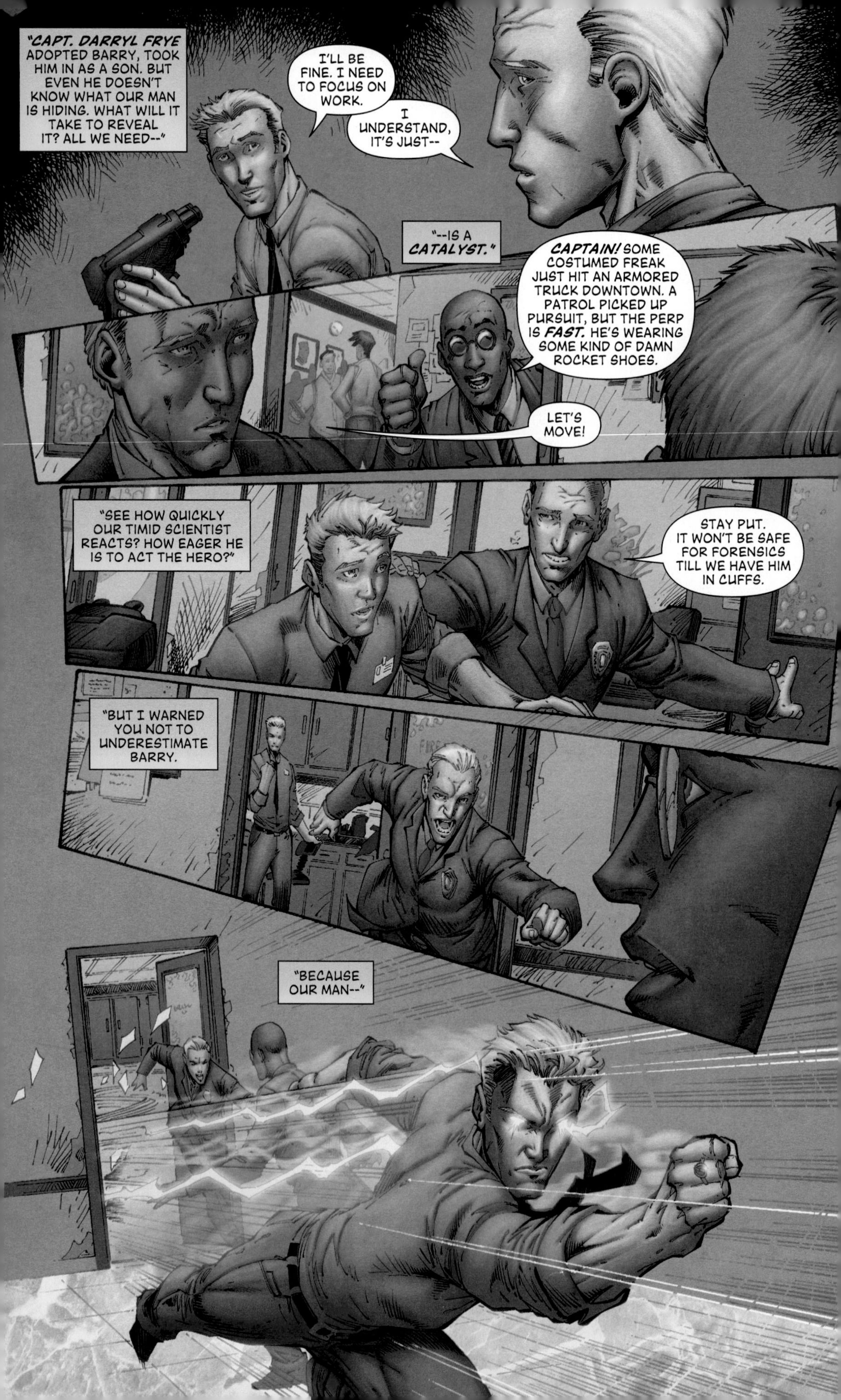
"CAPT. DARRYL FRYE ADOPTED BARRY, TOOK HIM IN AS A SON. BUT EVEN HE DOESN'T KNOW WHAT OUR MAN IS HIDING. WHAT WILL IT TAKE TO REVEAL IT? ALL WE NEED--"
I'LL BE FINE. I NEED TO FOCUS ON WORK.
I UNDERSTAND, IT'S JUST--
"--IS A CATALYST."
CAPTAIN! SOME COSTUMED FREAK JUST HIT AN ARMORED TRUCK DOWNTOWN. A PATROL PICKED UP PURSUIT, BUT THE PERP IS FAST. HE'S WEARING SOME KIND OF DAMN ROCKET SHOES.
LET'S MOVE!
"SEE HOW QUICKLY OUR TIMID SCIENTIST REACTS? HOW EAGER HE IS TO ACT THE HERO?"
STAY PUT. IT WON'T BE SAFE FOR FORENSICS TILL WE HAVE HIM IN CUFFS.
"BUT I WARNED YOU NOT TO UNDERESTIMATE BARRY.
"BECAUSE OUR MAN--"

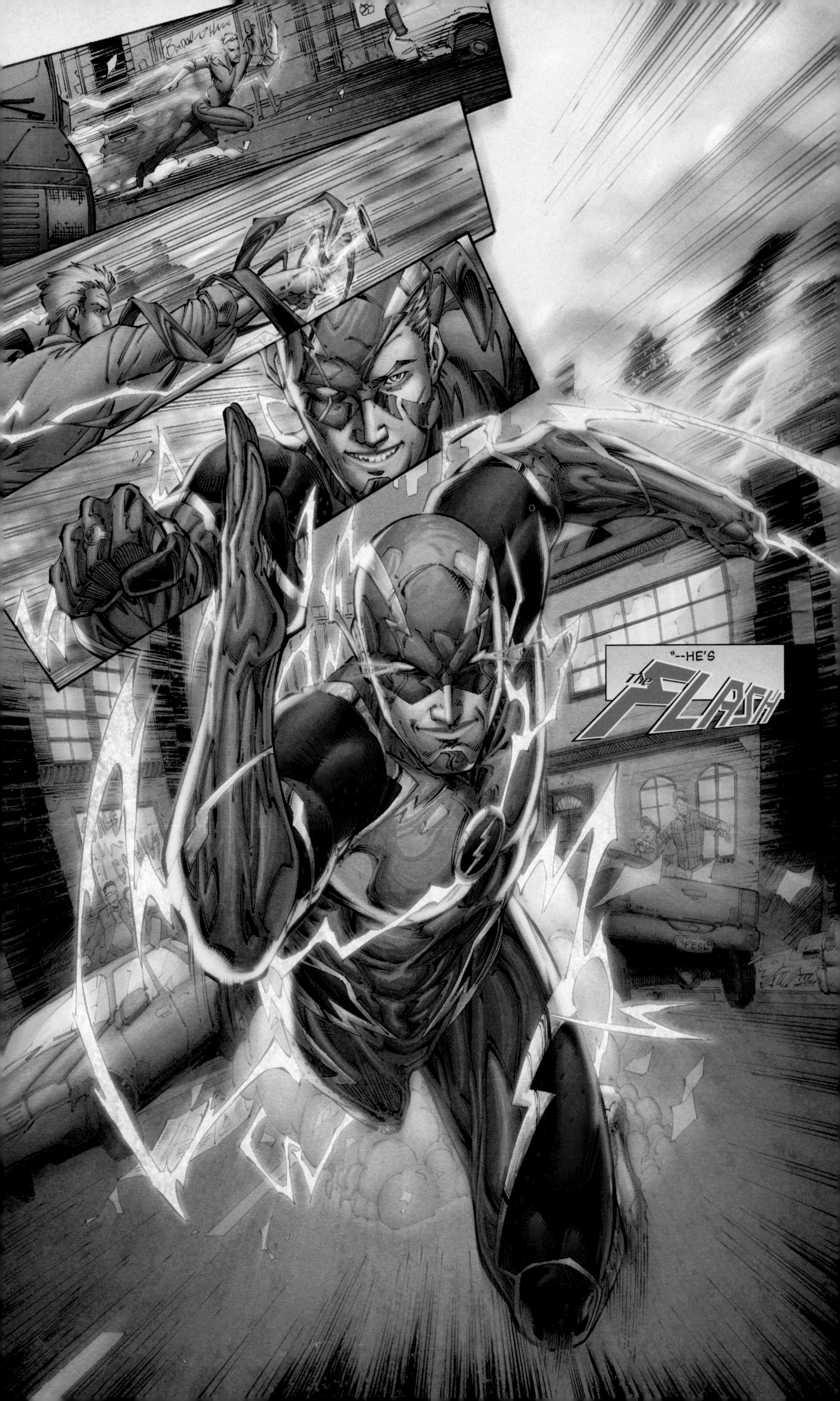
"--HE'S
The FLASH

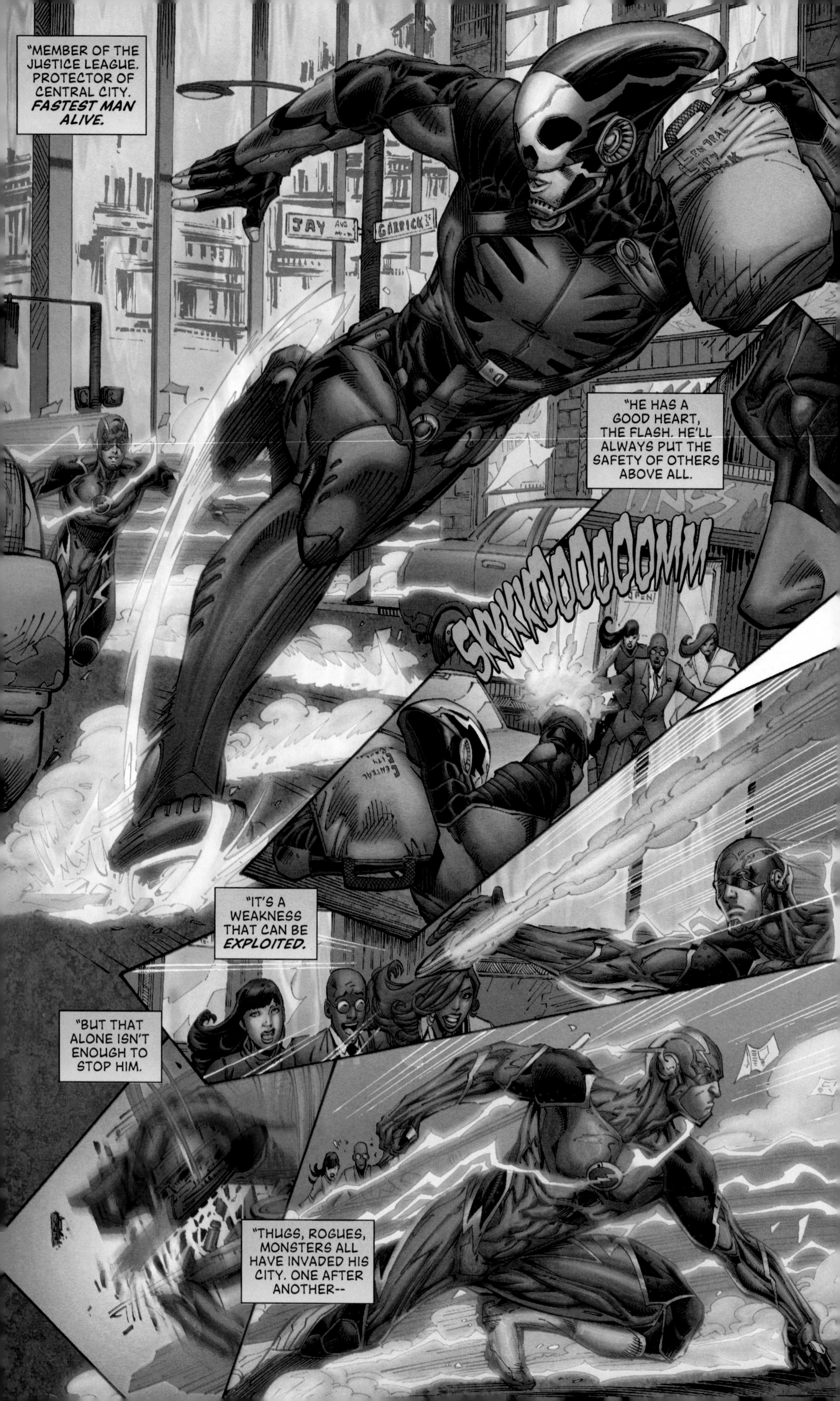
"MEMBER OF THE JUSTICE LEAGUE. PROTECTOR OF CENTRAL CITY. *FASTEST MAN ALIVE.*
JAY AVE
GARRICK ST
"HE HAS A GOOD HEART, THE FLASH. HE'LL ALWAYS PUT THE SAFETY OF OTHERS ABOVE ALL.
SKKKOOOOOOMM
"IT'S A WEAKNESS THAT CAN BE *EXPLOITED.*
"BUT THAT ALONE ISN'T ENOUGH TO STOP HIM.
"THUGS, ROGUES, MONSTERS ALL HAVE INVADED HIS CITY. ONE AFTER ANOTHER--

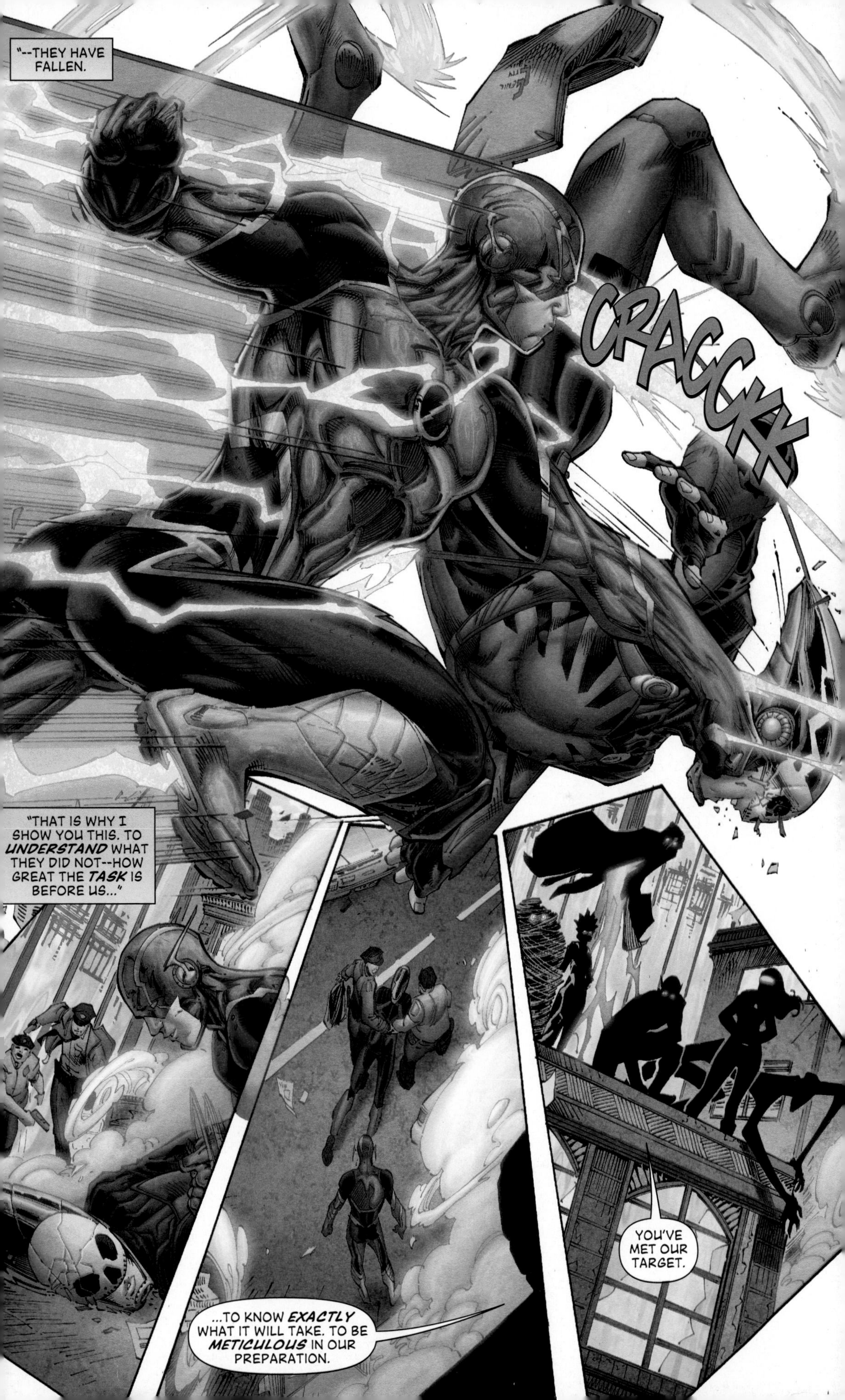
"--THEY HAVE FALLEN.
CRAGGKK
"THAT IS WHY I SHOW YOU THIS. TO UNDERSTAND WHAT THEY DID NOT--HOW GREAT THE TASK IS BEFORE US..."
...TO KNOW EXACTLY WHAT IT WILL TAKE. TO BE METICULOUS IN OUR PREPARATION.
YOU'VE MET OUR TARGET.

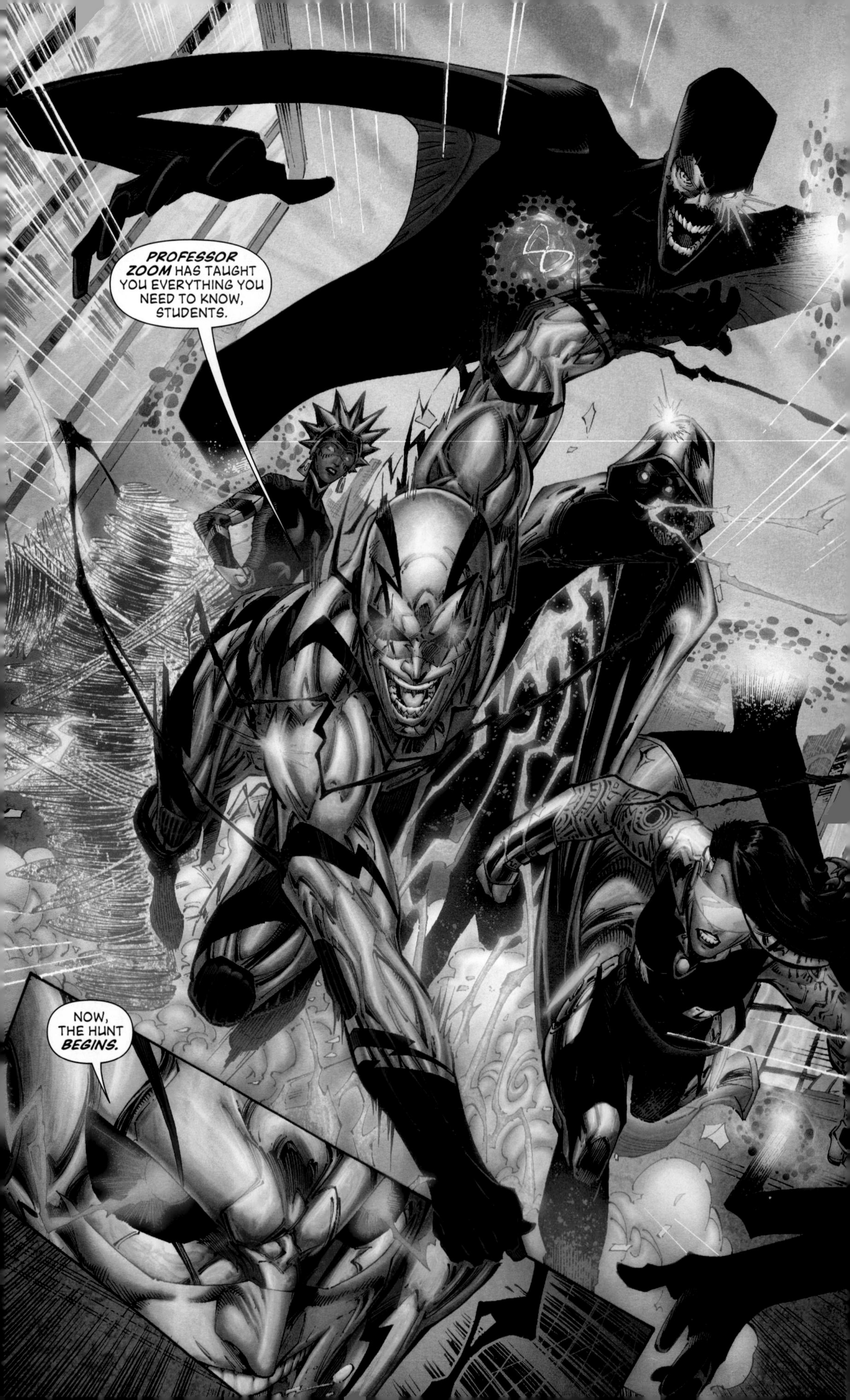

PROFESSOR ZOOM HAS TAUGHT YOU EVERYTHING YOU NEED TO KNOW, STUDENTS.
NOW, THE HUNT ***BEGINS.***

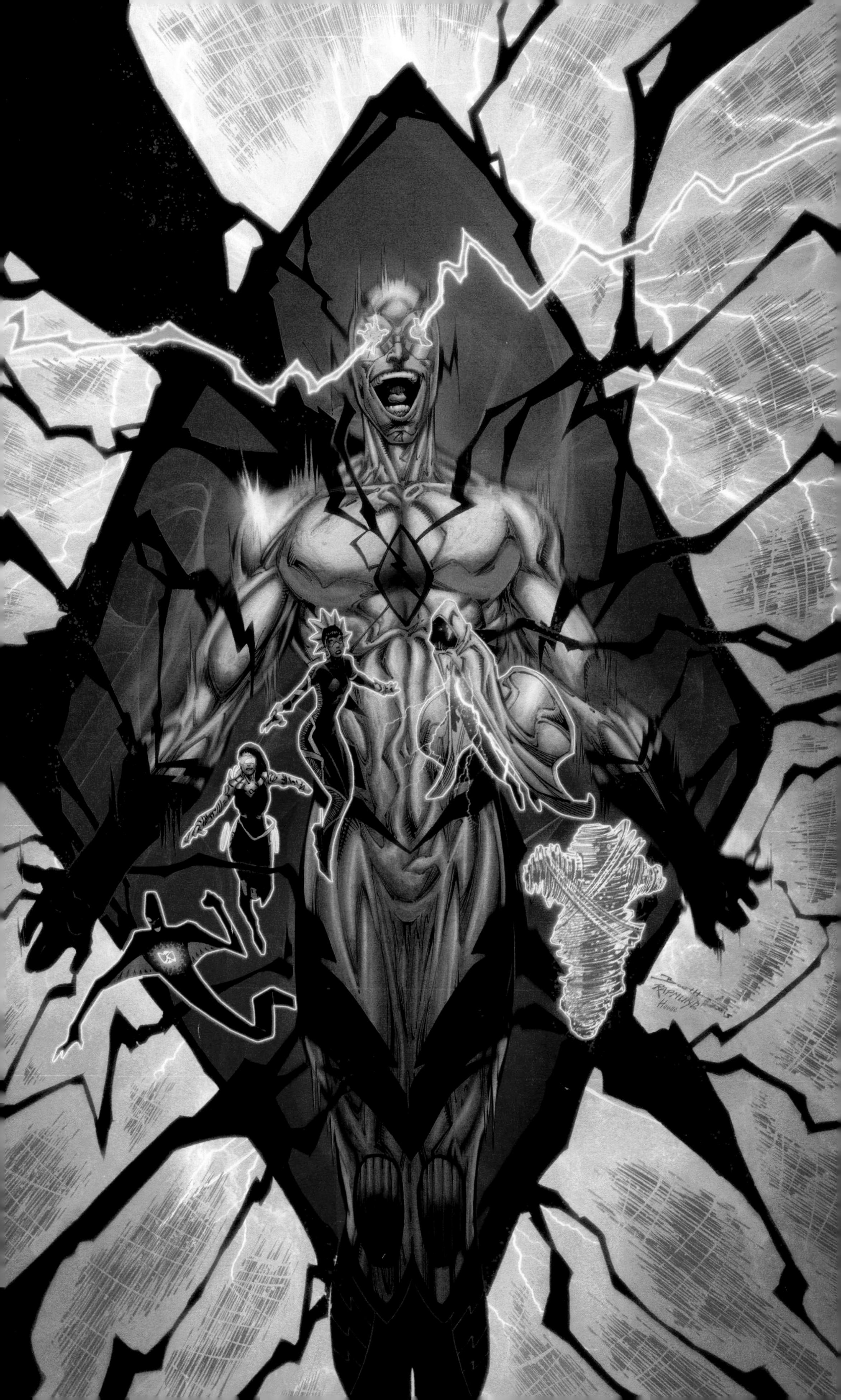

CREATION MYTHS

VAN JENSEN writer BONG DAZO penciller NORM RAPMUND inker ANDREW DALHOUSE colorist CARLOS M. MANGUAL letterer
cover by BRETT BOOTH, NORM RAPMUND, ANDREW DALHOUSE

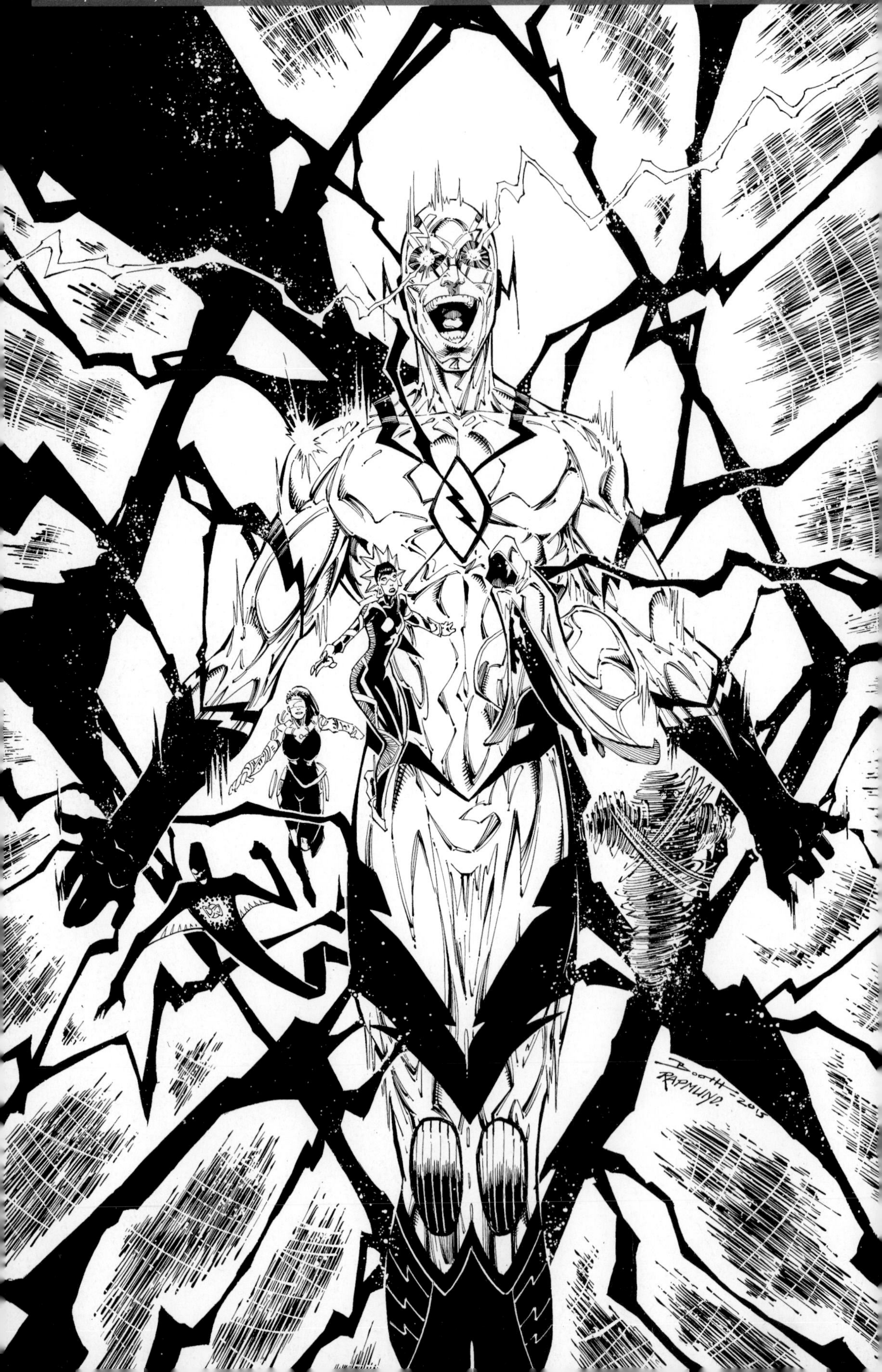
BOOTH - 2015
RAPMUND.

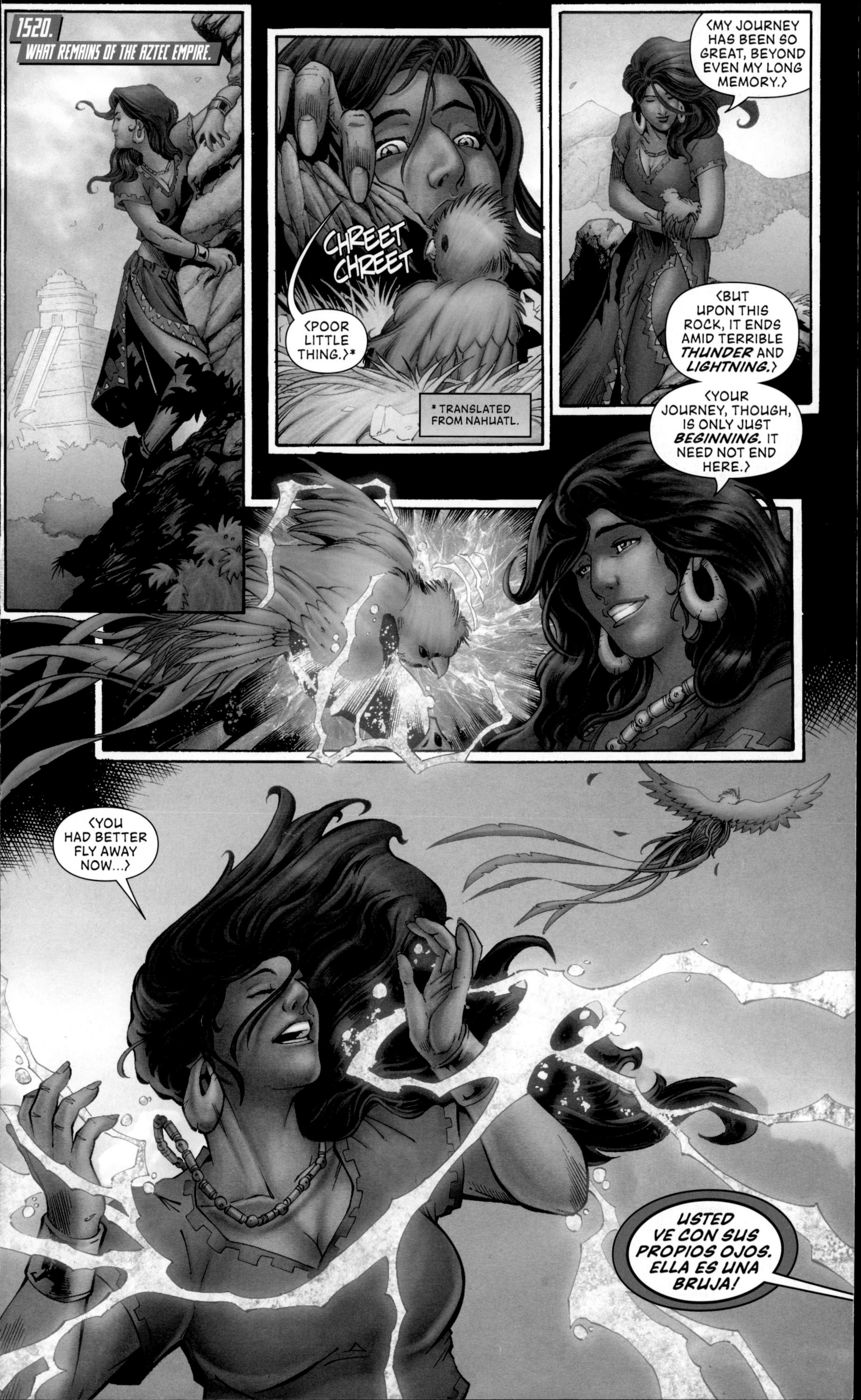
1520.
WHAT REMAINS OF THE AZTEC EMPIRE.
CHREET CHREET
<POOR LITTLE THING.>*
* TRANSLATED FROM NAHUATL.
<MY JOURNEY HAS BEEN SO GREAT, BEYOND EVEN MY LONG MEMORY.>
<BUT UPON THIS ROCK, IT ENDS AMID TERRIBLE THUNDER AND LIGHTNING.>
<YOUR JOURNEY, THOUGH, IS ONLY JUST BEGINNING. IT NEED NOT END HERE.>
<YOU HAD BETTER FLY AWAY NOW...>
USTED VE CON SUS PROPIOS OJOS. ELLA ES UNA BRUJA!

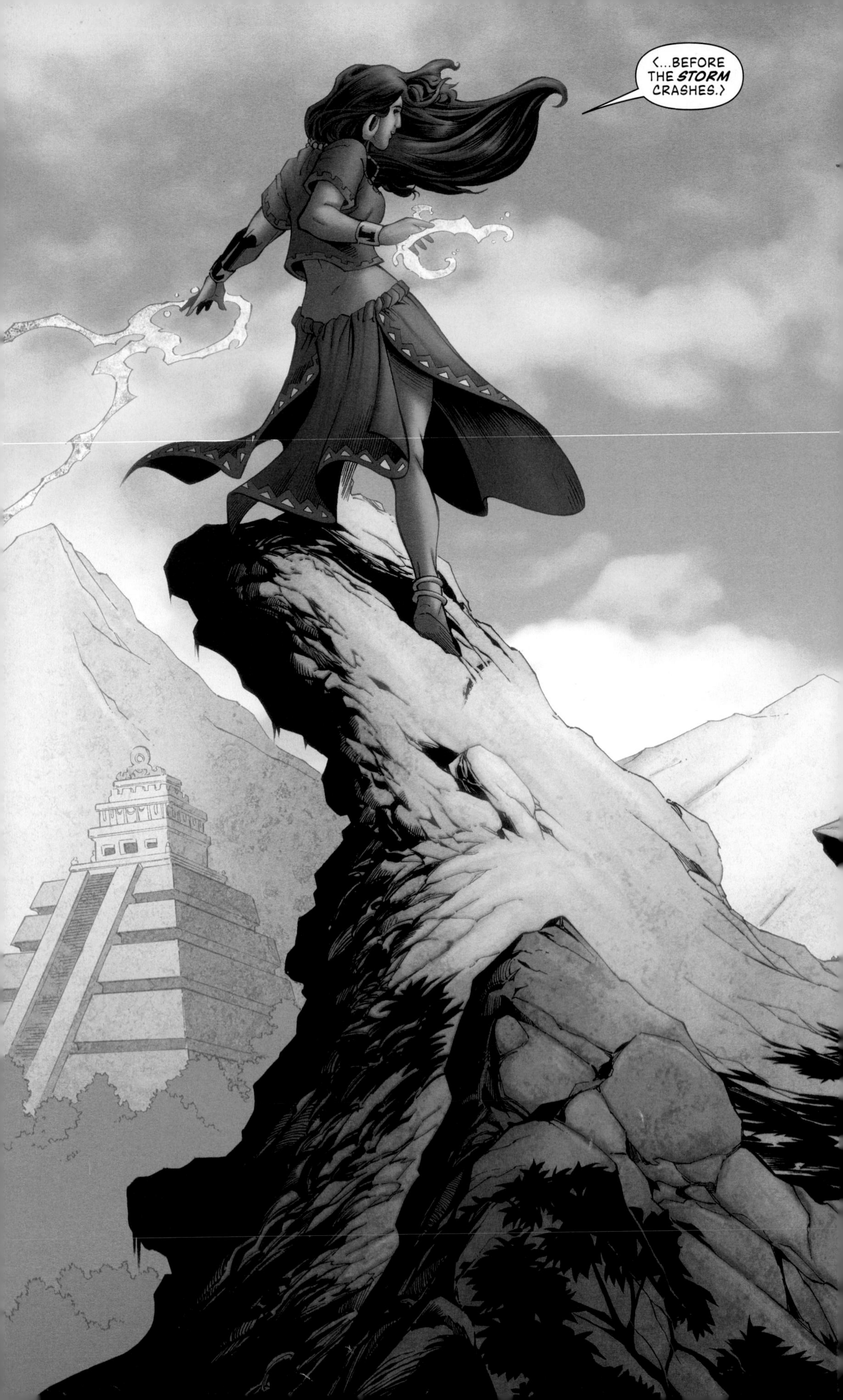

‹...BEFORE THE *STORM* CRASHES.›

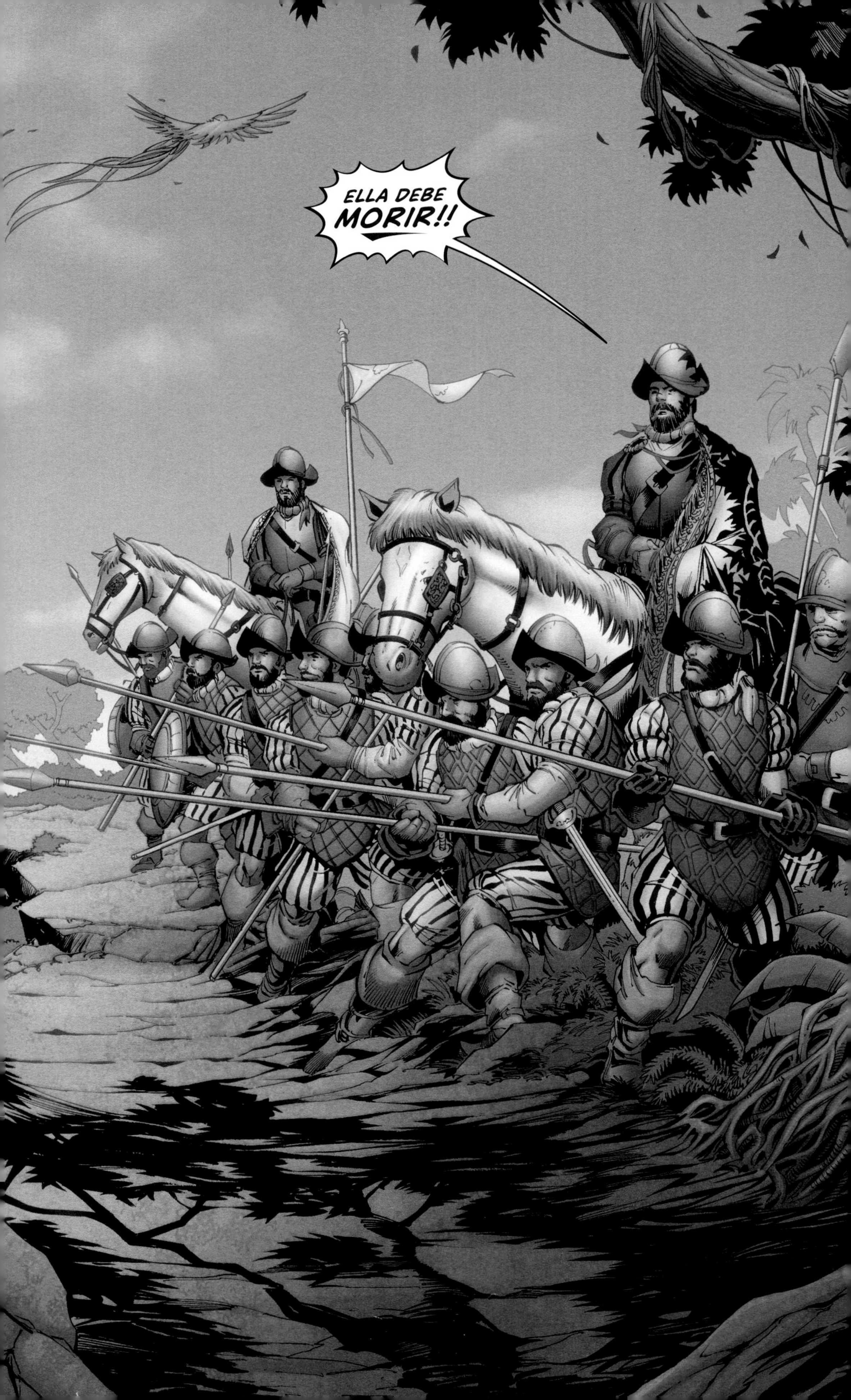
ELLA DEBE MORIR!!

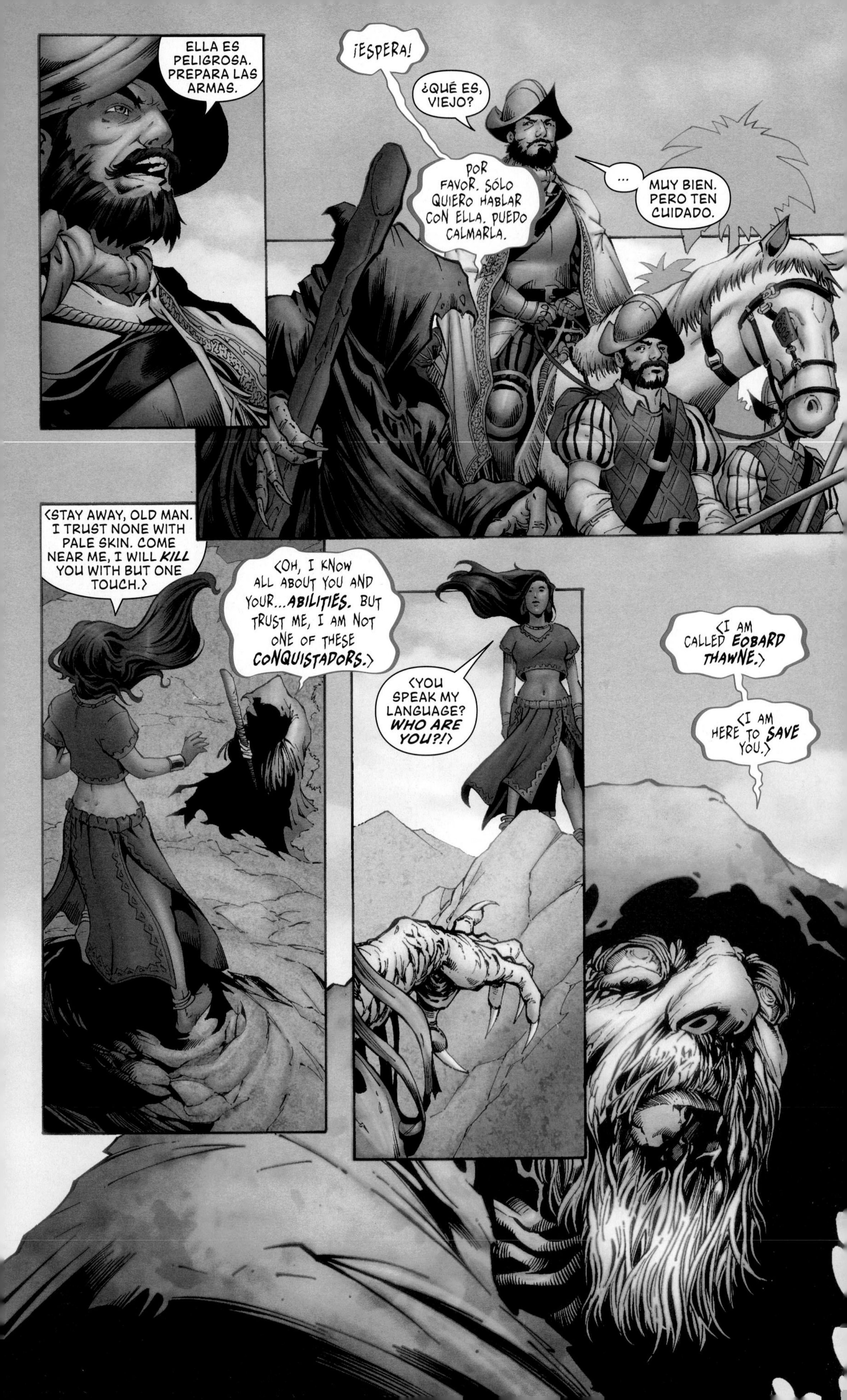
ELLA ES PELIGROSA. PREPARA LAS ARMAS.
¡ESPERA!
¿QUÉ ES, VIEJO?
POR FAVOR. SÓLO QUIERO HABLAR CON ELLA. PUEDO CALMARLA.
...
MUY BIEN. PERO TEN CUIDADO.
<STAY AWAY, OLD MAN. I TRUST NONE WITH PALE SKIN. COME NEAR ME, I WILL KILL YOU WITH BUT ONE TOUCH.>
<OH, I KNOW ALL ABOUT YOU AND YOUR...ABILITIES. BUT TRUST ME, I AM NOT ONE OF THESE CONQUISTADORS.>
<YOU SPEAK MY LANGUAGE? WHO ARE YOU?!>
<I AM CALLED EOBARD THAWNE.>
<I AM HERE TO SAVE YOU.>

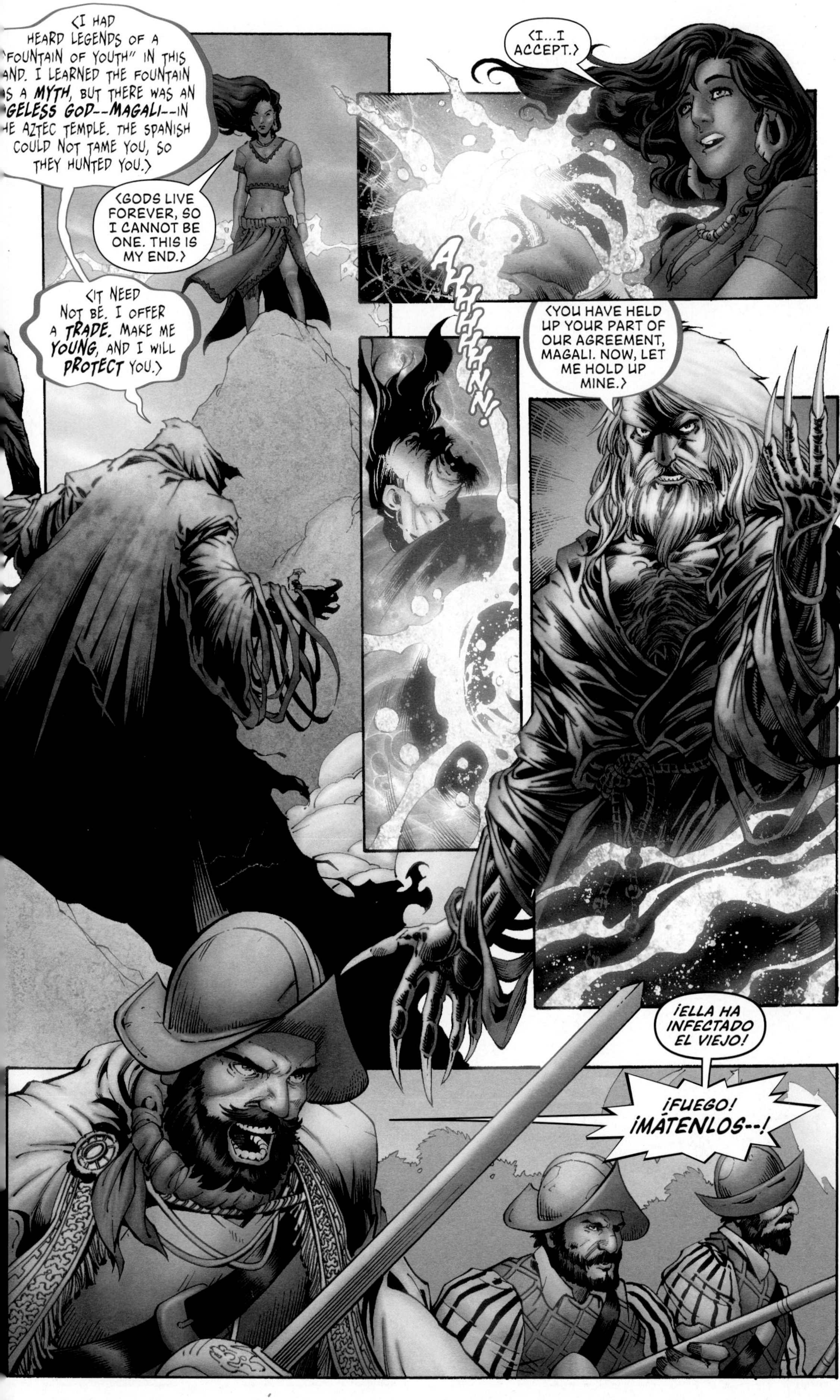
<I HAD HEARD LEGENDS OF A "FOUNTAIN OF YOUTH" IN THIS LAND. I LEARNED THE FOUNTAIN IS A MYTH, BUT THERE WAS AN AGELESS GOD--MAGALI--IN THE AZTEC TEMPLE. THE SPANISH COULD NOT TAME YOU, SO THEY HUNTED YOU.>
<GODS LIVE FOREVER, SO I CANNOT BE ONE. THIS IS MY END.>
<IT NEED NOT BE. I OFFER A TRADE. MAKE ME YOUNG, AND I WILL PROTECT YOU.>
<I...I ACCEPT.>
AHHHHHNN!
<YOU HAVE HELD UP YOUR PART OF OUR AGREEMENT, MAGALI. NOW, LET ME HOLD UP MINE.>
¡ELLA HA INFECTADO EL VIEJO!
¡FUEGO! ¡MÁTENLOS--!

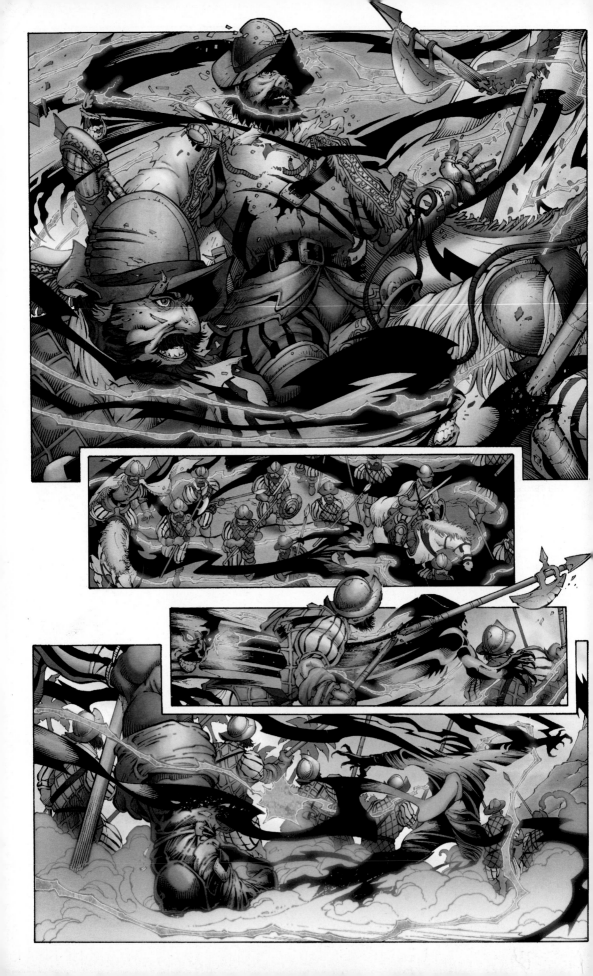

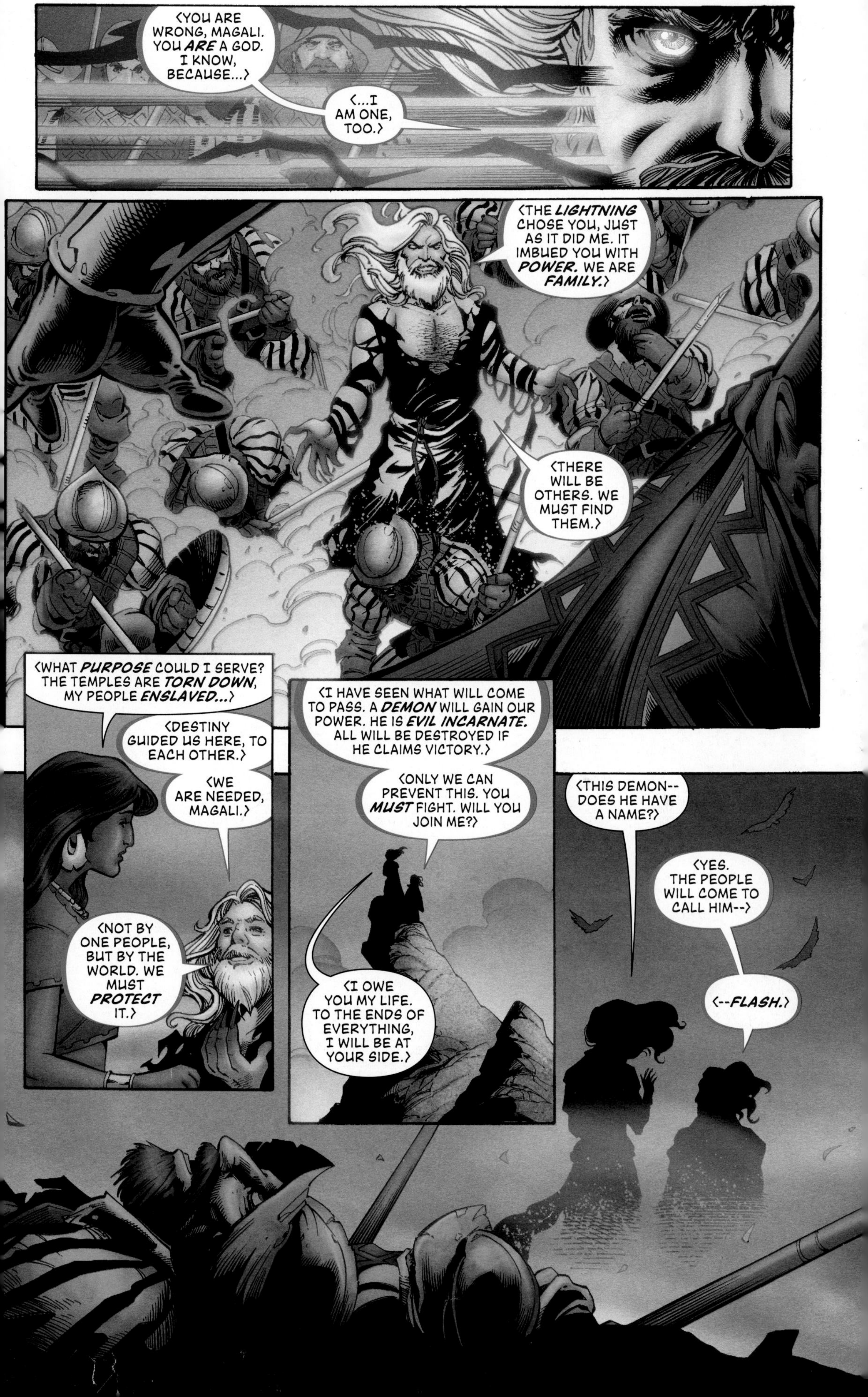
<YOU ARE WRONG, MAGALI. YOU *ARE* A GOD. I KNOW, BECAUSE...>
<...I AM ONE, TOO.>
<THE *LIGHTNING* CHOSE YOU, JUST AS IT DID ME. IT IMBUED YOU WITH *POWER.* WE ARE *FAMILY.*>
<THERE WILL BE OTHERS. WE MUST FIND THEM.>
<WHAT *PURPOSE* COULD I SERVE? THE TEMPLES ARE *TORN DOWN*, MY PEOPLE *ENSLAVED...*>
<DESTINY GUIDED US HERE, TO EACH OTHER.>
<WE ARE NEEDED, MAGALI.>
<NOT BY ONE PEOPLE, BUT BY THE WORLD. WE MUST *PROTECT* IT.>
<I HAVE SEEN WHAT WILL COME TO PASS. A *DEMON* WILL GAIN OUR POWER. HE IS *EVIL INCARNATE.* ALL WILL BE DESTROYED IF HE CLAIMS VICTORY.>
<ONLY WE CAN PREVENT THIS. YOU *MUST* FIGHT. WILL YOU JOIN ME?>
<I OWE YOU MY LIFE. TO THE ENDS OF EVERYTHING, I WILL BE AT YOUR SIDE.>
<THIS DEMON-- DOES HE HAVE A NAME?>
<YES. THE PEOPLE WILL COME TO CALL HIM-->
<--*FLASH.*>

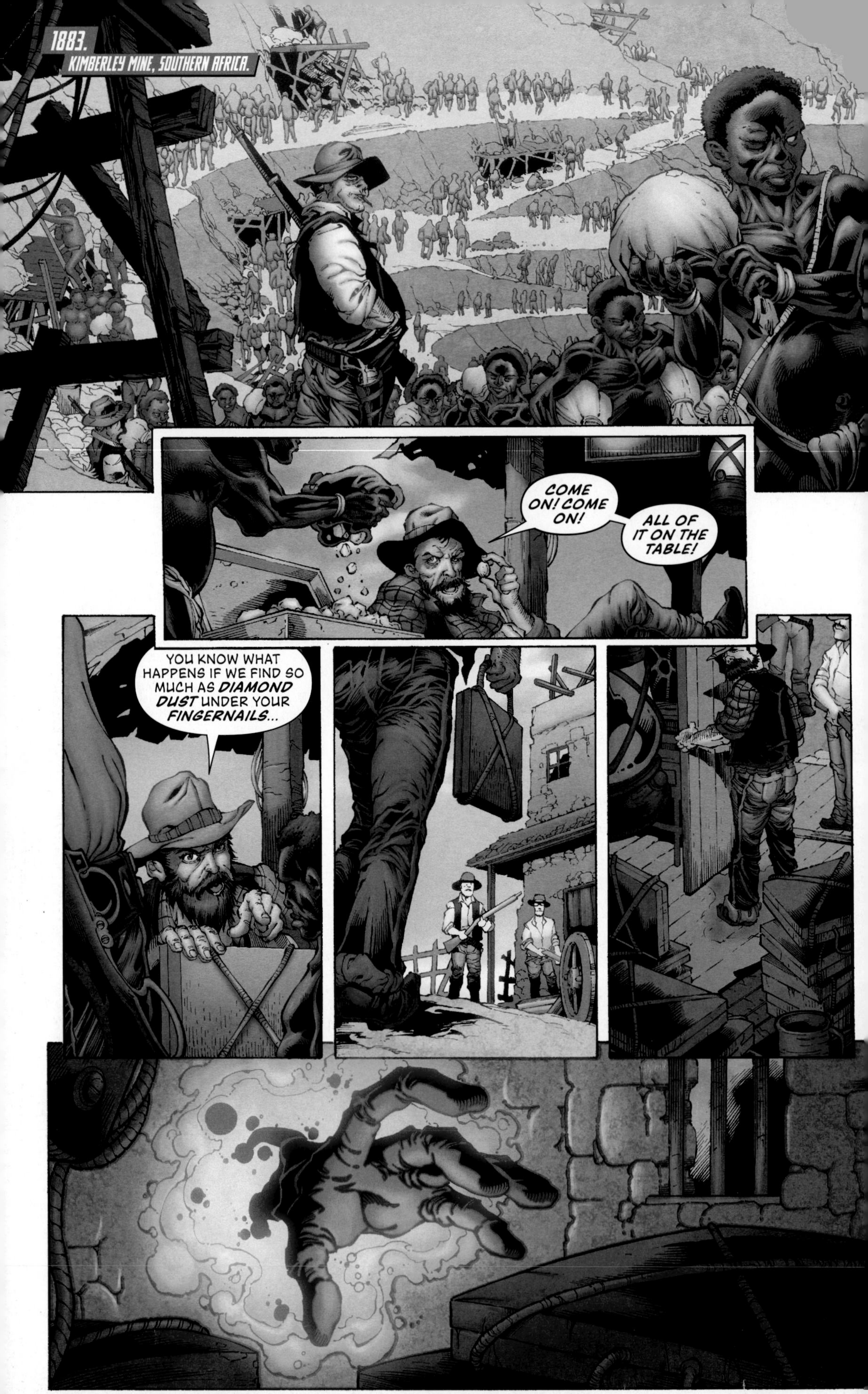
1883.
KIMBERLEY MINE, SOUTHERN AFRICA.
COME ON! COME ON!
ALL OF IT ON THE TABLE!
YOU KNOW WHAT HAPPENS IF WE FIND SO MUCH AS DIAMOND DUST UNDER YOUR FINGERNAILS...

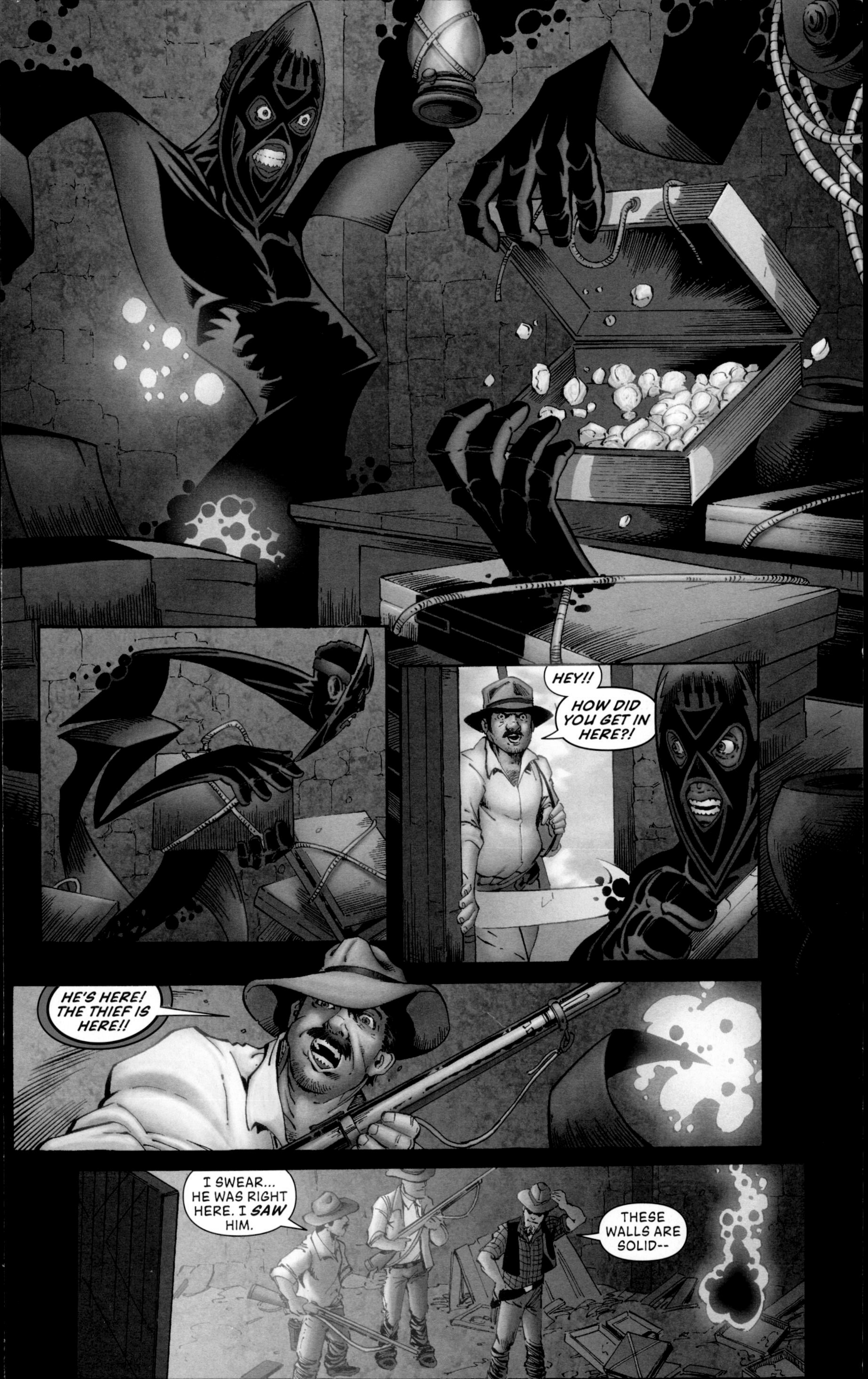
HEY!!
HOW DID YOU GET IN HERE?!
HE'S HERE! THE THIEF IS HERE!!
I SWEAR... HE WAS RIGHT HERE. I SAW HIM.
THESE WALLS ARE SOLID--

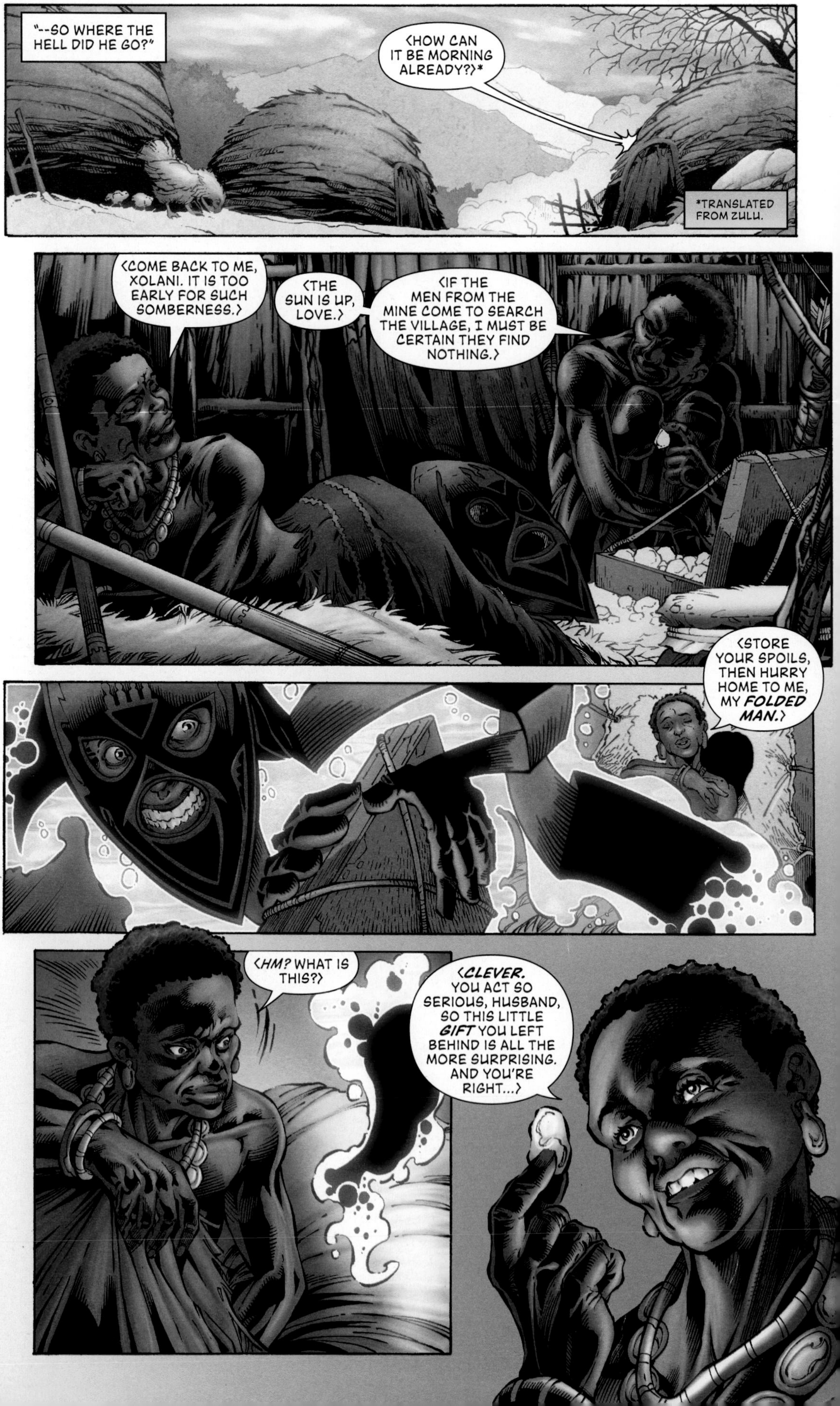

"--SO WHERE THE HELL DID HE GO?"
<HOW CAN IT BE MORNING ALREADY?>*
*TRANSLATED FROM ZULU.
<COME BACK TO ME, XOLANI. IT IS TOO EARLY FOR SUCH SOMBERNESS.>
<THE SUN IS UP, LOVE.>
<IF THE MEN FROM THE MINE COME TO SEARCH THE VILLAGE, I MUST BE CERTAIN THEY FIND NOTHING.>
<STORE YOUR SPOILS, THEN HURRY HOME TO ME, MY ***FOLDED MAN.***>
<***HM?*** WHAT IS THIS?>
<***CLEVER.*** YOU ACT SO SERIOUS, HUSBAND, SO THIS LITTLE ***GIFT*** YOU LEFT BEHIND IS ALL THE MORE SURPRISING. AND YOU'RE RIGHT...>

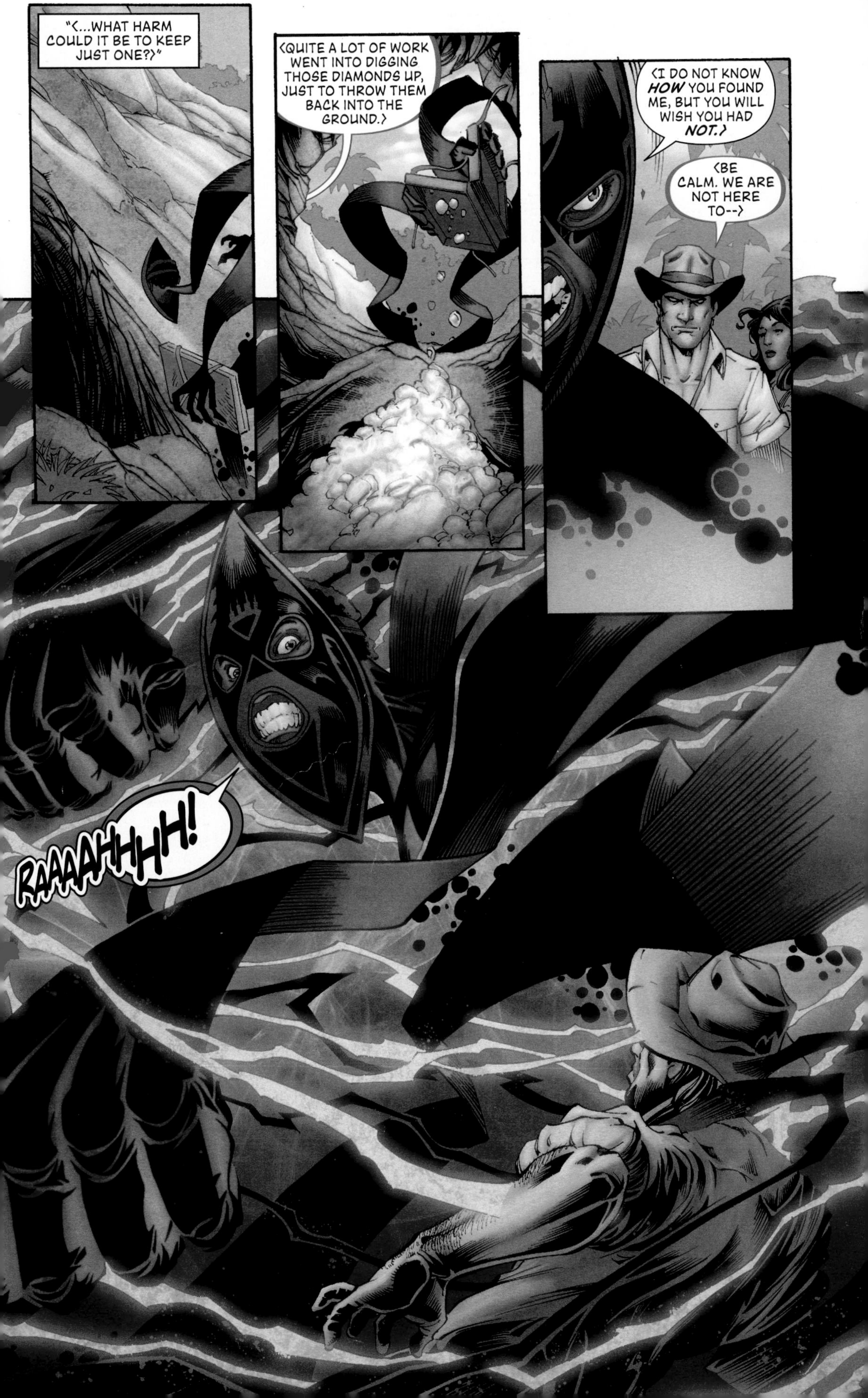
"<...WHAT HARM COULD IT BE TO KEEP JUST ONE?>"
<QUITE A LOT OF WORK WENT INTO DIGGING THOSE DIAMONDS UP, JUST TO THROW THEM BACK INTO THE GROUND.>
<I DO NOT KNOW **HOW** YOU FOUND ME, BUT YOU WILL WISH YOU HAD **NOT.**>
<BE CALM. WE ARE NOT HERE TO-->
RAAAAHHHH!

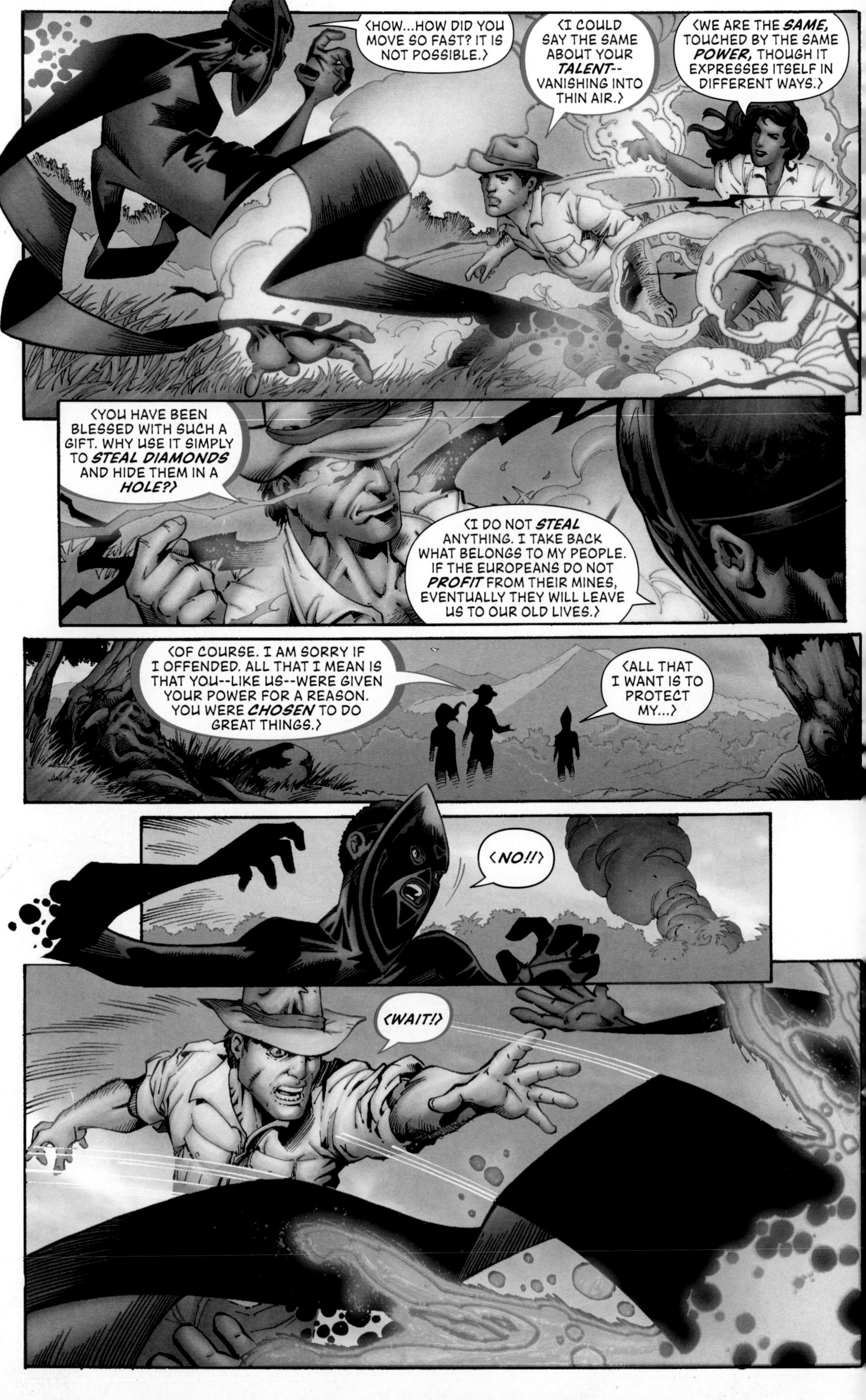
<HOW...HOW DID YOU MOVE SO FAST? IT IS NOT POSSIBLE.>
<I COULD SAY THE SAME ABOUT YOUR TALENT--VANISHING INTO THIN AIR.>
<WE ARE THE SAME, TOUCHED BY THE SAME POWER, THOUGH IT EXPRESSES ITSELF IN DIFFERENT WAYS.>
<YOU HAVE BEEN BLESSED WITH SUCH A GIFT. WHY USE IT SIMPLY TO STEAL DIAMONDS AND HIDE THEM IN A HOLE?>
<I DO NOT STEAL ANYTHING. I TAKE BACK WHAT BELONGS TO MY PEOPLE. IF THE EUROPEANS DO NOT PROFIT FROM THEIR MINES, EVENTUALLY THEY WILL LEAVE US TO OUR OLD LIVES.>
<OF COURSE. I AM SORRY IF I OFFENDED. ALL THAT I MEAN IS THAT YOU--LIKE US--WERE GIVEN YOUR POWER FOR A REASON. YOU WERE CHOSEN TO DO GREAT THINGS.>
<ALL THAT I WANT IS TO PROTECT MY...>
<NO!!>
<WAIT!>

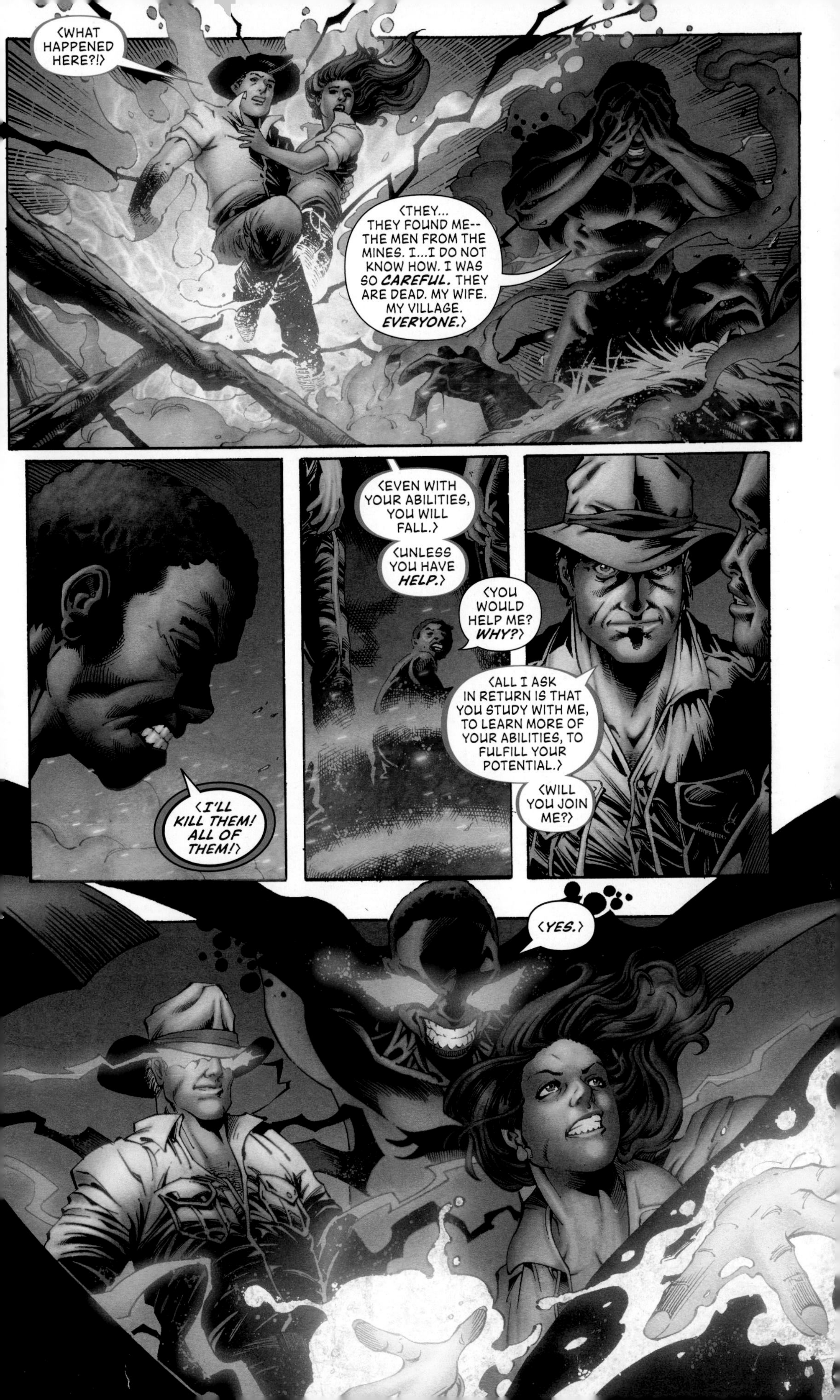

<WHAT HAPPENED HERE?!>
<THEY... THEY FOUND ME-- THE MEN FROM THE MINES. I...I DO NOT KNOW HOW. I WAS SO CAREFUL. THEY ARE DEAD. MY WIFE. MY VILLAGE. EVERYONE.>
<I'LL KILL THEM! ALL OF THEM!>
<EVEN WITH YOUR ABILITIES, YOU WILL FALL.>
<UNLESS YOU HAVE HELP.>
<YOU WOULD HELP ME? WHY?>
<ALL I ASK IN RETURN IS THAT YOU STUDY WITH ME, TO LEARN MORE OF YOUR ABILITIES, TO FULFILL YOUR POTENTIAL.>
<WILL YOU JOIN ME?>
<YES.>

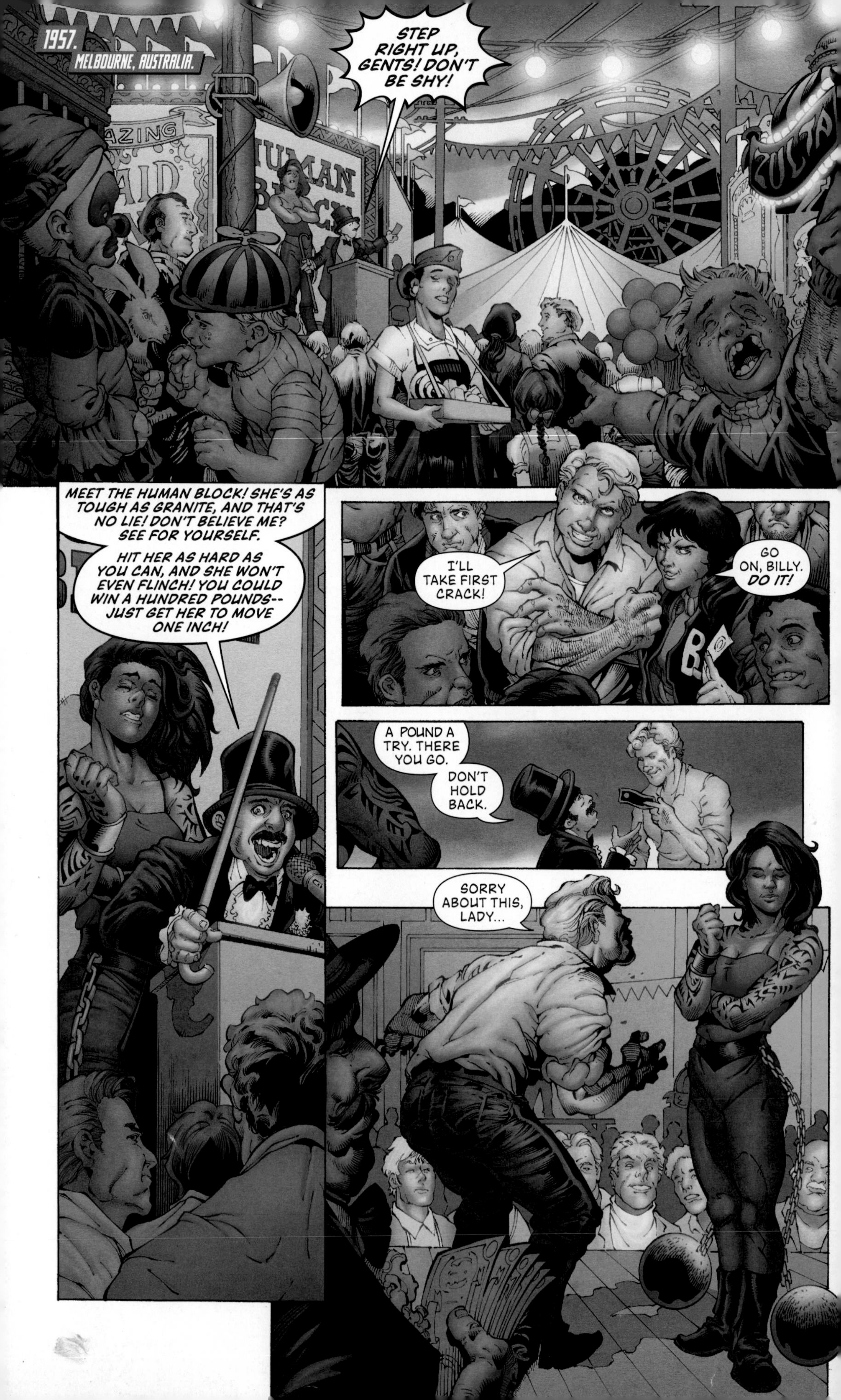

1957.
MELBOURNE, AUSTRALIA.
STEP RIGHT UP, GENTS! DON'T BE SHY!
AMAZING
HUMAN BLOCK
MEET THE HUMAN BLOCK! SHE'S AS TOUGH AS GRANITE, AND THAT'S NO LIE! DON'T BELIEVE ME? SEE FOR YOURSELF.
HIT HER AS HARD AS YOU CAN, AND SHE WON'T EVEN FLINCH! YOU COULD WIN A HUNDRED POUNDS-- JUST GET HER TO MOVE ONE INCH!
I'LL TAKE FIRST CRACK!
GO ON, BILLY. DO IT!
A POUND A TRY. THERE YOU GO.
DON'T HOLD BACK.
SORRY ABOUT THIS, LADY...

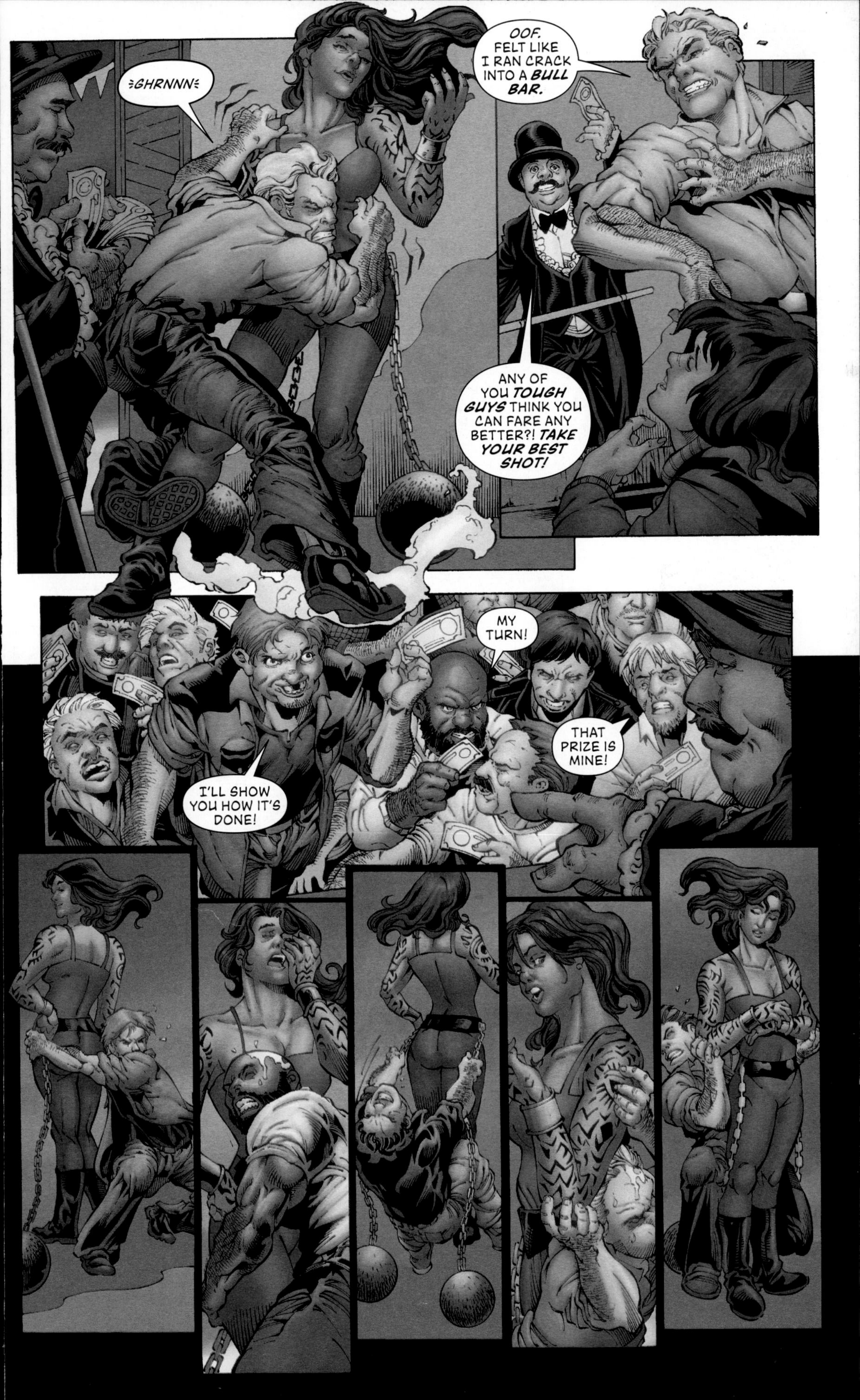

GHRNNN
OOF. FELT LIKE I RAN CRACK INTO A BULL BAR.
ANY OF YOU TOUGH GUYS THINK YOU CAN FARE ANY BETTER?! TAKE YOUR BEST SHOT!
MY TURN!
THAT PRIZE IS MINE!
I'LL SHOW YOU HOW IT'S DONE!

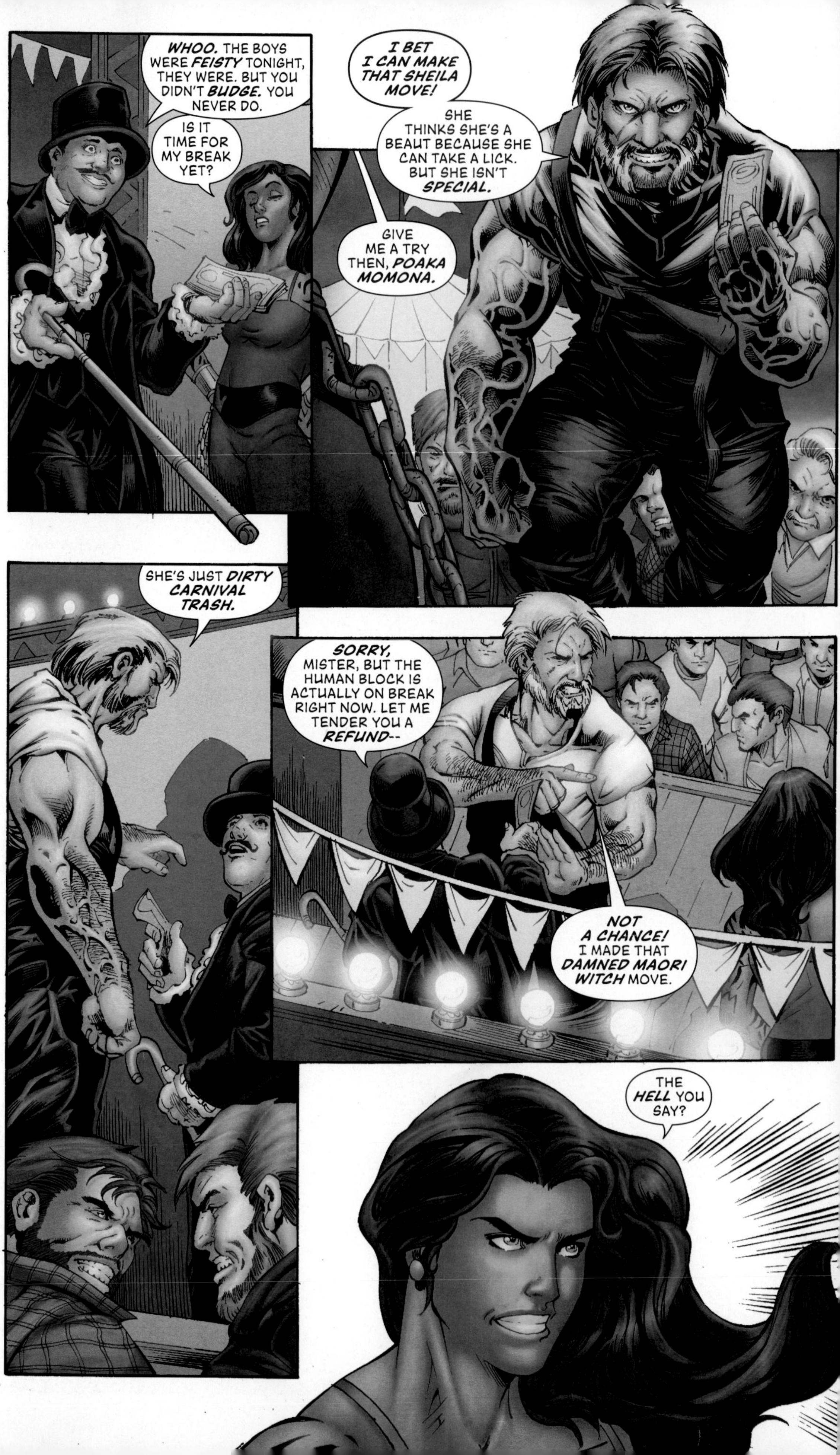
WHOO. THE BOYS WERE FEISTY TONIGHT, THEY WERE. BUT YOU DIDN'T BUDGE. YOU NEVER DO.
IS IT TIME FOR MY BREAK YET?
I BET I CAN MAKE THAT SHEILA MOVE!
SHE THINKS SHE'S A BEAUT BECAUSE SHE CAN TAKE A LICK. BUT SHE ISN'T SPECIAL.
GIVE ME A TRY THEN, POAKA MOMONA.
SHE'S JUST DIRTY CARNIVAL TRASH.
SORRY, MISTER, BUT THE HUMAN BLOCK IS ACTUALLY ON BREAK RIGHT NOW. LET ME TENDER YOU A REFUND--
NOT A CHANCE! I MADE THAT DAMNED MAORI WITCH MOVE.
THE HELL YOU SAY?

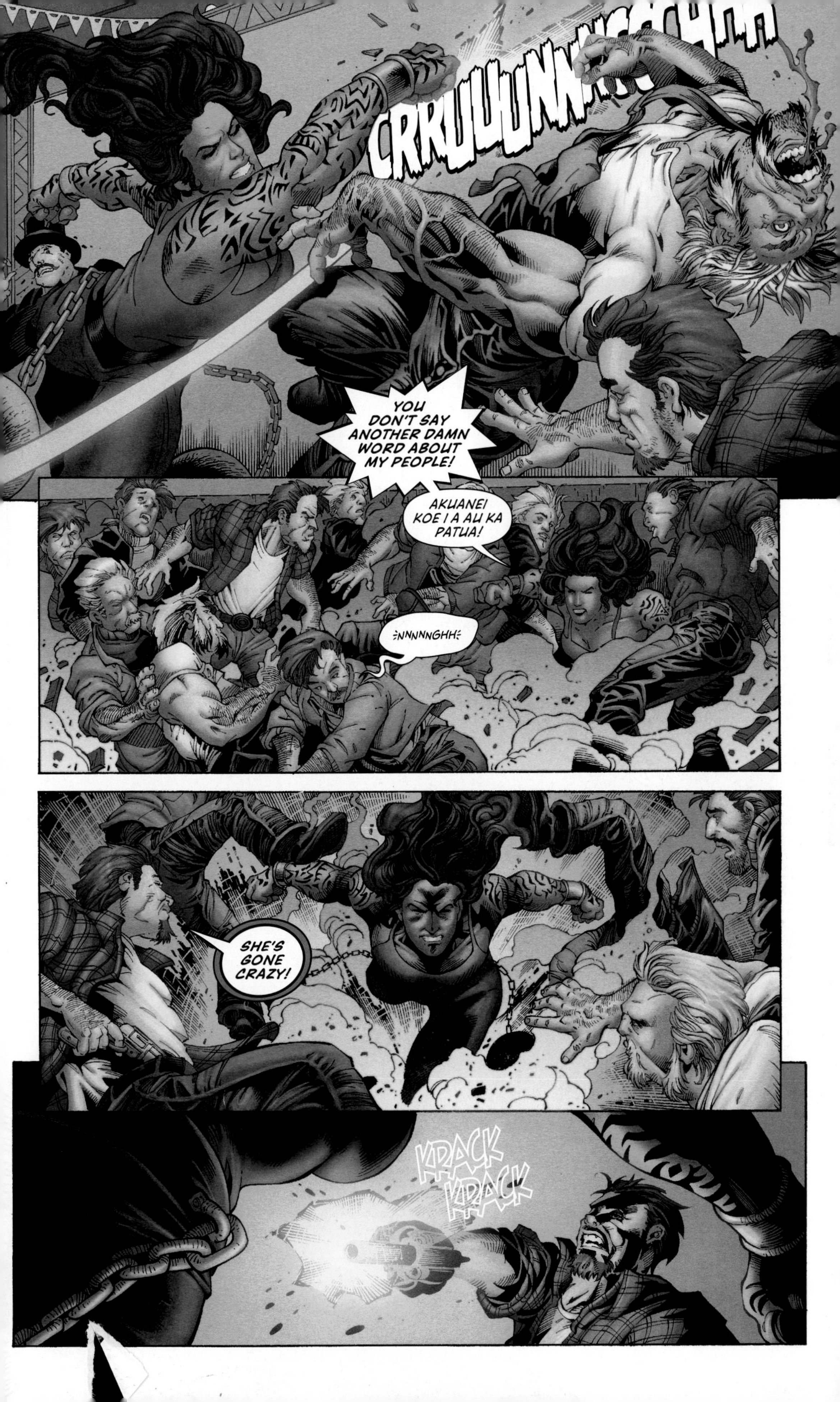
CRRUUUNNNGCHHH
YOU DON'T SAY ANOTHER DAMN WORD ABOUT MY PEOPLE!
AKUANEI KOE I A AU KA PATUA!
NNNNNGHH
SHE'S GONE CRAZY!
KRACK KRACK

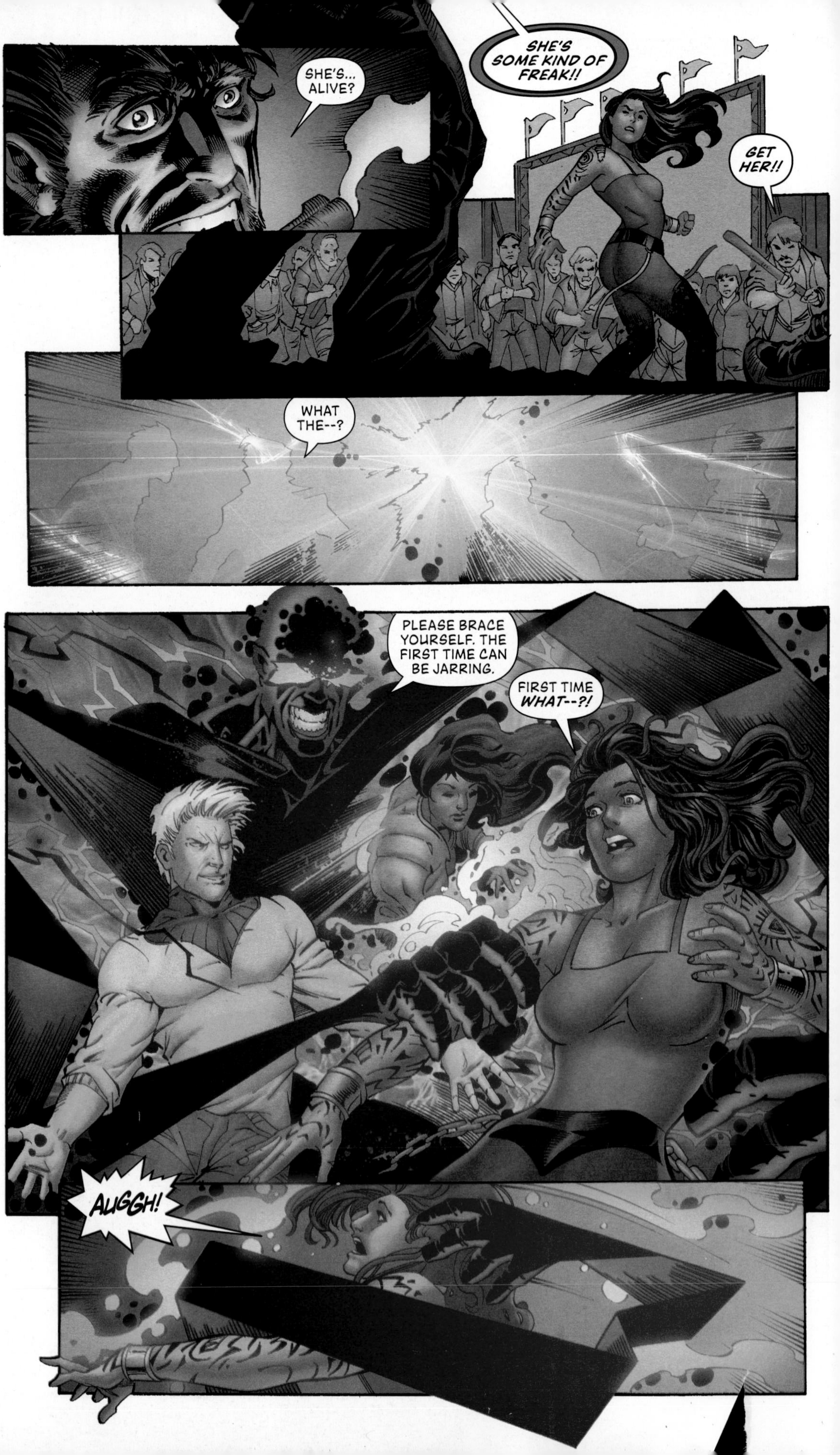
SHE'S... ALIVE?
SHE'S SOME KIND OF FREAK!!
GET HER!!
WHAT THE--?
PLEASE BRACE YOURSELF. THE FIRST TIME CAN BE JARRING.
FIRST TIME WHAT--?!
AUGGH!

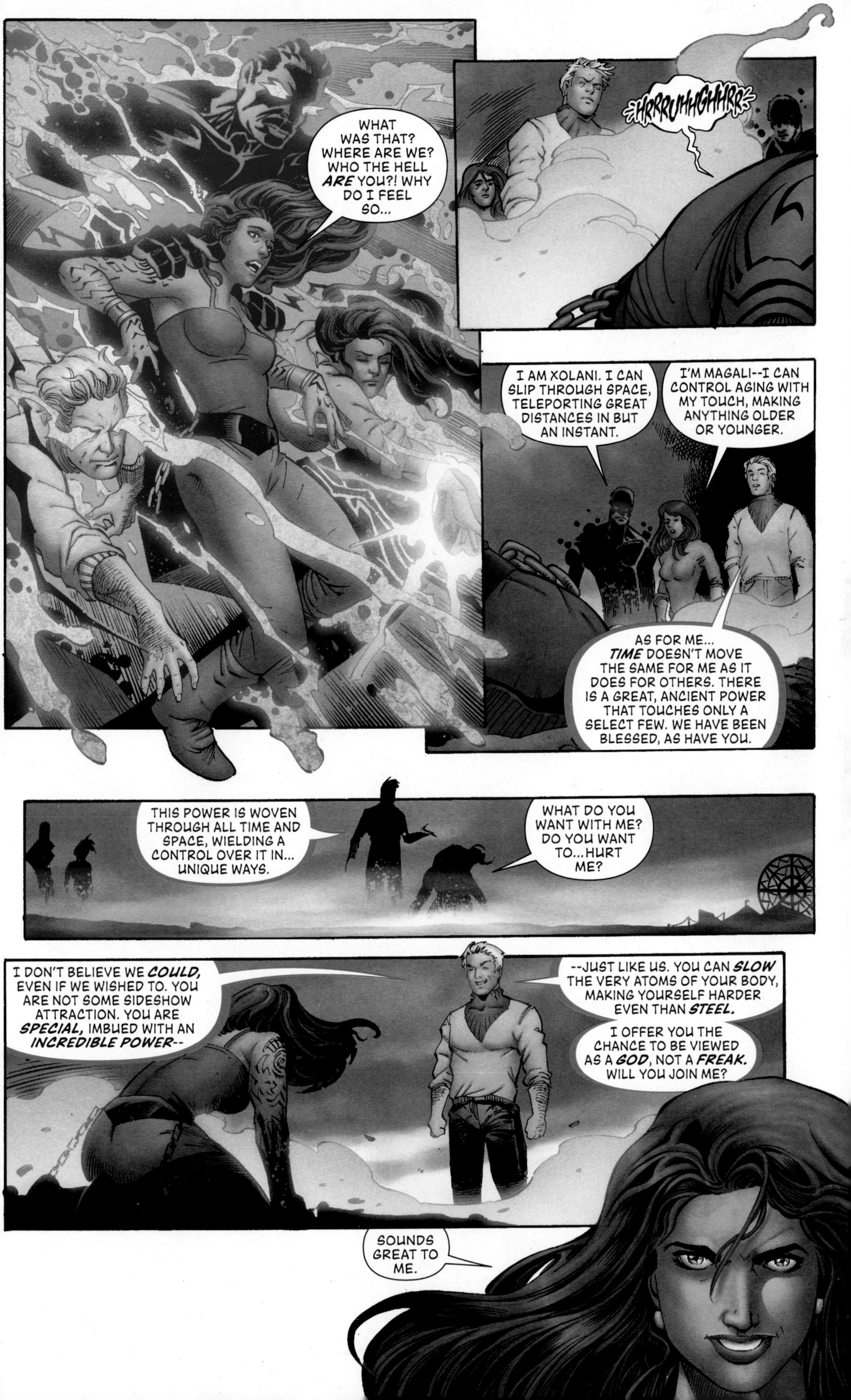
WHAT WAS THAT? WHERE ARE WE? WHO THE HELL ARE YOU?! WHY DO I FEEL SO...
HRRRUHHGHHRR
I AM XOLANI. I CAN SLIP THROUGH SPACE, TELEPORTING GREAT DISTANCES IN BUT AN INSTANT.
I'M MAGALI--I CAN CONTROL AGING WITH MY TOUCH, MAKING ANYTHING OLDER OR YOUNGER.
AS FOR ME... TIME DOESN'T MOVE THE SAME FOR ME AS IT DOES FOR OTHERS. THERE IS A GREAT, ANCIENT POWER THAT TOUCHES ONLY A SELECT FEW. WE HAVE BEEN BLESSED, AS HAVE YOU.
THIS POWER IS WOVEN THROUGH ALL TIME AND SPACE, WIELDING A CONTROL OVER IT IN... UNIQUE WAYS.
WHAT DO YOU WANT WITH ME? DO YOU WANT TO...HURT ME?
I DON'T BELIEVE WE COULD, EVEN IF WE WISHED TO. YOU ARE NOT SOME SIDESHOW ATTRACTION. YOU ARE SPECIAL, IMBUED WITH AN INCREDIBLE POWER--
--JUST LIKE US. YOU CAN SLOW THE VERY ATOMS OF YOUR BODY, MAKING YOURSELF HARDER EVEN THAN STEEL.
I OFFER YOU THE CHANCE TO BE VIEWED AS A GOD, NOT A FREAK. WILL YOU JOIN ME?
SOUNDS GREAT TO ME.

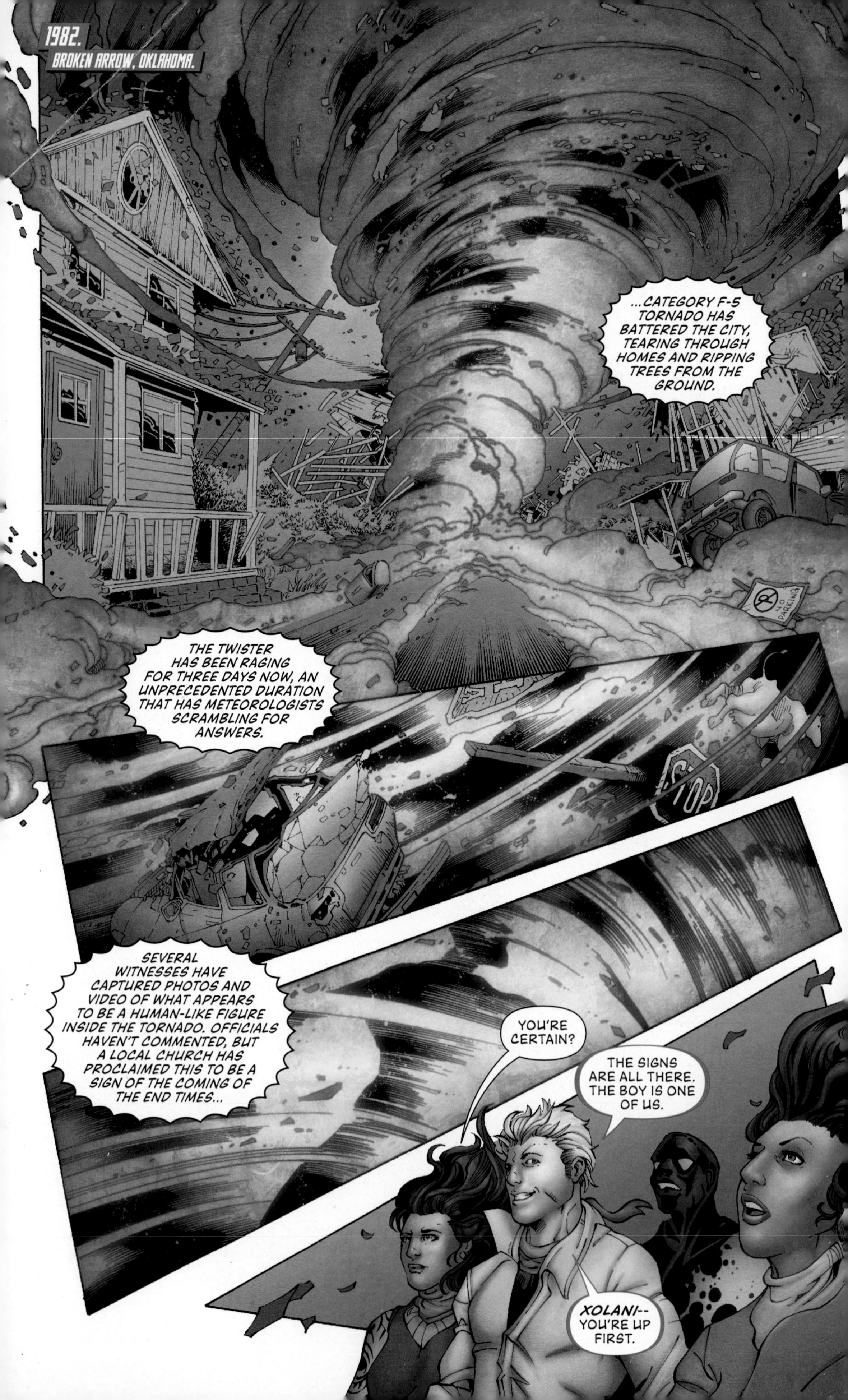
1982.
BROKEN ARROW, OKLAHOMA.
...CATEGORY F-5 TORNADO HAS BATTERED THE CITY, TEARING THROUGH HOMES AND RIPPING TREES FROM THE GROUND.
NO PARKING
THE TWISTER HAS BEEN RAGING FOR THREE DAYS NOW, AN UNPRECEDENTED DURATION THAT HAS METEOROLOGISTS SCRAMBLING FOR ANSWERS.
STOP
SEVERAL WITNESSES HAVE CAPTURED PHOTOS AND VIDEO OF WHAT APPEARS TO BE A HUMAN-LIKE FIGURE INSIDE THE TORNADO. OFFICIALS HAVEN'T COMMENTED, BUT A LOCAL CHURCH HAS PROCLAIMED THIS TO BE A SIGN OF THE COMING OF THE END TIMES...
YOU'RE CERTAIN?
THE SIGNS ARE ALL THERE. THE BOY IS ONE OF US.
XOLANI--YOU'RE UP FIRST.

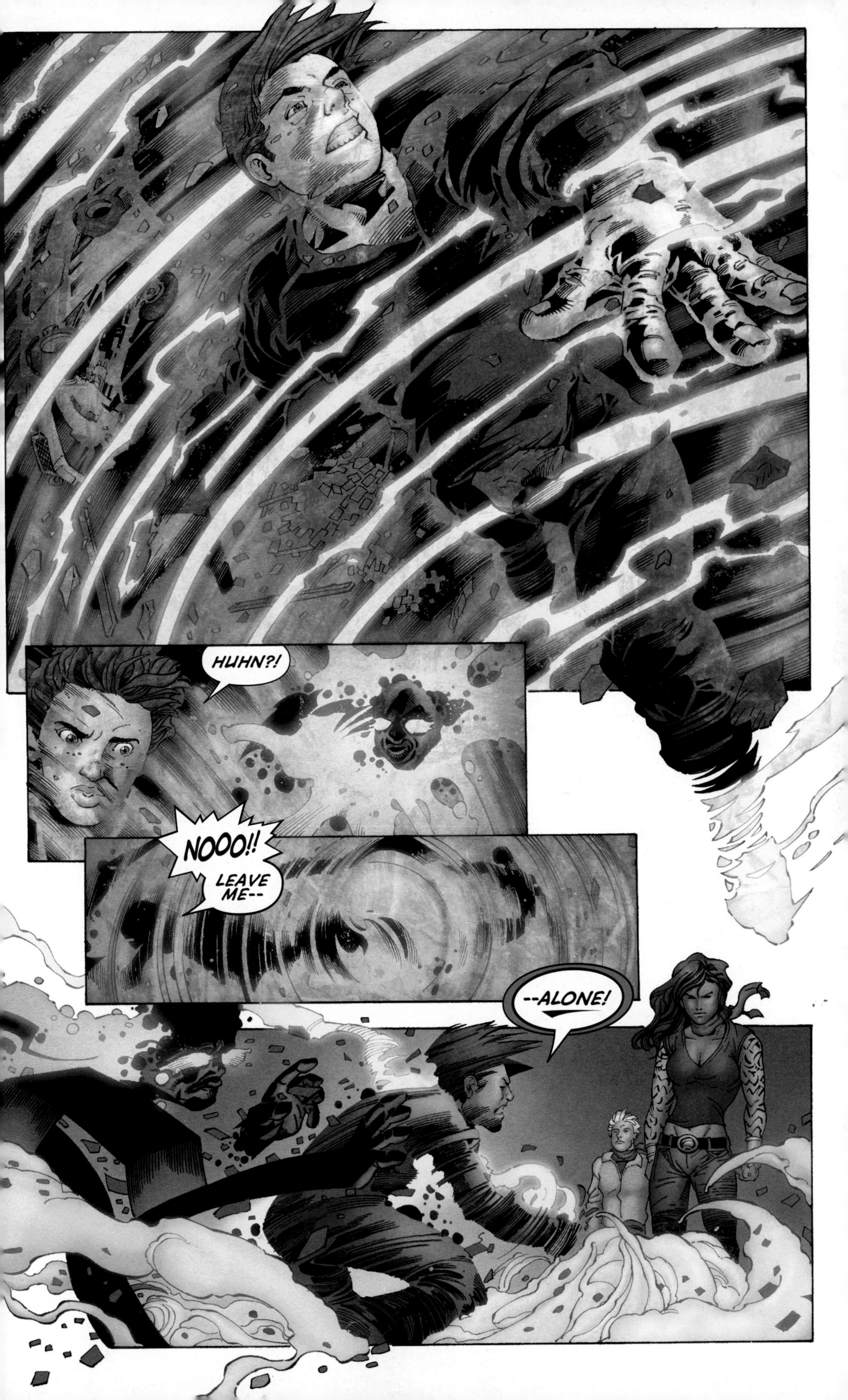
HUHN?!
NOOO!!
LEAVE ME--
--ALONE!

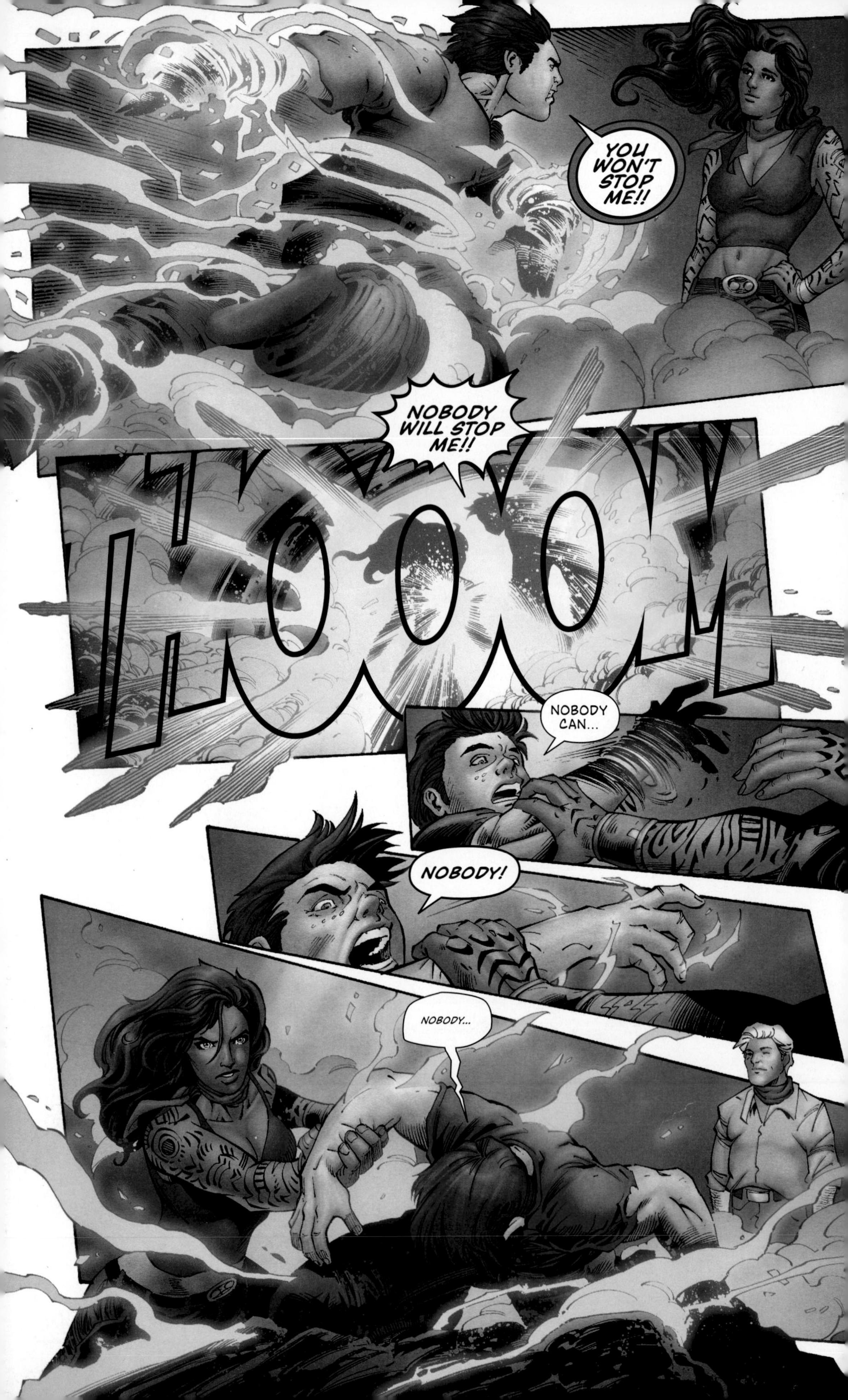
YOU WON'T STOP ME!!
NOBODY WILL STOP ME!!
THOOOM
NOBODY CAN...
NOBODY!
NOBODY...

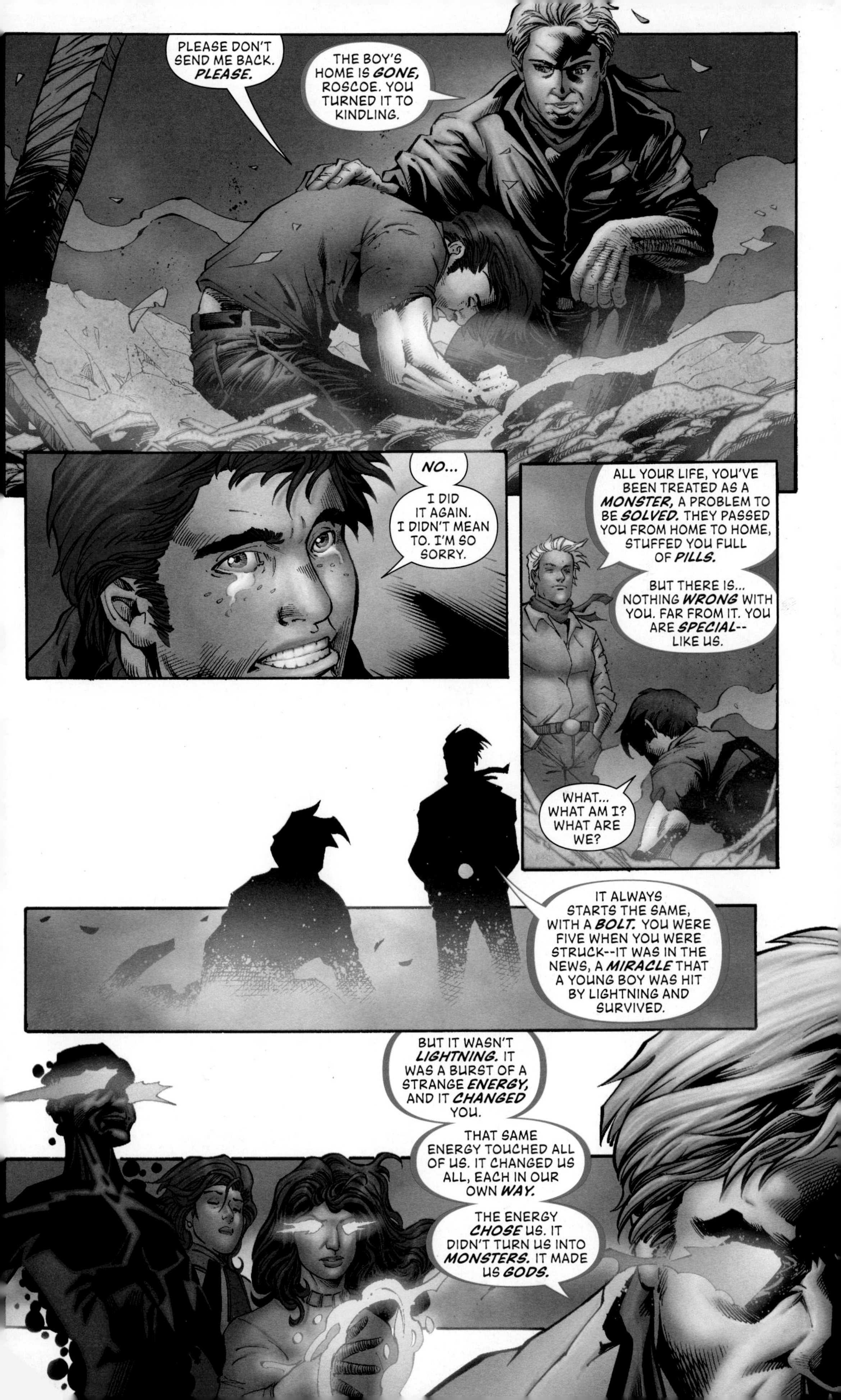
PLEASE DON'T SEND ME BACK. *PLEASE.*
THE BOY'S HOME IS *GONE,* ROSCOE. YOU TURNED IT TO KINDLING.
NO...
I DID IT AGAIN. I DIDN'T MEAN TO. I'M SO SORRY.
ALL YOUR LIFE, YOU'VE BEEN TREATED AS A *MONSTER,* A PROBLEM TO BE *SOLVED.* THEY PASSED YOU FROM HOME TO HOME, STUFFED YOU FULL OF *PILLS.*
BUT THERE IS... NOTHING *WRONG* WITH YOU. FAR FROM IT. YOU ARE *SPECIAL*-- LIKE US.
WHAT... WHAT AM I? WHAT ARE WE?
IT ALWAYS STARTS THE SAME, WITH A *BOLT.* YOU WERE FIVE WHEN YOU WERE STRUCK--IT WAS IN THE NEWS, A *MIRACLE* THAT A YOUNG BOY WAS HIT BY LIGHTNING AND SURVIVED.
BUT IT WASN'T *LIGHTNING.* IT WAS A BURST OF A STRANGE *ENERGY,* AND IT *CHANGED* YOU.
THAT SAME ENERGY TOUCHED ALL OF US. IT CHANGED US ALL, EACH IN OUR OWN *WAY.*
THE ENERGY *CHOSE* US. IT DIDN'T TURN US INTO *MONSTERS.* IT MADE US *GODS.*

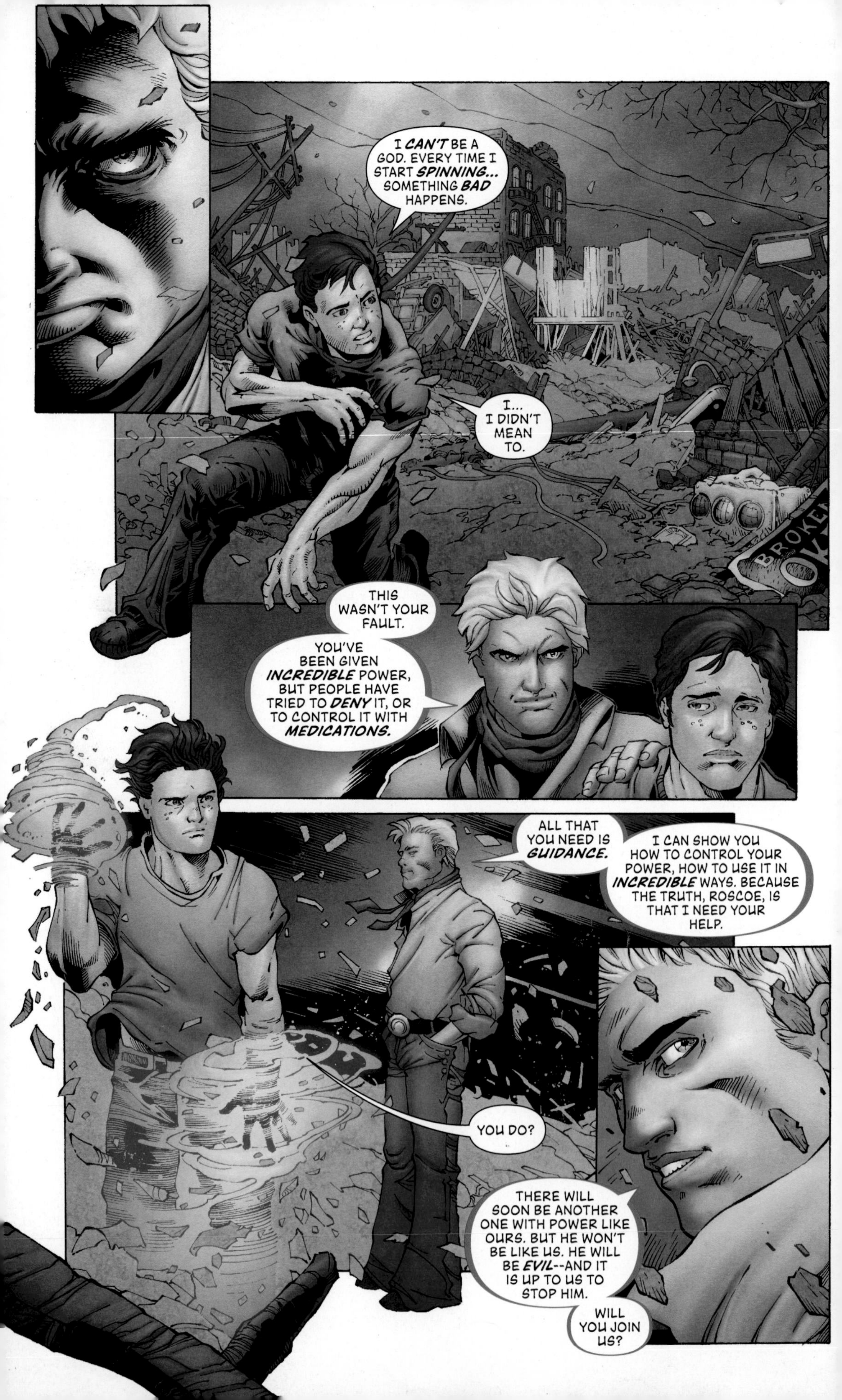
I CAN'T BE A GOD. EVERY TIME I START SPINNING... SOMETHING BAD HAPPENS.
I... I DIDN'T MEAN TO.
BROKEN
THIS WASN'T YOUR FAULT.
YOU'VE BEEN GIVEN INCREDIBLE POWER, BUT PEOPLE HAVE TRIED TO DENY IT, OR TO CONTROL IT WITH MEDICATIONS.
ALL THAT YOU NEED IS GUIDANCE.
I CAN SHOW YOU HOW TO CONTROL YOUR POWER, HOW TO USE IT IN INCREDIBLE WAYS. BECAUSE THE TRUTH, ROSCOE, IS THAT I NEED YOUR HELP.
YOU DO?
THERE WILL SOON BE ANOTHER ONE WITH POWER LIKE OURS. BUT HE WON'T BE LIKE US. HE WILL BE EVIL--AND IT IS UP TO US TO STOP HIM.
WILL YOU JOIN US?

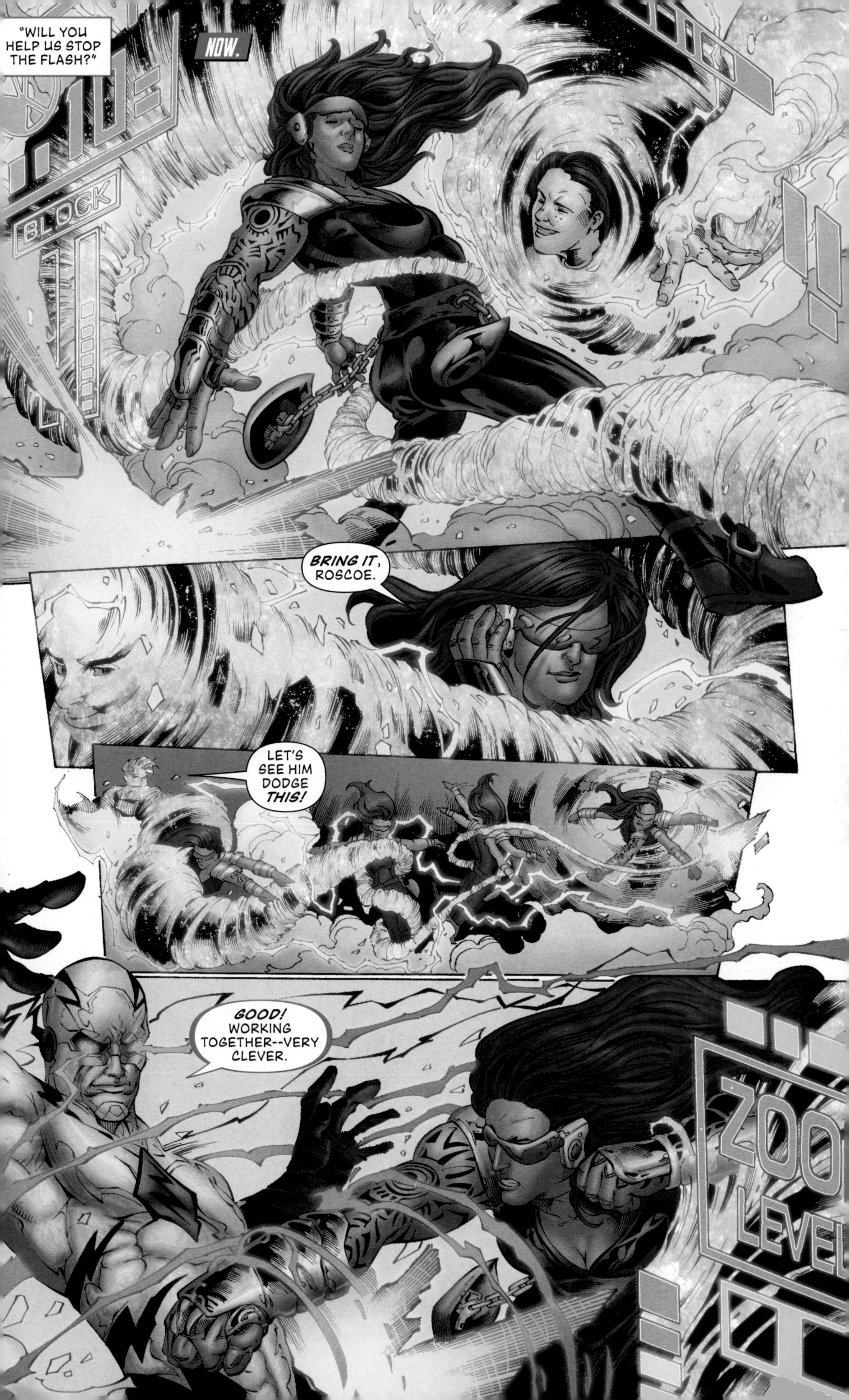
"WILL YOU HELP US STOP THE FLASH?"
NOW.
BLOCK
BRING IT, ROSCOE.
LET'S SEE HIM DODGE THIS!
GOOD! WORKING TOGETHER--VERY CLEVER.
ZOO LEVEL

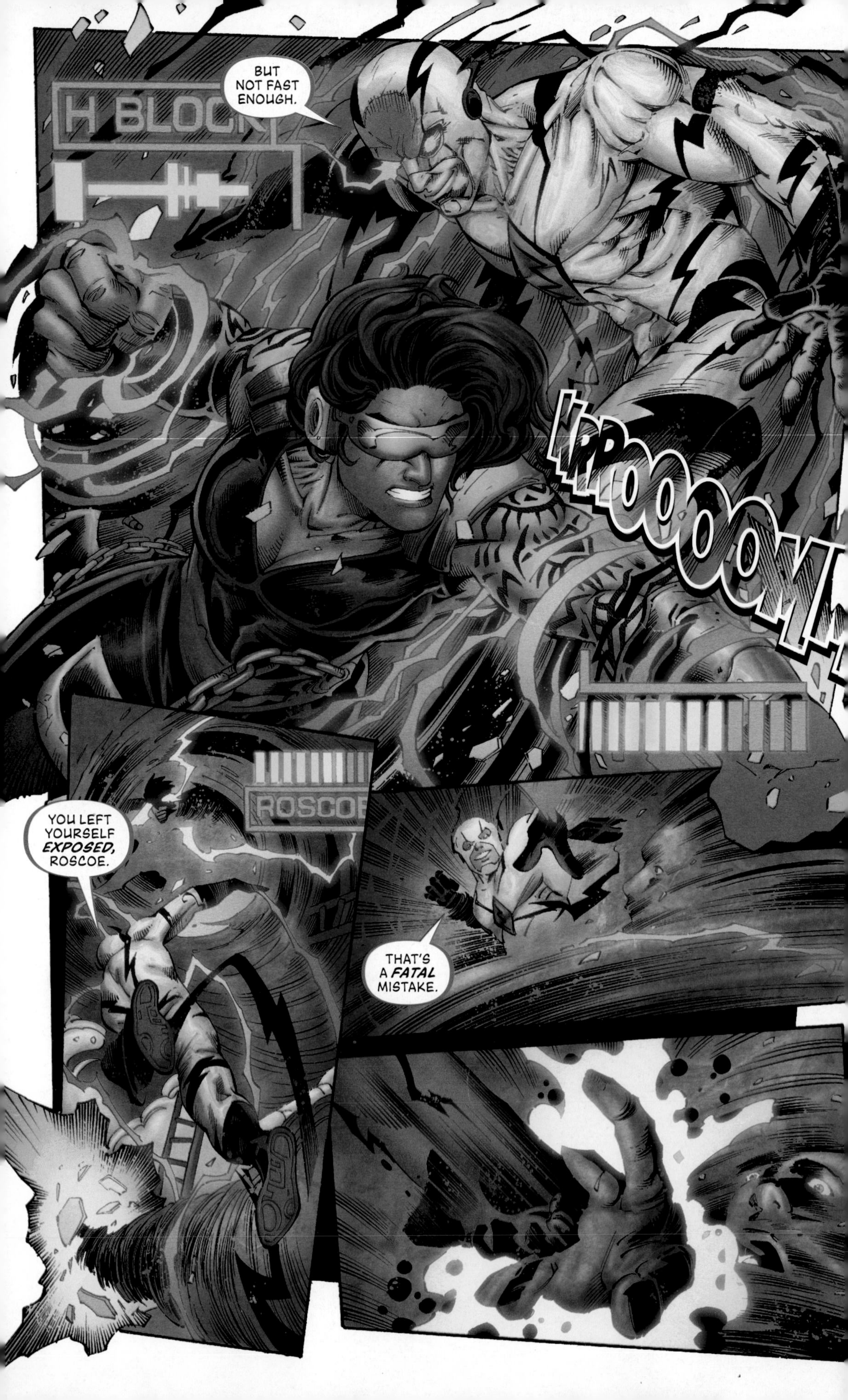
H BLOCK
BUT NOT FAST ENOUGH.
KRROOOOOM!
ROSCOE
YOU LEFT YOURSELF *EXPOSED,* ROSCOE.
THAT'S A *FATAL* MISTAKE.

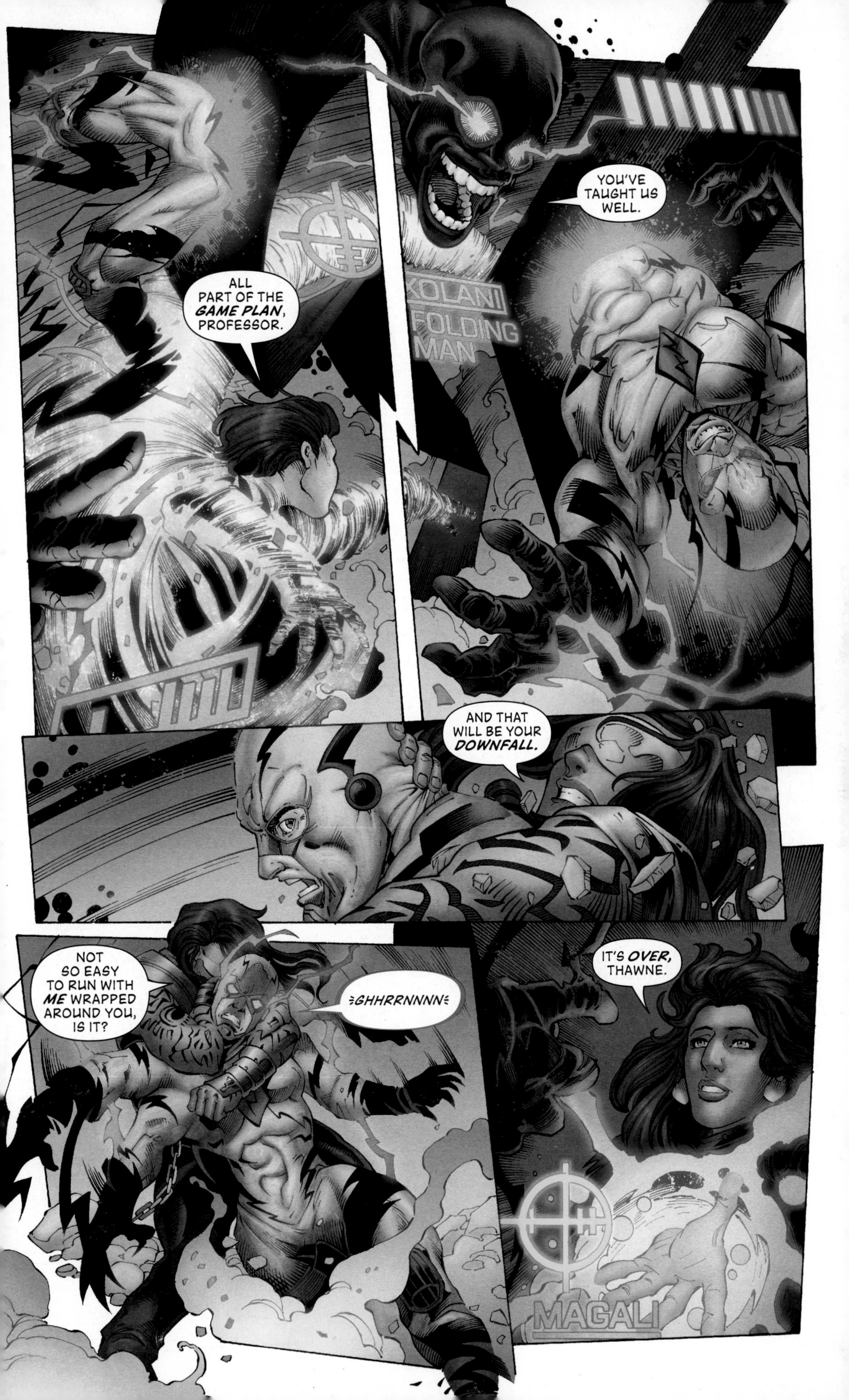
ALL PART OF THE *GAME PLAN*, PROFESSOR.
YOU'VE TAUGHT US WELL.
KOLANI FOLDING MAN
AND THAT WILL BE YOUR *DOWNFALL.*
NOT SO EASY TO RUN WITH *ME* WRAPPED AROUND YOU, IS IT?
GHHRRNNNN
IT'S *OVER,* THAWNE.
MAGALI

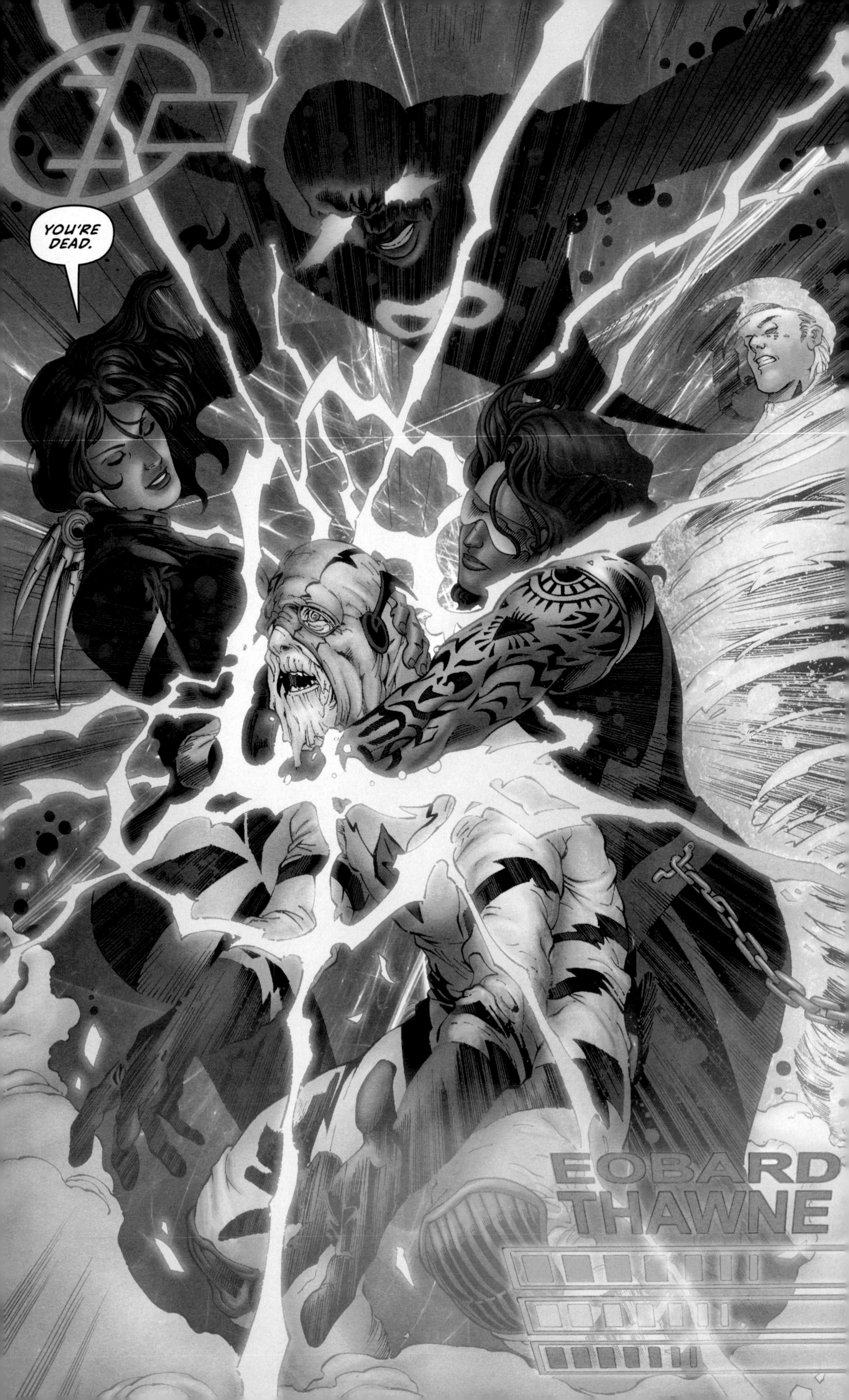
YOU'RE DEAD.
EOBARD THAWNE

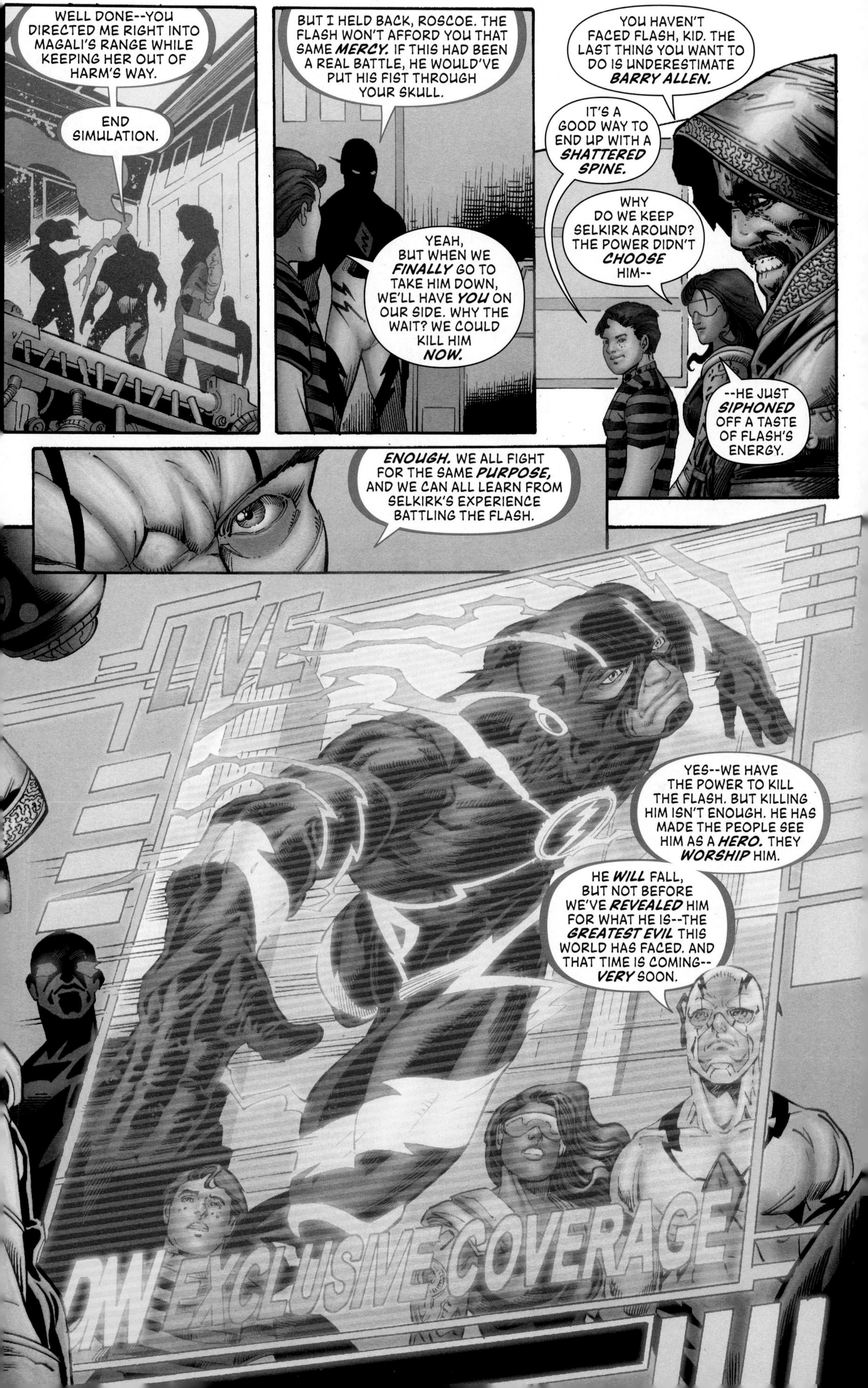
WELL DONE--YOU DIRECTED ME RIGHT INTO MAGALI'S RANGE WHILE KEEPING HER OUT OF HARM'S WAY.
END SIMULATION.
BUT I HELD BACK, ROSCOE. THE FLASH WON'T AFFORD YOU THAT SAME MERCY. IF THIS HAD BEEN A REAL BATTLE, HE WOULD'VE PUT HIS FIST THROUGH YOUR SKULL.
YEAH, BUT WHEN WE FINALLY GO TO TAKE HIM DOWN, WE'LL HAVE YOU ON OUR SIDE. WHY THE WAIT? WE COULD KILL HIM NOW.
YOU HAVEN'T FACED FLASH, KID. THE LAST THING YOU WANT TO DO IS UNDERESTIMATE BARRY ALLEN.
IT'S A GOOD WAY TO END UP WITH A SHATTERED SPINE.
WHY DO WE KEEP SELKIRK AROUND? THE POWER DIDN'T CHOOSE HIM--
--HE JUST SIPHONED OFF A TASTE OF FLASH'S ENERGY.
ENOUGH. WE ALL FIGHT FOR THE SAME PURPOSE, AND WE CAN ALL LEARN FROM SELKIRK'S EXPERIENCE BATTLING THE FLASH.
LIVE
YES--WE HAVE THE POWER TO KILL THE FLASH. BUT KILLING HIM ISN'T ENOUGH. HE HAS MADE THE PEOPLE SEE HIM AS A HERO. THEY WORSHIP HIM.
HE WILL FALL, BUT NOT BEFORE WE'VE REVEALED HIM FOR WHAT HE IS--THE GREATEST EVIL THIS WORLD HAS FACED. AND THAT TIME IS COMING--VERY SOON.
DW EXCLUSIVE COVERAGE

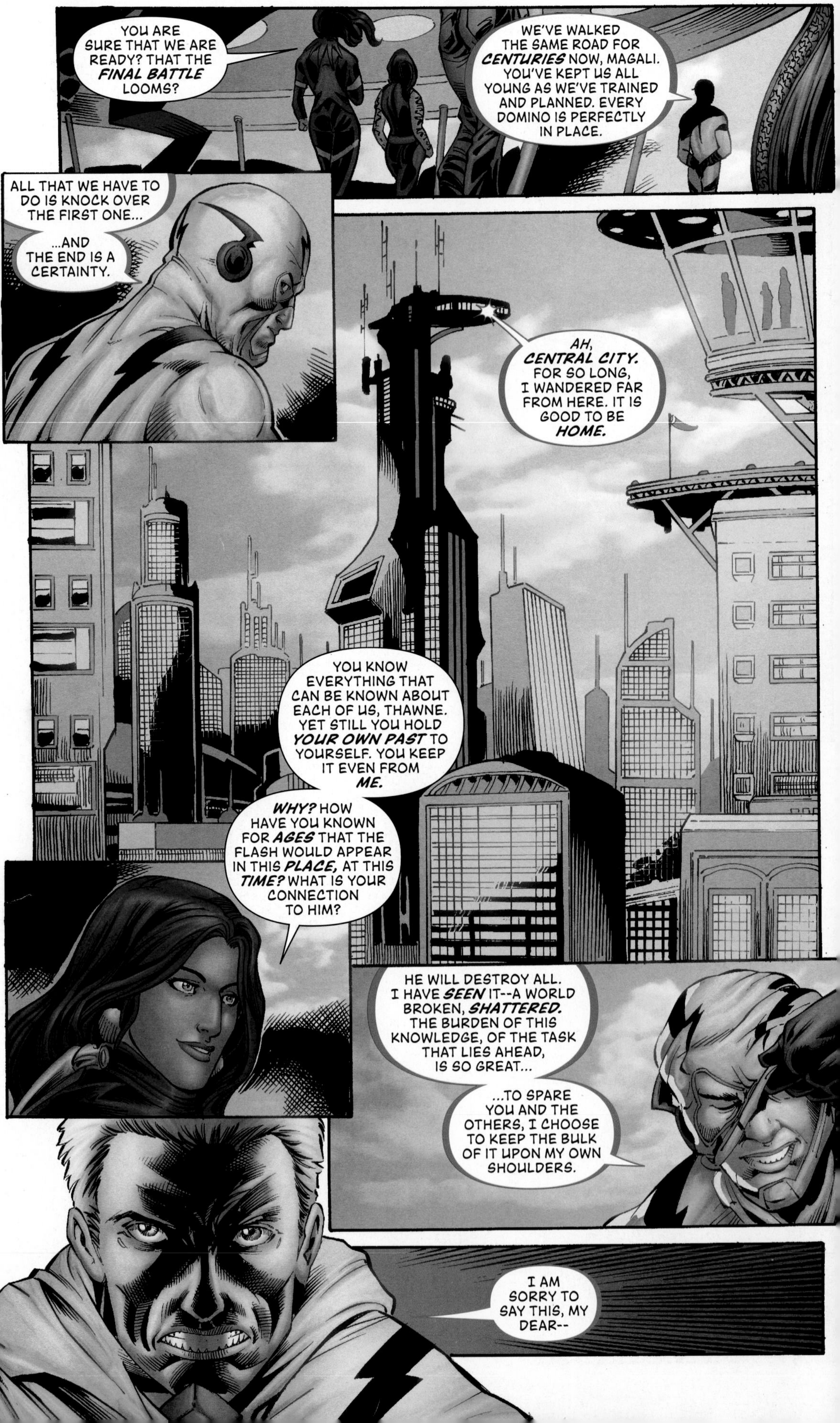
YOU ARE SURE THAT WE ARE READY? THAT THE FINAL BATTLE LOOMS?
WE'VE WALKED THE SAME ROAD FOR CENTURIES NOW, MAGALI. YOU'VE KEPT US ALL YOUNG AS WE'VE TRAINED AND PLANNED. EVERY DOMINO IS PERFECTLY IN PLACE.
ALL THAT WE HAVE TO DO IS KNOCK OVER THE FIRST ONE...
...AND THE END IS A CERTAINTY.
AH, CENTRAL CITY. FOR SO LONG, I WANDERED FAR FROM HERE. IT IS GOOD TO BE HOME.
YOU KNOW EVERYTHING THAT CAN BE KNOWN ABOUT EACH OF US, THAWNE. YET STILL YOU HOLD YOUR OWN PAST TO YOURSELF. YOU KEEP IT EVEN FROM ME.
WHY? HOW HAVE YOU KNOWN FOR AGES THAT THE FLASH WOULD APPEAR IN THIS PLACE, AT THIS TIME? WHAT IS YOUR CONNECTION TO HIM?
HE WILL DESTROY ALL. I HAVE SEEN IT--A WORLD BROKEN, SHATTERED. THE BURDEN OF THIS KNOWLEDGE, OF THE TASK THAT LIES AHEAD, IS SO GREAT...
...TO SPARE YOU AND THE OTHERS, I CHOOSE TO KEEP THE BULK OF IT UPON MY OWN SHOULDERS.
I AM SORRY TO SAY THIS, MY DEAR--

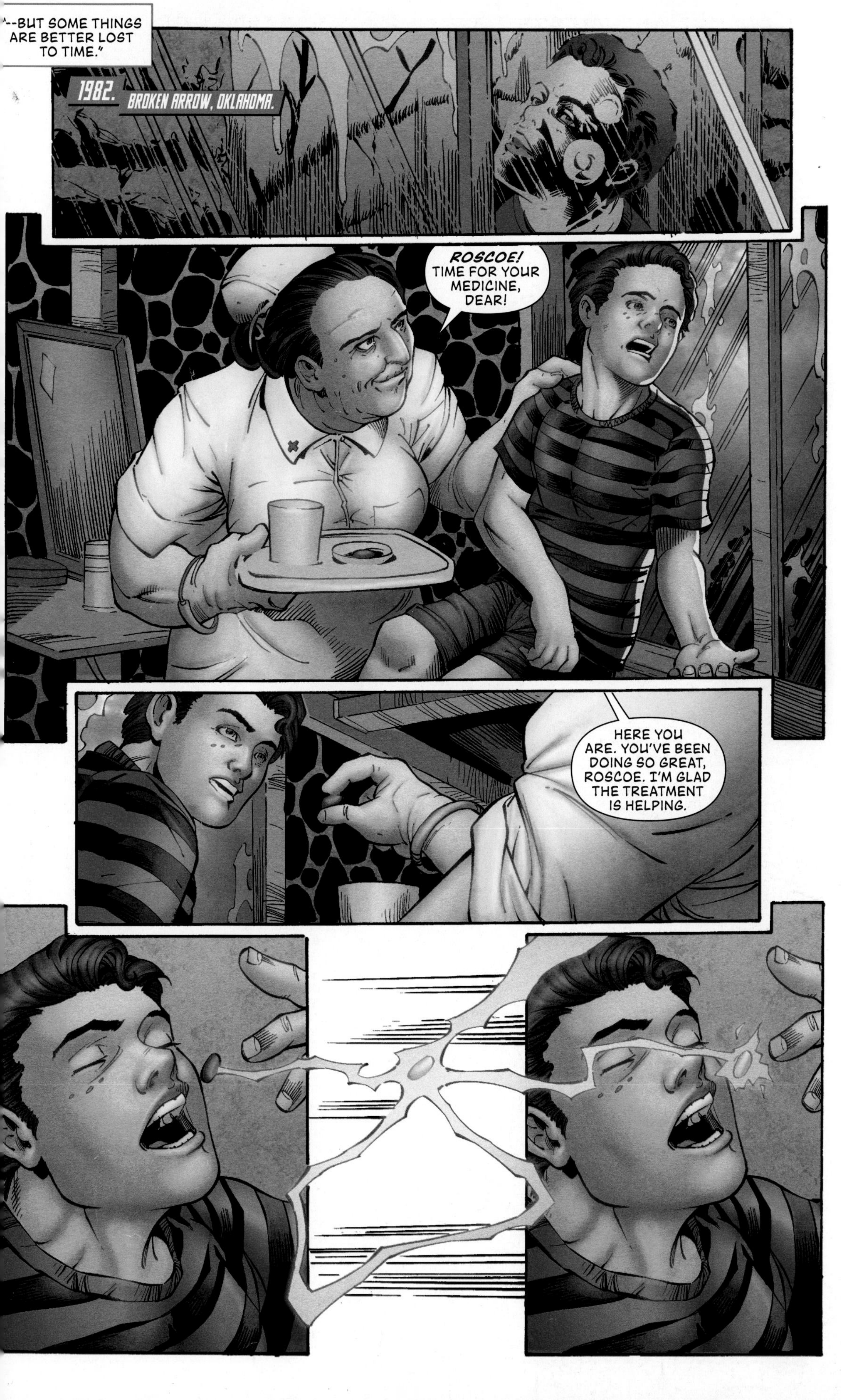
"--BUT SOME THINGS ARE BETTER LOST TO TIME."
1982. BROKEN ARROW, OKLAHOMA.
ROSCOE! TIME FOR YOUR MEDICINE, DEAR!
HERE YOU ARE. YOU'VE BEEN DOING SO GREAT, ROSCOE. I'M GLAD THE TREATMENT IS HELPING.

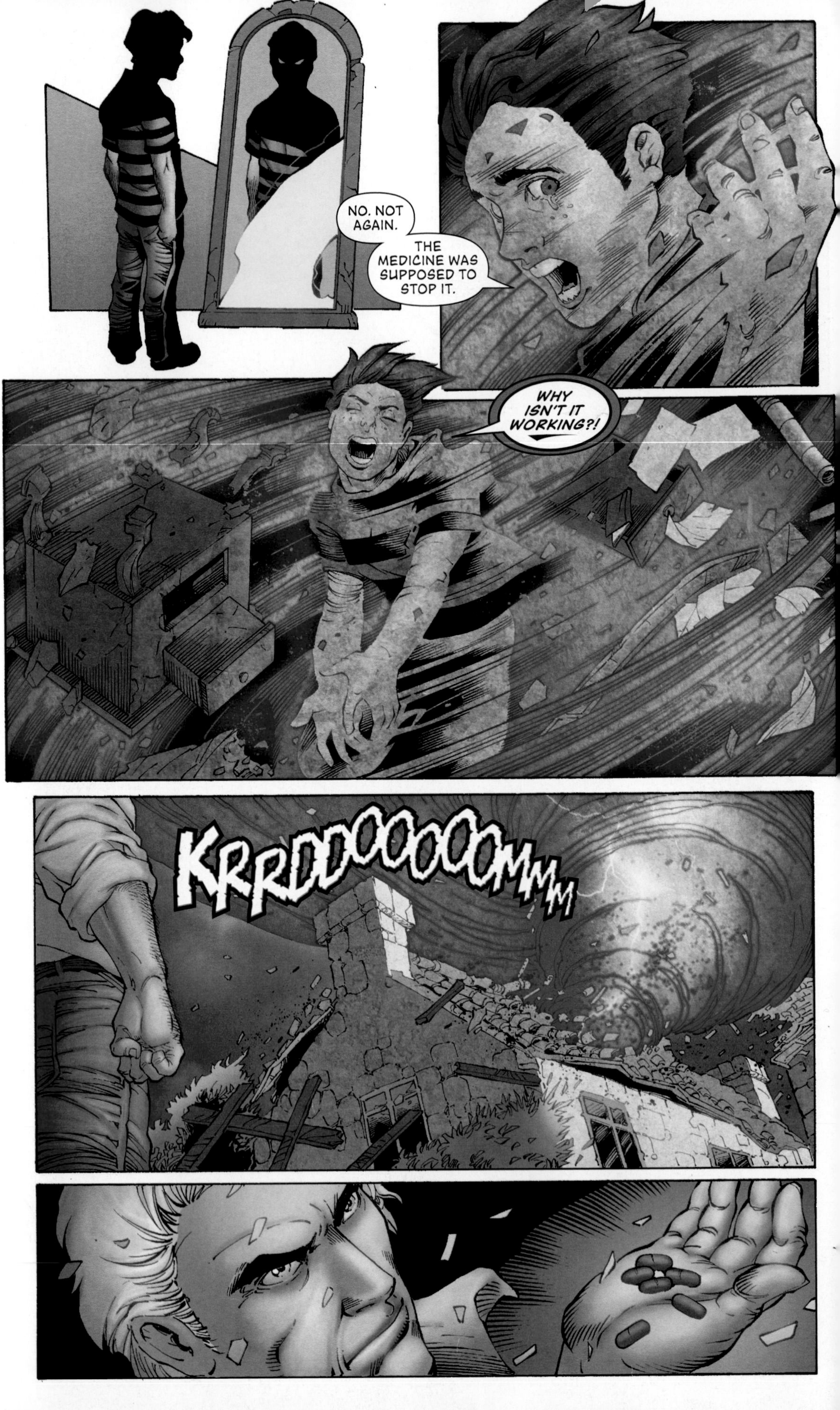
NO. NOT AGAIN.
THE MEDICINE WAS SUPPOSED TO STOP IT.
WHY ISN'T IT WORKING?!
KRRDDOOOOOOMMMM

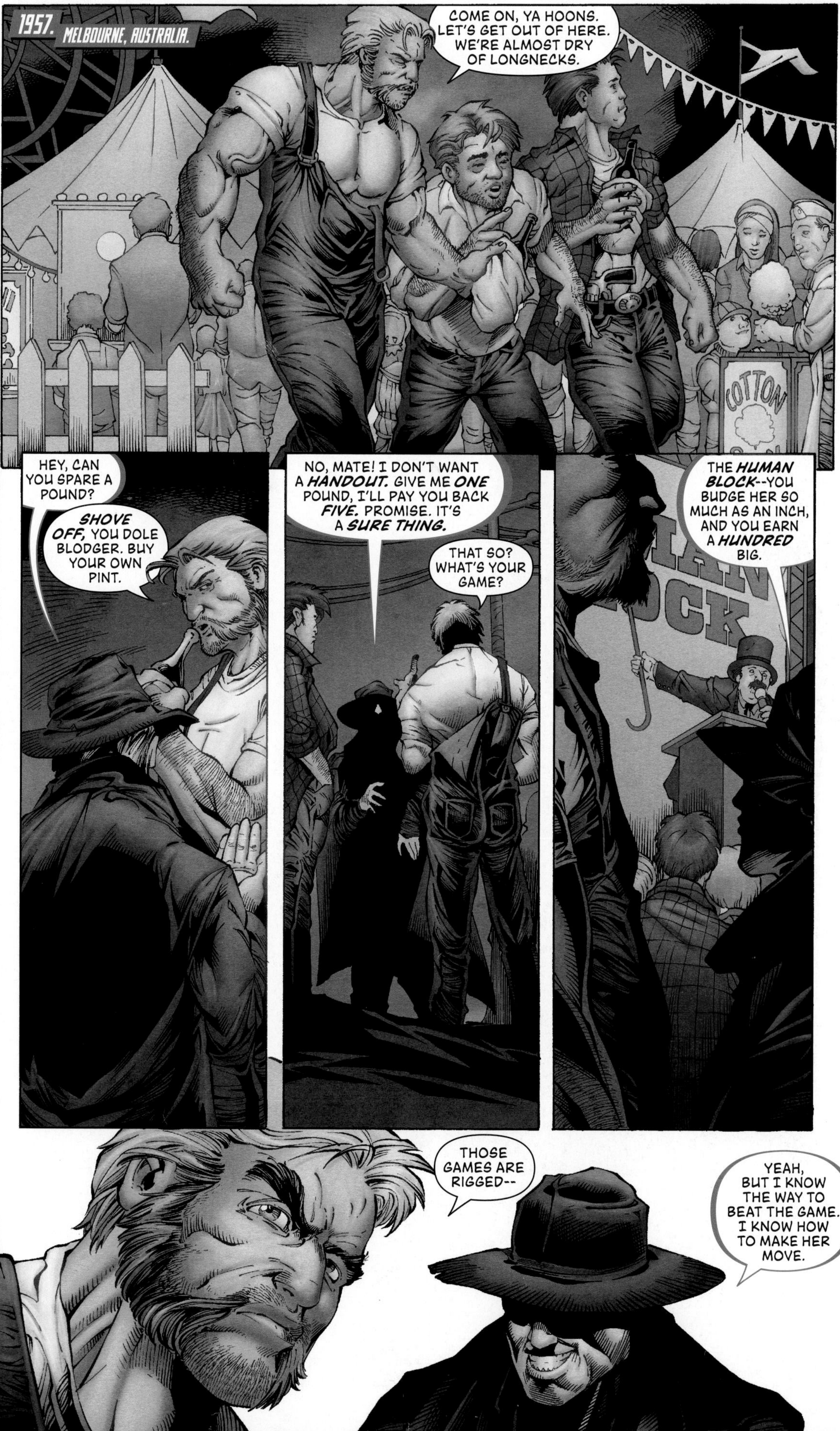
1957. MELBOURNE, AUSTRALIA.
COME ON, YA HOONS. LET'S GET OUT OF HERE. WE'RE ALMOST DRY OF LONGNECKS.
COTTON
HEY, CAN YOU SPARE A POUND?
SHOVE OFF, YOU DOLE BLODGER. BUY YOUR OWN PINT.
NO, MATE! I DON'T WANT A HANDOUT. GIVE ME ONE POUND, I'LL PAY YOU BACK FIVE. PROMISE. IT'S A SURE THING.
THAT SO? WHAT'S YOUR GAME?
THE HUMAN BLOCK--YOU BUDGE HER SO MUCH AS AN INCH, AND YOU EARN A HUNDRED BIG.
THOSE GAMES ARE RIGGED--
YEAH, BUT I KNOW THE WAY TO BEAT THE GAME. I KNOW HOW TO MAKE HER MOVE.

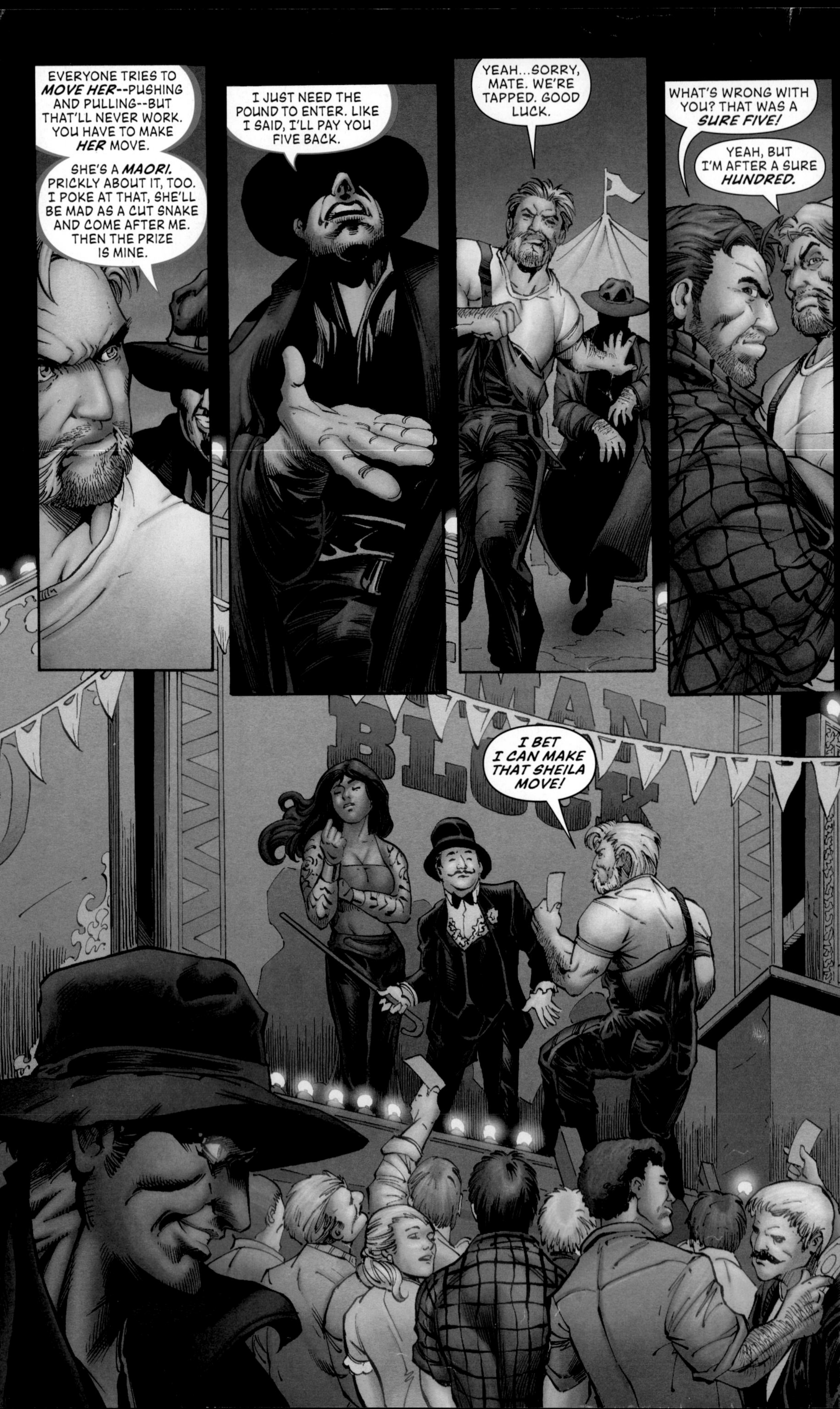
EVERYONE TRIES TO MOVE HER--PUSHING AND PULLING--BUT THAT'LL NEVER WORK. YOU HAVE TO MAKE HER MOVE.
SHE'S A MAORI. PRICKLY ABOUT IT, TOO. I POKE AT THAT, SHE'LL BE MAD AS A CUT SNAKE AND COME AFTER ME. THEN THE PRIZE IS MINE.
I JUST NEED THE POUND TO ENTER. LIKE I SAID, I'LL PAY YOU FIVE BACK.
YEAH...SORRY, MATE. WE'RE TAPPED. GOOD LUCK.
WHAT'S WRONG WITH YOU? THAT WAS A SURE FIVE!
YEAH, BUT I'M AFTER A SURE HUNDRED.
MAN
I BET I CAN MAKE THAT SHEILA MOVE!

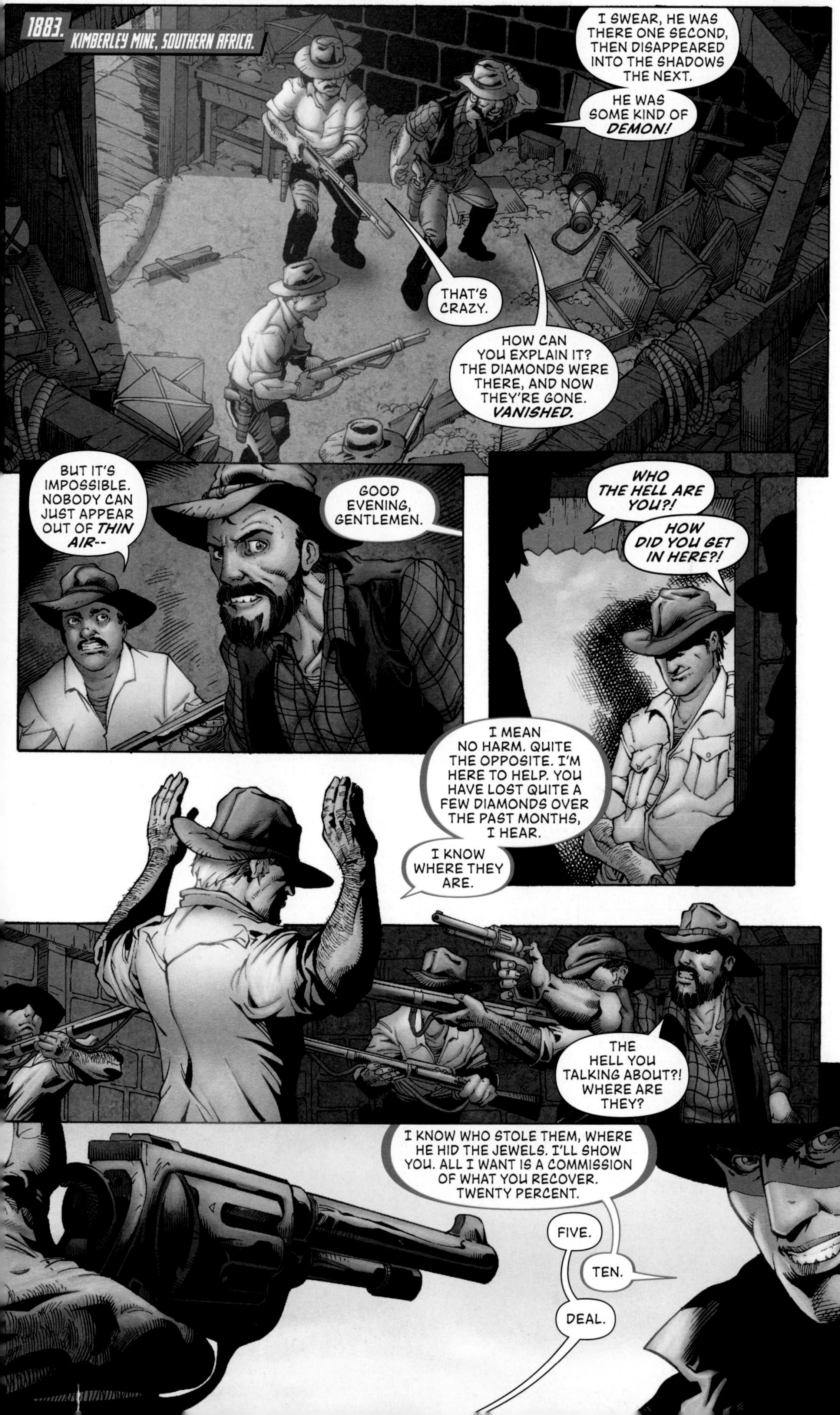
1883.
KIMBERLEY MINE, SOUTHERN AFRICA.
I SWEAR, HE WAS THERE ONE SECOND, THEN DISAPPEARED INTO THE SHADOWS THE NEXT.
HE WAS SOME KIND OF DEMON!
THAT'S CRAZY.
HOW CAN YOU EXPLAIN IT? THE DIAMONDS WERE THERE, AND NOW THEY'RE GONE. VANISHED.
BUT IT'S IMPOSSIBLE. NOBODY CAN JUST APPEAR OUT OF THIN AIR--
GOOD EVENING, GENTLEMEN.
WHO THE HELL ARE YOU?!
HOW DID YOU GET IN HERE?!
I MEAN NO HARM. QUITE THE OPPOSITE. I'M HERE TO HELP. YOU HAVE LOST QUITE A FEW DIAMONDS OVER THE PAST MONTHS, I HEAR.
I KNOW WHERE THEY ARE.
THE HELL YOU TALKING ABOUT?! WHERE ARE THEY?
I KNOW WHO STOLE THEM, WHERE HE HID THE JEWELS. I'LL SHOW YOU. ALL I WANT IS A COMMISSION OF WHAT YOU RECOVER. TWENTY PERCENT.
FIVE.
TEN.
DEAL.

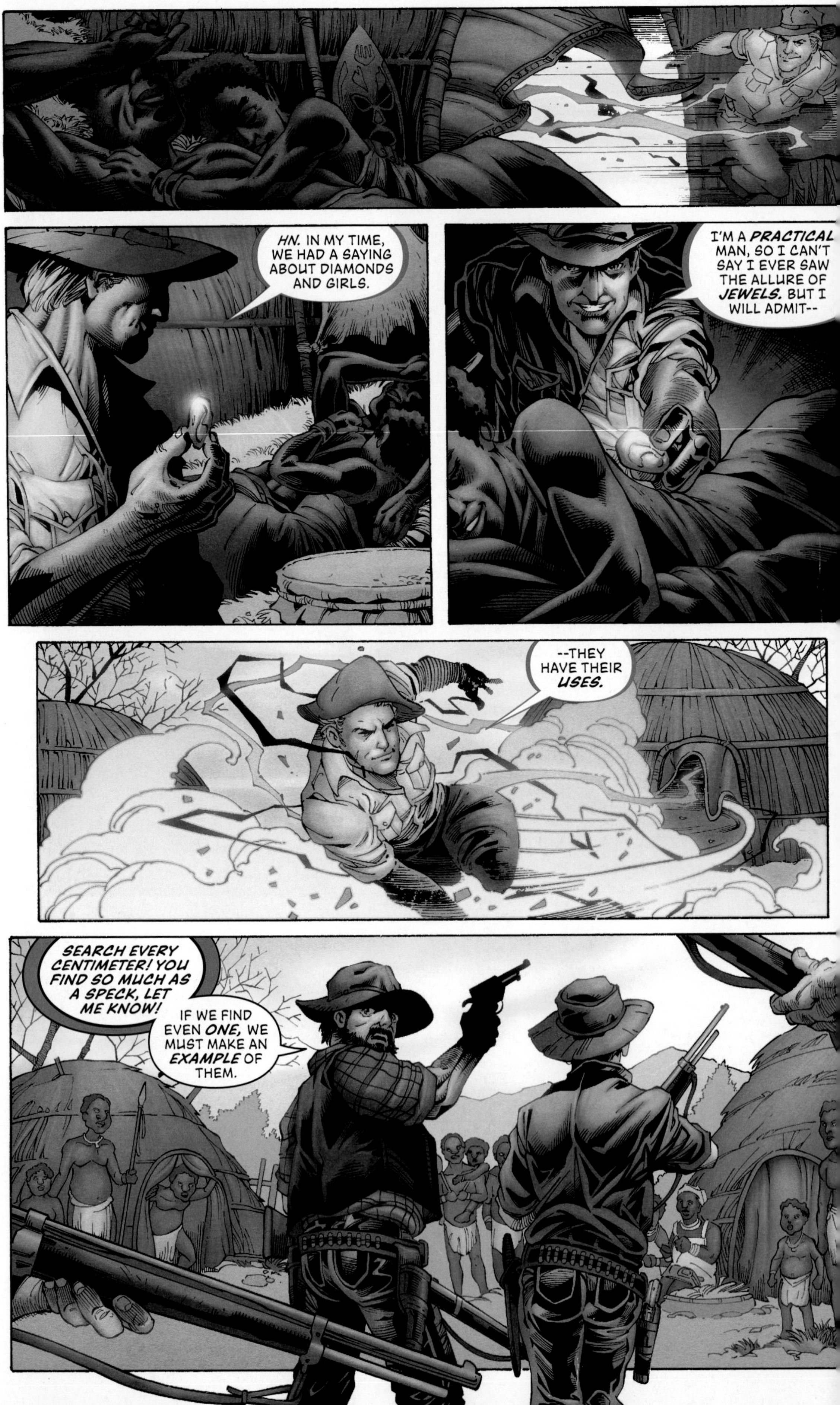
HN. IN MY TIME, WE HAD A SAYING ABOUT DIAMONDS AND GIRLS.
I'M A PRACTICAL MAN, SO I CAN'T SAY I EVER SAW THE ALLURE OF JEWELS. BUT I WILL ADMIT--
--THEY HAVE THEIR USES.
SEARCH EVERY CENTIMETER! YOU FIND SO MUCH AS A SPECK, LET ME KNOW!
IF WE FIND EVEN ONE, WE MUST MAKE AN EXAMPLE OF THEM.

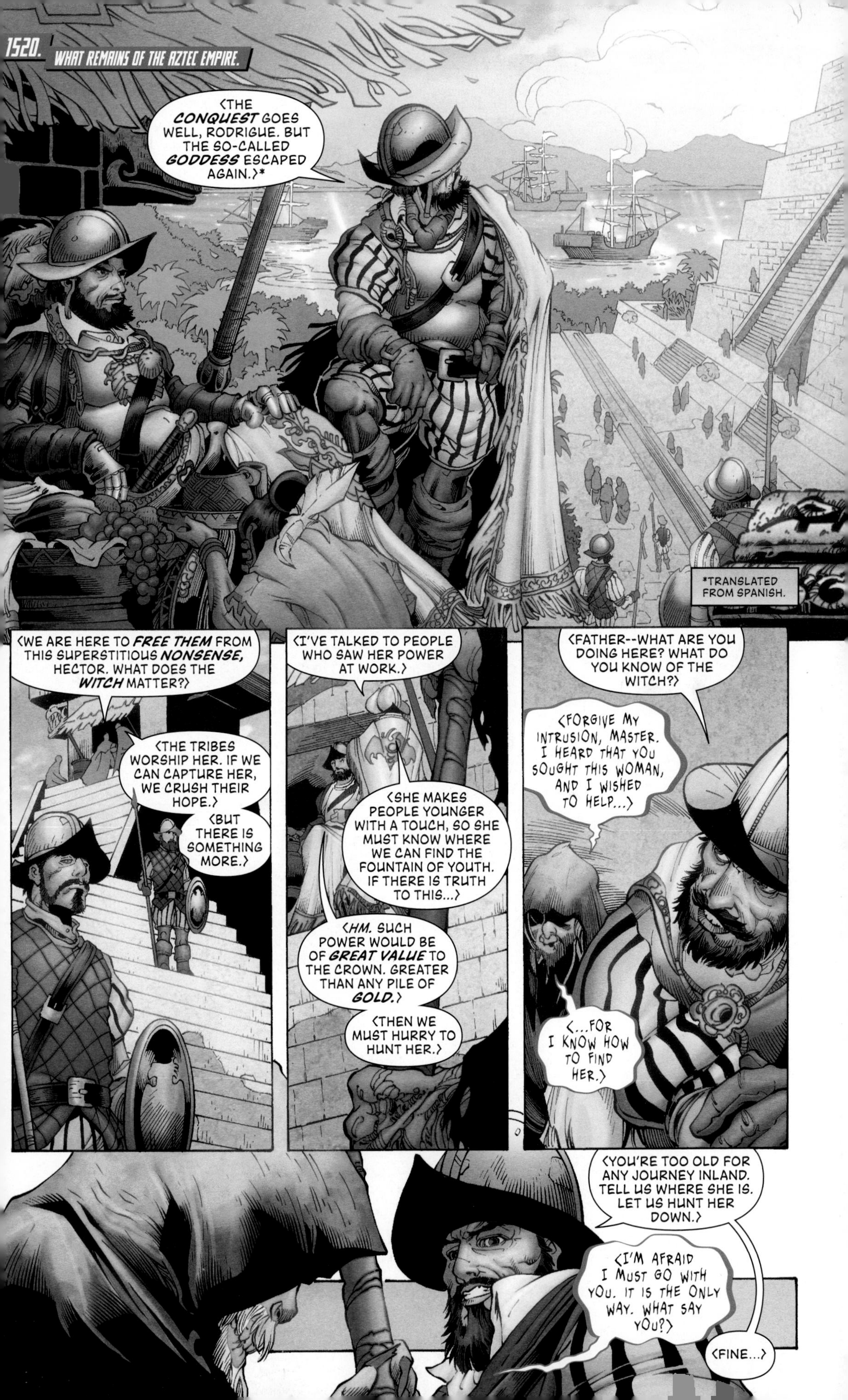
1520.
WHAT REMAINS OF THE AZTEC EMPIRE.
<THE CONQUEST GOES WELL, RODRIGUE. BUT THE SO-CALLED GODDESS ESCAPED AGAIN.>*
*TRANSLATED FROM SPANISH.
<WE ARE HERE TO FREE THEM FROM THIS SUPERSTITIOUS NONSENSE, HECTOR. WHAT DOES THE WITCH MATTER?>
<THE TRIBES WORSHIP HER. IF WE CAN CAPTURE HER, WE CRUSH THEIR HOPE.>
<BUT THERE IS SOMETHING MORE.>
<I'VE TALKED TO PEOPLE WHO SAW HER POWER AT WORK.>
<SHE MAKES PEOPLE YOUNGER WITH A TOUCH, SO SHE MUST KNOW WHERE WE CAN FIND THE FOUNTAIN OF YOUTH. IF THERE IS TRUTH TO THIS...>
<HM. SUCH POWER WOULD BE OF GREAT VALUE TO THE CROWN. GREATER THAN ANY PILE OF GOLD.>
<THEN WE MUST HURRY TO HUNT HER.>
<FATHER--WHAT ARE YOU DOING HERE? WHAT DO YOU KNOW OF THE WITCH?>
<FORGIVE MY INTRUSION, MASTER. I HEARD THAT YOU SOUGHT THIS WOMAN, AND I WISHED TO HELP...>
<...FOR I KNOW HOW TO FIND HER.>
<YOU'RE TOO OLD FOR ANY JOURNEY INLAND. TELL US WHERE SHE IS. LET US HUNT HER DOWN.>
<I'M AFRAID I MUST GO WITH YOU. IT IS THE ONLY WAY. WHAT SAY YOU?>
<FINE...>

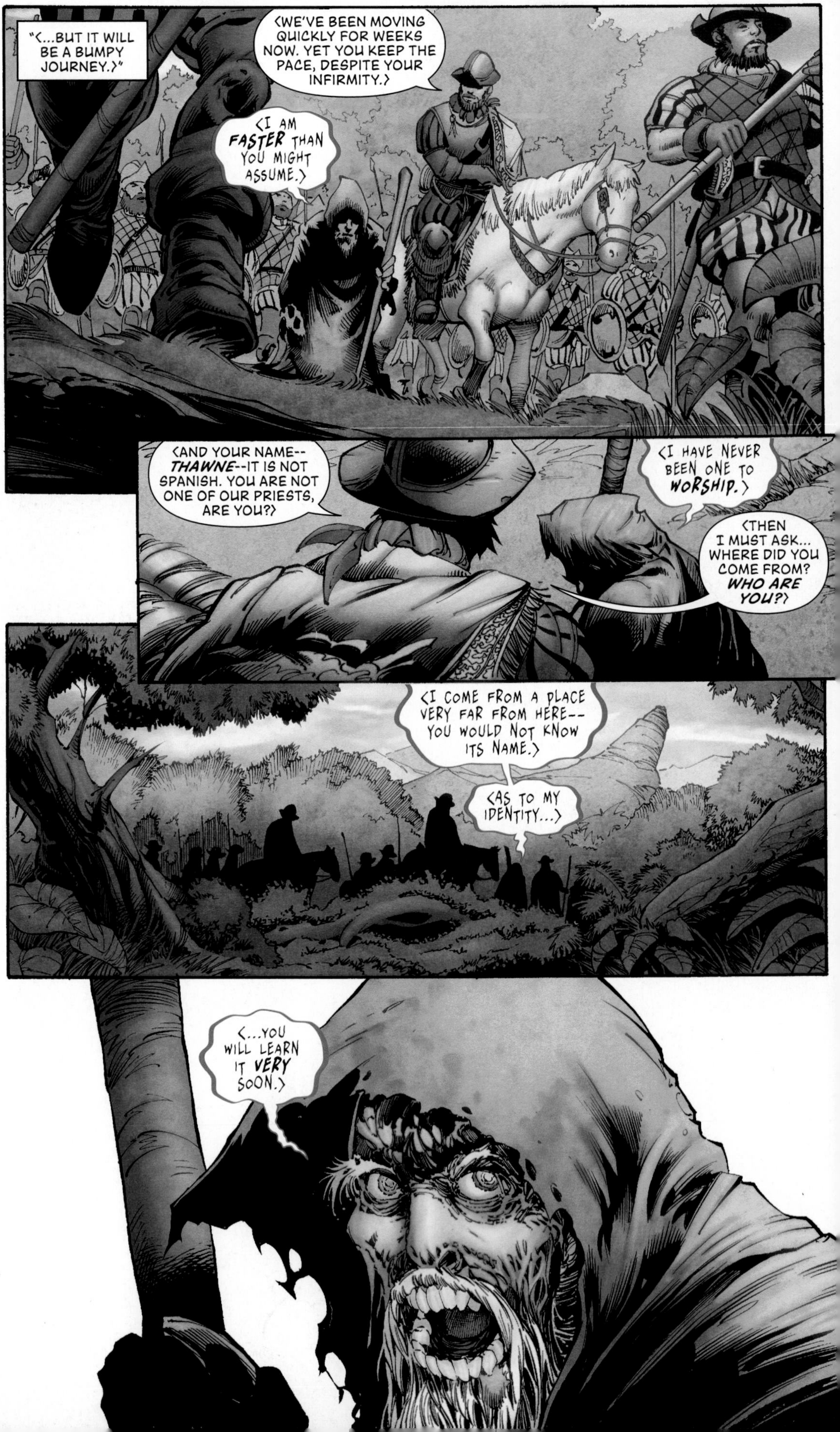
"<...BUT IT WILL BE A BUMPY JOURNEY.>"
<WE'VE BEEN MOVING QUICKLY FOR WEEKS NOW. YET YOU KEEP THE PACE, DESPITE YOUR INFIRMITY.>
<I AM FASTER THAN YOU MIGHT ASSUME.>
<AND YOUR NAME-- THAWNE--IT IS NOT SPANISH. YOU ARE NOT ONE OF OUR PRIESTS, ARE YOU?>
<I HAVE NEVER BEEN ONE TO WORSHIP.>
<THEN I MUST ASK... WHERE DID YOU COME FROM? WHO ARE YOU?>
<I COME FROM A PLACE VERY FAR FROM HERE-- YOU WOULD NOT KNOW ITS NAME.>
<AS TO MY IDENTITY...>
<...YOU WILL LEARN IT VERY SOON.>

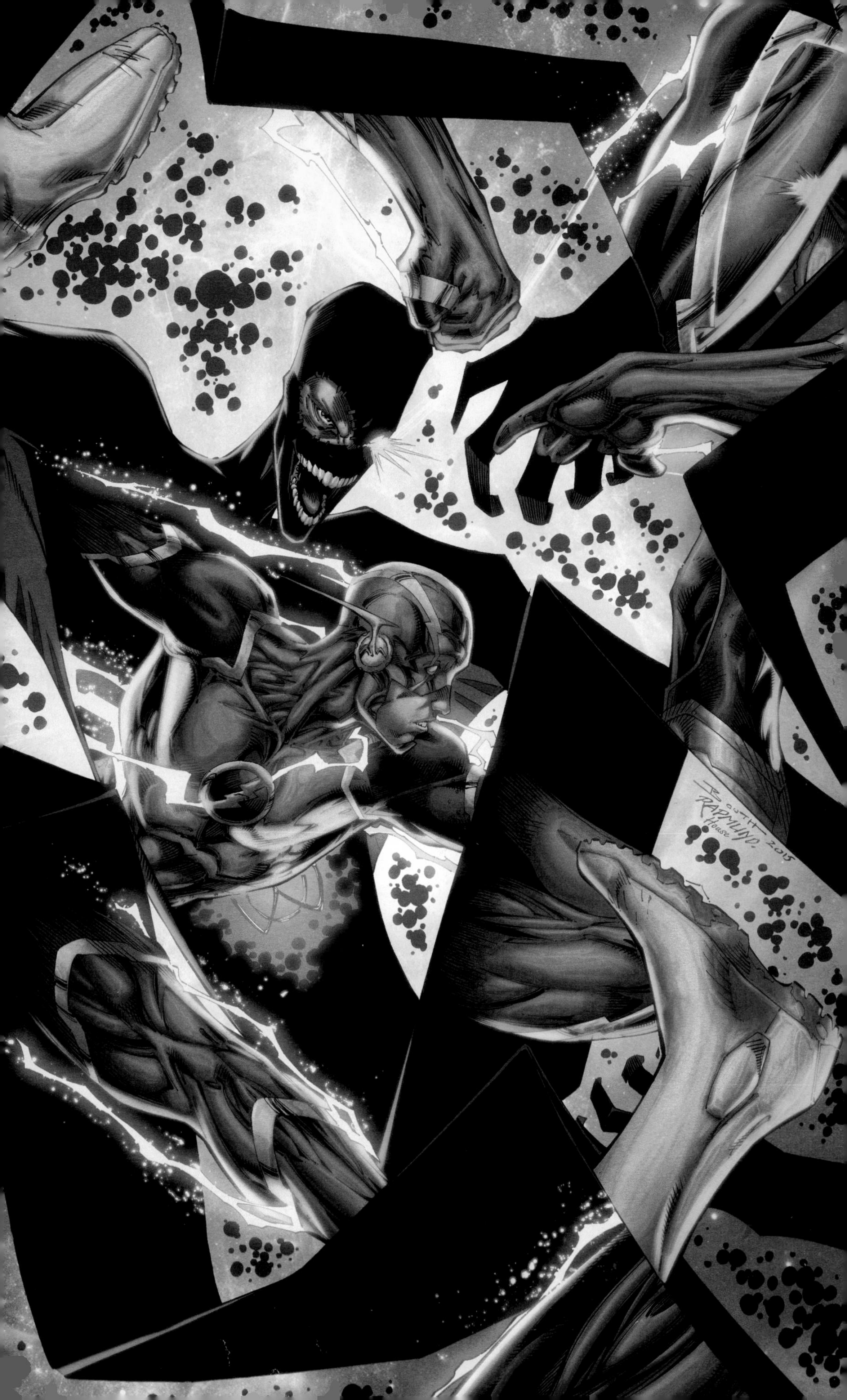

GETTING THE DROP

ROBERT VENDITTI, VAN JENSEN writers BRETT BOOTH penciller NORM RAPMUND inker ANDREW DALHOUSE, WENDY BROOME colorists PAT BROSSEAU letterer
cover by BRETT BOOTH, NORM RAPMUND, ANDREW DALHOUSE

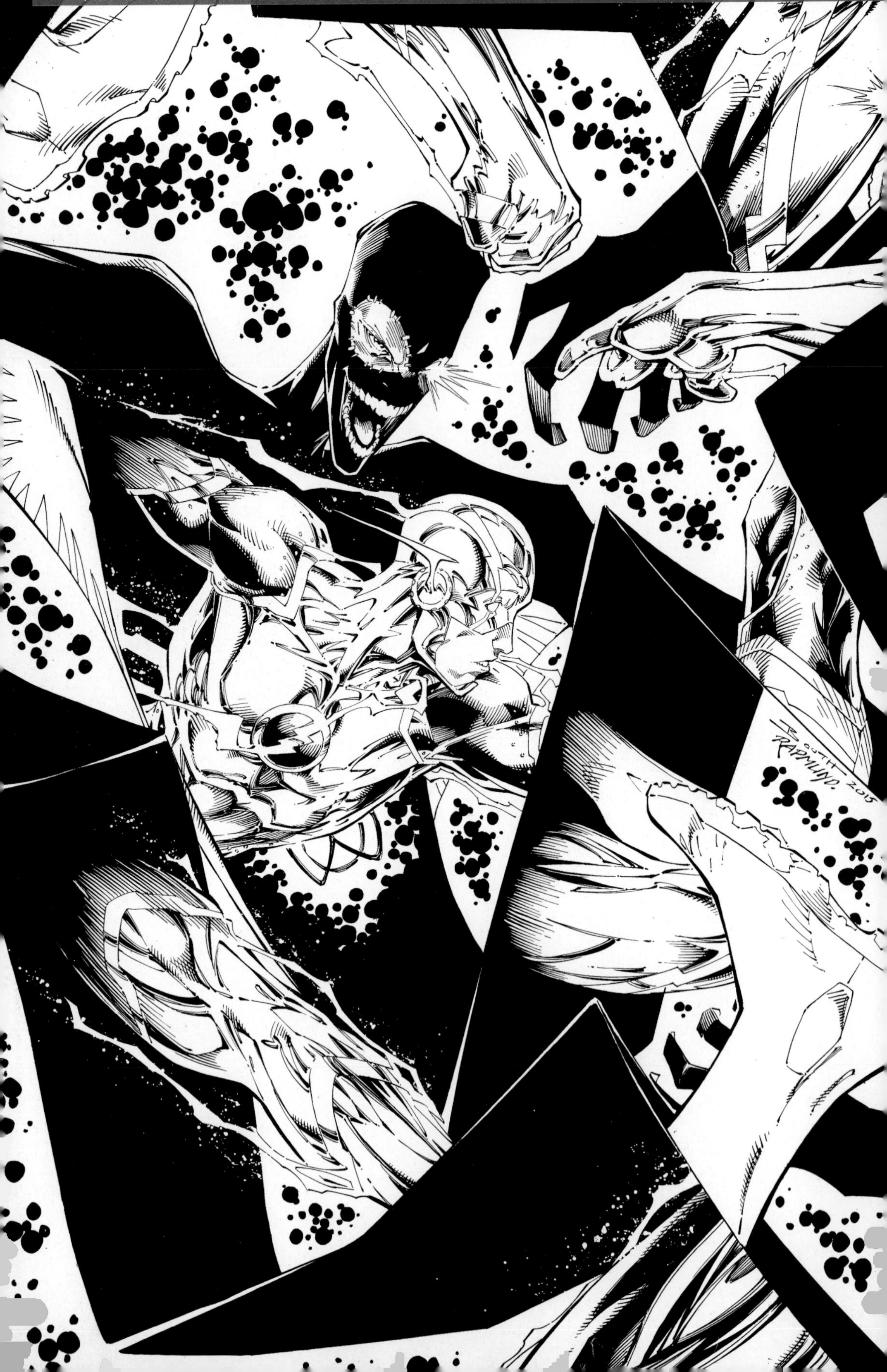
BOOTH
RAPMUND. 2015

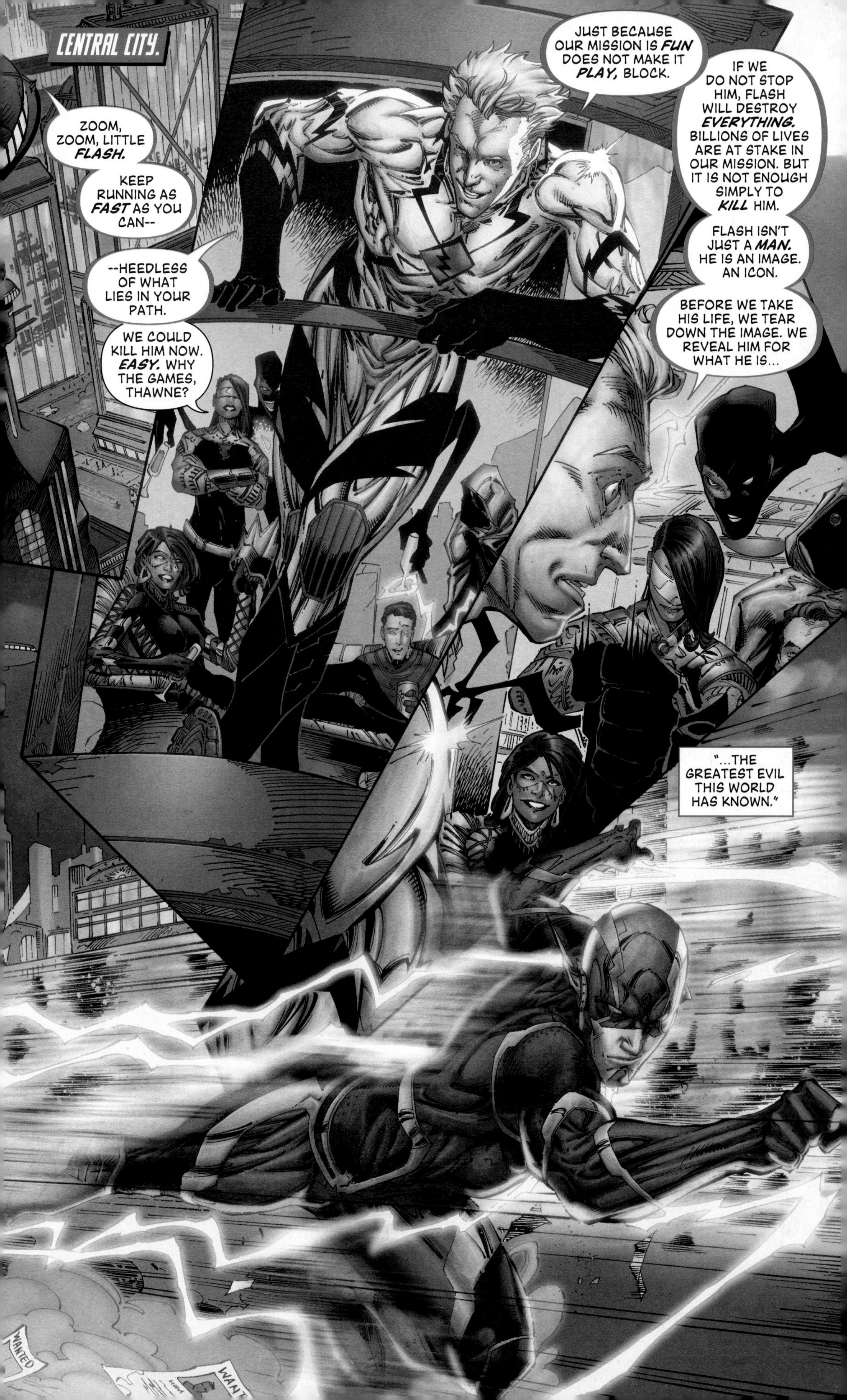
CENTRAL CITY.
ZOOM, ZOOM, LITTLE FLASH.
KEEP RUNNING AS FAST AS YOU CAN--
--HEEDLESS OF WHAT LIES IN YOUR PATH.
WE COULD KILL HIM NOW. EASY. WHY THE GAMES, THAWNE?
JUST BECAUSE OUR MISSION IS FUN DOES NOT MAKE IT PLAY, BLOCK.
IF WE DO NOT STOP HIM, FLASH WILL DESTROY EVERYTHING. BILLIONS OF LIVES ARE AT STAKE IN OUR MISSION. BUT IT IS NOT ENOUGH SIMPLY TO KILL HIM.
FLASH ISN'T JUST A MAN. HE IS AN IMAGE. AN ICON.
BEFORE WE TAKE HIS LIFE, WE TEAR DOWN THE IMAGE. WE REVEAL HIM FOR WHAT HE IS...
"...THE GREATEST EVIL THIS WORLD HAS KNOWN."
WANTED

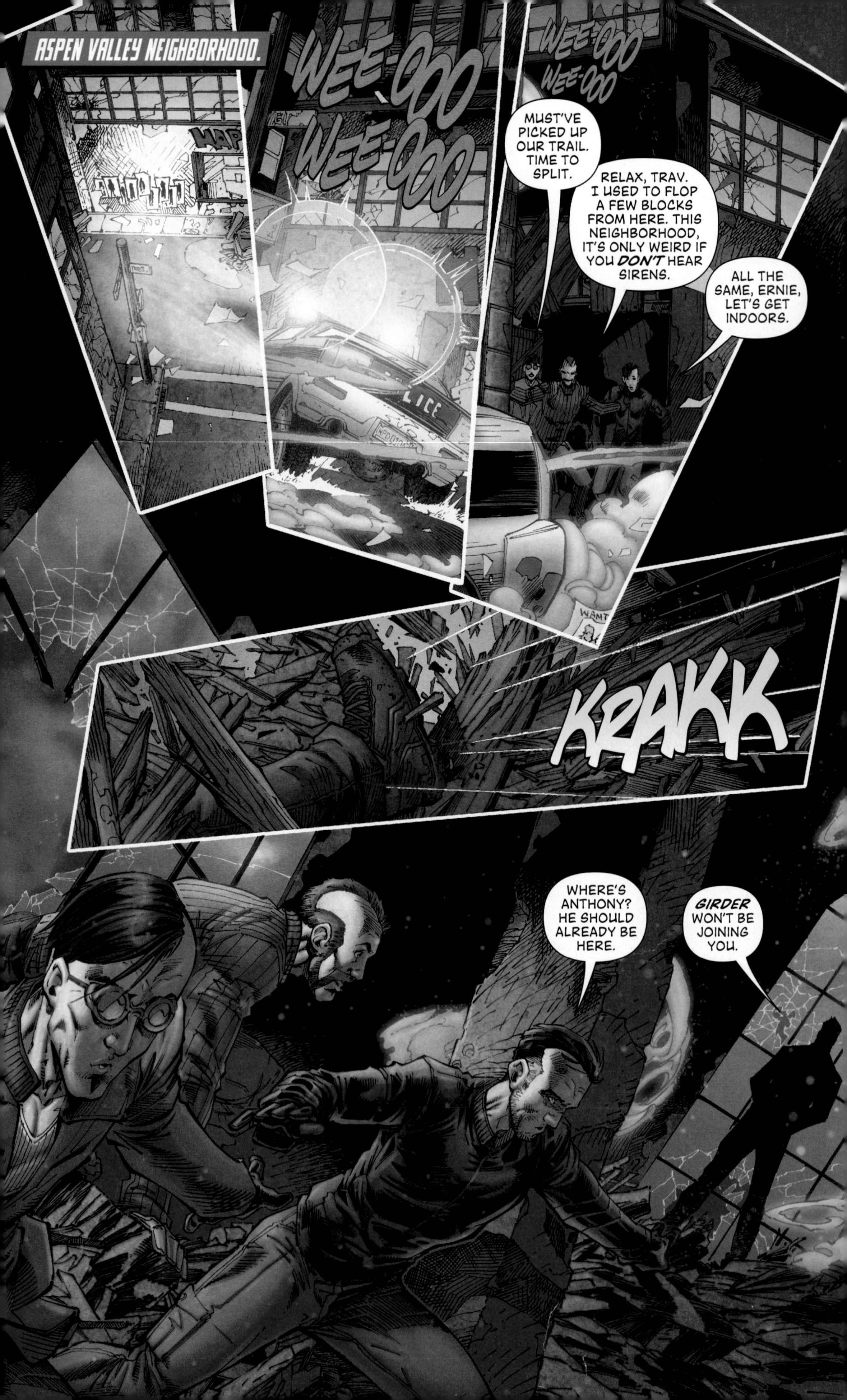
ASPEN VALLEY NEIGHBORHOOD.
WEE-OOO WEE-OOO
WEE-OOO WEE-OOO
MUST'VE PICKED UP OUR TRAIL. TIME TO SPLIT.
RELAX, TRAV. I USED TO FLOP A FEW BLOCKS FROM HERE. THIS NEIGHBORHOOD, IT'S ONLY WEIRD IF YOU *DON'T* HEAR SIRENS.
ALL THE SAME, ERNIE, LET'S GET INDOORS.
KRAKK
WHERE'S ANTHONY? HE SHOULD ALREADY BE HERE.
GIRDER WON'T BE JOINING YOU.

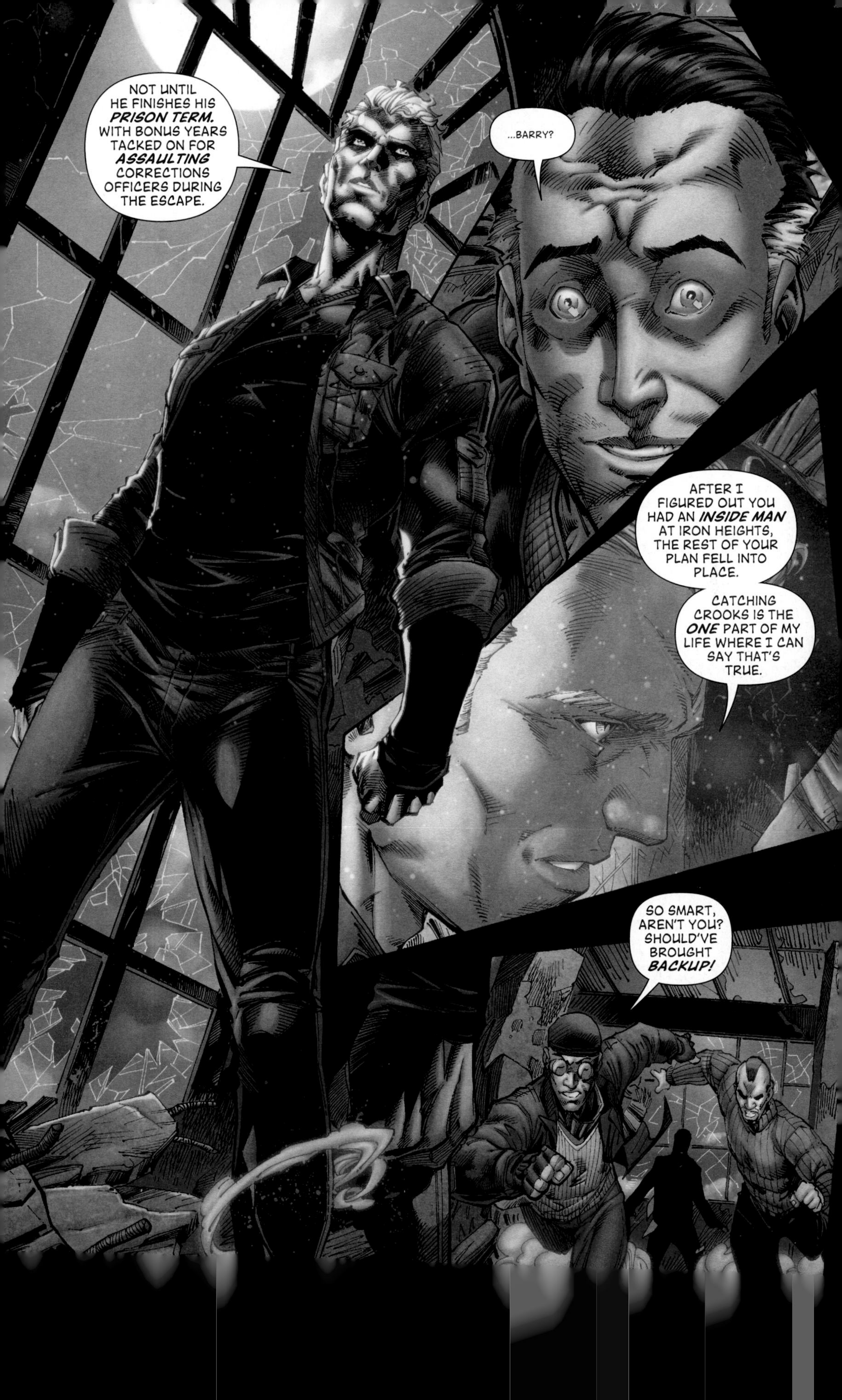
NOT UNTIL HE FINISHES HIS PRISON TERM. WITH BONUS YEARS TACKED ON FOR ASSAULTING CORRECTIONS OFFICERS DURING THE ESCAPE.
...BARRY?
AFTER I FIGURED OUT YOU HAD AN INSIDE MAN AT IRON HEIGHTS, THE REST OF YOUR PLAN FELL INTO PLACE.
CATCHING CROOKS IS THE ONE PART OF MY LIFE WHERE I CAN SAY THAT'S TRUE.
SO SMART, AREN'T YOU? SHOULD'VE BROUGHT BACKUP!

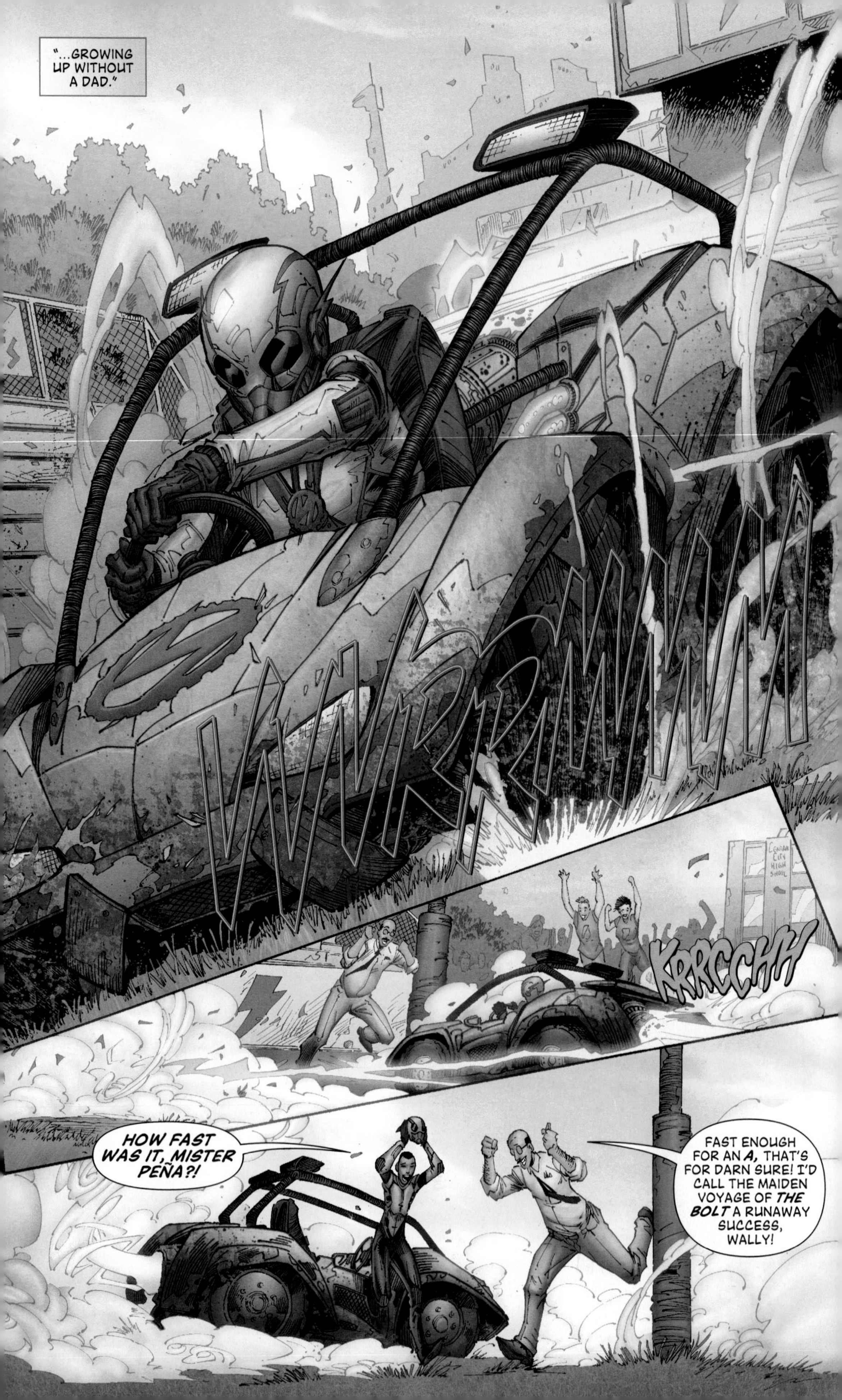
"...GROWING UP WITHOUT A DAD."
KRRCCHH
HOW FAST WAS IT, MISTER PEÑA?!
FAST ENOUGH FOR AN *A,* THAT'S FOR DARN SURE! I'D CALL THE MAIDEN VOYAGE OF *THE BOLT* A RUNAWAY SUCCESS, WALLY!

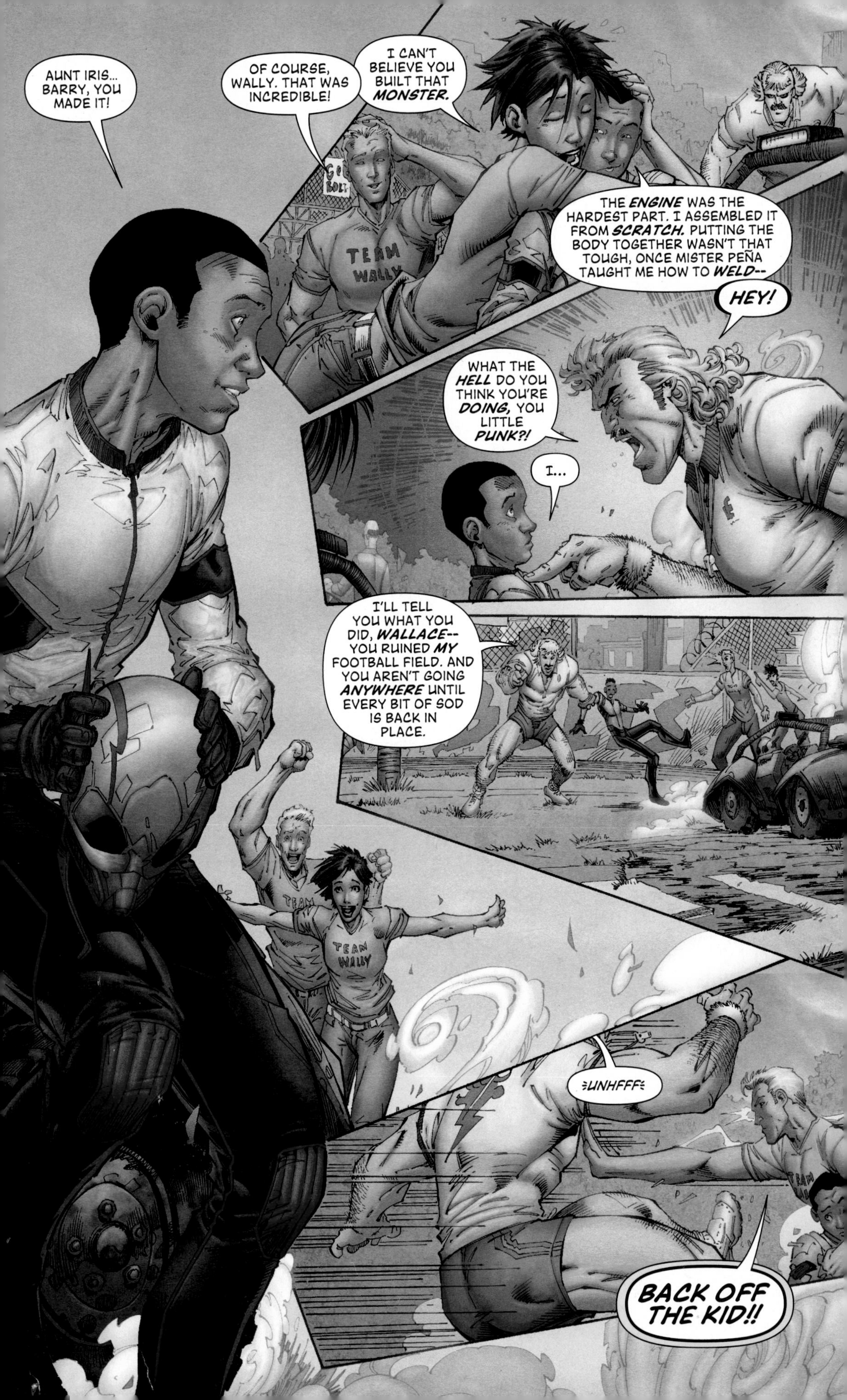
AUNT IRIS... BARRY, YOU MADE IT!
OF COURSE, WALLY. THAT WAS INCREDIBLE!
I CAN'T BELIEVE YOU BUILT THAT MONSTER.
THE ENGINE WAS THE HARDEST PART. I ASSEMBLED IT FROM SCRATCH. PUTTING THE BODY TOGETHER WASN'T THAT TOUGH, ONCE MISTER PEÑA TAUGHT ME HOW TO WELD--
HEY!
WHAT THE HELL DO YOU THINK YOU'RE DOING, YOU LITTLE PUNK?!
I...
I'LL TELL YOU WHAT YOU DID, WALLACE-- YOU RUINED MY FOOTBALL FIELD. AND YOU AREN'T GOING ANYWHERE UNTIL EVERY BIT OF SOD IS BACK IN PLACE.
UNHFFF
BACK OFF THE KID!!

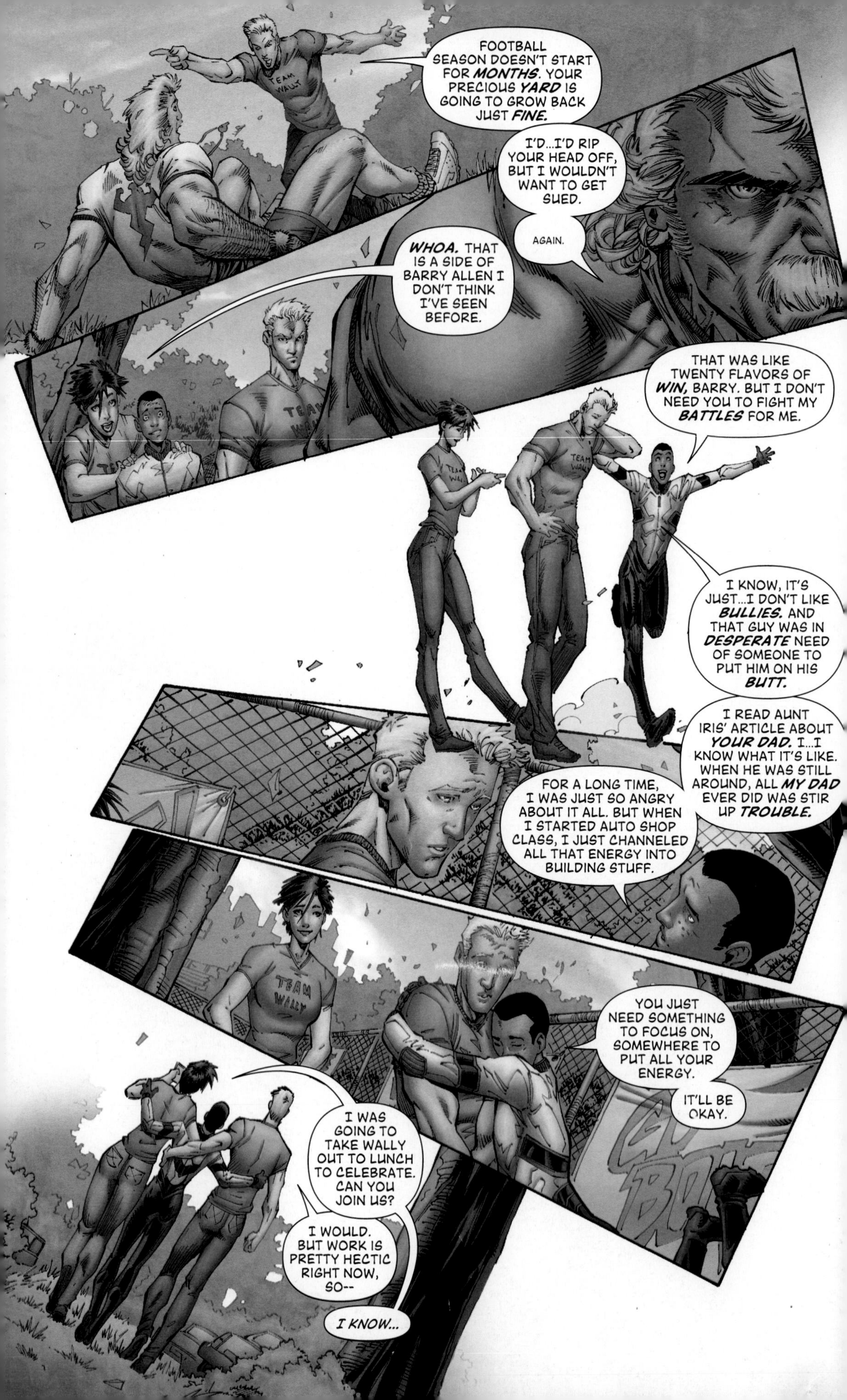
FOOTBALL SEASON DOESN'T START FOR MONTHS. YOUR PRECIOUS YARD IS GOING TO GROW BACK JUST FINE.
I'D...I'D RIP YOUR HEAD OFF, BUT I WOULDN'T WANT TO GET SUED.
AGAIN.
WHOA. THAT IS A SIDE OF BARRY ALLEN I DON'T THINK I'VE SEEN BEFORE.
TEAM WALLY
THAT WAS LIKE TWENTY FLAVORS OF WIN, BARRY. BUT I DON'T NEED YOU TO FIGHT MY BATTLES FOR ME.
I KNOW, IT'S JUST...I DON'T LIKE BULLIES. AND THAT GUY WAS IN DESPERATE NEED OF SOMEONE TO PUT HIM ON HIS BUTT.
I READ AUNT IRIS' ARTICLE ABOUT YOUR DAD. I...I KNOW WHAT IT'S LIKE. WHEN HE WAS STILL AROUND, ALL MY DAD EVER DID WAS STIR UP TROUBLE.
FOR A LONG TIME, I WAS JUST SO ANGRY ABOUT IT ALL. BUT WHEN I STARTED AUTO SHOP CLASS, I JUST CHANNELED ALL THAT ENERGY INTO BUILDING STUFF.
TEAM WALLY
YOU JUST NEED SOMETHING TO FOCUS ON, SOMEWHERE TO PUT ALL YOUR ENERGY.
IT'LL BE OKAY.
I WAS GOING TO TAKE WALLY OUT TO LUNCH TO CELEBRATE. CAN YOU JOIN US?
I WOULD. BUT WORK IS PRETTY HECTIC RIGHT NOW, SO--
I KNOW...

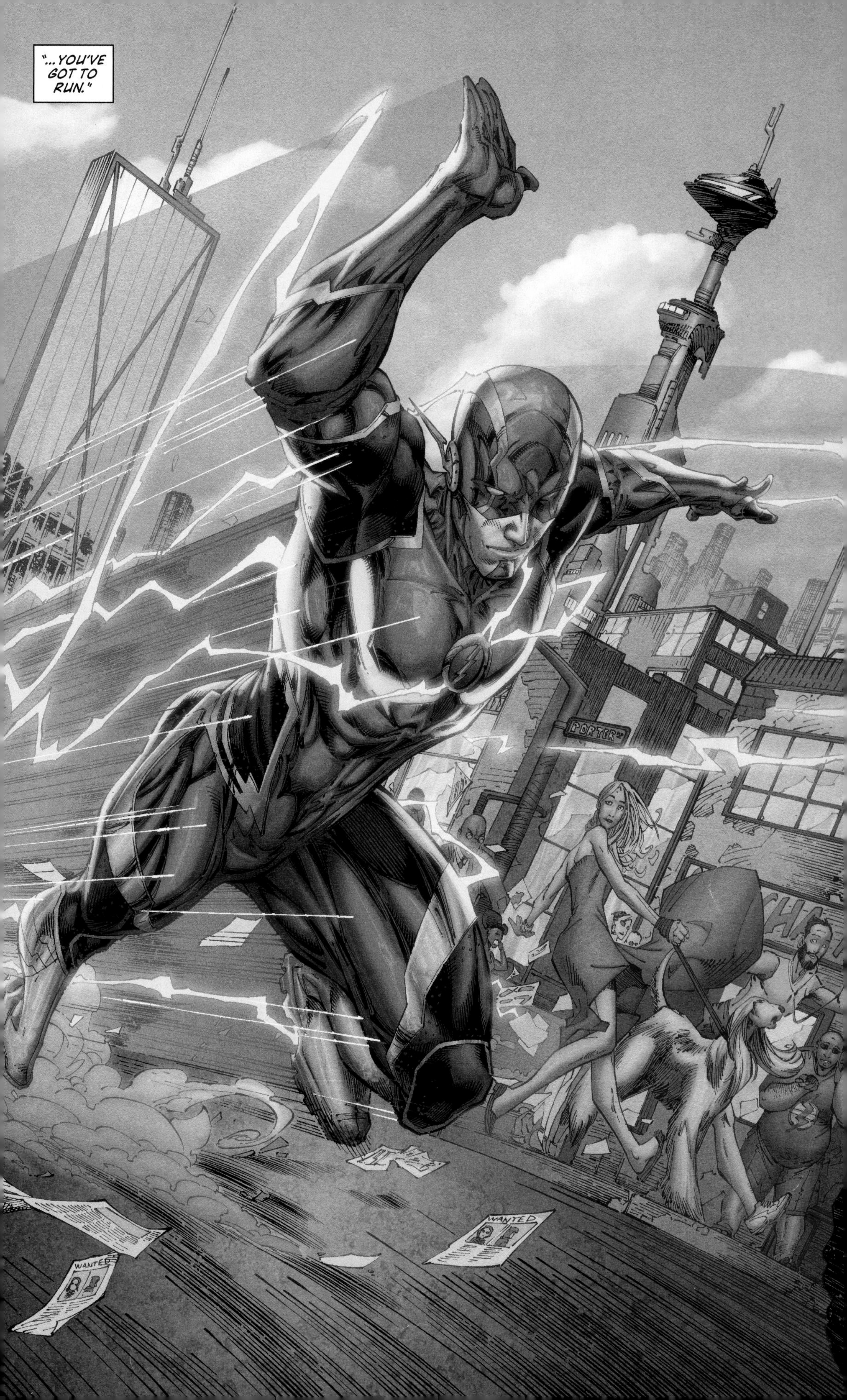
"...YOU'VE GOT TO RUN."
PORTER
WANTED
WANTED

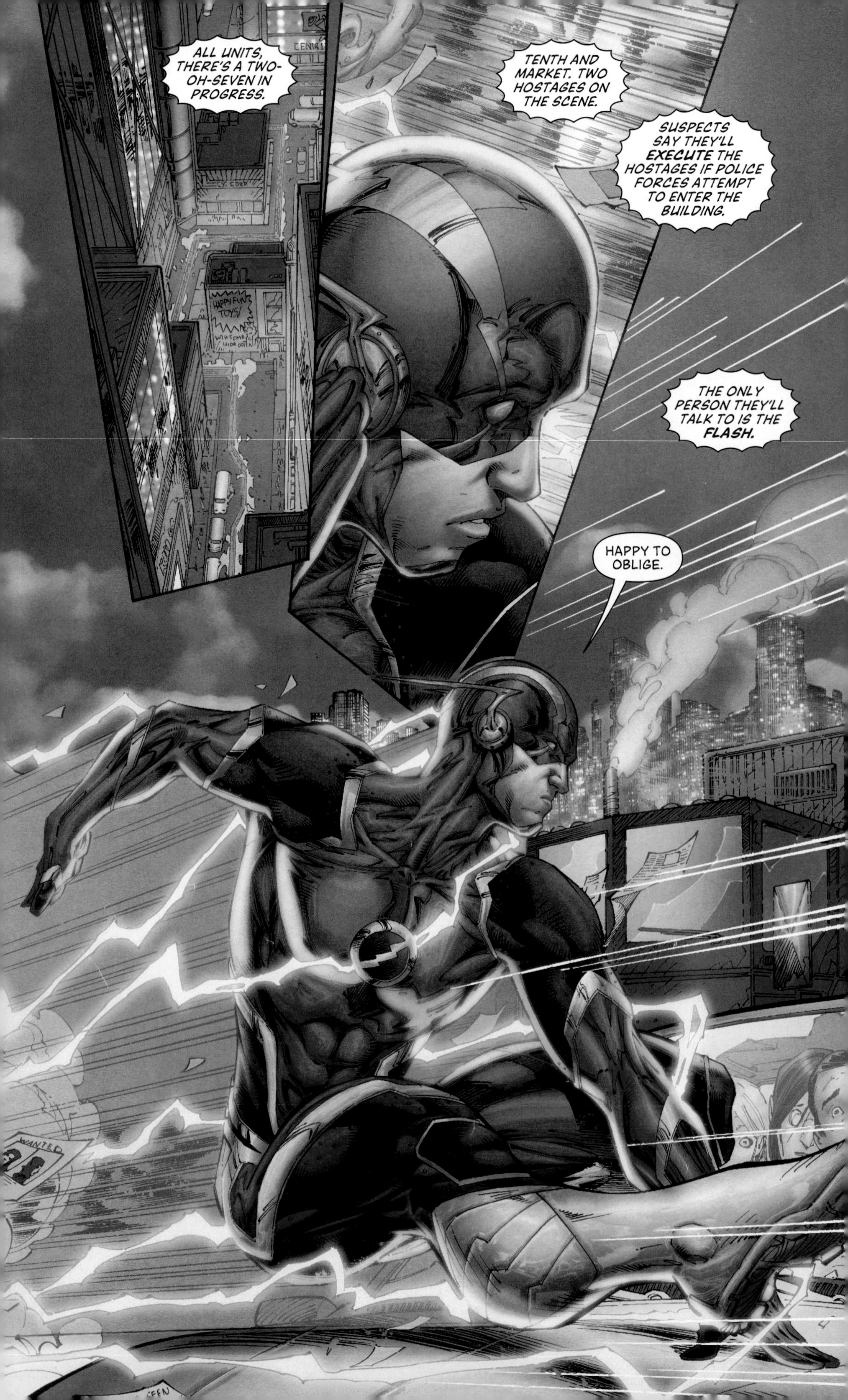
ALL UNITS, THERE'S A TWO-OH-SEVEN IN PROGRESS.
TENTH AND MARKET. TWO HOSTAGES ON THE SCENE.
SUSPECTS SAY THEY'LL **EXECUTE** THE HOSTAGES IF POLICE FORCES ATTEMPT TO ENTER THE BUILDING.
THE ONLY PERSON THEY'LL TALK TO IS THE **FLASH.**
HAPPY TO OBLIGE.
HAPPY FUN TOYS!
WANTED

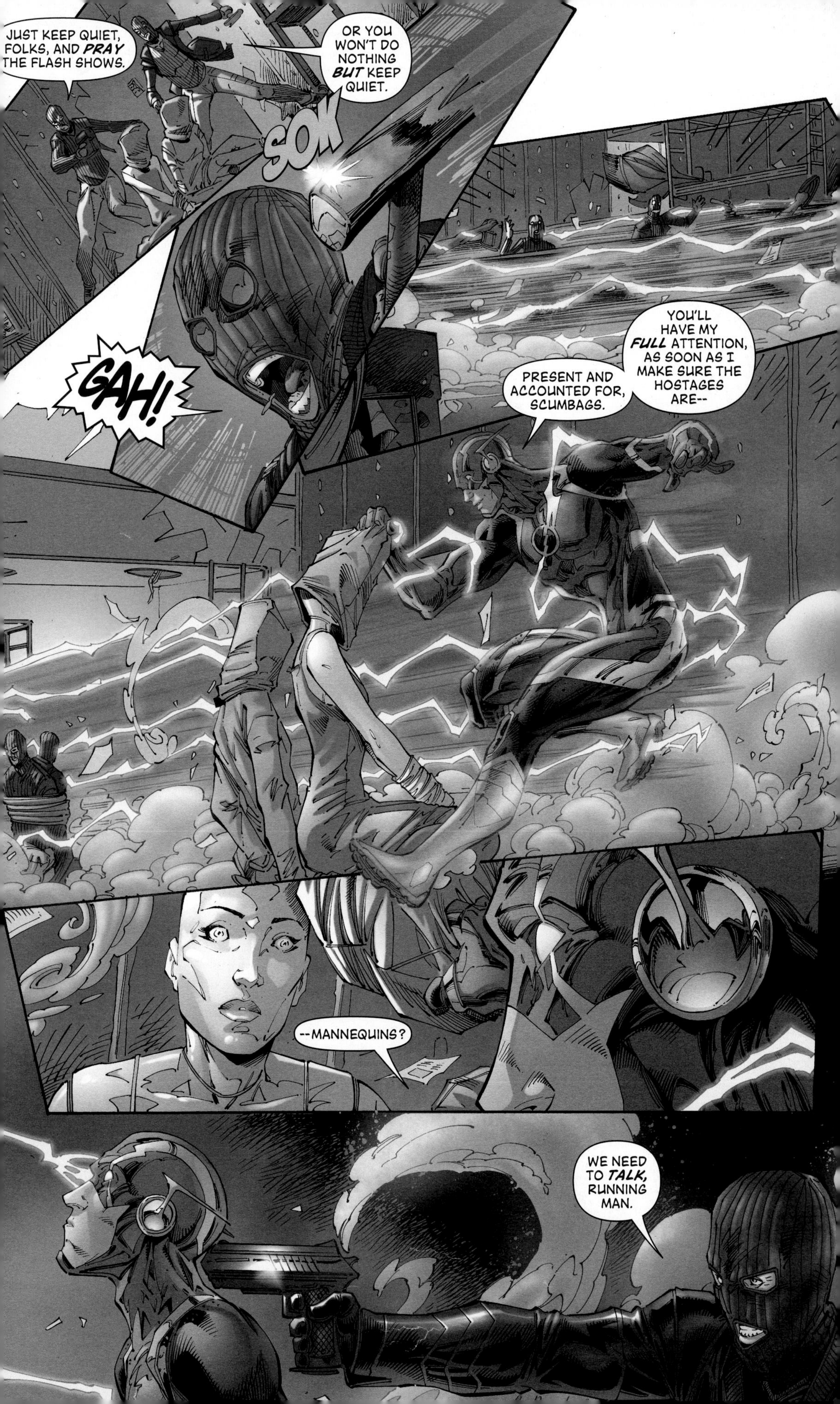

JUST KEEP QUIET, FOLKS, AND *PRAY* THE FLASH SHOWS.
OR YOU WON'T DO NOTHING *BUT* KEEP QUIET.
SOK
GAH!
PRESENT AND ACCOUNTED FOR, SCUMBAGS.
YOU'LL HAVE MY *FULL* ATTENTION, AS SOON AS I MAKE SURE THE HOSTAGES ARE--
--MANNEQUINS?
WE NEED TO *TALK,* RUNNING MAN.

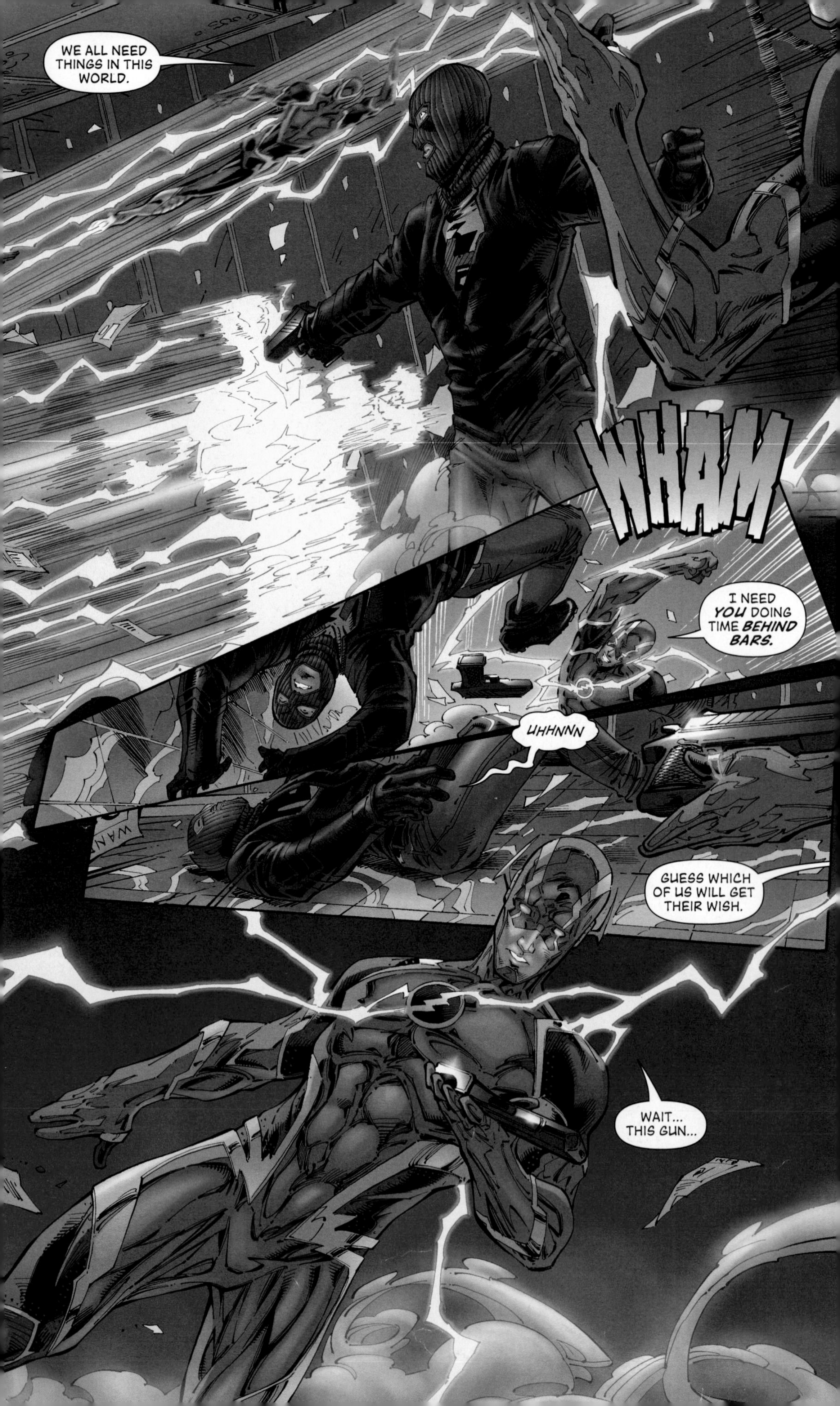
WE ALL NEED THINGS IN THIS WORLD.
WHAM
I NEED *YOU* DOING TIME *BEHIND BARS.*
UHHNNN
GUESS WHICH OF US WILL GET THEIR WISH.
WAIT... THIS GUN...

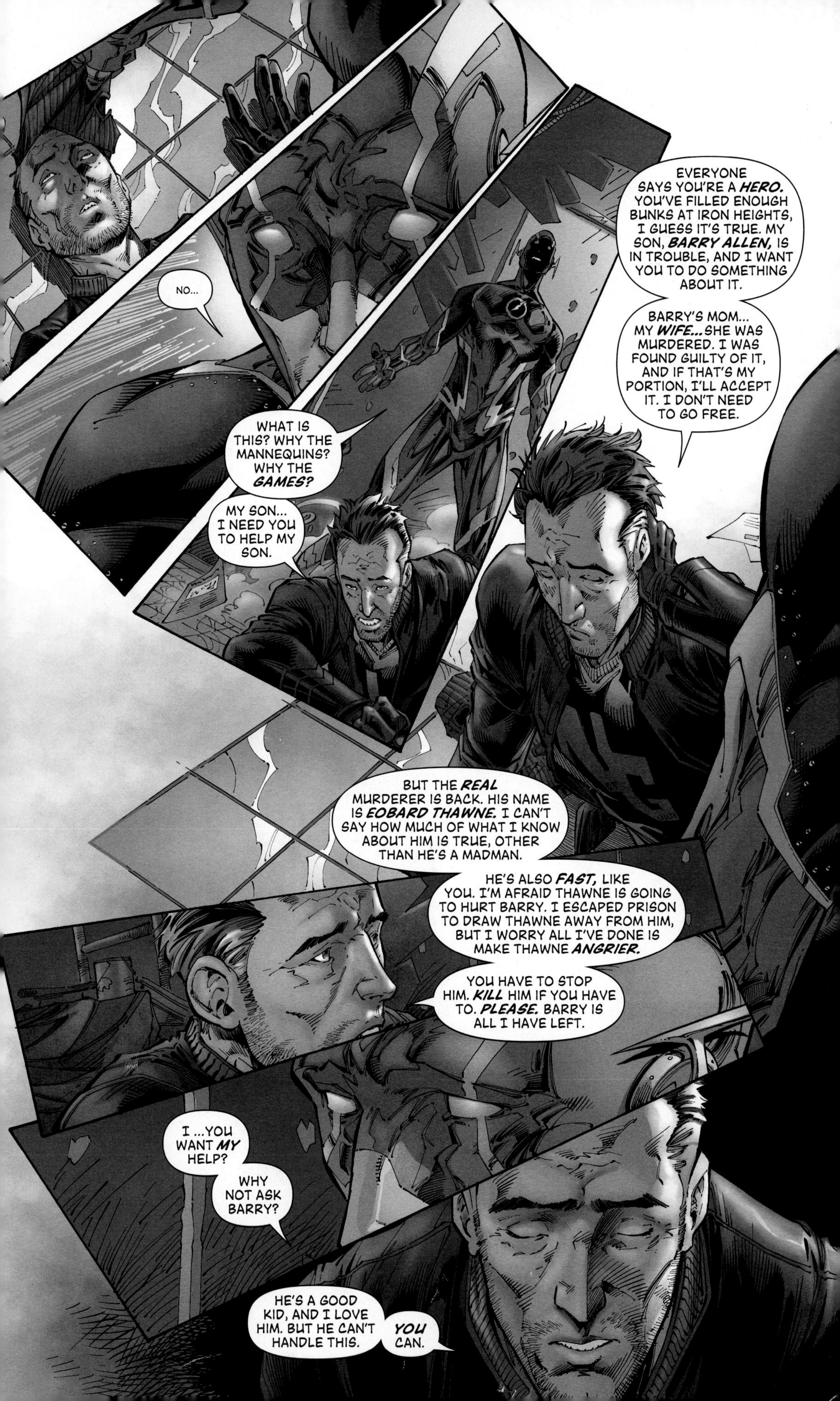
NO...
EVERYONE SAYS YOU'RE A HERO. YOU'VE FILLED ENOUGH BUNKS AT IRON HEIGHTS, I GUESS IT'S TRUE. MY SON, BARRY ALLEN, IS IN TROUBLE, AND I WANT YOU TO DO SOMETHING ABOUT IT.
BARRY'S MOM... MY WIFE... SHE WAS MURDERED. I WAS FOUND GUILTY OF IT, AND IF THAT'S MY PORTION, I'LL ACCEPT IT. I DON'T NEED TO GO FREE.
WHAT IS THIS? WHY THE MANNEQUINS? WHY THE GAMES?
MY SON... I NEED YOU TO HELP MY SON.
BUT THE REAL MURDERER IS BACK. HIS NAME IS EOBARD THAWNE. I CAN'T SAY HOW MUCH OF WHAT I KNOW ABOUT HIM IS TRUE, OTHER THAN HE'S A MADMAN.
HE'S ALSO FAST, LIKE YOU. I'M AFRAID THAWNE IS GOING TO HURT BARRY. I ESCAPED PRISON TO DRAW THAWNE AWAY FROM HIM, BUT I WORRY ALL I'VE DONE IS MAKE THAWNE ANGRIER.
YOU HAVE TO STOP HIM. KILL HIM IF YOU HAVE TO. PLEASE. BARRY IS ALL I HAVE LEFT.
I ...YOU WANT MY HELP?
WHY NOT ASK BARRY?
HE'S A GOOD KID, AND I LOVE HIM. BUT HE CAN'T HANDLE THIS.
YOU CAN.

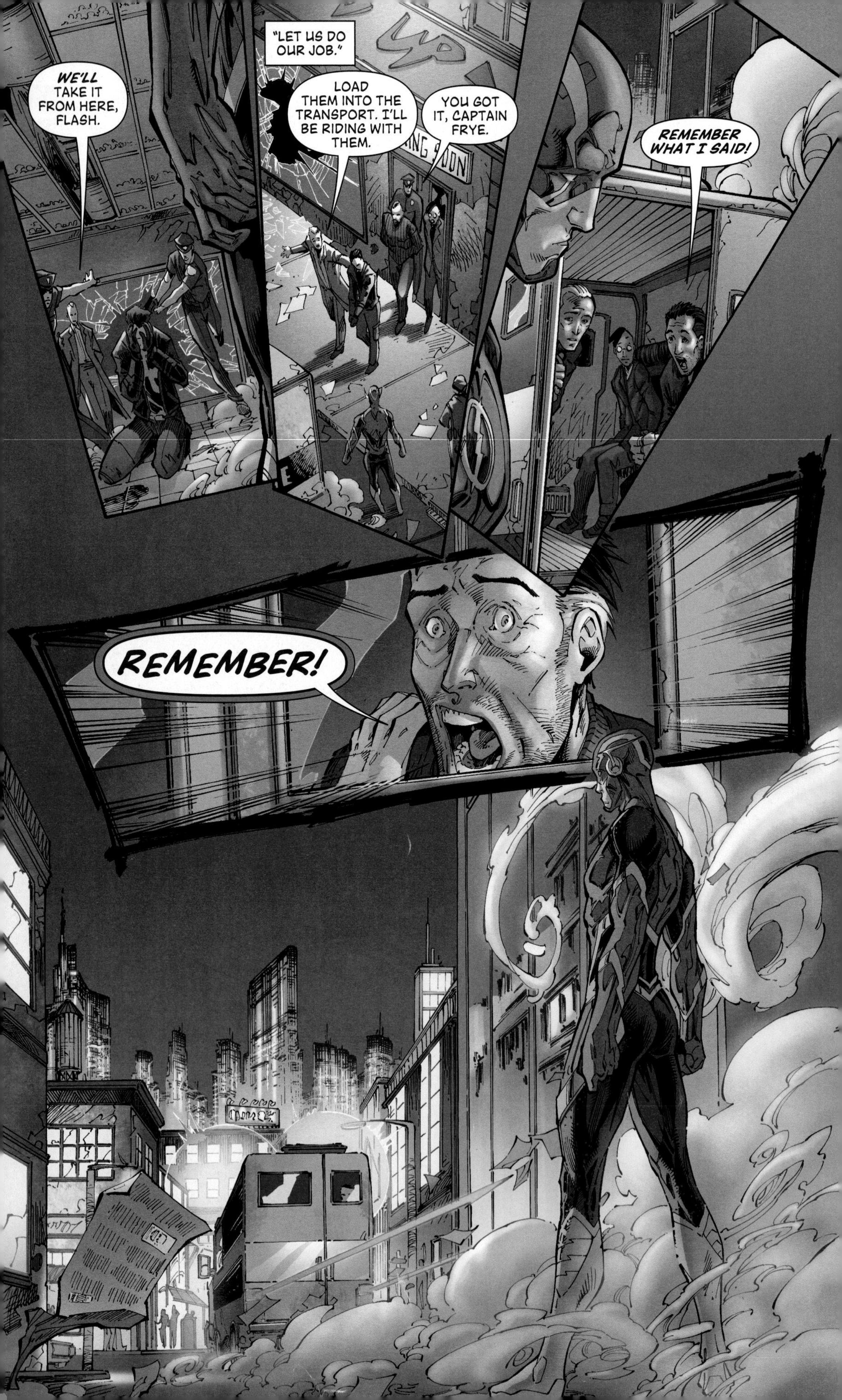

WE'LL TAKE IT FROM HERE, FLASH.
"LET US DO OUR JOB."
LOAD THEM INTO THE TRANSPORT. I'LL BE RIDING WITH THEM.
YOU GOT IT, CAPTAIN FRYE.
REMEMBER WHAT I SAID!
REMEMBER!

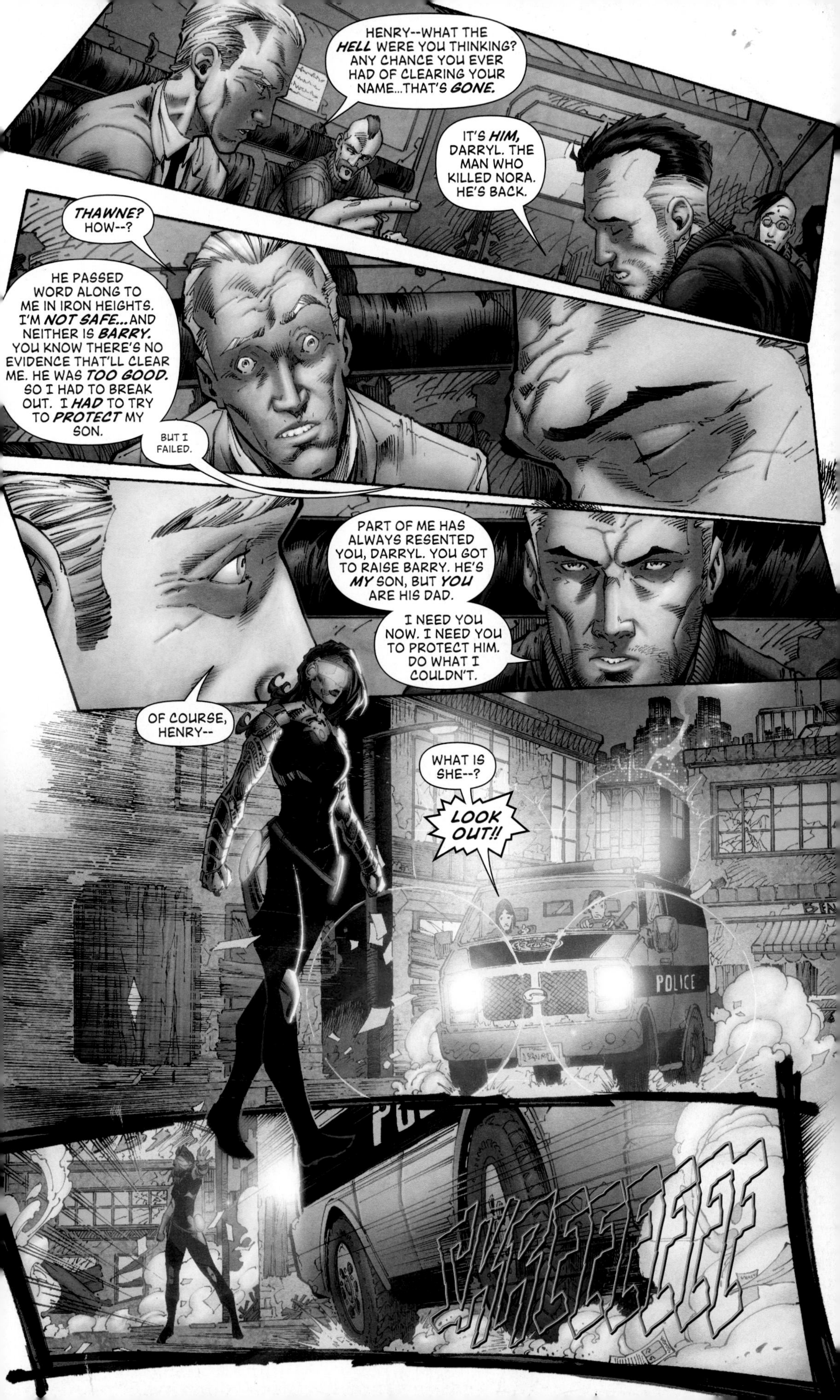
HENRY--WHAT THE HELL WERE YOU THINKING? ANY CHANCE YOU EVER HAD OF CLEARING YOUR NAME...THAT'S GONE.
IT'S HIM, DARRYL. THE MAN WHO KILLED NORA. HE'S BACK.
THAWNE? HOW--?
HE PASSED WORD ALONG TO ME IN IRON HEIGHTS. I'M NOT SAFE...AND NEITHER IS BARRY. YOU KNOW THERE'S NO EVIDENCE THAT'LL CLEAR ME. HE WAS TOO GOOD. SO I HAD TO BREAK OUT. I HAD TO TRY TO PROTECT MY SON.
BUT I FAILED.
PART OF ME HAS ALWAYS RESENTED YOU, DARRYL. YOU GOT TO RAISE BARRY. HE'S MY SON, BUT YOU ARE HIS DAD.
I NEED YOU NOW. I NEED YOU TO PROTECT HIM. DO WHAT I COULDN'T.
OF COURSE, HENRY--
WHAT IS SHE--?
LOOK OUT!!
POLICE

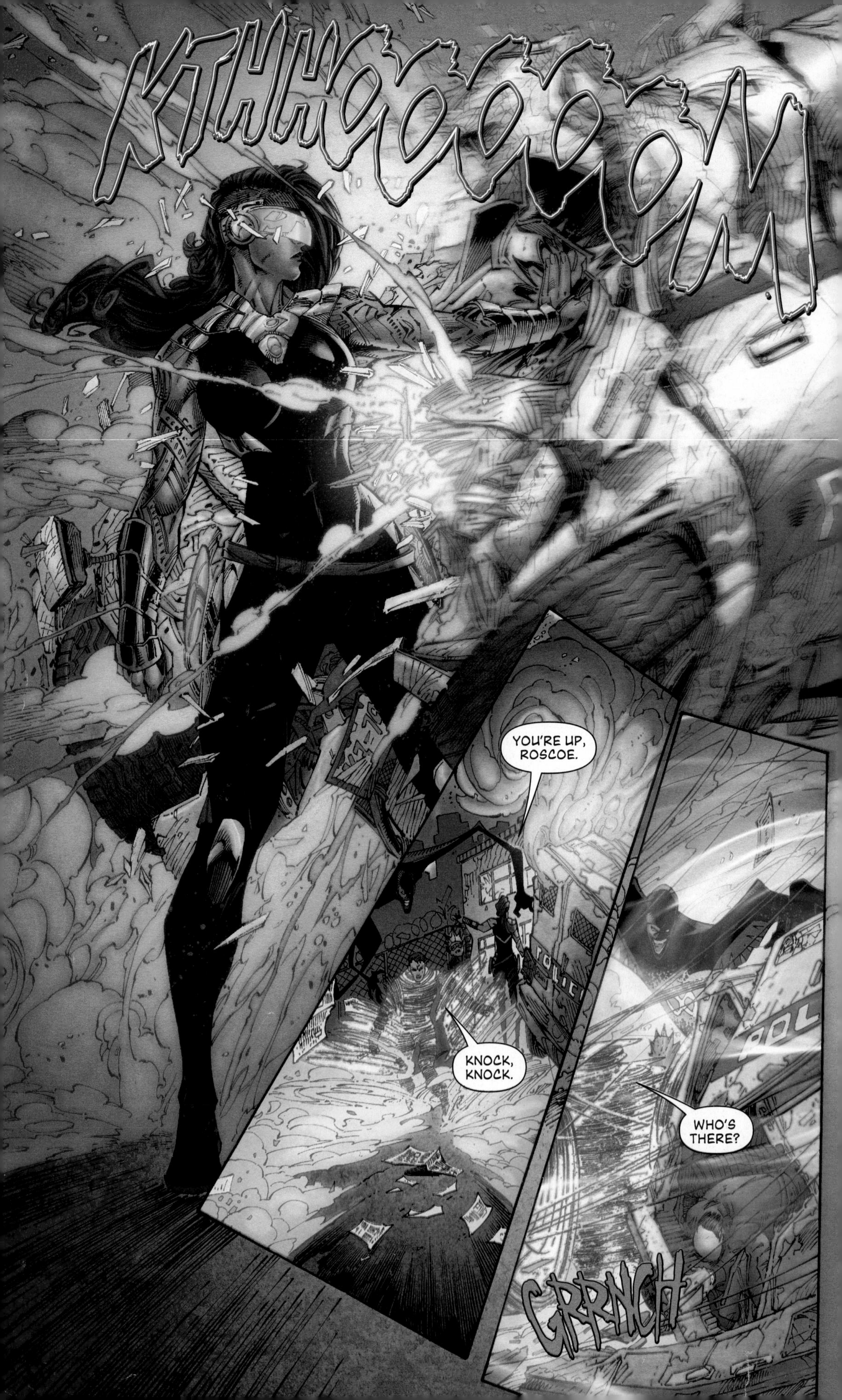
KTHHOOOOOM
YOU'RE UP, ROSCOE.
KNOCK, KNOCK.
WHO'S THERE?
GRRNCH

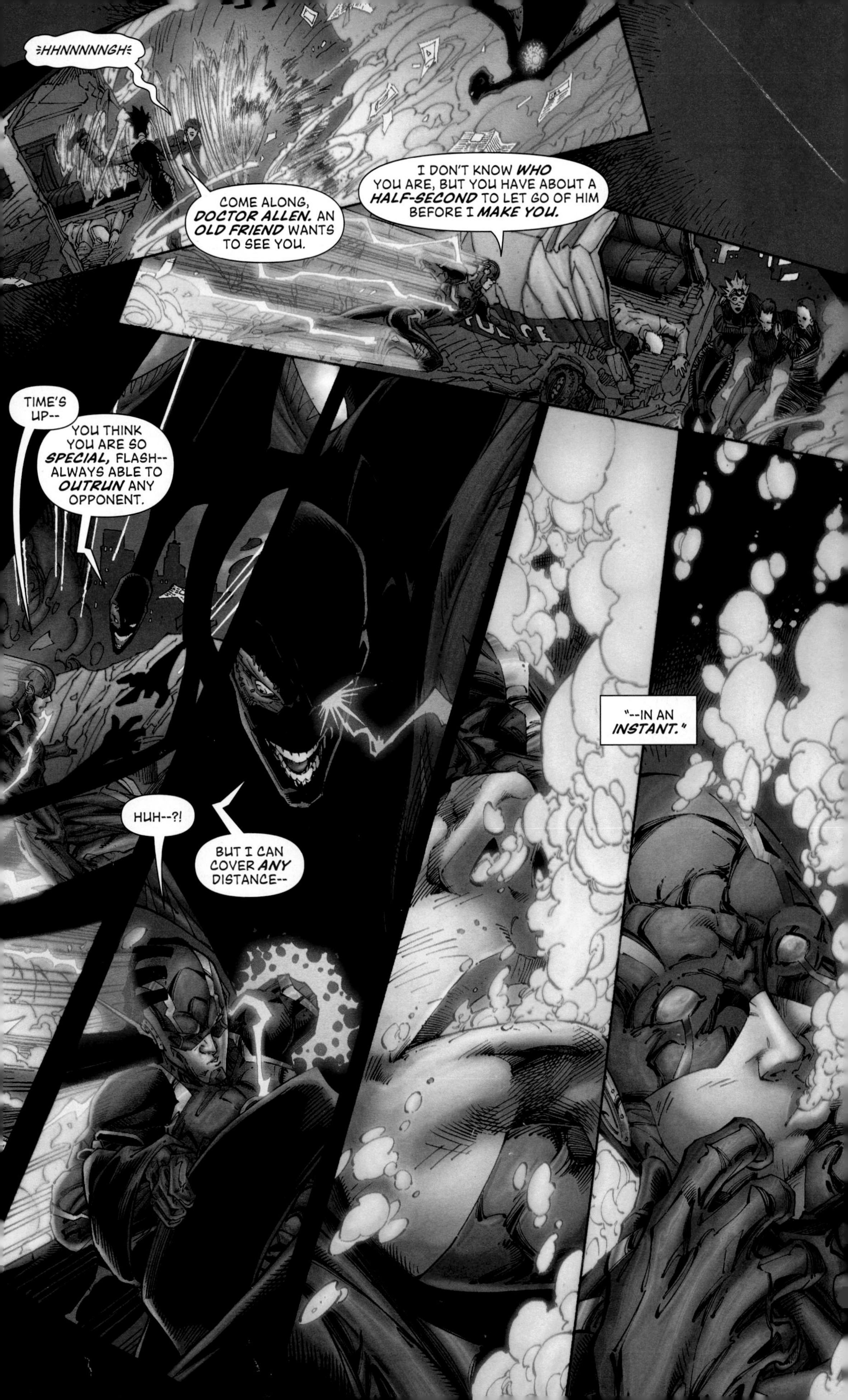

HHNNNNNNGH
COME ALONG, DOCTOR ALLEN. AN OLD FRIEND WANTS TO SEE YOU.
I DON'T KNOW WHO YOU ARE, BUT YOU HAVE ABOUT A HALF-SECOND TO LET GO OF HIM BEFORE I MAKE YOU.
TIME'S UP--
YOU THINK YOU ARE SO SPECIAL, FLASH-- ALWAYS ABLE TO OUTRUN ANY OPPONENT.
HUH--?!
BUT I CAN COVER ANY DISTANCE--
"--IN AN INSTANT."

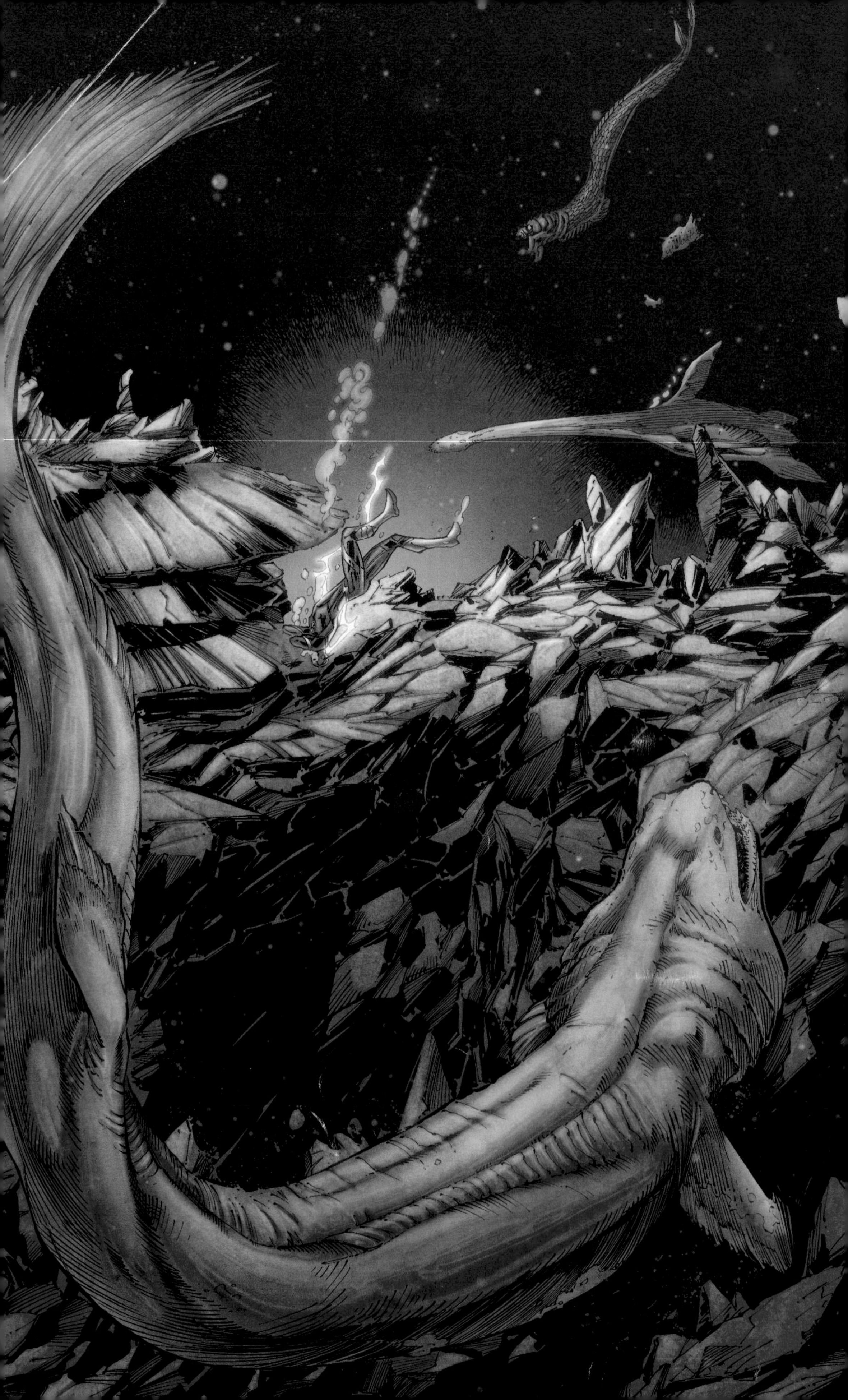

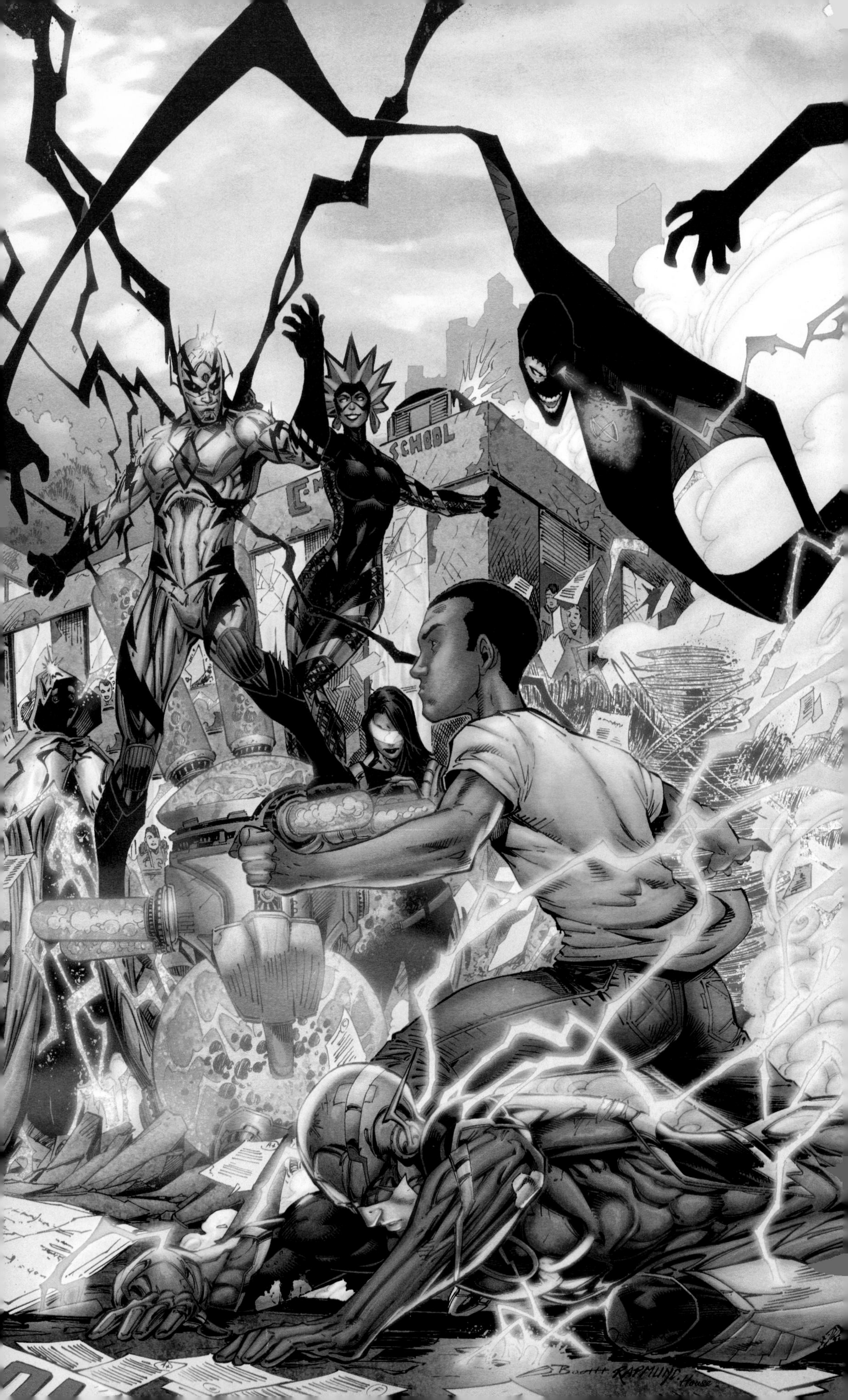
SCHOOL

BUBBLE

ROBERT VENDITTI, VAN JENSEN writers BRETT BOOTH penciller NORM RAPMUND inker ANDREW DALHOUSE colorist PAT BROSSEAU letterer
cover by BRETT BOOTH, NORM RAPMUND, ANDREW DALHOUSE

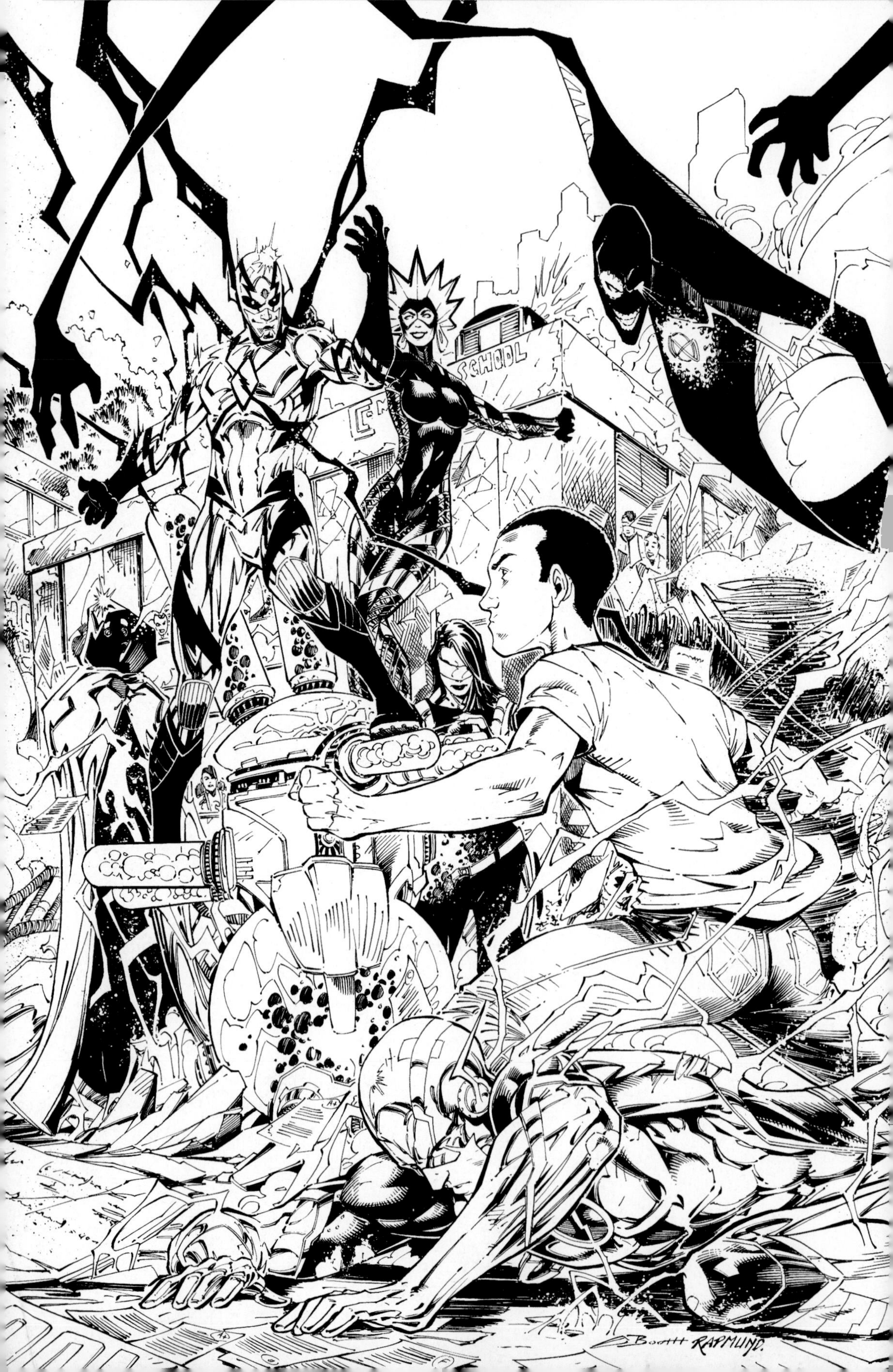
SCHOOL

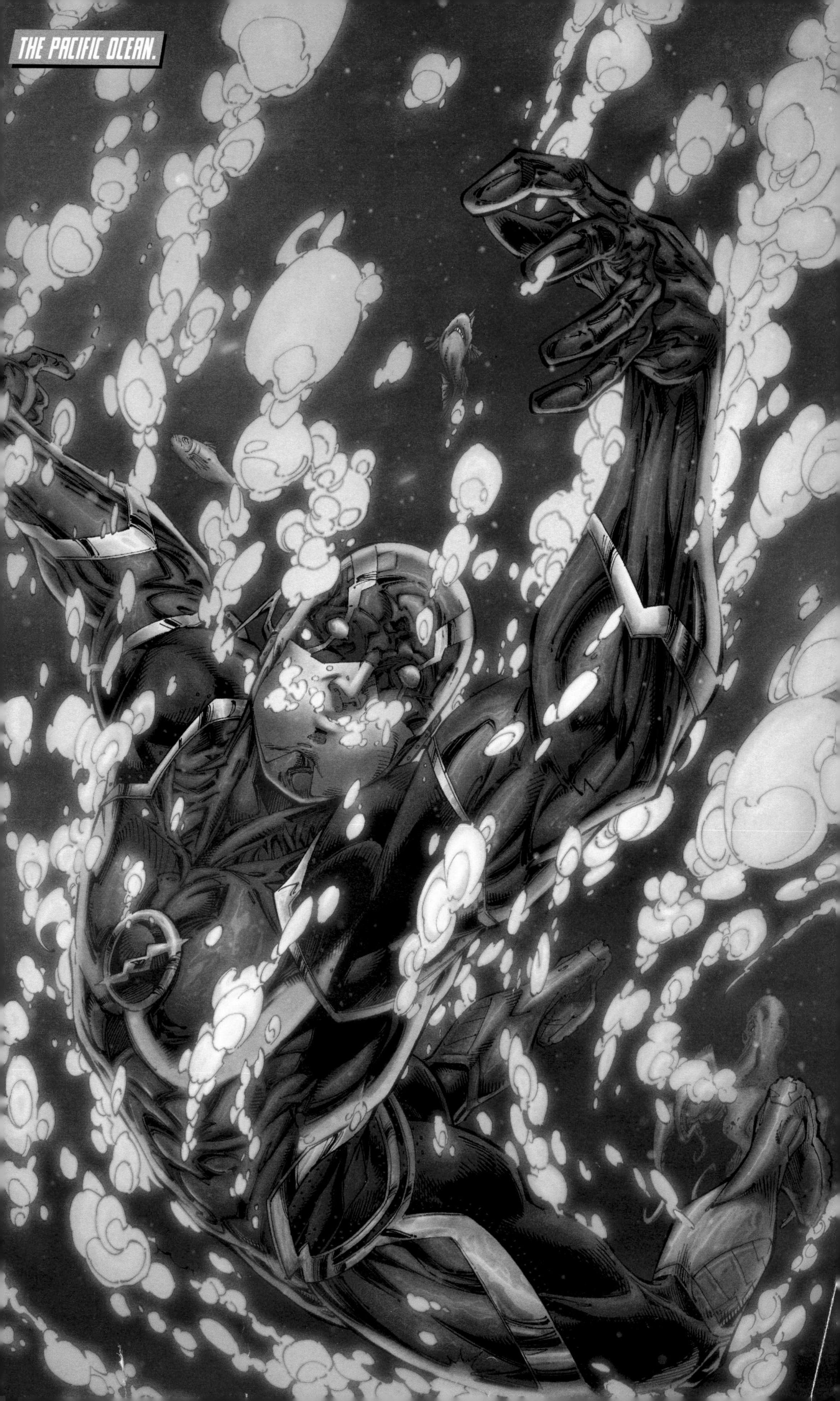
THE PACIFIC OCEAN.

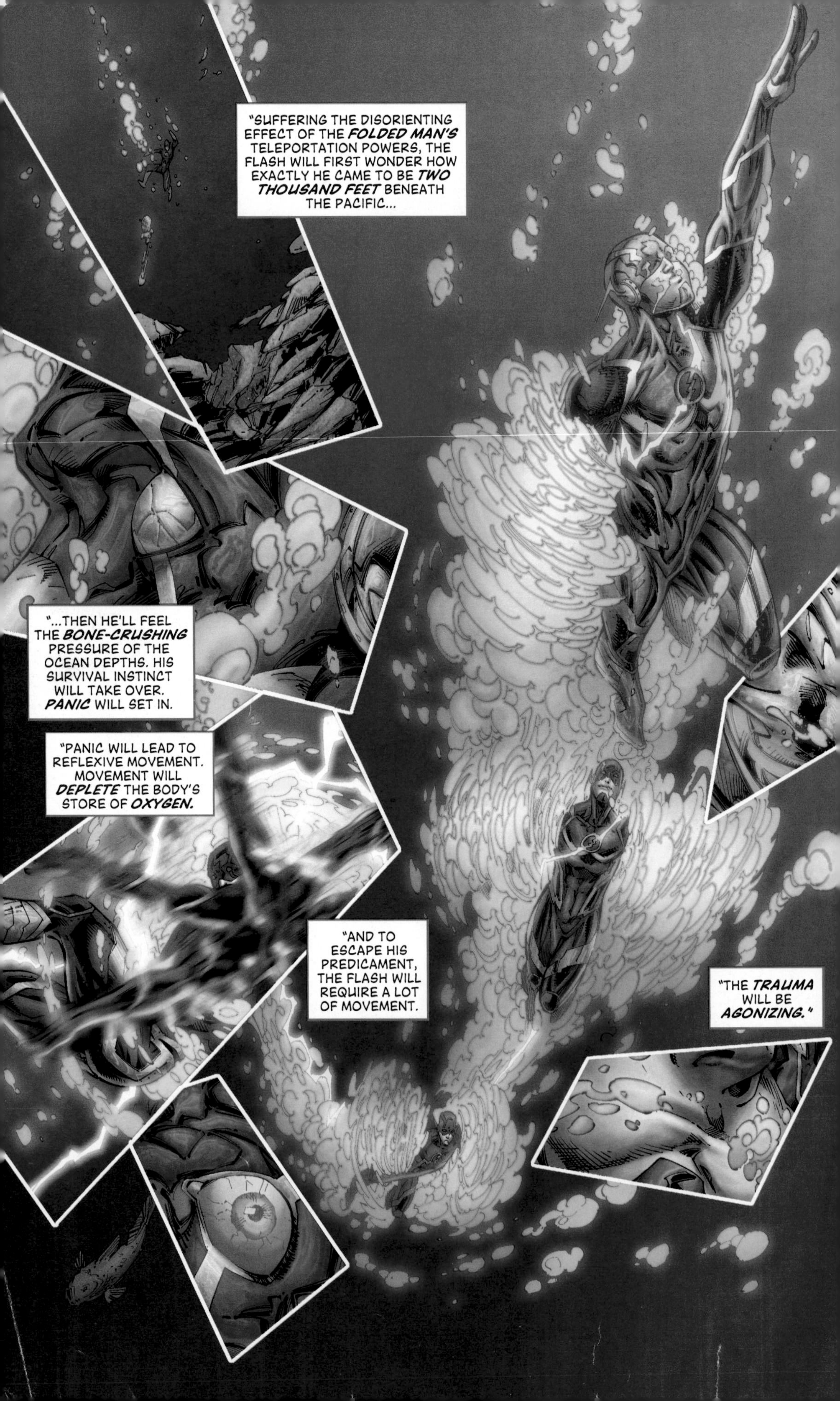
"SUFFERING THE DISORIENTING EFFECT OF THE *FOLDED MAN'S* TELEPORTATION POWERS, THE FLASH WILL FIRST WONDER HOW EXACTLY HE CAME TO BE *TWO THOUSAND FEET* BENEATH THE PACIFIC...
"...THEN HE'LL FEEL THE *BONE-CRUSHING* PRESSURE OF THE OCEAN DEPTHS. HIS SURVIVAL INSTINCT WILL TAKE OVER. *PANIC* WILL SET IN.
"PANIC WILL LEAD TO REFLEXIVE MOVEMENT. MOVEMENT WILL *DEPLETE* THE BODY'S STORE OF *OXYGEN.*
"AND TO ESCAPE HIS PREDICAMENT, THE FLASH WILL REQUIRE A LOT OF MOVEMENT.
"THE *TRAUMA* WILL BE *AGONIZING.*"

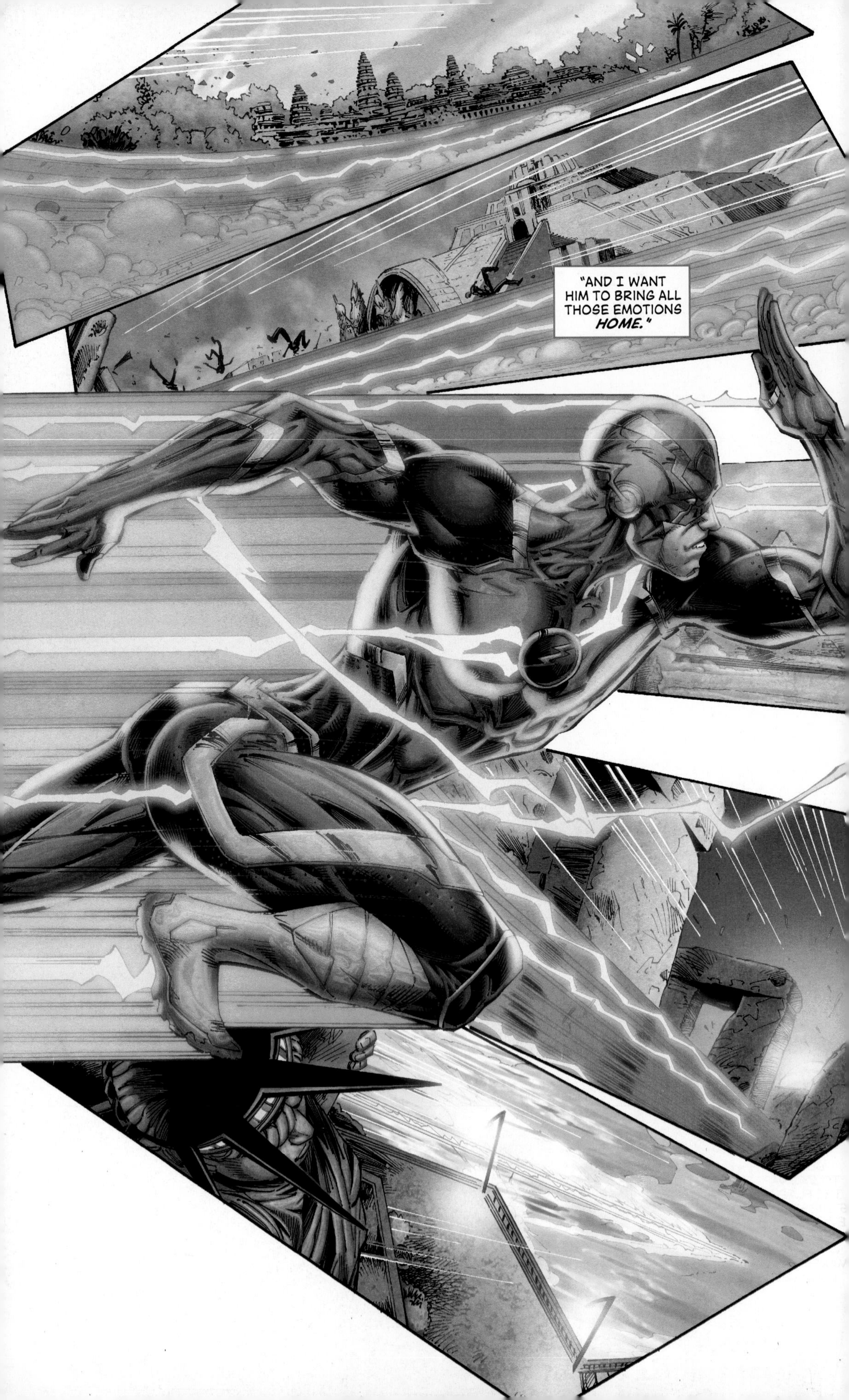
"AND I WANT HIM TO BRING ALL THOSE EMOTIONS *HOME.*"

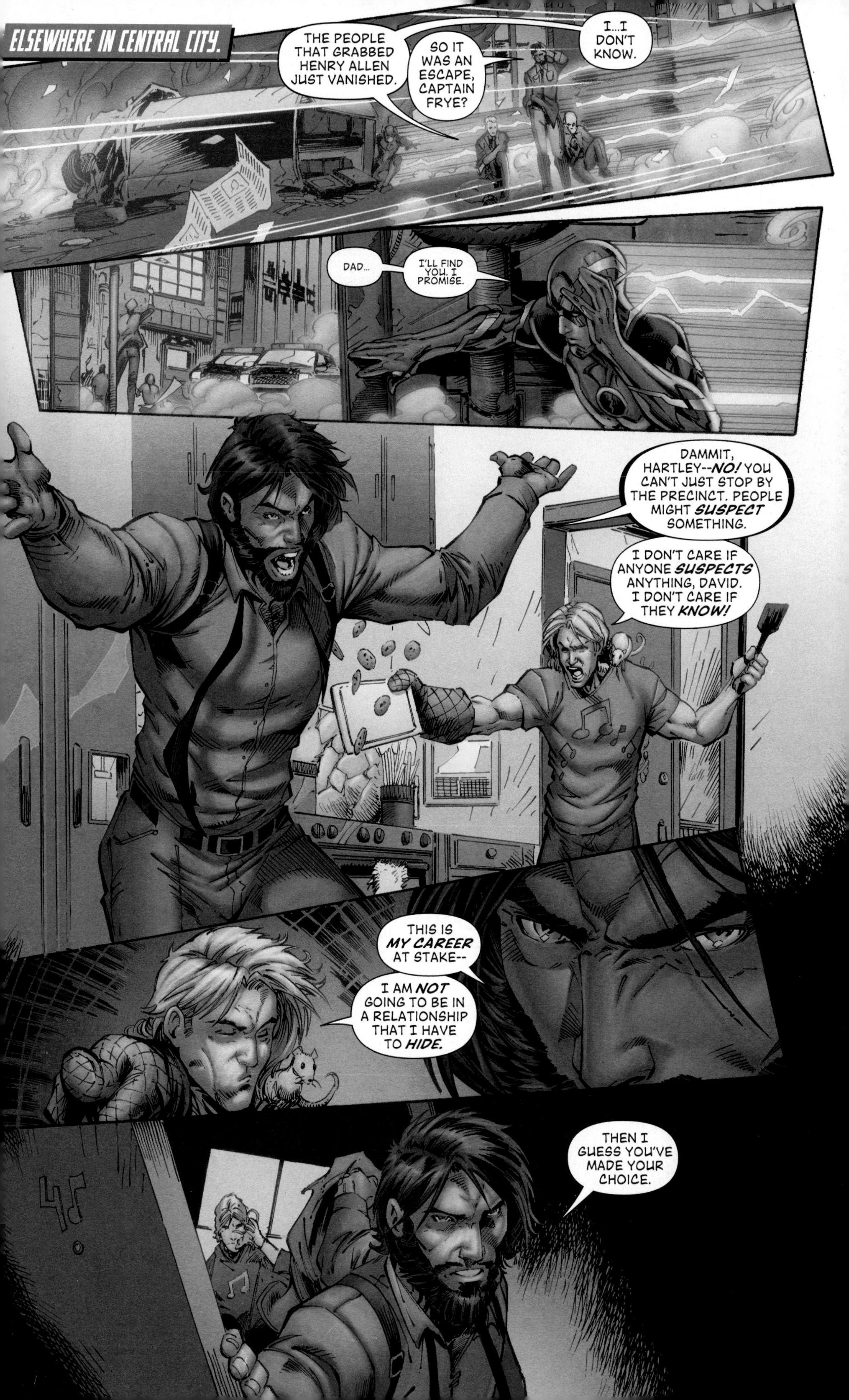
ELSEWHERE IN CENTRAL CITY.
THE PEOPLE THAT GRABBED HENRY ALLEN JUST VANISHED.
SO IT WAS AN ESCAPE, CAPTAIN FRYE?
I...I DON'T KNOW.
DAD...
I'LL FIND YOU. I PROMISE.
DAMMIT, HARTLEY--NO! YOU CAN'T JUST STOP BY THE PRECINCT. PEOPLE MIGHT SUSPECT SOMETHING.
I DON'T CARE IF ANYONE SUSPECTS ANYTHING, DAVID. I DON'T CARE IF THEY KNOW!
THIS IS MY CAREER AT STAKE--
I AM NOT GOING TO BE IN A RELATIONSHIP THAT I HAVE TO HIDE.
THEN I GUESS YOU'VE MADE YOUR CHOICE.

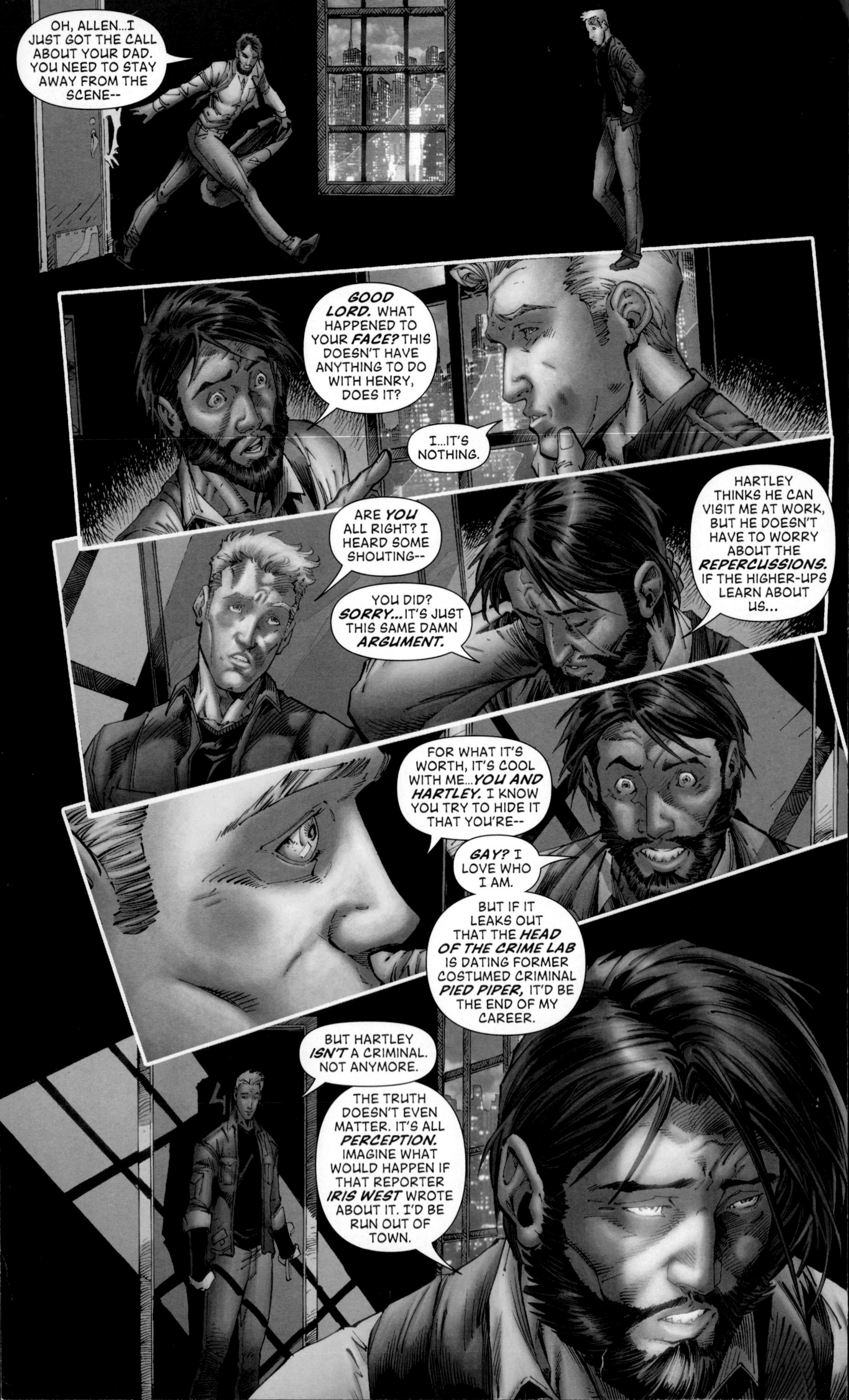
OH, ALLEN...I JUST GOT THE CALL ABOUT YOUR DAD. YOU NEED TO STAY AWAY FROM THE SCENE--
GOOD LORD. WHAT HAPPENED TO YOUR FACE? THIS DOESN'T HAVE ANYTHING TO DO WITH HENRY, DOES IT?
I...IT'S NOTHING.
ARE YOU ALL RIGHT? I HEARD SOME SHOUTING--
YOU DID? SORRY...IT'S JUST THIS SAME DAMN ARGUMENT.
HARTLEY THINKS HE CAN VISIT ME AT WORK, BUT HE DOESN'T HAVE TO WORRY ABOUT THE REPERCUSSIONS. IF THE HIGHER-UPS LEARN ABOUT US...
FOR WHAT IT'S WORTH, IT'S COOL WITH ME...YOU AND HARTLEY. I KNOW YOU TRY TO HIDE IT THAT YOU'RE--
GAY? I LOVE WHO I AM.
BUT IF IT LEAKS OUT THAT THE HEAD OF THE CRIME LAB IS DATING FORMER COSTUMED CRIMINAL PIED PIPER, IT'D BE THE END OF MY CAREER.
BUT HARTLEY ISN'T A CRIMINAL. NOT ANYMORE.
THE TRUTH DOESN'T EVEN MATTER. IT'S ALL PERCEPTION. IMAGINE WHAT WOULD HAPPEN IF THAT REPORTER IRIS WEST WROTE ABOUT IT. I'D BE RUN OUT OF TOWN.

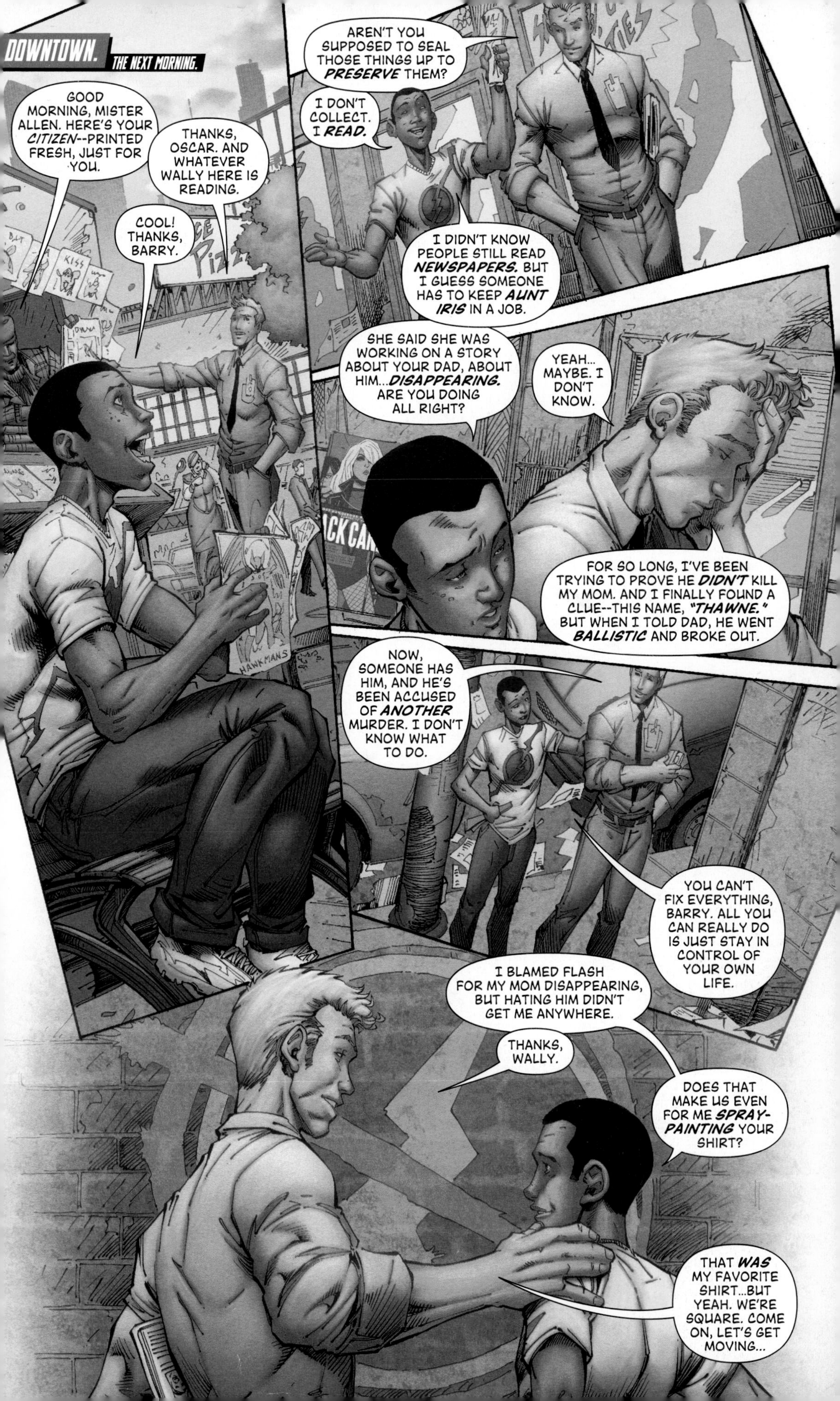
DOWNTOWN.
THE NEXT MORNING.
GOOD MORNING, MISTER ALLEN. HERE'S YOUR CITIZEN--PRINTED FRESH, JUST FOR YOU.
THANKS, OSCAR. AND WHATEVER WALLY HERE IS READING.
COOL! THANKS, BARRY.
AREN'T YOU SUPPOSED TO SEAL THOSE THINGS UP TO PRESERVE THEM?
I DON'T COLLECT. I READ.
I DIDN'T KNOW PEOPLE STILL READ NEWSPAPERS. BUT I GUESS SOMEONE HAS TO KEEP AUNT IRIS IN A JOB.
SHE SAID SHE WAS WORKING ON A STORY ABOUT YOUR DAD, ABOUT HIM...DISAPPEARING. ARE YOU DOING ALL RIGHT?
YEAH... MAYBE. I DON'T KNOW.
FOR SO LONG, I'VE BEEN TRYING TO PROVE HE DIDN'T KILL MY MOM. AND I FINALLY FOUND A CLUE--THIS NAME, "THAWNE." BUT WHEN I TOLD DAD, HE WENT BALLISTIC AND BROKE OUT.
NOW, SOMEONE HAS HIM, AND HE'S BEEN ACCUSED OF ANOTHER MURDER. I DON'T KNOW WHAT TO DO.
YOU CAN'T FIX EVERYTHING, BARRY. ALL YOU CAN REALLY DO IS JUST STAY IN CONTROL OF YOUR OWN LIFE.
I BLAMED FLASH FOR MY MOM DISAPPEARING, BUT HATING HIM DIDN'T GET ME ANYWHERE.
THANKS, WALLY.
DOES THAT MAKE US EVEN FOR ME SPRAY-PAINTING YOUR SHIRT?
THAT WAS MY FAVORITE SHIRT...BUT YEAH. WE'RE SQUARE. COME ON, LET'S GET MOVING...

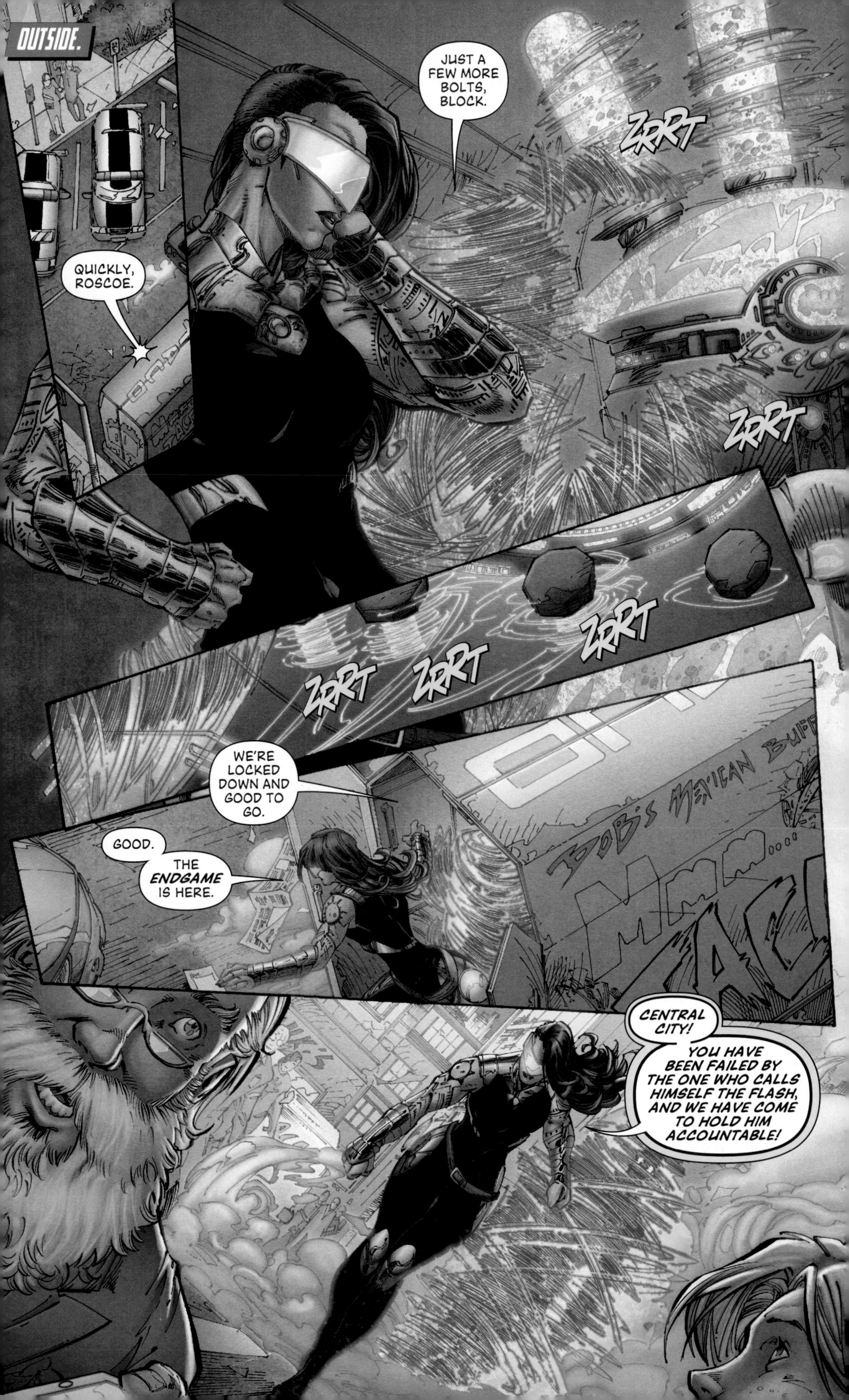
OUTSIDE.
JUST A FEW MORE BOLTS, BLOCK.
ZRRT
QUICKLY, ROSCOE.
ZRRT
ZRRT
ZRRT
ZRRT
WE'RE LOCKED DOWN AND GOOD TO GO.
BOB'S MEXICAN BUFF
GOOD.
THE *ENDGAME* IS HERE.
CENTRAL CITY!
YOU HAVE BEEN FAILED BY THE ONE WHO CALLS HIMSELF THE FLASH, AND WE HAVE COME TO HOLD HIM ACCOUNTABLE!

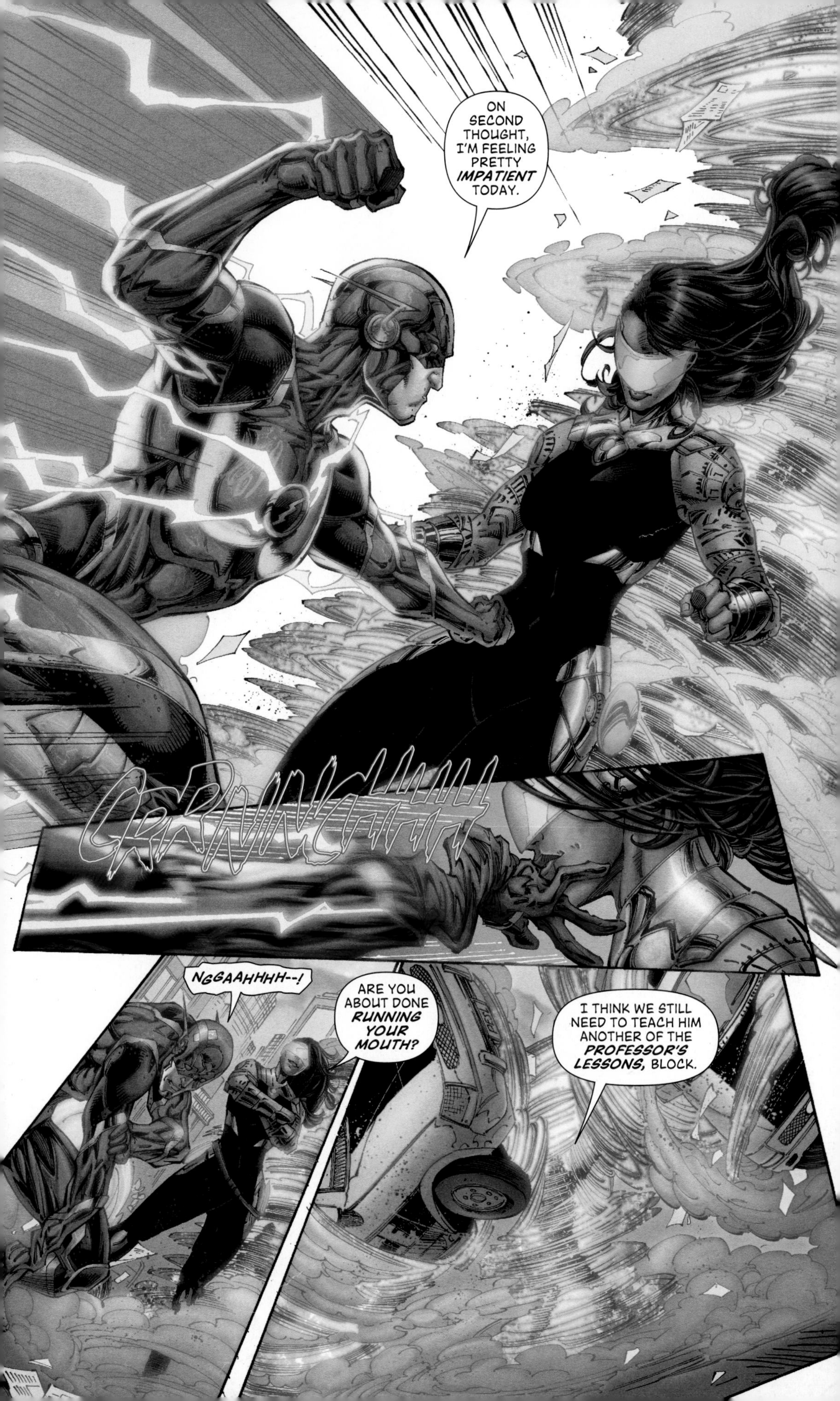
ON SECOND THOUGHT, I'M FEELING PRETTY *IMPATIENT* TODAY.
NGGAAHHHH--!
ARE YOU ABOUT DONE *RUNNING YOUR MOUTH?*
I THINK WE STILL NEED TO TEACH HIM ANOTHER OF THE *PROFESSOR'S LESSONS,* BLOCK.

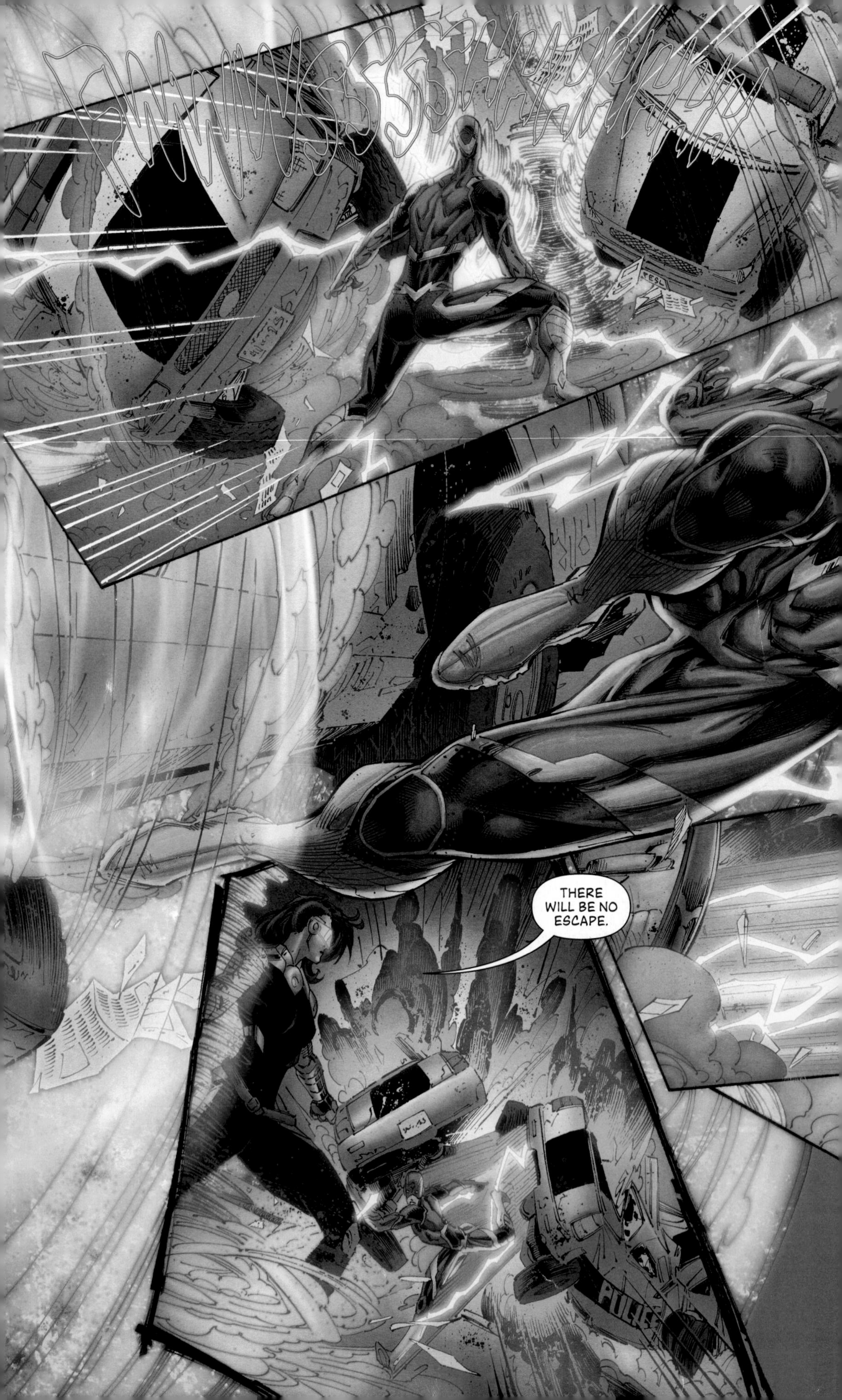
THERE WILL BE NO ESCAPE.

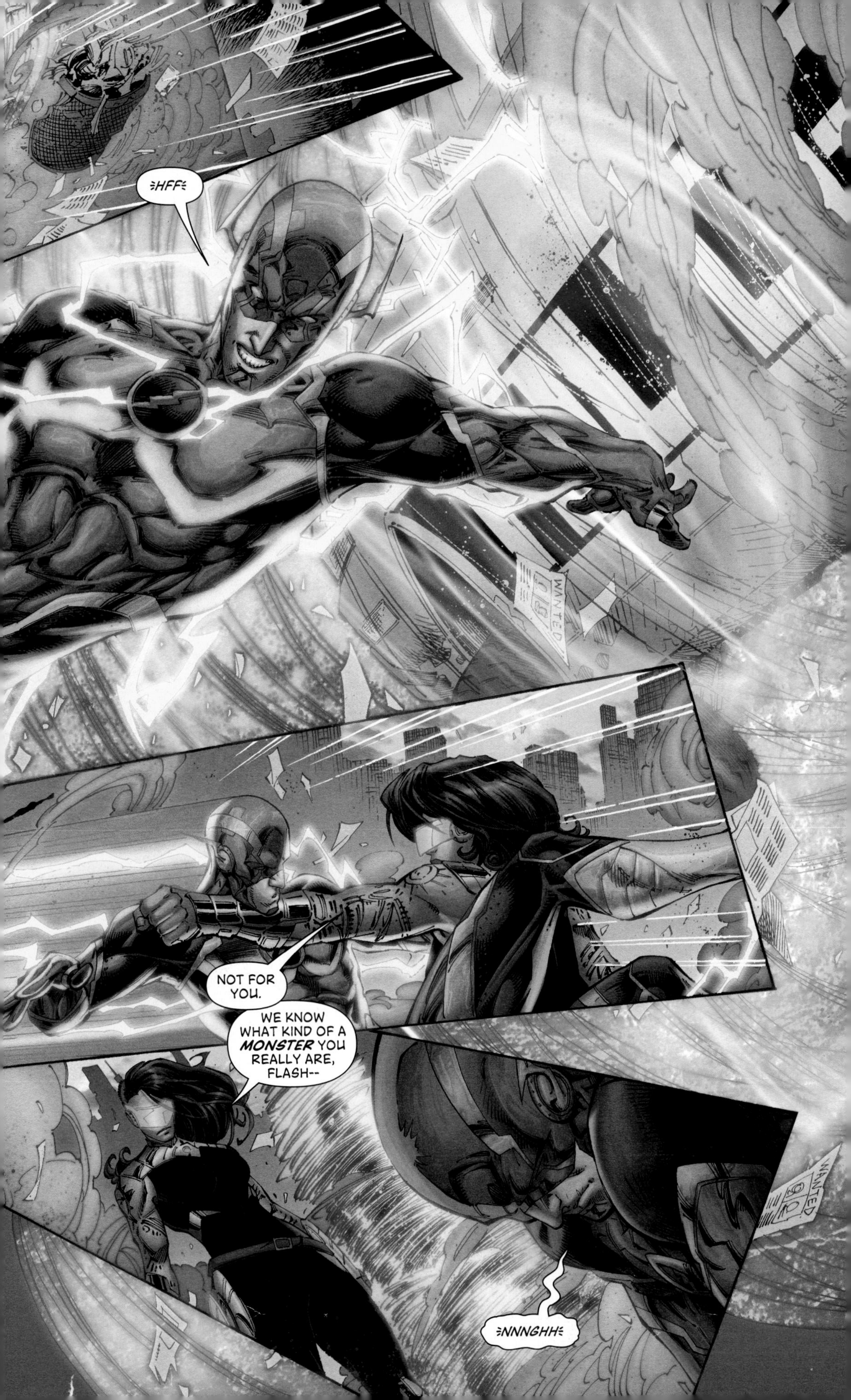
HFF
NOT FOR YOU.
WE KNOW WHAT KIND OF A MONSTER YOU REALLY ARE, FLASH--
NNNGHH
WANTED

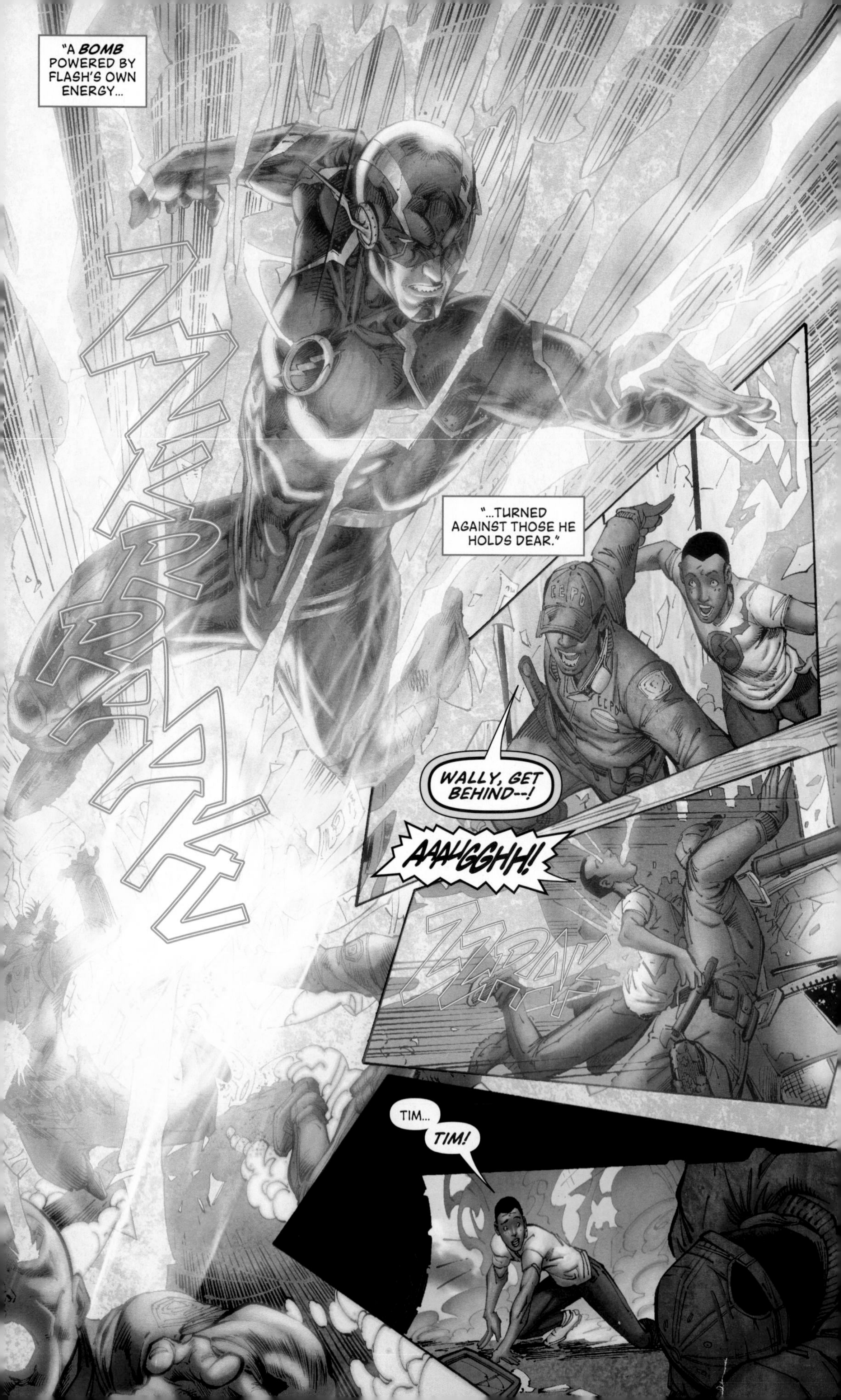
"A BOMB POWERED BY FLASH'S OWN ENERGY...
"...TURNED AGAINST THOSE HE HOLDS DEAR."
WALLY, GET BEHIND--!
AAAUGGHH!
TIM...
TIM!

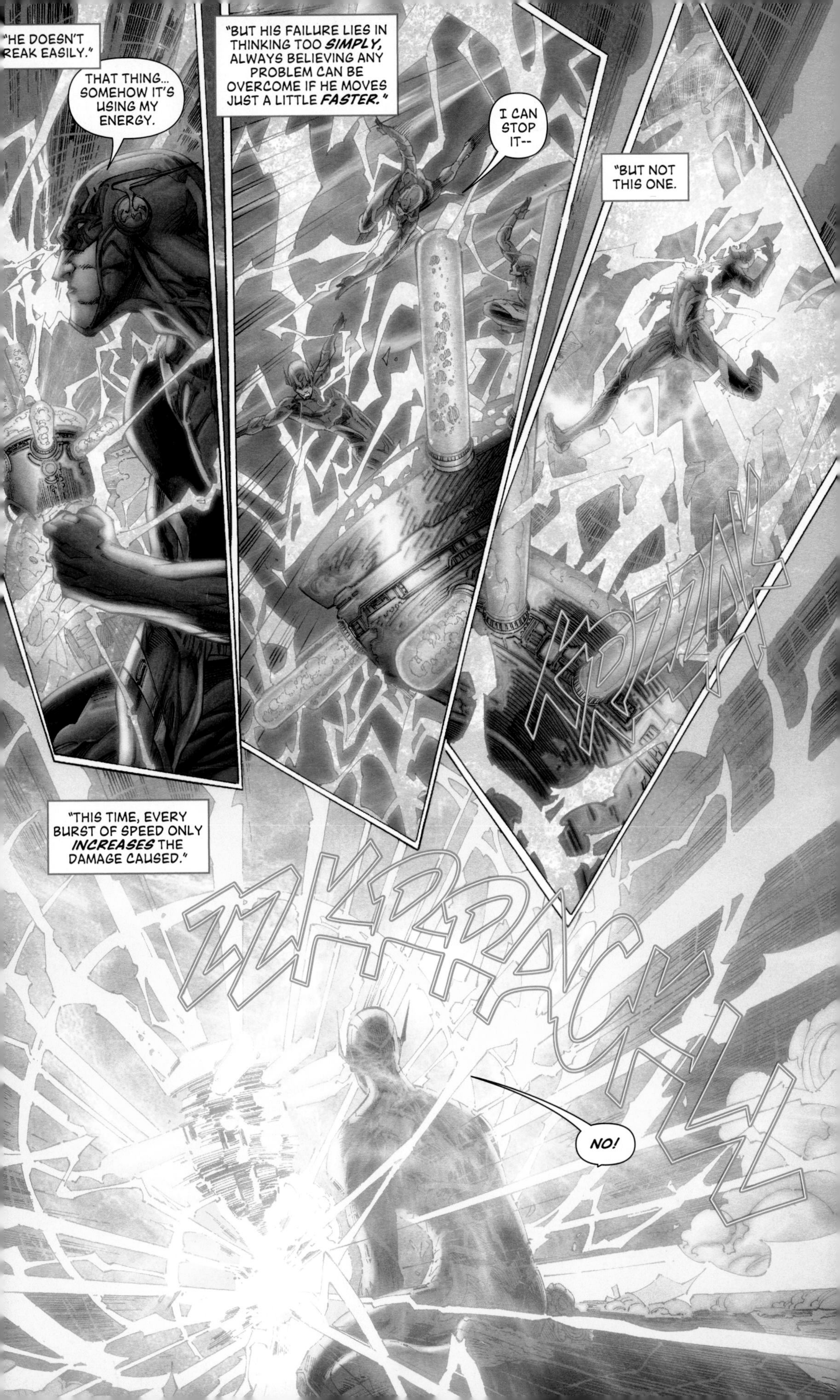
"HE DOESN'T
REAK EASILY."
THAT THING... SOMEHOW IT'S USING MY ENERGY.
"BUT HIS FAILURE LIES IN THINKING TOO SIMPLY, ALWAYS BELIEVING ANY PROBLEM CAN BE OVERCOME IF HE MOVES JUST A LITTLE FASTER."
I CAN STOP IT--
"BUT NOT THIS ONE.
KRZZAK
"THIS TIME, EVERY BURST OF SPEED ONLY INCREASES THE DAMAGE CAUSED."
ZZKRRACKL
NO!

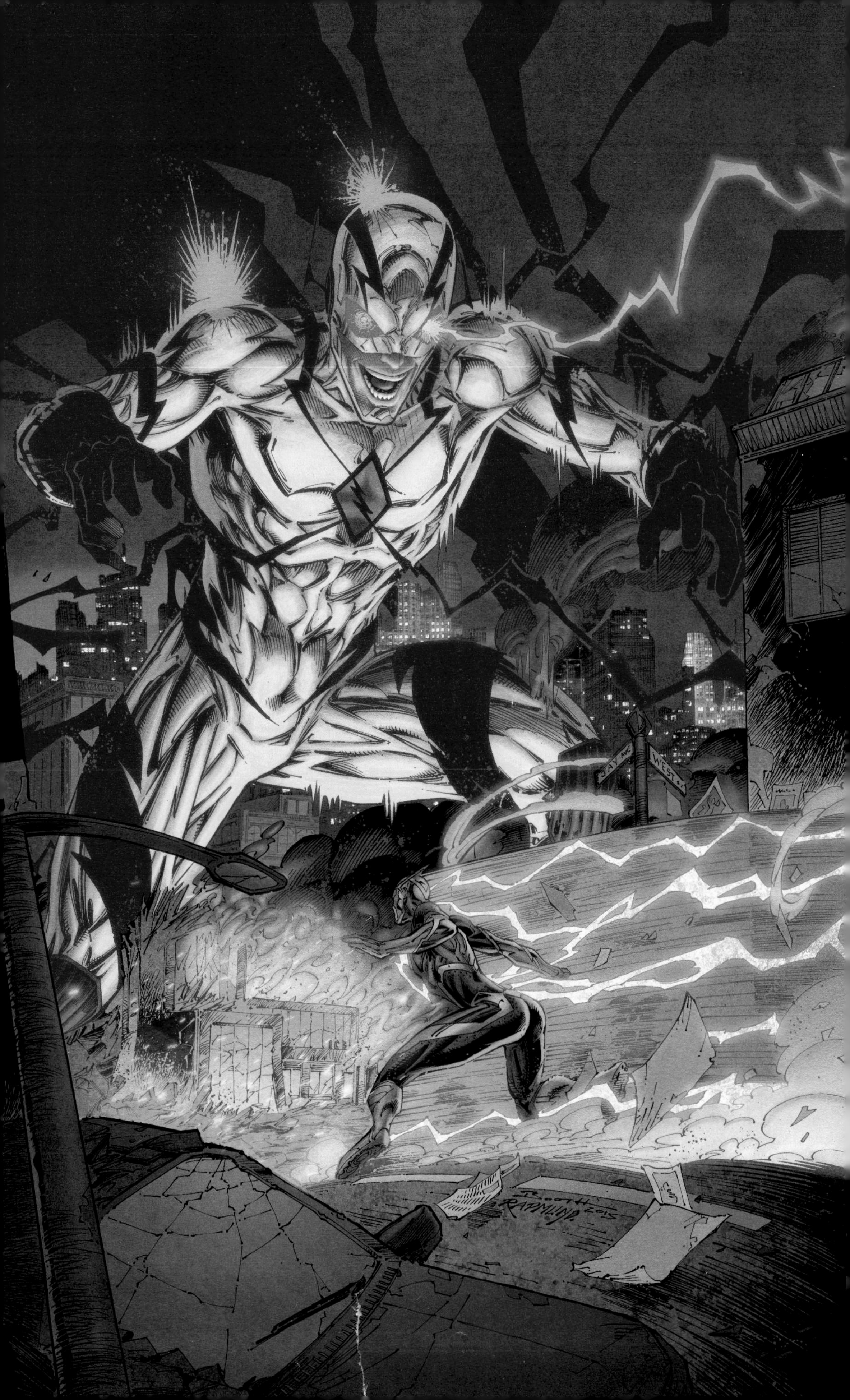
JAY AVE
WEST ST.
BOOTH
RAPMUND 2015

THUNDERDOME

ROBERT VENDITTI, VAN JENSEN writers **BRETT BOOTH, VICENTE CIFUENTES, ALÉ GARZA** pencillers **NORM RAPMUND** inker **ANDREW DALHOUSE** colorist **PAT BROSSEAU** letterer
cover by **BRETT BOOTH, NORM RAPMUND, ANDREW DALHOUSE**

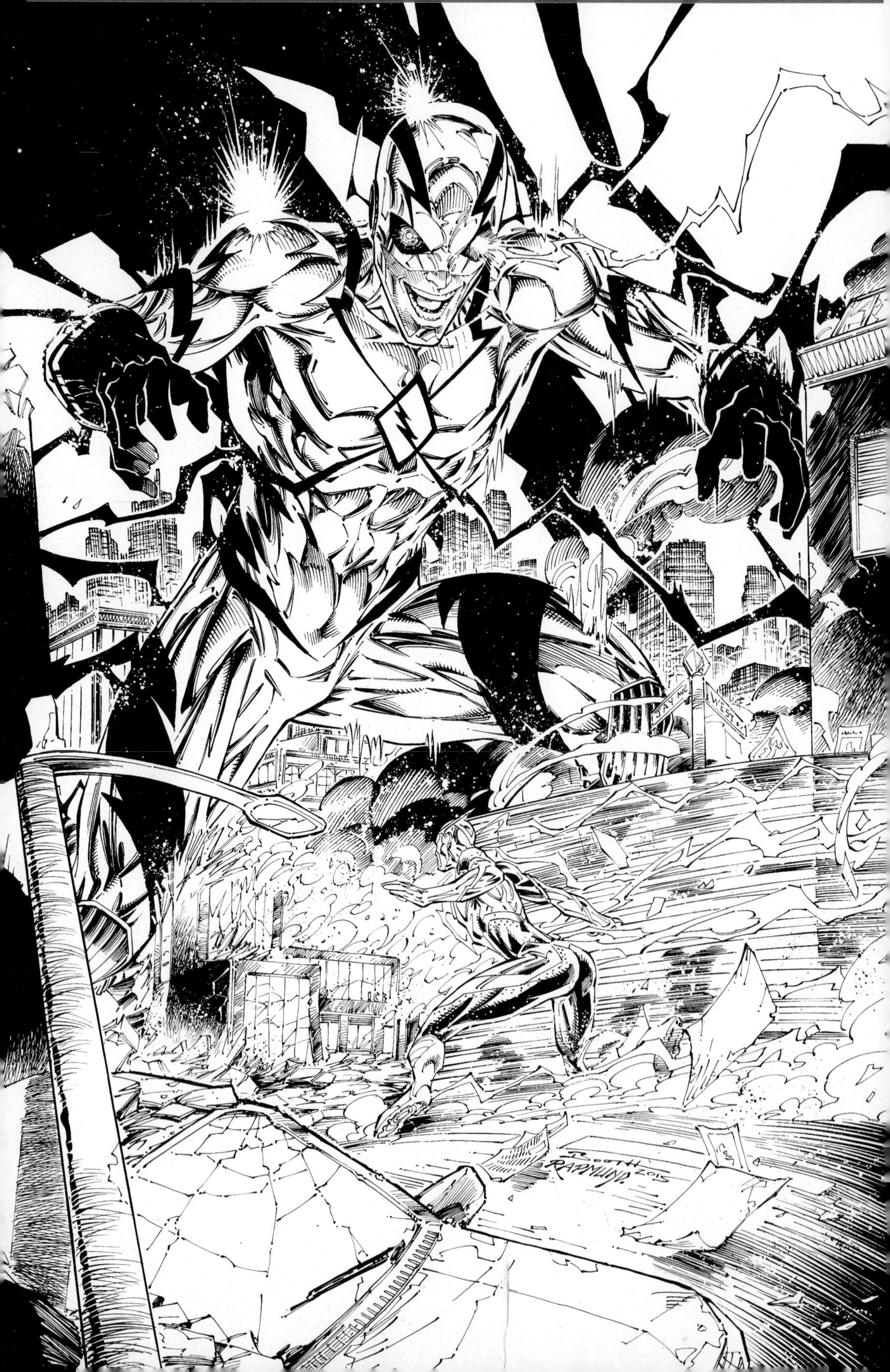
BOOTH
RAPMUND 2015

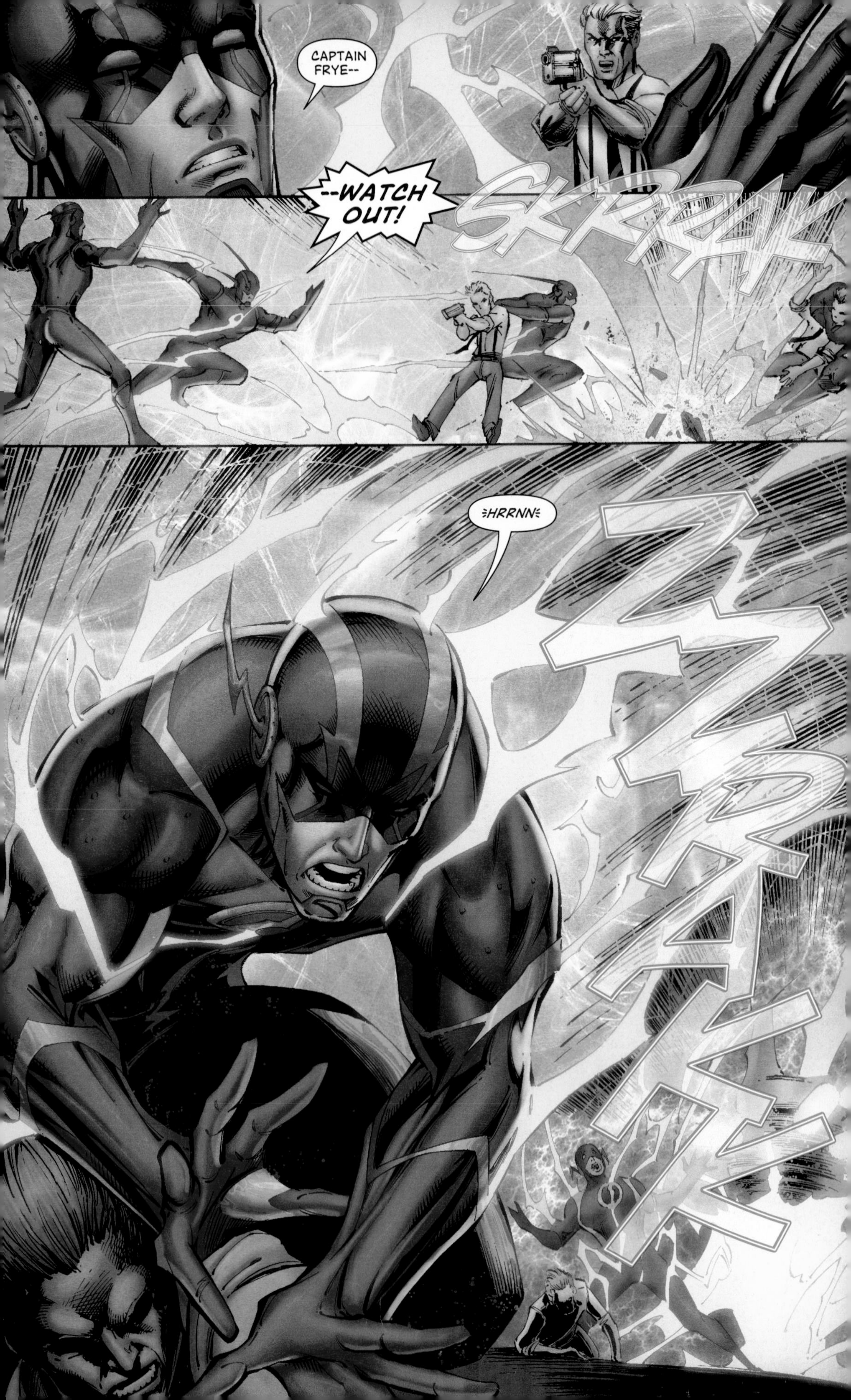
CAPTAIN FRYE--
--WATCH OUT!
SKRRAK
HRRNN

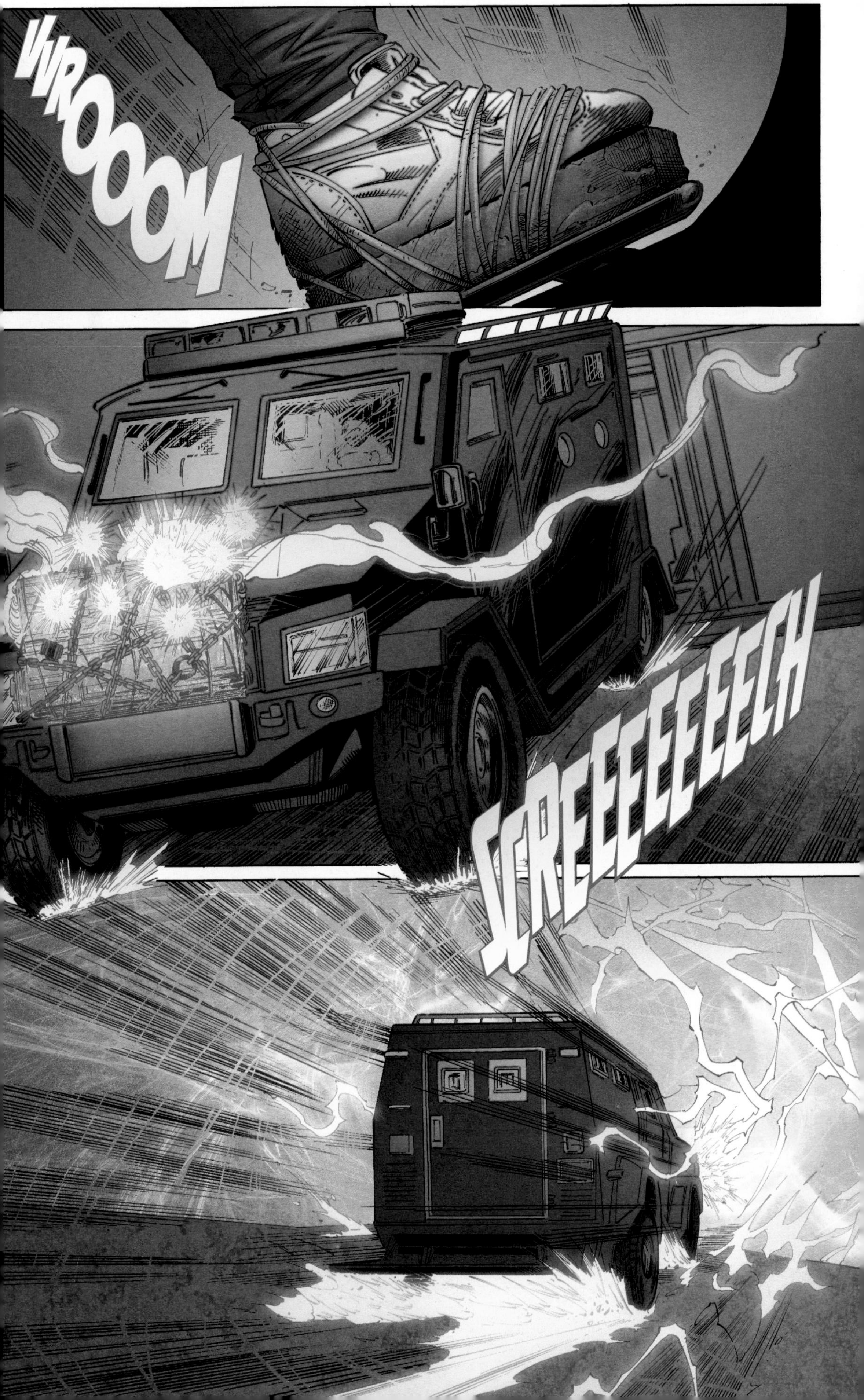
VVROOOM
SCREEEEEEECH

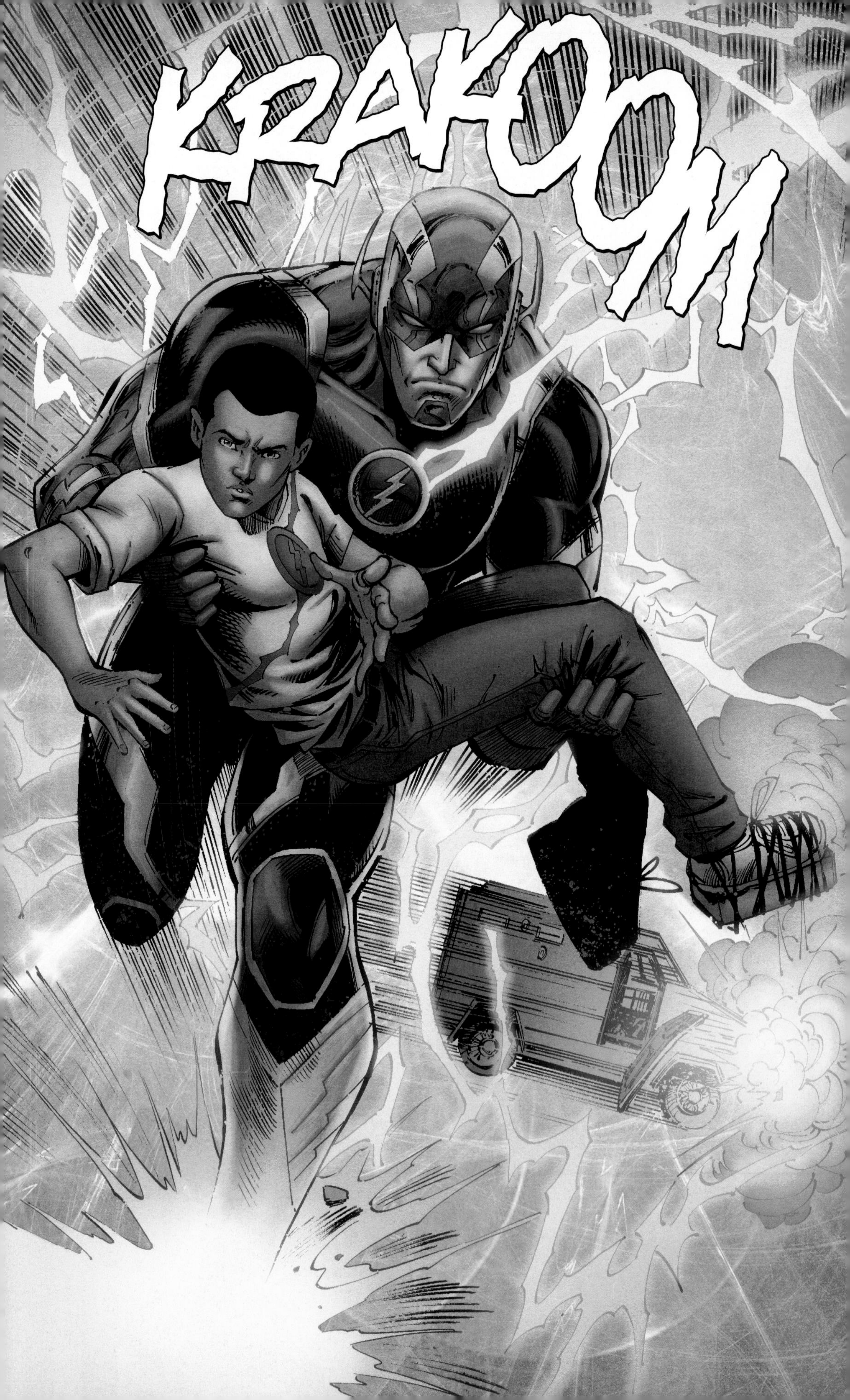
KRAKOOM

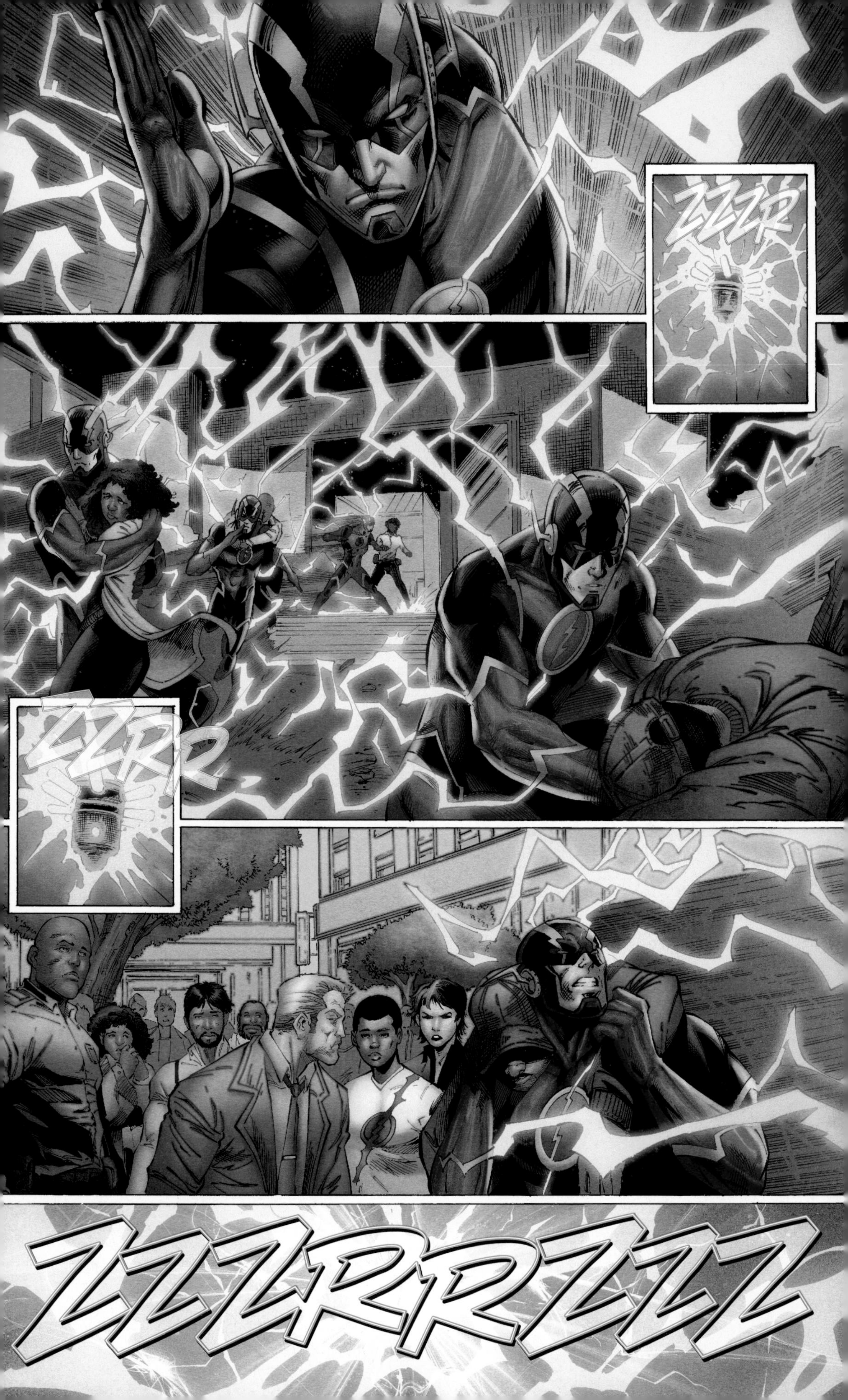
ZZZR
ZZRR
ZZZRRZZZ

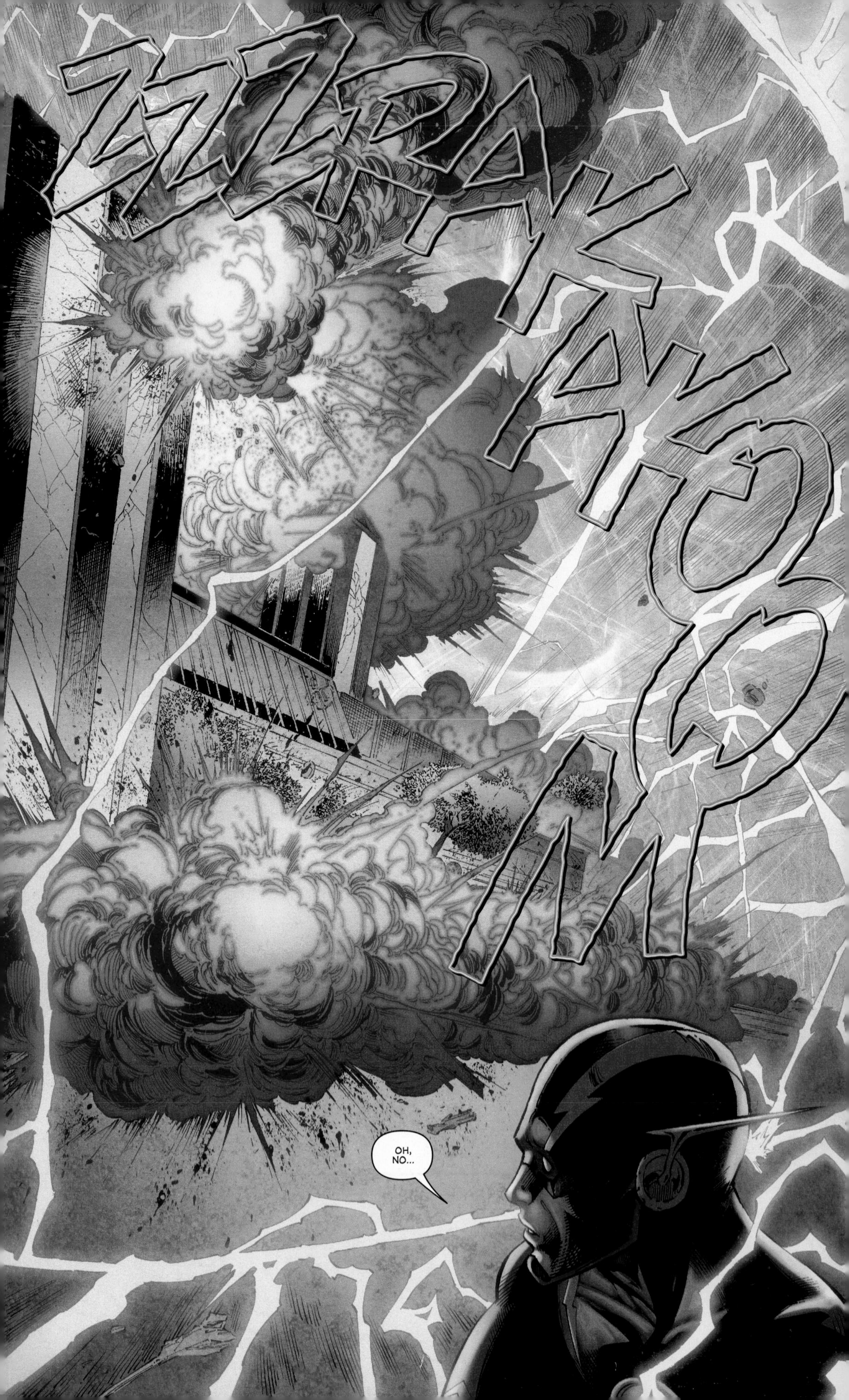
ZZZRAKATOOM
OH, NO...

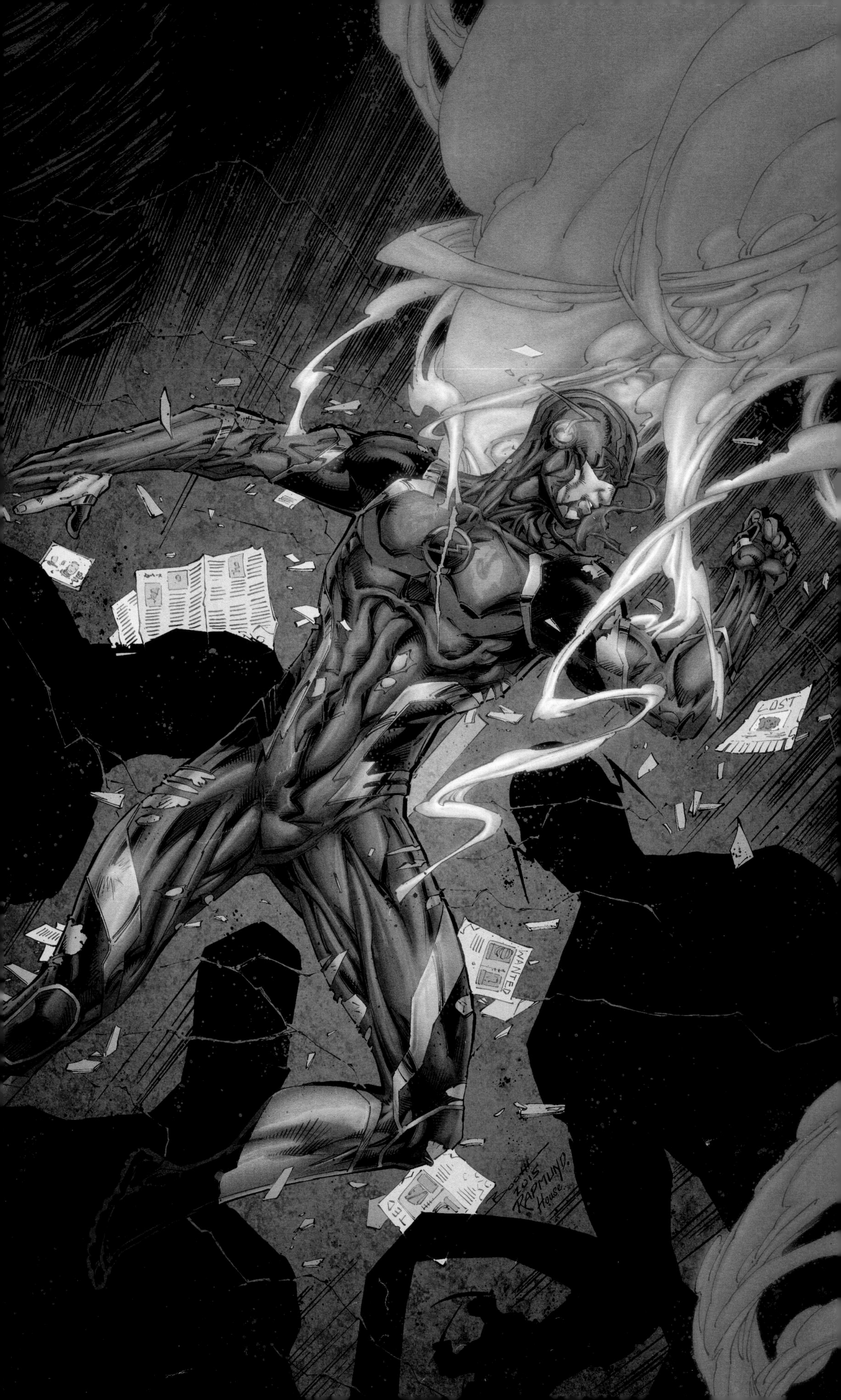
LOST
WANTED
BOOTH 2015 RAPMUND. House

END OF THE HUNT

ROBERT VENDITTI, VAN JENSEN writers BRETT BOOTH penciller NORM RAPMUND inker ANDREW DALHOUSE colorist PAT BROSSEAU letterer
cover by BRETT BOOTH, NORM RAPMUND, ANDREW DALHOUSE

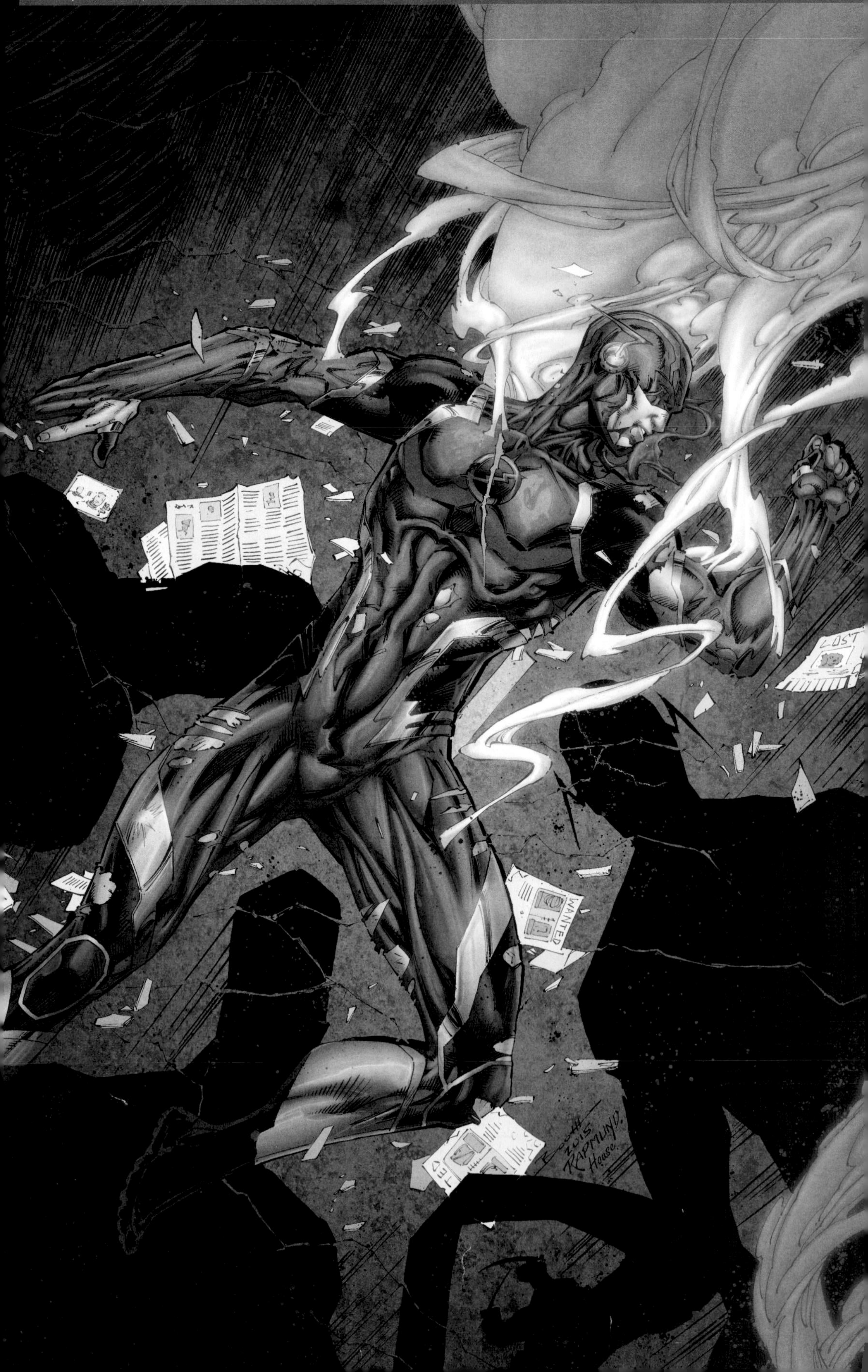
LOST
WANTED

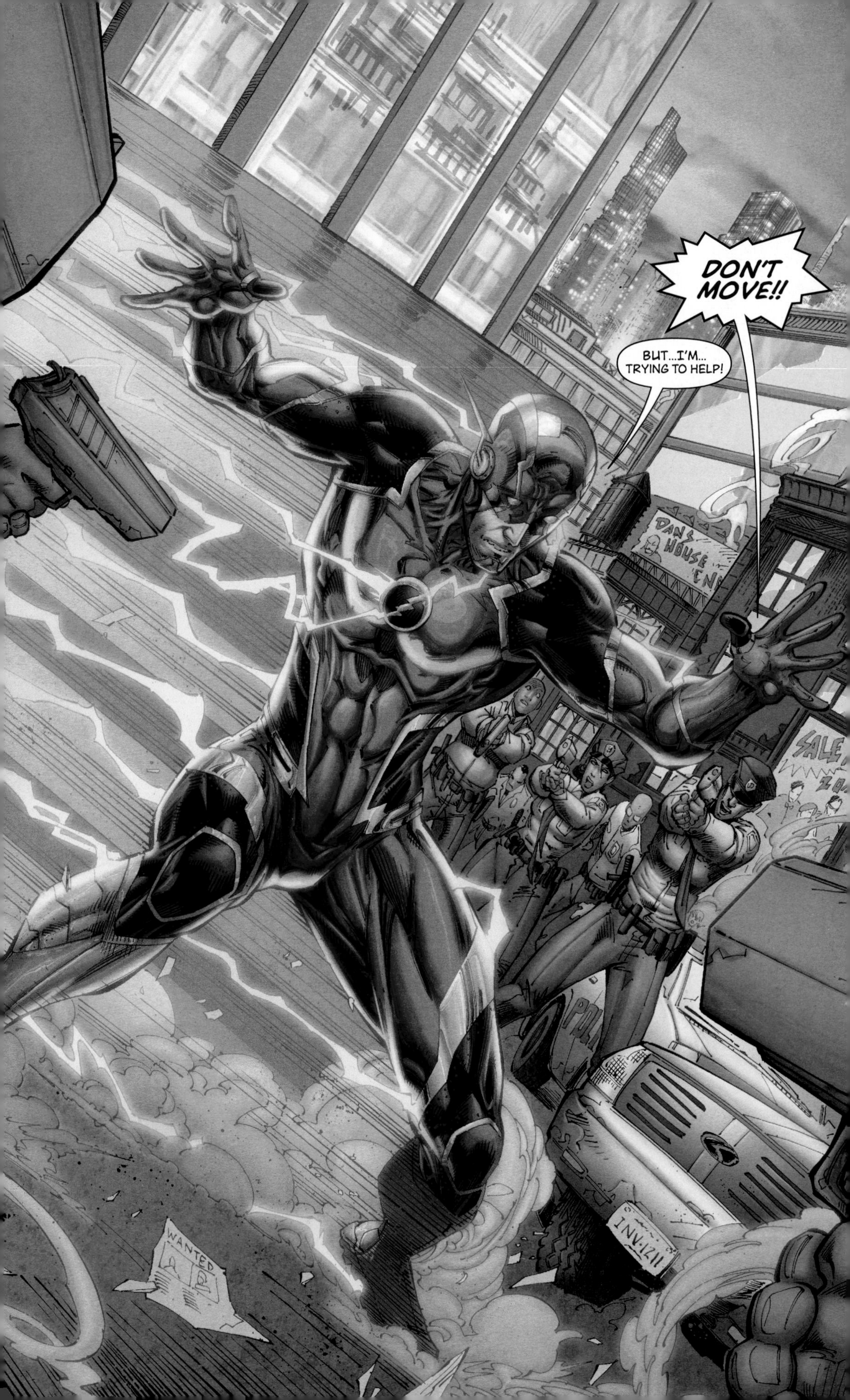
DON'T MOVE!!
BUT...I'M... TRYING TO HELP!
DAN'S HOUSE
SALE
WANTED
INV-1211

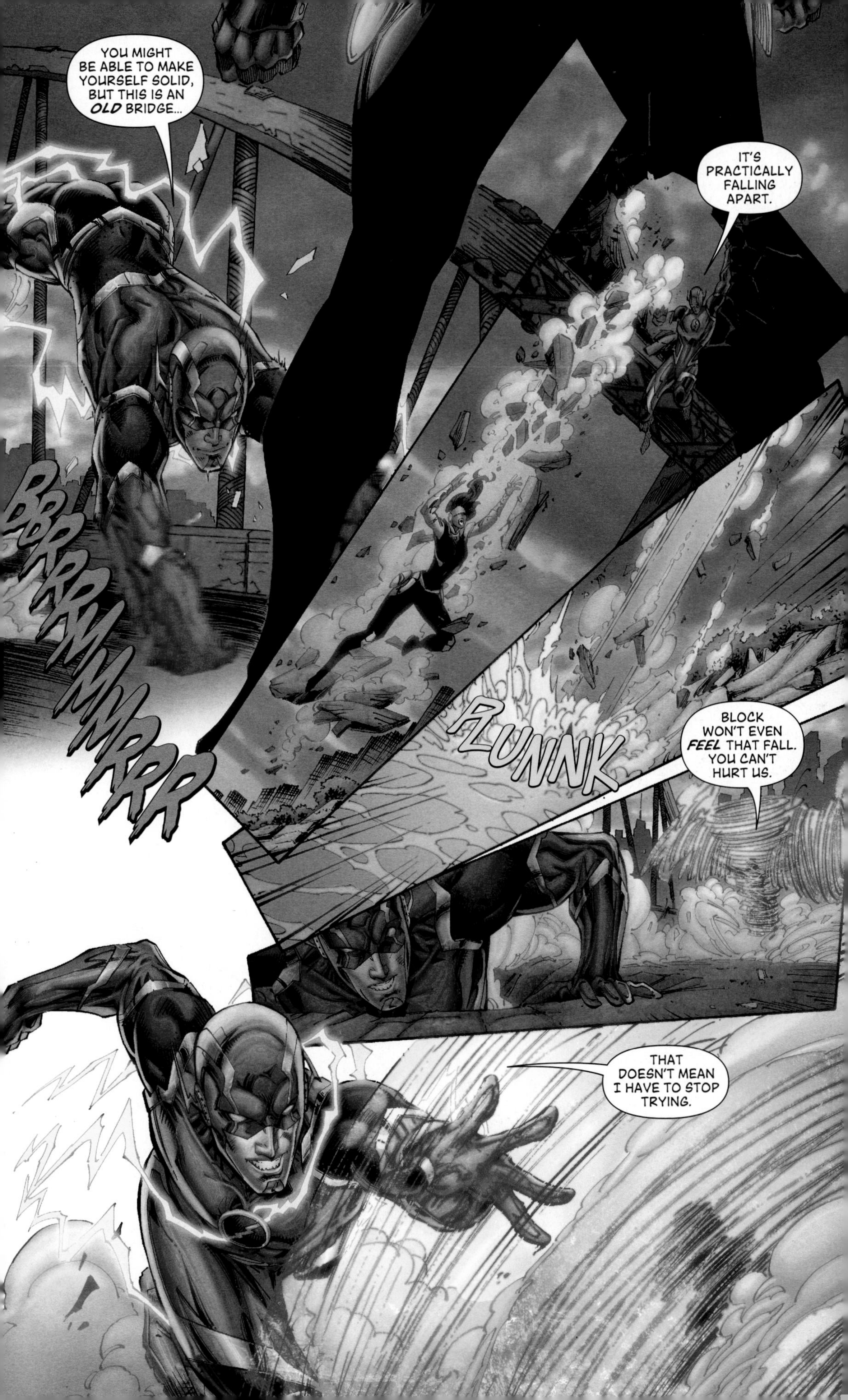
YOU MIGHT BE ABLE TO MAKE YOURSELF SOLID, BUT THIS IS AN OLD BRIDGE...
IT'S PRACTICALLY FALLING APART.
BBRRRMMMMRRR
FLUNNK
BLOCK WON'T EVEN FEEL THAT FALL. YOU CAN'T HURT US.
THAT DOESN'T MEAN I HAVE TO STOP TRYING.

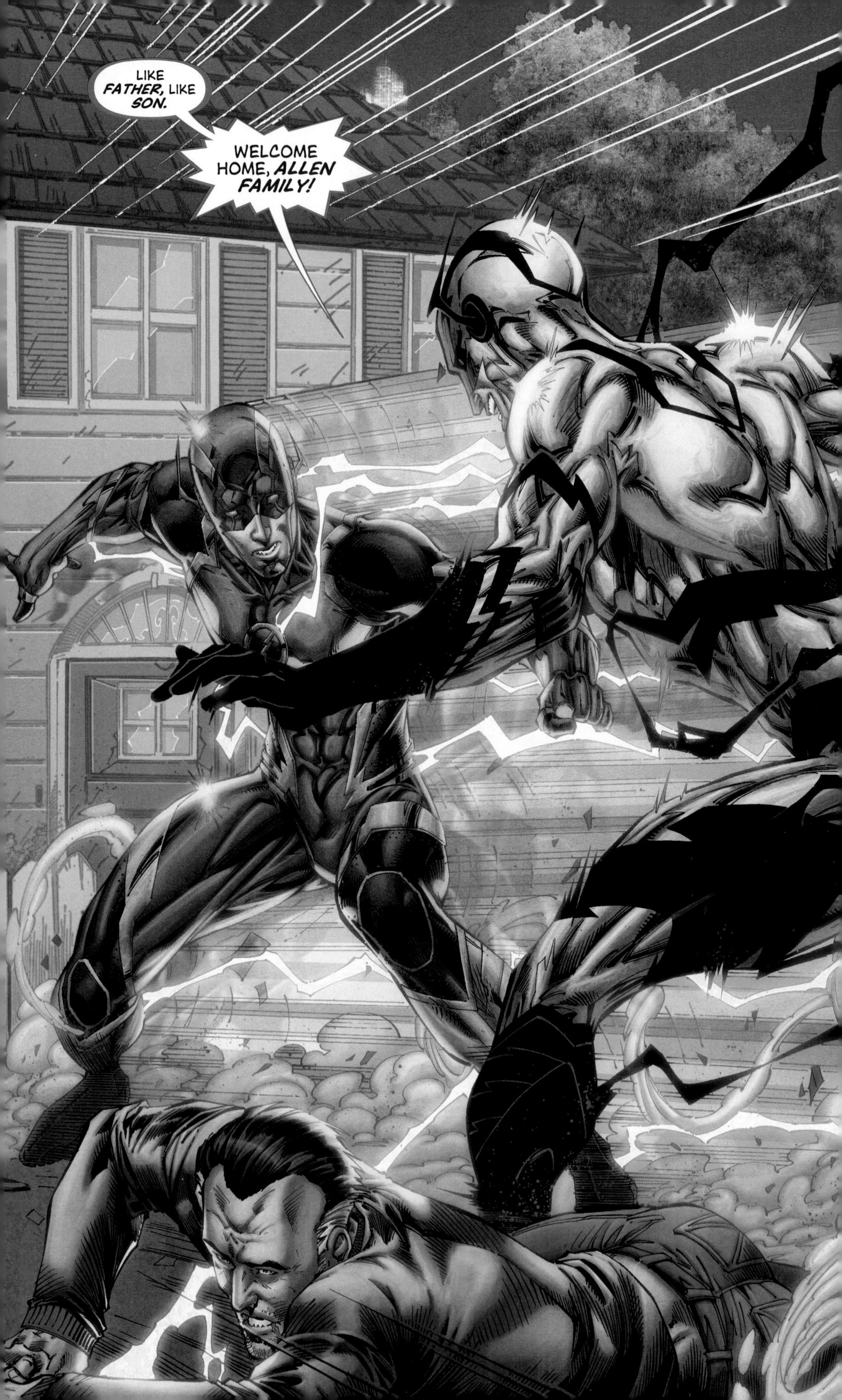
LIKE FATHER, LIKE SON.
WELCOME HOME, ALLEN FAMILY!

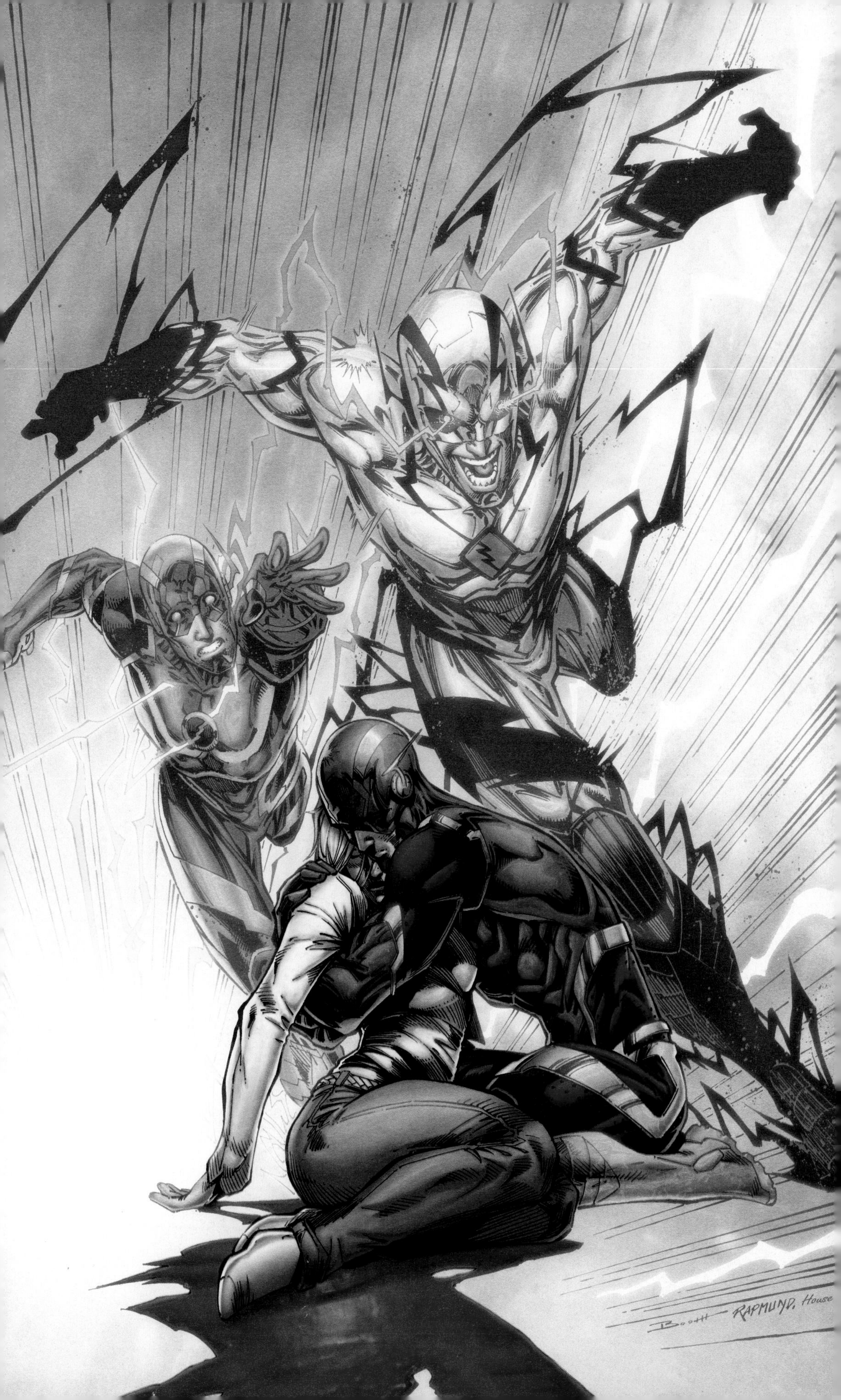
Booth
RAPMUND, House

REUNION

ROBERT VENDITTI, VAN JENSEN writers BRETT BOOTH penciller NORM RAPMUND inker ANDREW DALHOUSE, JEROMY COX colorists PAT BROSSEAU letterer
cover by BRETT BOOTH, NORM RAPMUND, ANDREW DALHOUSE

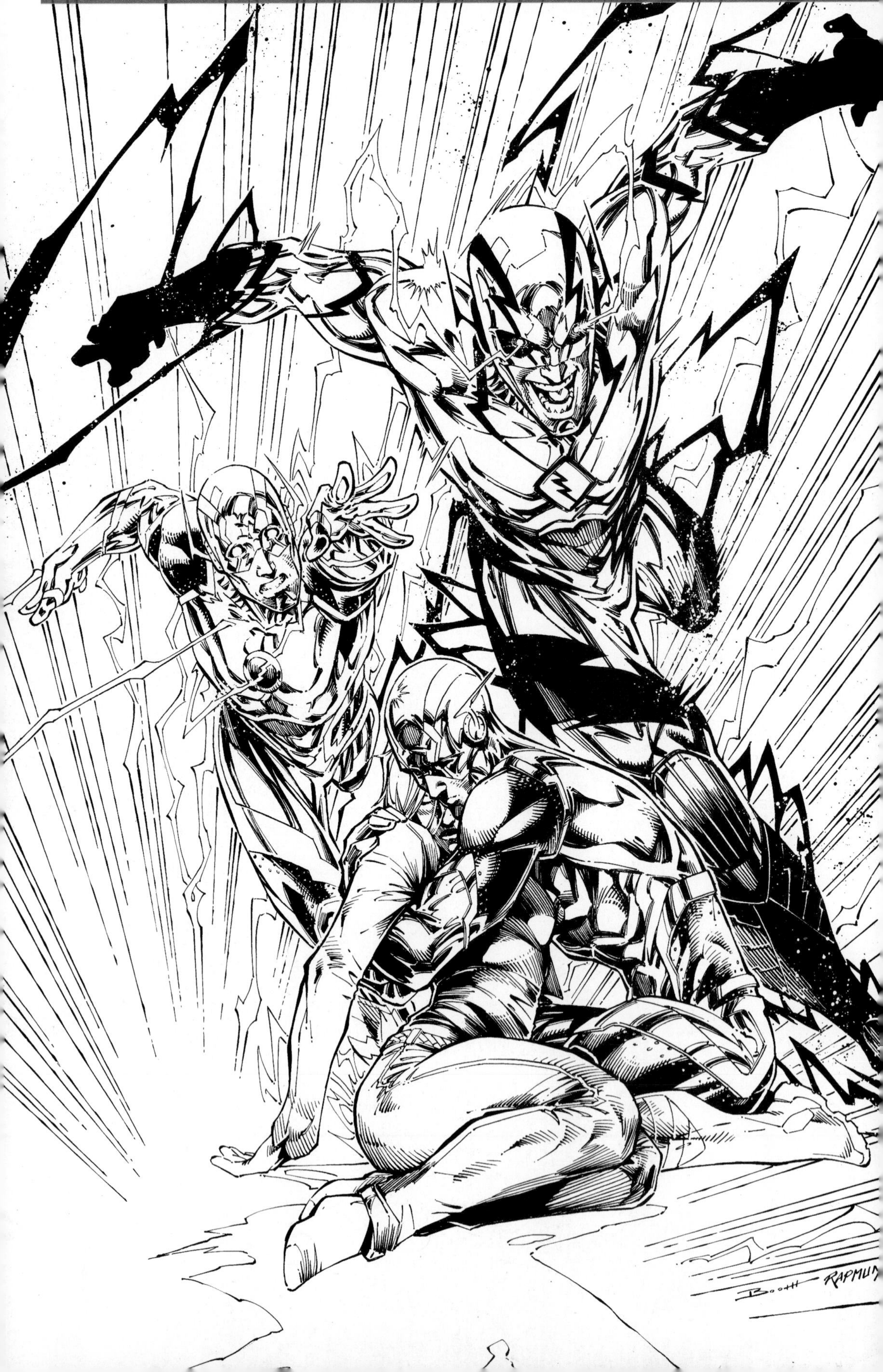

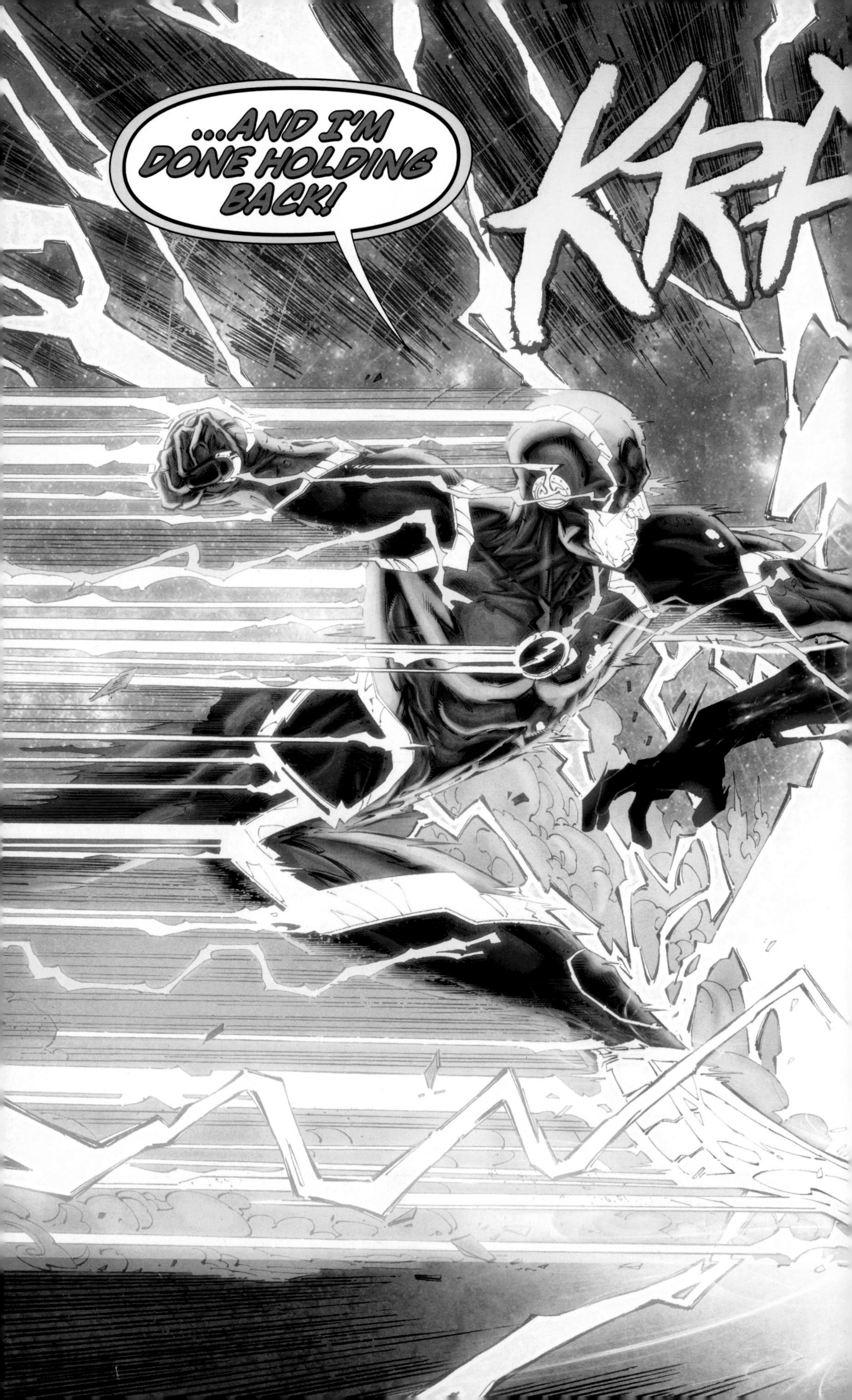
...AND I'M DONE HOLDING BACK!
KRA

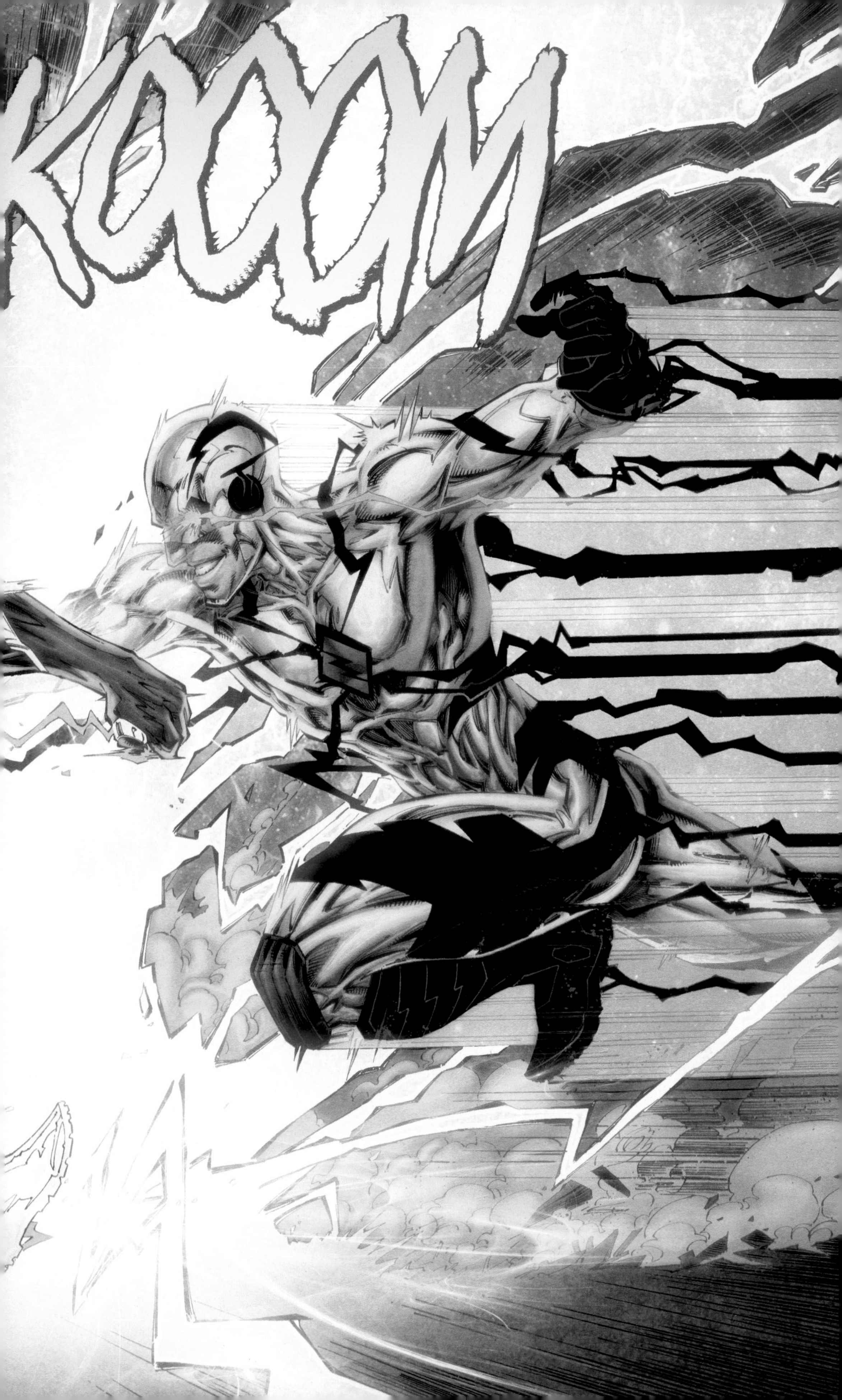
KOOM

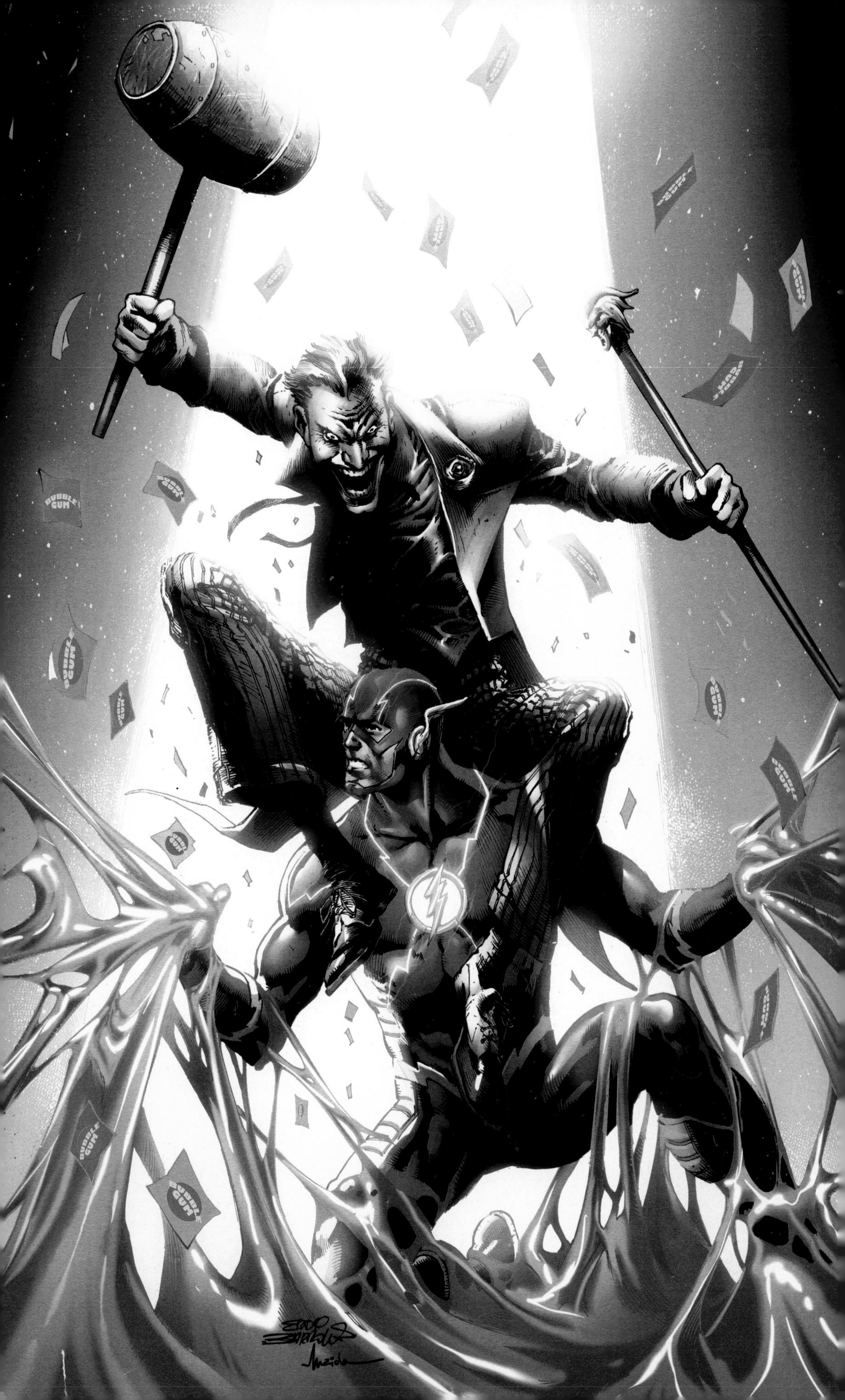
BUBBLE GUM
BUBBLE GUM
BUBBLE GUM

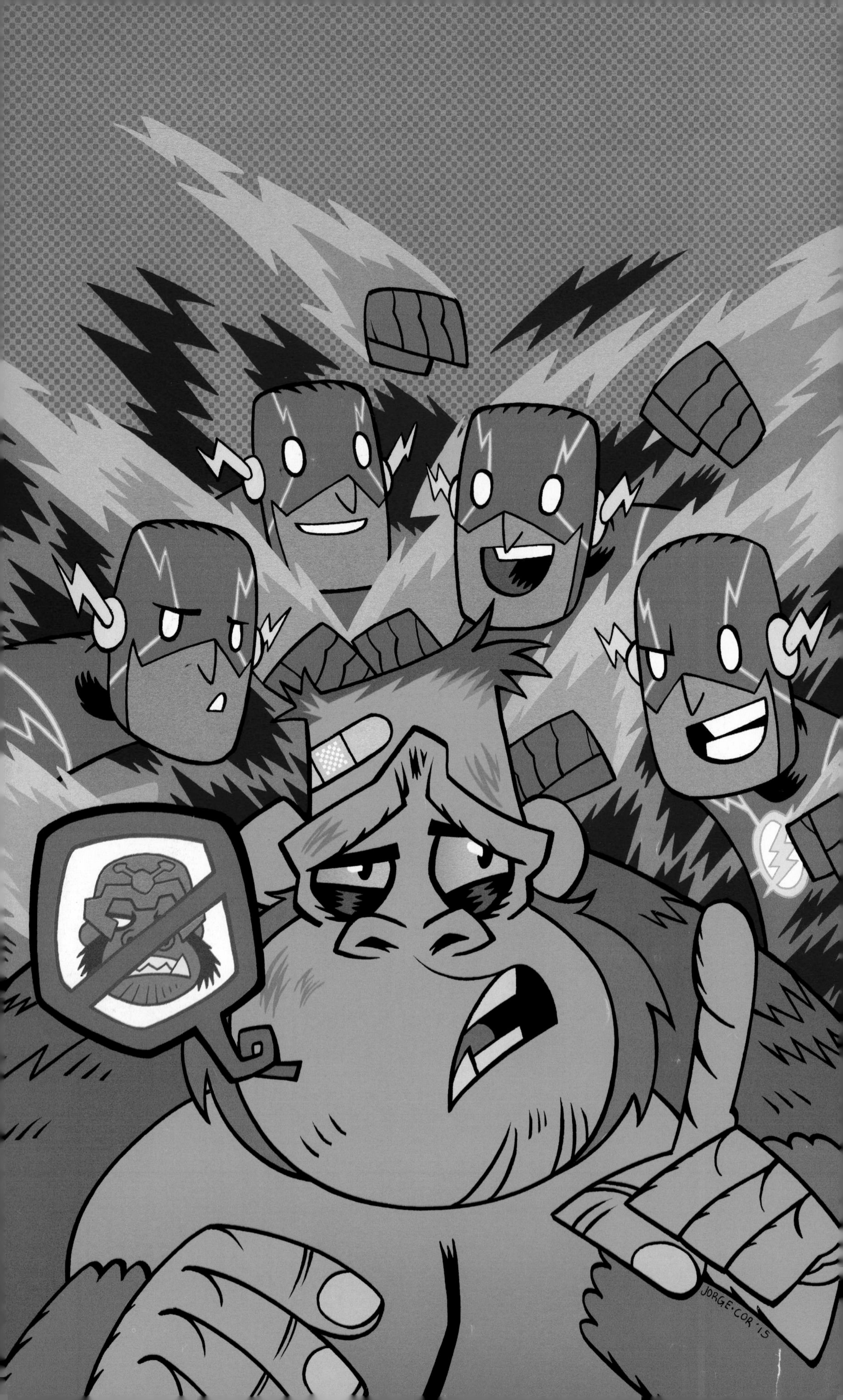
JORGE·COR '15

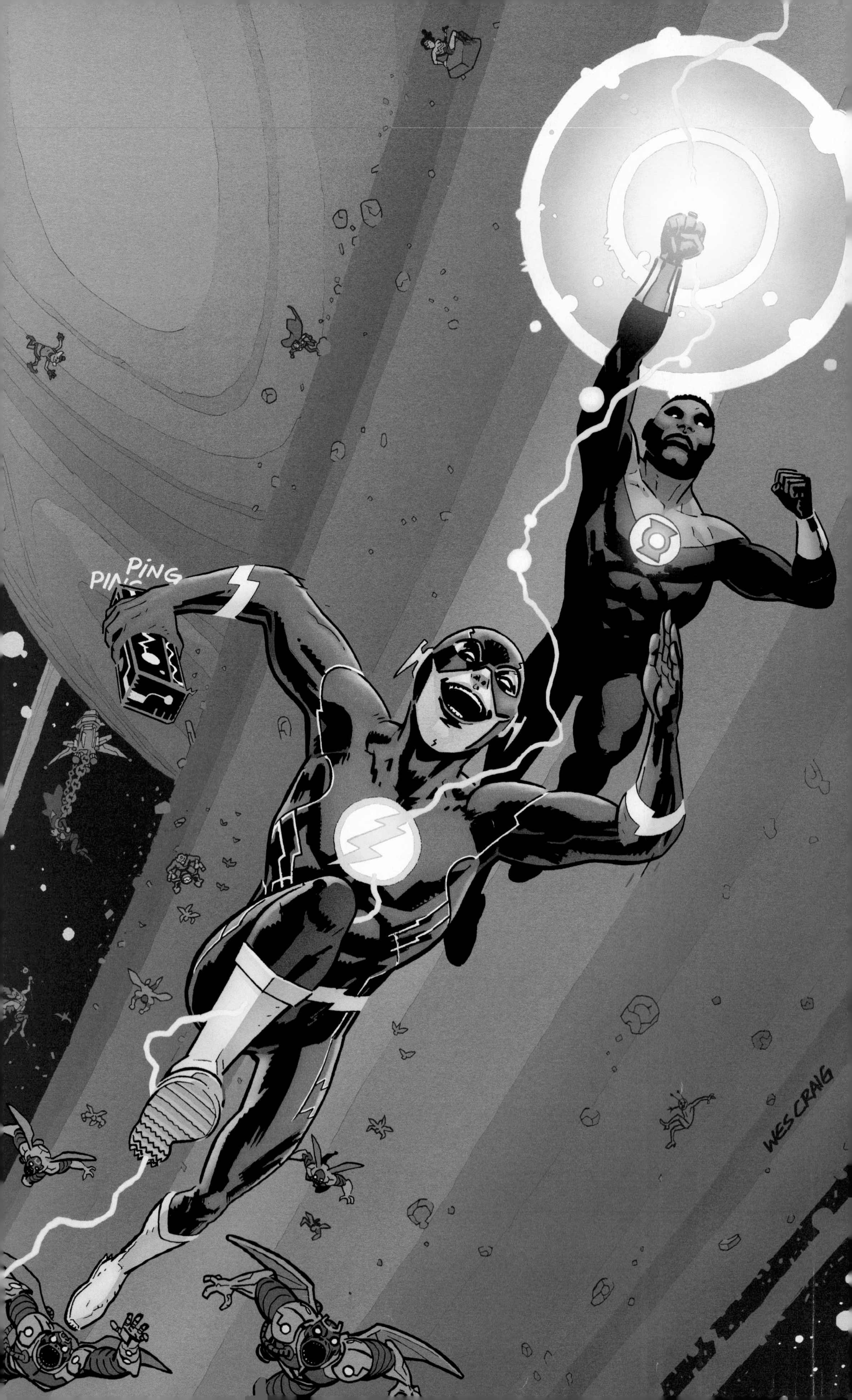
PING
WES CRAIG

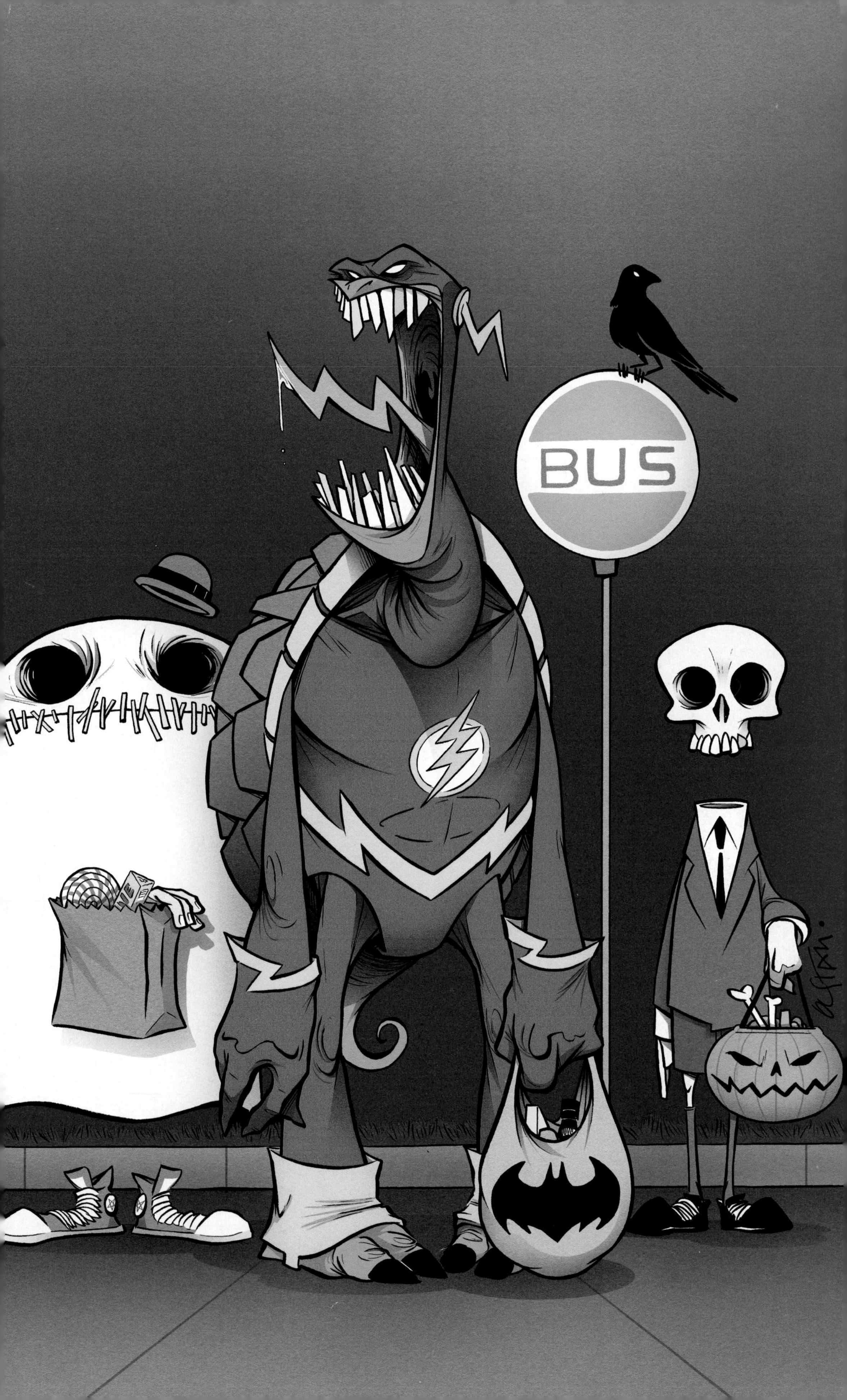
BUS

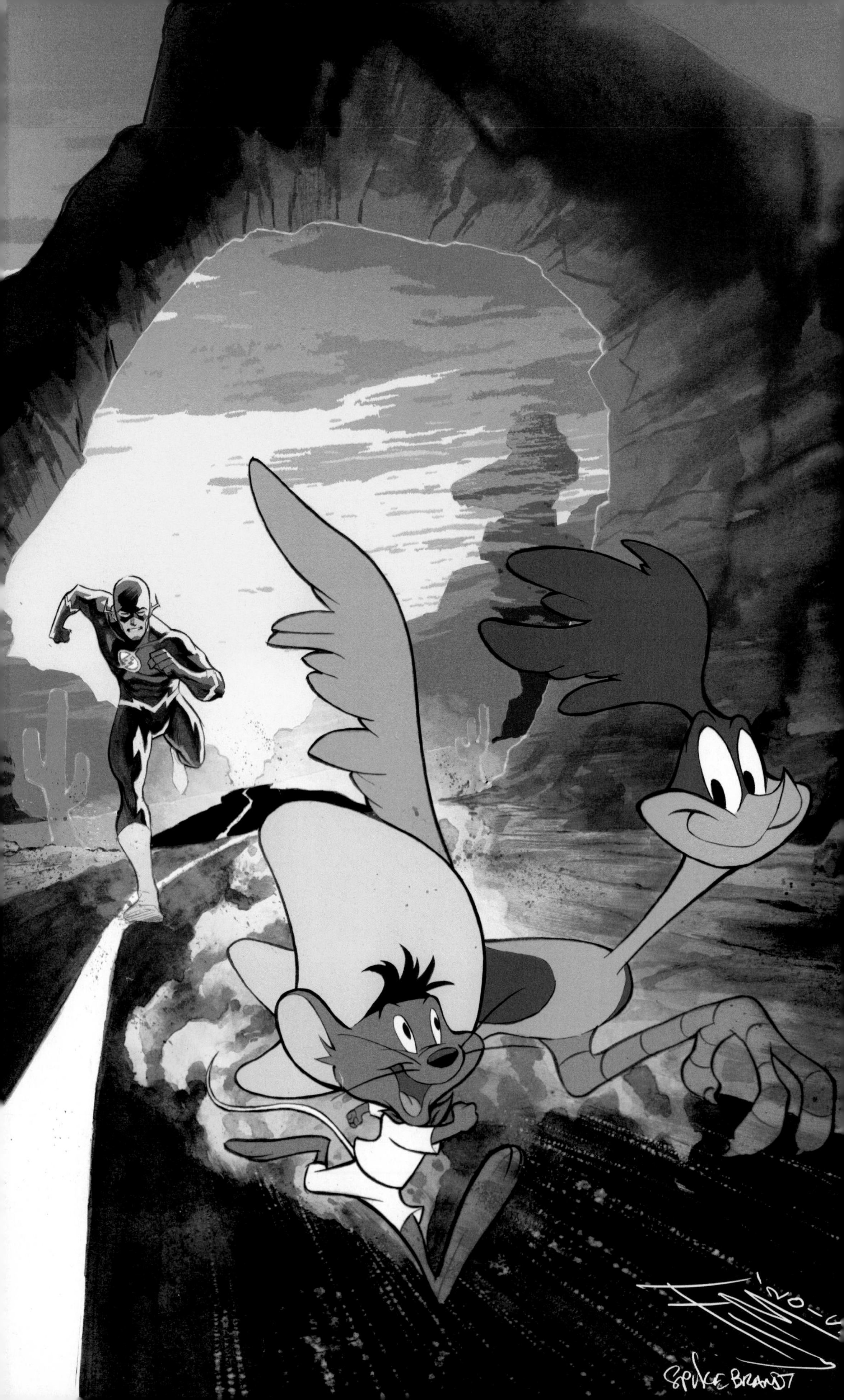
SPIKE BRANDT

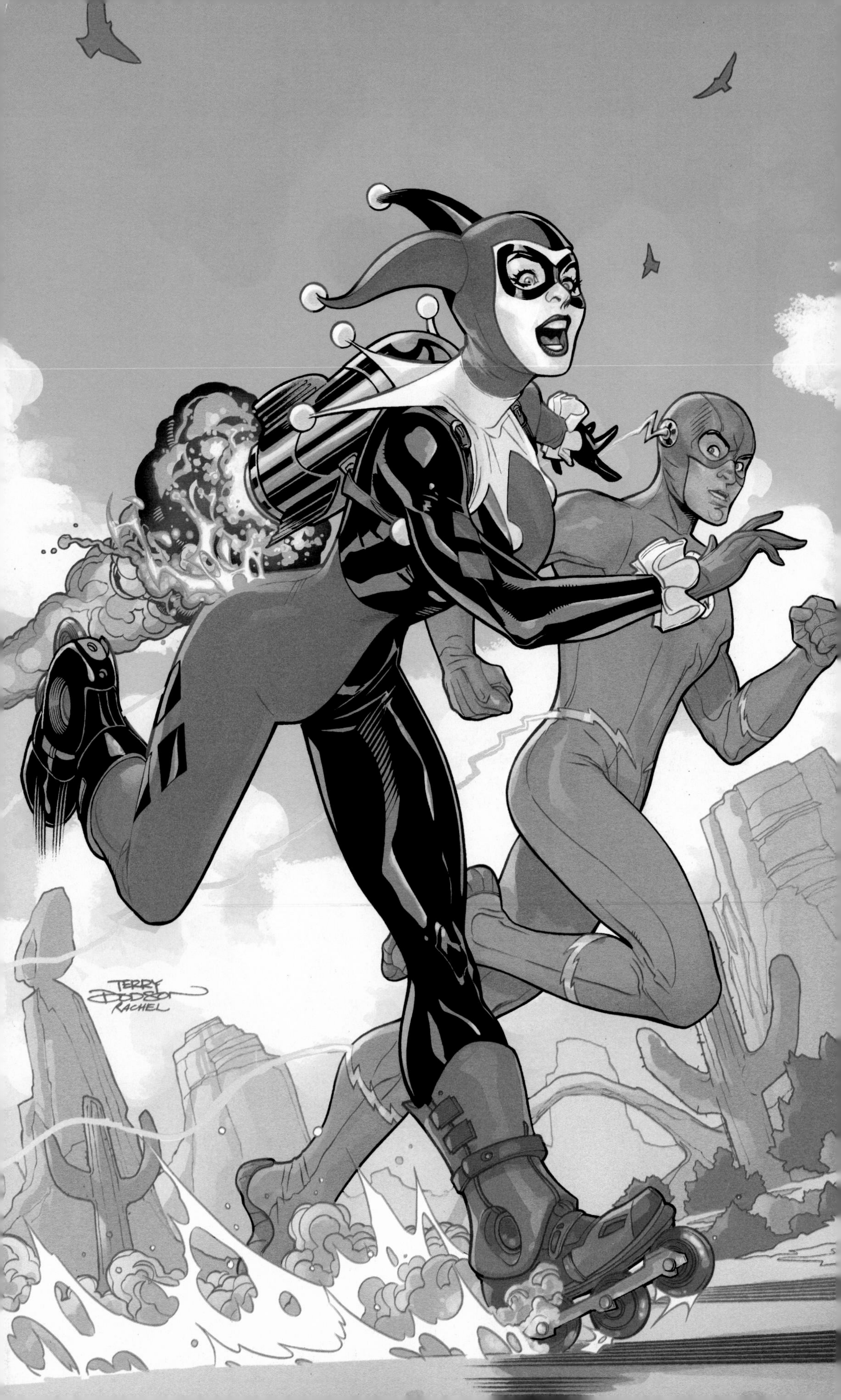
TERRY DODSON
RACHEL

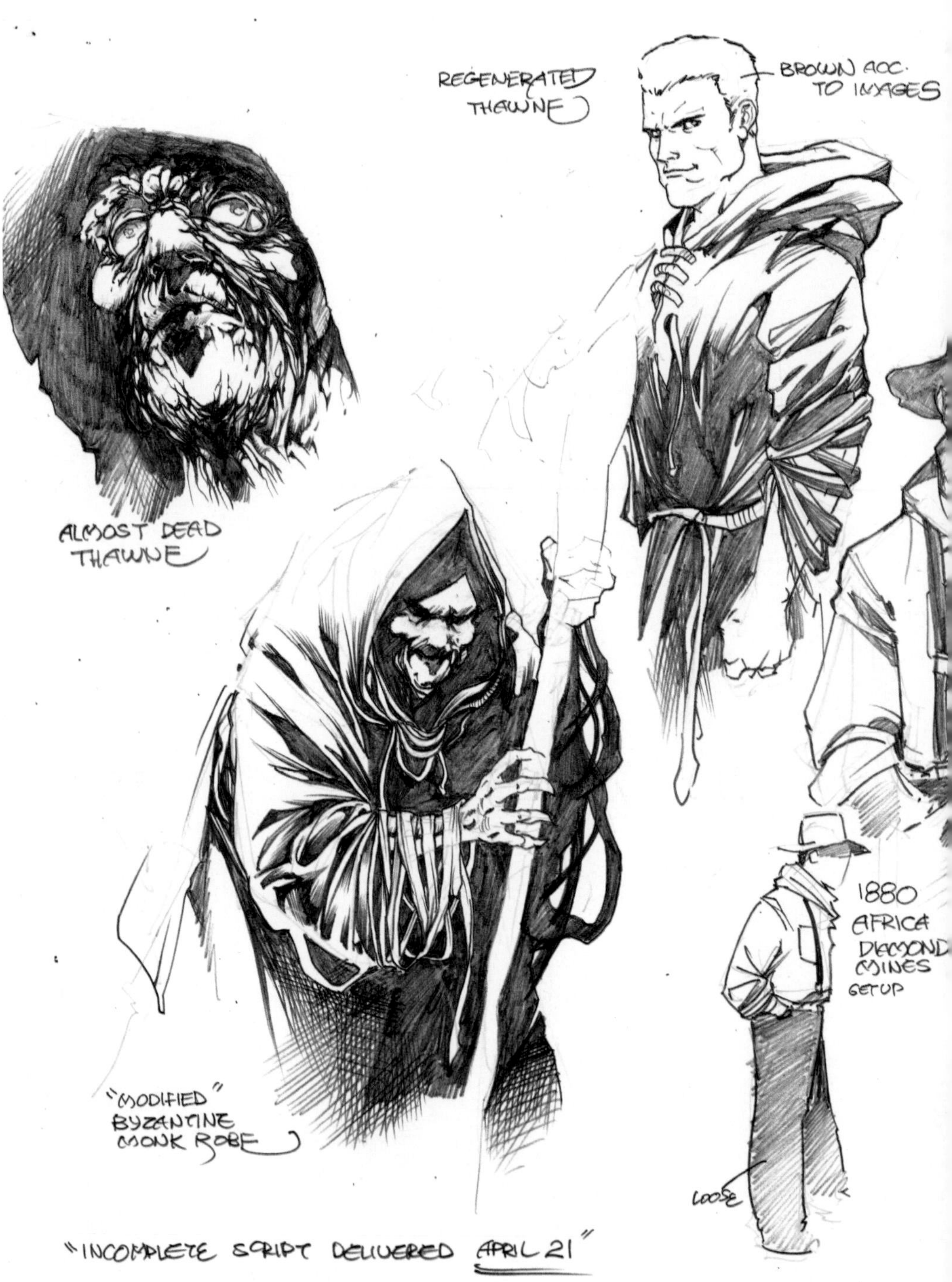
REGENERATED THAWNE
BROWN ACC. TO IMAGES
ALMOST DEAD THAWNE
"MODIFIED" BYZANTINE MONK ROBE
1880 AFRICA DIAMOND MINES GETUP
LOOSE
"INCOMPLETE SCRIPT DELIVERED APRIL 21"

"THAWNE"

EOBARD THAWNE

1980
OKLAHOMA

'DRAGONFLY'
EYEGLASS

PIMP
VEST

SHEMAG

1950
AUSTRALIA
CIRCUS IN
TOWN

BELL BOTTOM
BLUES

TRAINING DAYS
→1990?

"INCOMPLETE SCRIPT"
NO GUIDES ON "COSTUME"
IN THE TRAINING DAYS ON
LAST PAGES....

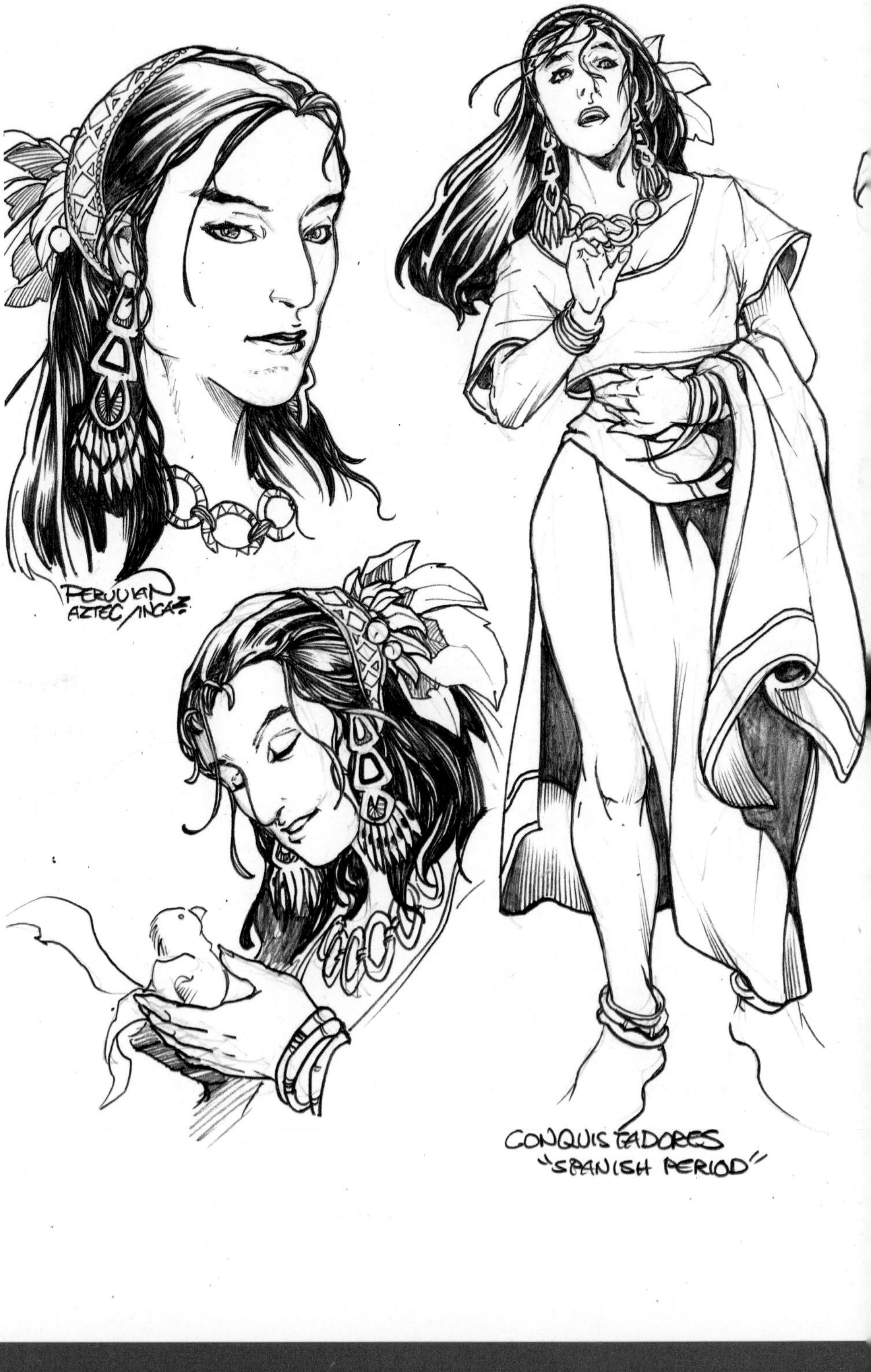
PERUVIAN
AZTEC/INCA?
CONQUISTADORES
"SPANISH PERIOD"

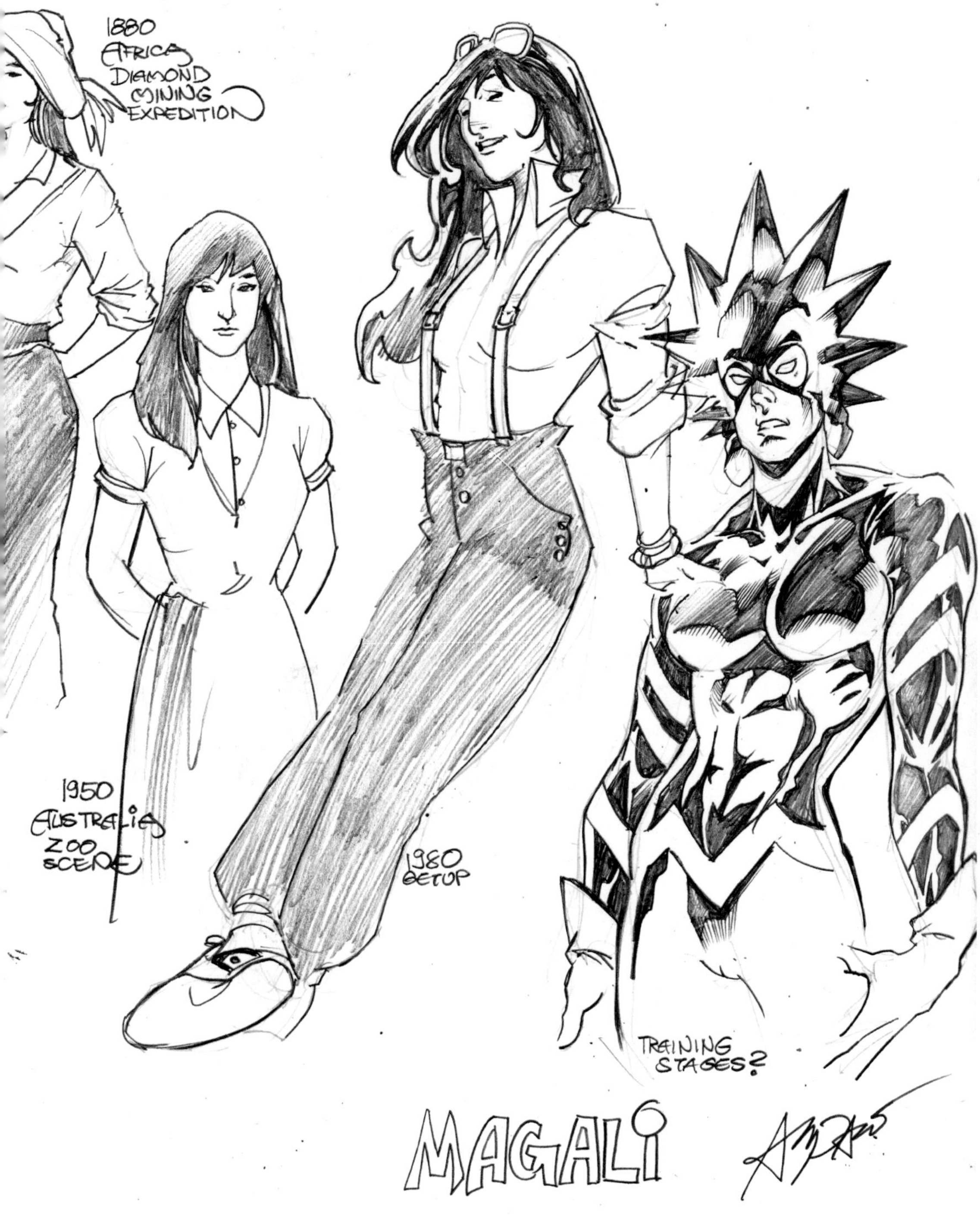
1880
AFRICA
DIAMOND
MINING
EXPEDITION
1950
AUSTRALIA
ZOO
SCENE
1980
GETUP
TRAINING
STAGES?
MAGALI

CONCEPT ART FOR THE FOLDED MAN, SELKIRK & ROSCOE DILLON BY
BONG DAZO

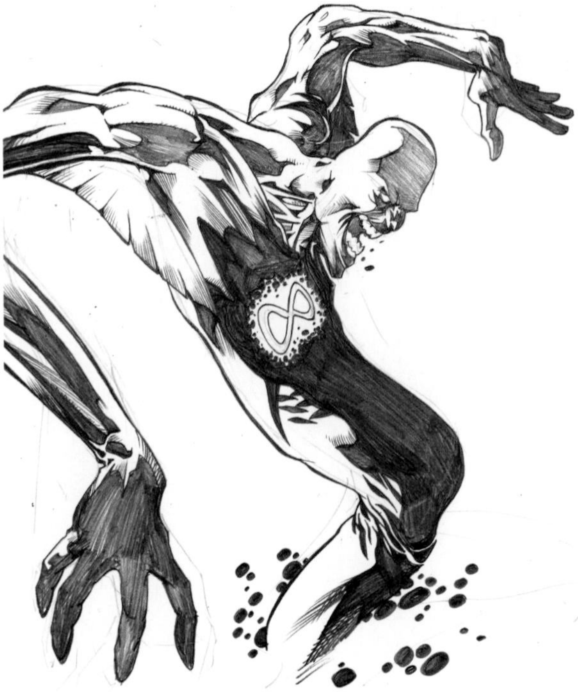

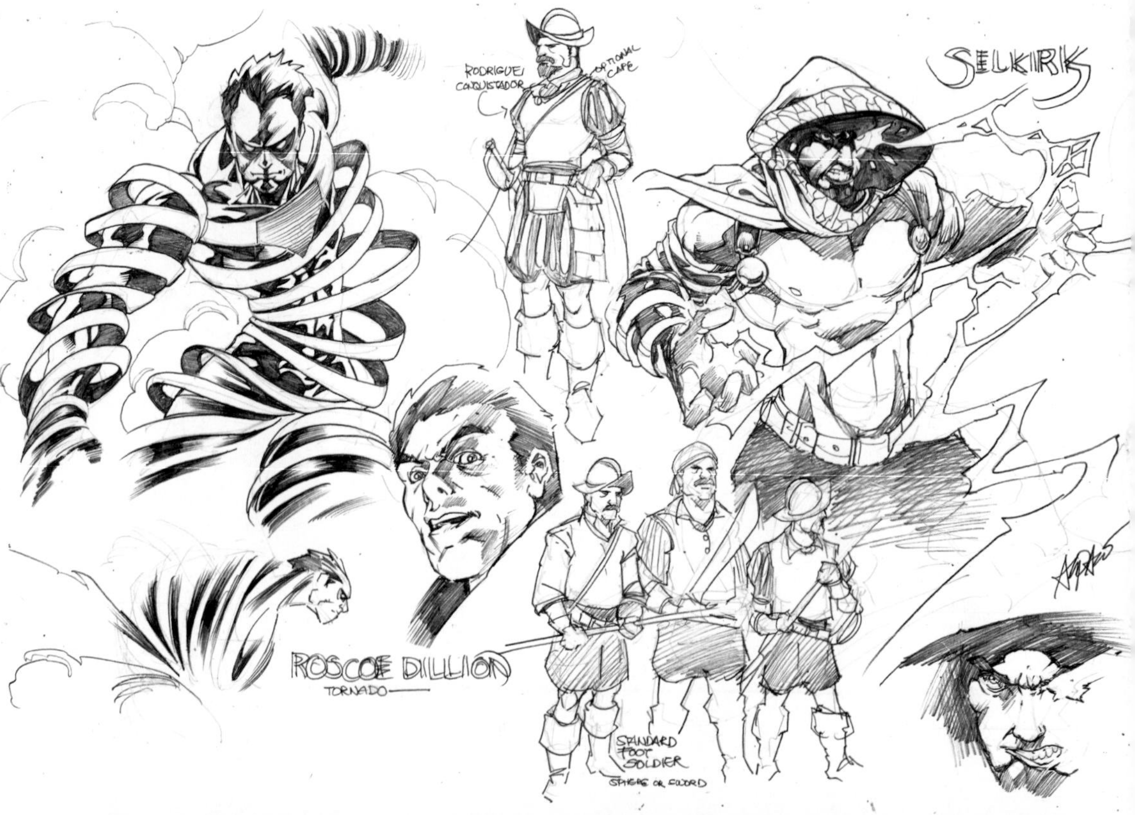

RODRIGUE/ CONQUISTADOR
OPTIONAL CAPE
SELKIRK
ROSCOE DILLION
TORNADO
STANDARD FOOT SOLDIER